Scientific Methods
in Medieval Archaeology

Published under the auspices of the
CENTER FOR MEDIEVAL AND RENAISSANCE STUDIES
University of California, Los Angeles

Contributions of the
UCLA CENTER FOR MEDIEVAL AND RENAISSANCE STUDIES

UCLA CENTER FOR
MEDIEVAL AND RENAISSANCE STUDIES
CONTRIBUTIONS: IV

Scientific Methods in Medieval Archaeology

Edited by

RAINER BERGER

UNIVERSITY OF CALIFORNIA PRESS

BERKELEY, LOS ANGELES, LONDON, 1970

University of California Press
Berkeley and Los Angeles, California
University of California Press, Ltd.
London, England

MARIONI IOHANNAE CONLEGAE ET ADIVTRICI PULCHERRIMAE,
ELEGANTISSIMAE ET DOCTISSIMAE . . .

THE CONTRIBUTORS

MARTIN J. AITKEN, Research Laboratory for Archaeology and the History of Art, Oxford University, Oxford, England.

FRANK ASARO, Lawrence Radiation Laboratory, University of California, Berkeley, California.

RAINER BERGER, Institute of Geophysics and Planetary Physics, Center for Medieval and Renaissance Studies, Department of History, and Department of Anthropology, University of California, Los Angeles, California.

HARRY BOWMAN, Lawrence Radiation Laboratory, University of California, Berkeley, California.

ROBERT H. BRILL, The Corning Museum of Glass, Corning Glass Center, Corning, New York.

FRED W. B. CHARLES, F. W. B. Charles Architect, Worcester, England.

TSAIHWA J. CHOW, Ocean Research Division, Scripps Institution of Oceanography, University of California, San Diego, California.

ISRAEL CORNET, Department of Mechanical Engineering, University of California, Berkeley, California.

PAUL E. DAMON, Department of Geochronology, University of Arizona, Tucson, Arizona.

C. WESLEY FERGUSON, Laboratory of Tree-Ring Research, University of Arizona, Tucson, Arizona.

JOHN M. FLETCHER, Department of Forestry, Oxford University, Oxford, England.

JAY D. FRIERMAN, Museum and Laboratories of Ethnic Arts and Technology, and Center for Medieval and Renaissance Studies, University of California, Los Angeles, California.

ROBERT D. GIAUQUE, Department of Nuclear Chemistry, University of California, Berkeley, California.

VERONIKA GIERTZ, Forstbotanisches Institut, Universität München, Germany.

DONALD C. GREY, Department of Geochronology, University of Arizona, Tucson, Arizona.

MARK C. HAN, Applied Science Center for Archaeology, The University Museum, University of Pennsylvania, Philadelphia, Pennsylvania.

WALTER HORN, Department of Art, University of California, Berkeley, California.

BRUNO HUBER, Forstbotanisches Institut, Universität München, Germany.

WILLARD F. LIBBY, Institute of Geophysics and Planetary Physics, and Department of Chemistry and Space Center, University of California, Los Angeles, California.

MASAYO MUROZUMI, Muroran Institute of Technology, Hokkaido, Japan.

CLAIR C. PATTERSON, Department of Geology, California Institute of Technology, Pasadena, California.

ISADORE PERLMAN, Lawrence Radiation Laboratory and Department of Chemistry, University of California, Berkeley, California.

ELIZABETH K. RALPH, Applied Science Center for Archaeology, The University Museum, University of Pennsylvania, Philadelphia, Pennsylvania.

JOHN T. SMITH, Royal Commission for Ancient Monuments, Westminster, London, England.

HANS E. SUESS, Department of Chemistry, University of California, San Diego, California.

SIGURDUR THORARINSSON, Museum of National History, Reykjavik, Iceland.

LYNN WHITE, jr, Center for Medieval and Renaissance Studies and Department of History, University of California, Los Angeles, California.

It is my pleasant task to introduce the reader to novel proceedings at the University of California at Los Angeles. In so doing it is perhaps appropriate to take note of their very special character.

In my rather brief experience in academic administration I believe to have discovered what appears to be a valid application of the principle of pluralism which might be phrased in the following fashion: The more specialized the discipline, the more wide-ranging its implications. Certainly the agenda before us would seem to provide an excellent illustration. Here the natural scientists and the humanists find common cause in the exploration of problems of mutual concern, to the advantage of us all. Indeed, it can be suggested that specialization properly pursued is a route to general understanding and a cure for the ills of the two worlds of C. P. Snow.

FOSTER SHERWOOD
Chancellor's Office and
Department of Political Science
University of California
Los Angeles, California

An international conference on the application of science to medieval archaeology was held on 26–28 October 1967 at the University of California at Los Angeles under the auspices of the Center for Medieval and Renaissance Studies and the Isotope Laboratory of the Institute of Geophysics and Planetary Physics.

The primary aim of the conference was to illustrate with concrete results how the latest scientific methods might be used in research on medieval Europe and the Near East. In addition to the various papers delivered, we decided to include appropriate methods in this volume where particular problems of methodology were deemed relevant to the period under study (ca. A.D. 300–1600).

The term "archaeology" is used in its widest sense herein to include any physical object such as, for example, a manuscript or an existing building surviving from the period. In many cases the methods discussed are also applicable to other space-time intervals in the world's past such as the contemporaneous civilizations in Mesoamerica, Africa, Asia, and Oceania.

The conference provided a successful forum in the best manner of an interdisciplinary systems approach to the solution of archaeologic research problems in the humanities and the physical and social sciences. Besides acquainting scientists in the different classical disciplines with the present state of research, the conference occasioned consideration of one very important aspect of the archaeologic research problem.

Normally, sophisticated archaeologic studies encompass the collection of the most relevant and best-suited samples to a problem, their physical measurement and cultural evaluation, and finally interpretation of all the varied significant factors. For optimum results closest to reality, a comprehensive knowledge of the degree of exactness of the field methods and the analytical laboratory procedures is of the essence, as neither can alleviate the shortcomings of the other. In the following pages the subtleties of modern methods and techniques of measurement and interpretation in the historical and physical sciences emerge. Often their inherent qualitative and quantitative potential can easily elucidate a particular problem. Sometimes the analytical results are less clear-cut, and not infrequently we realize our inability to obtain perfect answers. Thus a number of detailed questions may remain unresolved.

As is to be expected, several of the scientific techniques discussed are still in the experimental stage and only the years will reveal their ultimate potential. Realizing this, most members of the conference agreed to review the state of the art in a few years at a similar meeting in order to update their assessments. The present evaluation, however, for the reader with specific demands is not likely to be surpassed in the immediately foreseeable future. At the same time, its incompleteness challenges strongly indeed.

This conference would not have been possible without the generous spiritual championship of Lynn White, jr, and the financial backing of the University, especially Vice-Chancellor Foster H. Sherwood, for which I am indeed grateful. Thanks are due the other members of the conference committee, Jay D. Frierman and Philip Levine, for their active support, and to W. F. Libby for his encouragement. My senior colleague Walter Horn provided generously invaluable cooperation in all phases of the arrangements. Throughout, Mmes. Wanda Schmukler, Gwen Holley, and Sophia Wyatt provided their very competent assistance. Finally, I very much appreciate the editorial assistance of Robert Y. Zachary, Alain L. Hénon, Ernest J. Kubeck, and especially Vincent J. Ryan for his painstaking thoroughness and excellent literary editing of the manuscript, and the assistance of Reiner Protsch in preparing the index.

RAINER BERGER

The arrangements for the Conference on
SCIENTIFIC METHODS IN MEDIEVAL ARCHAEOLOGY
upon which this volume is based rested in the hands of:
WILLARD F. LIBBY and LYNN WHITE, JR, *Honorary Cochairmen*

Conference Committee:
RAINER BERGER, *Chairman*
JAY D. FRIERMAN
PHILIP LEVINE
LYNN WHITE, JR

Conference Advisor:
WALTER HORN

CONTENTS

PART TWO: TRACING METHODS

Introduction

INTRODUCTION:

THE RETICENCES OF THE MIDDLE AGES

Lynn White, jr

*T*HE GREATEST single defect in most historical scholarship is its greater preoccupation with written records than with other kinds of evidence. Thanks to Renaissance enthusiasm for Greek and Roman art, and to the nineteenth-century effort to solve the riddle of the Sphinx, archaeology is taken for granted, on a par with the analysis of texts, by those who are devoted to understanding mankind in the millennia before the victory of Christianity. But the thinking and technical training of the far larger body of humanists devoted to study of the Middle Ages and more recent times is word-bound, almost entirely focused on the extant documents. We shall continue to have a badly distorted view of the last sixteen centuries until this myopia is corrected.

The eighteenth and early nineteenth centuries, for example, are generally called the age of the Industrial Revolution, and businssmen and engineers obviously had a great deal to do with the radical change in our culture about that time. Yet, even today businessmen and engineers are notoriously nonverbal types: they seldom write books saying exactly what they are thinking and doing, and why. Perhaps there is an unconscious defense mechanism in this taciturnity, because self-examination would lead to awareness that they are, and long have been, the basic revolutionary class, profoundly disrupting all the world's traditions.

Even the casual written materials needed for the daily operations of such men (in contrast, for example, with those of statesmen) have been considered expendable: they survive only by the merest chance. The result is that the history of the Industrial Revolution is today scarcely above the level of mythology. It is factually and conceptually far inferior to such topics as the political histories of the American or French revolutions, or the literary history of Romanticism, for which written records are available in great quantity.

To grasp the Industrial Revolution and its human implications in-

tellectually, we must in some measure adopt the methods of the pre-
historian. The realization of this situation has led not only to a rapid
growth of museums for the history of technology but also, more recently,
to a movement for industrial archaeology attempting to recover and
understand the debris of the vanished machines and factories, railroads,
canals, tunnels, and the like, of the fairly recent past that are *not* "one
with Nineveh and Tyre" only because Nineveh and Tyre are archaeologically better known.

In the present paper we shall be talking about medieval archaeology.
During a large part of the twelve hundred very diversified years that
we usually lump together as the Middle Ages, reading and writing, at
least in the geographic area of Latin Catholicism, were largely skills of
the clergy—a fact fossilized today in our habit of calling any blunder in
recording rightly or wrongly "a clerical error." Even when laymen could
write, it was not part of their self-image to do so. Just as the president of
the United States can drive an automobile but habitually is driven, so in
Ruodlieb, a Latin verse novelette produced in South Germany ca. 1050,
the king knows how to read, and does read in private; but in public he
is read to. The secular aristocracy of the Middle Ages produced an elaborate and sophisticated culture parallel to, and fairly independent of, the
Latin culture of the clergy. But until the later thirteenth century it was
largely an oral culture. The symbol of this is the fact that two of the
most famous literary masterpieces produced by secular society in the
twelfth century, the French *Song of Roland* and the Spanish *Cid*, not to
mention the Provençal *Flamenca* of the early thirteenth century, survive
in single manuscripts. And below the social level of the feudal class were
the generally mute merchants, the craftsmen, and the peasants. Since
most Europeans and Americans today are directly descended from these
people, we have prime genetic evidence that they were not stupid. But
with rare exceptions they did not create the sort of written records that
historians love. Only the clergy provided many records, and naturally
what the clergy wrote normally reflected churchly interests and ways of
seeing things. Yet according to the best estimates, even in the early fourteenth century, after the great expansion of the new orders of friars, the
clergy amounted to only about 1.5 percent of the total population.[1] If
we want to view the remaining 98.5 percent of humanity through other
than ecclesiastical eyes, we must resort as best we can to archaeology.

[1] D. Hay, *Europe in the Fourteenth and Fifteenth Centuries* (New York, 1966),
pp. 58–59.

Only so can the vast silences of medieval written records be made resonant with historical meaning.

We have not entirely lacked profitable work in this field; for, as the great Merovingian archaeologist Edouard Salin has said, "Graves know how to whisper to those who bend over them."[2] Since most postclassical humanists seem to feel that archaeology is limited to exposing the merely physical aspects of life, it is worthwhile to insist that Salin's sensitive labors penetrate deep into the psychic existence of kinds of people who have left us scarcely a recorded word. One is appalled at the archaeological picture of the state of superstition faced by early Christian evangelists in northern Europe: it exceeds anything that the literate clergy themselves have told us. The Frankish warrior's marvelously laminated sword blade was designed to deal with visible foes, but, whether among pagans or nominal converts, the patterns on his sword belt were amulets equally directed to fending off invisible foes. Both barbarian religion and the cult of the newly baptized Germans were intensely practical devices for manipulating ambient powers to get security and physical well-being. Religion was a branch of technology.

Moreover, the sort of archaeology that Salin illustrates opens wide problems of cultural history of which the texts give scarcely a hint: for example, a Chinese belt hook turned up in a Merovingian burial.[3] And one of the most curious of Salin's findings is the consistent allergy of the Franks to representational art. Even when they used the form of an animal, god, or saint, the natural aspect tended to fragment itself and to develop into an abstract pattern with only vestigial representative elements. That this should have occurred in Gaul and Germany simultaneously with the rise of iconoclasm in the Christian Orient and with the banning of images of men and beasts from Islamic art, raises questions of connections among group psychologies which Salin himself does not broach but which historians must eventually face.

It may be no coincidence that Salin was trained as a mining engineer and metallurgist before he became an archaeologist. He knows how to combine the erudition of a scholar with the laboratory techniques of a scientist. It is in the fusion of such disciplines that many new adventures in medieval studies may be found.

Unfortunately, much of the best medieval archaeology—like Kenneth

[2] E. Salin, *La civilisation merovingienne d'après les sepultures, les textes et le laboratoire,* IV (Paris, 1959), 442.

[3] Ibid., p. 498.

Conant's excavations at Cluny—consists of specialized projects conducted to illuminate a famous monument, often a church. But since the written records of that age mostly come from churchmen, churches are the last things we need to know more about, save for architectural history. Personally, as a general. historian, I would swap an abbey for a village any day. I find deep excitement in the superb Russian dig at Novgorod which has exposed so much of the life of that teeming commercial republic of the later Middle Ages, including a most welcome mass of fugitive letters and documents in vernacular Slavic on birch bark miraculously preserved in the acidic soil.[4] At the other end of Europe, in 1962 and 1963 excavations of parts of the town of Winchester produced, at separate sites, a Byzantine lead seal of ca. 1060 and a seal of Sophronios, patriarch of Jesusalem, who died in 1059.[5] Clearly, on the eve of the Norman Conquest the Anglo-Saxons were getting about somewhat more nimbly than the written records would lead us to expect.

Indeed, all sorts of quite unexpected insights are coming out of medieval archaeology. In Hungary, excavations of Avar graves at Ullo produced a much higher proportion of Mongol physical types among women than among men.[6] The only explanation is the practice not only of exogamy but of exogamy among settlements of different ethnic groups. What chronicler of the seventh or eighth century gives us any hint of such a situation? Again, historians have been contemptuous of folk traditions about historic events that lack documentation. In north-central Sweden a local legend asserted that a certain small log cabin used as a farm building was originally a chapel built by a woman who was the first convert to Christianity in that region. This would have placed it in the very early eleventh century, and since there was no written confirmation, the story was rejected by scholars. However, carbon-14 tests run in Stockholm show that, while the roof is fairly recent, the body of the structure dates from A.D. 975 ± 80.[7] The lore of peasants may at times enshrine more history than we had thought. Yet from the Middle Ages there survives a vast mass of documentation. Is it really conceivable

[4] For a brief English account, see A. L. Mongait, *Archaeology in the USSR* (London, 1961), pp. 296–303.

[5] *Medieval Archaeol.*, VIII (1963), 265–266.

[6] M. R. Sauter, "Quelques contributions de l'anthropologie a la connaissance du haut moyen age," *Memoires et documents publiées par la Société d'Histoire et d'Archéologie de Genève*, XL (1961), 5.

[7] "A Viking Age Log Cabin in Jamtland," *Amer. Scandinavian Rev.*, LII (1964), 176–177.

that there are *significant* problems that defy solution through the texts simply because they were the sort of thing which people did not normally bother to mention in writing? Such is in fact the case. Let me give two examples from the not unimportant field of transportation.

In 1963 Lional Casson, professor of classics at New York University and the leading authority of Greco-Roman ships, published an unexpected discovery.[8] It was known that the Viking shipwrights, like those of the Indian Ocean, built up the shell of a hull by attaching each plank to the one below it, and that only after the skin of the hull was complete did they insert whatever ribbing or braces were deemed necessary. It had been assumed, however, that the Greeks and Romans constructed their vessels in the more efficient modern sequence, that is, by building first a skeleton of keel and ribs, and then nailing the planks of the hull to that frame. On the basis, however, of a relief on the tombstone of a Roman shipwright, a hitherto enigmatic passage in the Odyssey, and above all on the underwater examination of ancient shipwrecks, Casson has established beyond doubt that from the beginning to as late as the first half of the seventh century after Christ, Mediterranean ships were built by the skin-first procedure.

This old method was very costly. While the Norse ships were clinker-built, that is, with overlapping planks that could be riveted together through the overlap, those of the classical world were built smooth on the exterior. This meant that the planks were joined along their edges, which is the "Corinthian" construction of today. Every plank was chiseled with the care of a cabinetmaker, so that it had mortises and tenons on opposite edges, and when the planks were assembled to form the hull, dowels or pins were set through the mortise-and-tenon joints to keep them from working loose. Then, when the entire skin of the boat was finished, massive ribs were sculptured and inserted to reinforce the skin. This produced a very strong vessel, but at a staggering expenditure of labor, which means a high capital investment even in the slave economy of Antiquity.

Clearly, Casson has raised an entirely new question in the history of European commerce: when and where was the sequence of building a

---

[8] L. Casson, "Ancient Shipbuilding: New Light on an Old Source," *Trans. and Proc. Amer. Philol. Assoc.,* XCIV (1963), 28–33; "Odysseus' Boat (Od. V. 244–257)," *Amer. J. Philol.,* LXXXV (1964), 61–64; "New Light on Ancient Rigging and Boatbuilding," *Amer. Neptune,* XXIV (1964), 81–94; "The River Boats of Mesopotamia," *Mariner's Mirror,* LIII (1967), 286–288.

ship reversed by adoption of the labor-saving and cheaper method of constructing the skeleton of ribs first? The profits on marine commerce would obviously shoot up in relation to capital employed. Can this have had anything to do with the surge of prosperity and vitality in the Italian maritime cities of the later tenth century: Amalfi and Pisa, Genoa and Venice? I know of no texts that might be helpful. Indeed, even for Italy in that period, the texts are almost entirely from clerical quills, and the details of shipbuilding are the sort of thing that would not concern many clergy.

It occurred to me that the episode of the building of Noah's ark might have produced informative pictures. So I consulted the Princeton Index of Christian Art, which contains photographs of all published works of Christian art to 1400, with high hopes that were soon dashed. Through the centuries, every artist was so eager to get those animals safely aboard before the rains began, that not a single representation of the ark permits one to judge what he thought about the sequence in its construction. That master of the history of Venetian shipping, Frederick C. Lane of Johns Hopkins, finds no unquestionable evidence of skeleton building there before 1410.[9] It appears that this major problem in the history of medieval economics which Casson has identified will not be solved either by documents or by iconology: we must rely on archaeology, presumably supplemented by laboratory dating devices.

That progress will be made is indicated by careful reports published in 1965 and 1967[10] of two Roman shallow-bottomed barges, probably of the second century, recently found at separate sites in or near the Thames. In both of these the planks of the hulls are *not* joined at the edges, but are nailed directly to the beams of the frame. The only other Roman barges thus far discovered, those from Lake Nemi of the first century and from Fumicino of the third to fourth century,[11] have edge-joined planking. Perhaps the modern sequence in shipbuilding began on the long, placid rivers of the northern provinces of the Roman Empire, where structural

[9] F. C. Lane, *Navires et constructeurs a Venise pendant la Renaissance* (Paris, 1965), p. 7, n. 3.

[10] P. R. V. Marsden, "A Boat of the Roman Period Discovered on the Site of New Guy's House, Bermondsey, 1958," *Trans. London and Middlesex Archaeol. Soc.,* XXI (1965), 118–131, and P. R. V. Marsden, *A Roman Ship from Blackfriars, London* (Guildhall Museum Publication) (London, 1967), esp. pp. 34–35.

[11] G. Ucelli, *Le navi di Nemi,* 2d ed. (Rome, 1950), pp. 152–159, 380; *Amer. Neptune,* XXIV (1964), 86–87.

strength in boats seemed less important than it was on the salt seas or on the often turbulent streams of the Mediterranean. For economic history the critical question, still to be answered by archaeology, is when this technique was adapted to commerce on the high seas.

My second example of a basic problem in the history of transportation, which must be solved less from the texts than by sophisticated archaeology, is the horseshoe. The part which the horse has played in the technology of the West is symbolized by the traditional engineering term "horsepower" to designate the standard theoretical unit of the rate of work in a power machine. It is now generally recognized that the Romans were incredibly inefficient in their use of horses, and that one of the most significant cultural advances of the early Middle Ages was the conquest of horsepower[12] by means of tandem harnessing in the late Roman period, the arrival of the stirrup from China ca. 730, the emergence of both the breast-strap and the rigid-collar types of harness with lateral traces by the year 800 (probably as borrowings from Asia), and the whippletree in the eleventh century. But especially in moist climates— and most of Europe is chronically damp—the hooves of a horse become soft and subject to breakage and rapid wear. The first person to nail iron shoes onto a horse was a bold spirit and a great benefactor of our race. When and where did he live?

During the nineteenth century not only Roman but also Celtic horseshoes were exhibited in many European museums. But doubt of their dating gradually increased.[13] The veterinary literature of Antiquity is much concerned with the care of horses' hooves, yet there is no hint in writing of the nailed horseshoe before a Latin poem written in Germany in the 890s and a Byzantine military treatise of about the same date. Thereafter, casual references to horseshoes are increasingly common. Although the horse is found everywhere in early art, no one has spotted nailed horseshoes in a picture or sculpture until a miniature, probably from Liége, of the middle of the eleventh century, was critically evaluated.

My personal skepticism of Celtic, Greco-Roman, and even early Frankish horseshoes grew rapidly when, in the course of studying the history of the stirrup and its implications for cavalry warfare, I went through great masses of archaeological reports on pagan burials in Ger-

---

[12] Lynn White, jr, *Medieval Technology and Social Change* (Oxford, 1962), pp. 1–28, 59–69.

[13] Ibid., pp. 57–59.

many and eastern Europe during the early Middle Ages. Until Christianity brought in the idea that "you can't take it with you," warriors with enough social status to ride to battle were often buried with a horse fully equipped. Only once did I find any hint of a horseshoe fragment "Hufeisenstück mit Nagel" credited to a seventh-century grave. Where were the other three shoes? Was this fragment properly identified? If so, did some medieval horse intrude it?

Anyone who has seen a horse bogged in mud knows that he may leave a shoe two or three feet down, pulled off by the suction of his struggles to lift his feet. Inevitably that shoe, in Europe, is deposited next to a coin of Vespasian. A horse stepping into a rodent's hole at times loses a shoe that the denizen of the burrow is as likely to draw in deeper as to push out; and down there, invariably, is also a fragment of Aretine pottery. Likewise, rodent tunnels normally slant considerably, so that objects drawn downward may end up directly beneath far earlier objects or structures, thus creating a false stratification after the burrow has filled again and vanished. The earthworm also causes trouble. In moist soil with a heavy population of worms, a quarter-inch of droppings may be deposited annually on the surface, with the result that small heavy objects like horseshoes tend to work downward into the earth at varying rates and to varying depths, all to the confusion of stratification. Since the first unambiguous evidence of nailed horseshoes in rider burials comes from the Yenisei valley in Siberia about the year 900, and since that coincides with the first Greek and Latin literary references, I concluded by 1962 that nailed horseshoes were an invention of the later ninth century which spread from an unknown source with great rapidity, much as the stirrup had been diffused two hundred years earlier. A quick run through several European museums in 1966 failed to reveal any surviving earlier horseshoes: the consensus, although recent, seems to be fairly complete.

The only dissidents are the British. This may be explained in part by the great personal prestige of Sir Mortimer Wheeler who, while digging at Maiden Castle, found what he claims are "clearly stratified" nailed horseshoes of the late fourth or early fifth century.[14] Wheeler has ranged archaeologically from the Irish Sea to the Bay of Bengal, and the historical profession is much in his debt. He writes magnificently. He is, however, at times cavalier in the treatment of his own finds: he does not

[14] R. E. M. Wheeler, "Maiden Castle, Dorset," *Rep. of the Res. Comm. of the Soc. of Antiquaries of London*, XII (1943), p. 290, pl. 30*b*.

always ponder all their interesting implications. For example, as at Maiden Castle, he reports without comment three "cheese-shaped" grindstones,[15] all associated with Belgic pottery of the first century A.D. He should have noticed that, if his dating is accurate, these are indeed buried treasure: the first rotary grindstones in the world by a margin of eight hundred years. And this is a matter of some importance in the history of machine design, since the cranked grindstone is one of the first examples of the conversion of reciprocating motion into continuous rotary motion. Since grindstones are as indestructible as millstones, it is curious that no other archaeologist has found one of any comparable age. One wonders therefore whether the dating of Wheeler's horseshoes is more cautious.

As of the present writing, the latest English commentator on the horseshoe problem is obviously troubled by "the preponderance of Romano-British horseshoes over those from other provinces," and tries to explain it by proposing that "Britain was the Roman province with the most humid climate."[16] Those who have endured the perpetual drip of northern France and Belgium, or who recall Heine's description of the German summer as "winter painted green," will demur, quite apart from meteorological statistics. However, a single specimen with impeccable stratification is enough to establish a fact, despite the difficulty that in excavation the digger destroys the context of his evidence. Late in 1966 a reputable English archaeologist asserted that he personally "extracted the half of a lobate horseshoe from the gravelly top-dressing refill of a rut" in a Roman road running under a Middle Saxon cemetery; moreover "a body lay directly over the spot where the shoe was later found."[17] I am in no position to contradict such an assertion. If it is correct, we are compelled to accept the difficult hypothesis that during the Roman occupation of Britain a Celtic blacksmith of genius invented the nailed iron horseshoe, but that technological timidity on the Continent blocked the diffusion of this very useful device across the Channel for some six centuries. I suspect that the French and Germans will remain obdurate in their disbelief. This is a problem which will not be settled by texts, or by pictures, or even by the archaeology of erudition. We must wait for some labora-

---

[15] Ibid., pp. 321–322. These are sharply distinguished from the 63 querns (7 saddle and 56 rotary) from the same site.

[16] A. A. Dent, "The Early Horseshoe," *Antiquity,* XLI (1967), 62.

[17] C. Green, "The Purpose of the Early Horseshoe," ibid., XL (1966), 306–307.

tory analyses of dating iron objects, perhaps by the recently developed carbon-14 method since most iron contains some carbon.[18]

Simply because everyone is agreed that transportation has profound influence on economic and social developments, I have chosen to dwell on two cases in the history of transportation in which I feel that the taciturnity of medieval written records is not going to be circumvented without archaeological aid. But there are innumerable other potentialities particularly related to the newer laboratory techniques. Let me offer a possibility in a more ethereal topic that intrigues me.

The most charming and famous work of English medieval music is the round *Sumer is icumen in* preserved by the British Museum's Harley MS 978, fol. 11. Primarily, but not entirely, on palaeographic grounds, Sir Frederick Madden dated it ca. 1240. Then in 1944 that master of the medieval musical art, the lamented Manfred Bukofzer of Berkeley, re-dated the composition ca. 1310, using musicological arguments and largely dismissing the palaeographic evidence as irrelevant.[19] Bukofzer's attack joggled the palaeographers into reexamination of their data, with the result that most of them seem in a mood to push Harley 978 up to about 1260, but not a week further!

Because humanistic scholarship, in contrast to natural science, deals so largely with the complex variables and unpredictabilities of personality, a high proportion of its judgments must be based on connoisseurship, that is, on immensely well educated guesses. Yet the more magistral the scholar, the more aware he is of the possibility of error: Bernard Berenson used to drive Sir Joseph Duveen to apoplexy by occasionally changing his mind about the ascription of a Renaissance picture that Duveen, on the basis of Berenson's earlier accreditation, had sold to some millionaire at a fat profit. Essentially, both palaeographers and musicologists are connoisseurs, which means that after they have collected and weighed all the available facts about a problem they must sometimes call upon their carefully honed sensibilities for a decision. The dating of *Sumer is icumen in* is a matter of importance for an understanding of the dynamics of thirteenth-century culture. Bukofzer felt that to place it about 1240 was as incongruous as to make the Stravinsky of *The Firebird* a con-temporary of Berlioz, and 1260 was no great improvement. I believe that the question which Bukofzer raised has not been settled, and that it can

[18] M. Stuiver and N. J. van der Merwe, *Current Anthropol.* 9 (1968), p. 48.

[19] M. F. Bukofzer, "'Sumer is icumen in,': a Revision," *University of California Pub. in Music,* II, ii (1944), 79–114.

only be decided by precision carbon-14 dating. But what are the chances of persuading the good gray officials of the British Museum to give us some snippets of blank parchment, if not from the margins of fol. 11 at least from a less famous leaf of Harley 978?

We should not even approach them until the preparatory work has been done, since librarians rightly have a custodial attitude toward the treasures placed in their care. Almost no efforts have been made at carbon-14 dating of medieval manuscripts, because the standard deviations in carbon-14 dates have been at least as large as the variables admitted by good palaeographers in their ascriptions. (Incidentally, carbon-14 is worthless for medieval paper, since the latter was made largely of linen rags that may have been in use for two or three generations before they reached the pulping mill.) We are beginning, however, to suspect fluctuations in the formation of carbon-14 in the earth's atmosphere. When these variations have been accurately chartered, we should be able to predict the periods in the Middle Ages for which we can get a sharp carbon-14 date, as well as the decades for which such dating will be blurred. In the present state of the evidence, the entire thirteenth and also fifteenth centuries look like periods of fairly sharp dating. Greater exactness in our information about changes in the production rate of carbon-14 can be secured by testing the blank margins of some of the innumerable and snippable precisely dated notarial documents and charters of this period. Such parchments would be preferable in carbon-14 tests even to segments of accurately dated tree rings, since there remains the suspicion, at least for some species of trees, that the cellulose or lignin of the growth year may be contaminated by the sap of later years, thus giving a carbon-14 date that is a bit too young. Since vellum and parchment were costly, they were probably not stockpiled for any great period before use, and consequently the date on a charter should be only slightly later than the date of the slaughter of the animal providing the hide from which the sheet was made. When we can show repeatedly that radiocarbon measurements give results that would be significant for the dating of Harley 978, we can reasonably approach the British Museum for our snippet.

I believe that there are many other historical problems which might yield their secrets to similar methods. In 1921 Poul Nørlund excavated a graveyard in Greenland which had preserved by far our best specimens of late medieval, nonceremonial, everyday clothing. The fact that these garments echo changes in style occurring in Flanders and France is not surprising for the fourteenth century when, after all, a bishop was still often resident at the settlement of Gardar and contacts with Europe were frequent. But some of the dress seems to reflect fashions even of the second half of the fifteenth century, whereas the last medieval ship known to have reached Greenland sailed home in 1410.[20] If the Copenhagen Museum would provide us with an inconspicuous bit of one of these supposedly late fifteen-century costumes, we might be able to settle the question of whether communication between medieval Europe and its North American outpost continued almost to the time of Columbus' voyage.

A point has been reached in the intellectual adventure of our race in which a more conscious blending of the interests and methods of humanists and natural scientists is strongly indicated. The symbol of the new situation is Willard Libby who, as has so often been remarked, won "the first Nobel Prize for history." A good scholar is as eager as any scientist to get all the hard facts he can, and to evaluate them as objectively as he can. A creative scientist is as vividly aware as any humanist can be of the elements of art, the quest for conceptual elegance, the role of educated intuition, in expanding insights in his field. All of us in the learned world are concerned with a single task: the understanding of nature. People classed as scientists deal mostly, although not entirely, with the world external to man. People called humanists specialize in studying that most enigmatic, unpredictable, and undisciplined phenomenon of nature, as it is now known to us, *Homo sapiens*. Our task is single. The purpose of the present symposium is to explore that singleness and singularity.[21]

[20] Pøul Norlund, "Buried Norsemen at Herjolfnes," *Meddelelser om Grønland*, LXVII, i (1924), 87–190, 253–254.

[21] The preceding chapter was originally given as the dinner address of 26 October 1967.

Part One

Dating Methods

I

THE PHYSICAL SCIENCE OF RADIOCARBON DATING

W. F. Libby

$\mathcal{A}$ S THE radiocarbon dating method has been perfected, and accuracies have increased, it has been discovered, as might have been anticipated, that there are significant deviations between radiocarbon and true dates, but during the early years of the development of the method good checks were found by the author's group, since the measurement errors gave dates accurate to only two centuries or so.[1] Apparently, and fortunately, the deviations are normally small in the periods of recorded history, being on the order of 1 or 2 percent in radiocarbon content. A curve of correction has been published by Suess and others which can be used over the period of the Middle Ages to give results that are apparently fully concordant.[2]

It is very intriguing to try and understand what it is about the basic assumptions of radiocarbon which causes these deviations. A phase is now being entered where radiocarbon dates are used to test the validity of the geophysical parameters involved; for example, the constancy of the earth's magnetic field, as was pointed out years ago by Elsasser, Ney, and Winkler.[3] Changes in the earth's magnetic dipole would cause a change in the production rate of carbon-14 through changing the degree

---

[1] W. F. Libby, Radioactive Dating and Methods of Low-Level Counting, Proceedings of a Symposium, Monaco, 2–10 March 1967, held by the International Atomic Energy Agency, Vienna, 1967. This address has been largely adapted from the original presentation at Monaco.

[2] P. E. Damon, A. Long, and D. C. Grey, in *J. Geophys. Res. 71* (1966), p. 1055, and Sixth International Carbon-14 and Tritium Dating Conference (June 1965), USAEC CONF. 650652 (Washington, D. C.: Clearing House of Technical Information, Nat. Bur. Standards), (1965), p. 415; K. Kigoshi, ibid., p. 429; H. E. Suess, ibid., 439; M. Stuiver, ibid., p. 452, and in *Science 149* (1965), p. 533; H. E. Suess, in *J. Geophys. Res. 70* (1965), p. 5937; M. Stuiver and H. E. Suess, in *Radiocarbon 8* (1966), p. 534.

[3] W. Elsasser, E. P. Ney, and J. R. Winkler, in *Nature 178* (1956), p. 1226.

to which incoming cosmic rays are deflected away from the earth and, therefore, agreement between radiocarbon and historical dates is indirect evidence for the constancy of the earth's magnetic dipole.[4] Of course, there is the matter of sensitivity for each effect. With a lifetime of 8300 years considerable inertia exists in the system, and one cannot expect to record changes immediately as change in the production rate occurs.[5]

As for possible sources of deviation, other than the earth's dipole, Suess and others[6] suggested that it is quite conceivable that deviations are a measure of solar activity, the correlation being with climate. Thus deviations during warm periods, when the sun is active, correspond to additional shielding of the cosmic rays by the solar wind, which the sun then emits in higher intensity, with the result that the production rate of radiocarbon is reduced, the opposite being the case during cold periods.

A new set of samples from the first twelve dynasties of Egypt was recently obtained by the British Museum to test whether, by chance, the Egyptian samples previously used were misleading. In general, measurements of these samples confirmed earlier work, and there appears to be a deviation in the fifth millennium of about five or six hundred years, the radiocarbon date being younger than the historical date. It is conjectural whether the deviation is real or whether the Egyptian historical dates are incorrect, or both. In any case, deviations during the time period of the Middle Ages are very much smaller than those encountered in the early dynastic periods of Egypt.

Other evidence indicates that it is the radiocarbon which deviates toward being too young. This evidence is from the bristlecone pine tree rings. These trees live to be very ancient and, when carefully studied, can give tree-ring dates. Although the method of dating with these trees has not been so certainly established, especially in the fifth millennium, as the dating with other kinds of trees in the first three millennia has been,

[4] R. Ramaty, "Influence of Geomagnetism on Radiocarbon Production and Content," *Magnetism: The Cosmos* (Proc. NATO Conf. Planetary and Stellar Magnetism), ed. S. K. Runcorn (Edinburgh, 1966: Oliver and Boyd); W. F. Libby, "Radiocarbon and Paleomagnetism," *Magnetism: The Cosmos,* ed. S. K. Runcorn (Edinburgh, 1966: Oliver and Boyd), p. 13; L. Wood and W. F. Libby, in *Isotopic and Cosmic Chemistry,* H. Craig, S. L. Miller, and G. J. Wasserburg, eds. (Amsterdam, 1964: Holland Publishing Co.), p. 205.

[5] L. Wood and W. F. Libby, in *Isotopic and Cosmic Chemistry,* H. Craig, S. L. Miller, and G. J. Wasserburg, eds. (Amsterdam, 1964: Holland Publishing Co.), p. 205.

[6] H. E. Suess, in *J. Geophys. Res. 71* (1966), p. 439; M. Stuiver, ibid., p. 452, and in *Science 149* (1965), p. 533; J. R. Bray, in *Nature 209* (1965), p. 1065.

TABLE I

Chronologies of the Egyptian Dynasties I-XII in Years B.C.

Beginning of dynasty	Historical chronologies			Radiocarbon chronologies $t_{1/2} = 5730$		
	Hayes [1]	Helck [2]		Arizona [3]	British Museum [4]	UCLA [5]
I	c.3100	2950	Beginning	2500	2490	2695
			Early		2690	2465
			Middle			2410
			End			2320
II	—	—		2540		2335
						2225
III	2691	2650		2330		(Early) 2140
IV	2617	2579		2340		2220
V	2497	2460				2185
VI	2347	2322			1910	
VII–X	—	—				
XI	—	—				1655
XII	1991	1995			1480,1550	1650

[1] W. C. Hayes, in *Cambridge Ancient History*, I, chap. vi (1962).
[2] W. Helck, in *Handbuch der Orientalistik* (1967).
[3] P. Damon et al., uncorrected dates, *Radiocarbon 10* (1968).
[4] I. E. S. Edwards et al., uncorrected dates, British Museum, Radiocarbon Advisory Committee Mtg. (Dec. 7, 1966) (MS).
[5] R. Berger and W. F. Libby, *Radiocarbon 9*, 477 (1967).

there is a tendency for the radiocarbon dates to be younger than the bristlecone pine tree-ring dates, as the radiocarbon dates are younger than the historical dates of the Egyptian fifth millennium. Some radiocarbon-dating experts believe that the discrepancy in the fifth millennium is about 10 percent, or about 800 years. The question is open at the moment, because the bristlecone pine dating technique remains to be established to the point of certainty needed, and the historical dates are themselves uncertain during the period 2000 to 3000 B.C.

The cosmic-ray flux is one possible cause of deviation. However, studies of meteorites by Arnold and others[7] have shown that the most likely cosmic rays have been quite constant. Although the accuracies are less than desired, there seems to be no systematic tendency for cosmic rays to change in intensity over periods of hundreds of years. This is judged by the relative amounts of cosmic ray–produced radioactivities of lifetimes varying between a few years and hundreds of millions of years. The meteorites traveling outside the earth's magnetic shield are subject to solar wind shielding only, and thus serve more closely as a measure of the true extraterrestrial flux. Therefore, questions may arise regarding variation in the terrestrial and solar magnetic shields. The solar shield acts mainly through patches of plasma which are sent out by the sun, called solar wind, and which serve to scatter the cosmic rays[8] away from the solar system. On this basis, as Suess has pointed out, there may be a correlation between the activity of the sun and the production rate of radiocarbon. On the other hand, the earth's magnetic dipole may have undergone changes. (It is noted that its direction is known to have changed; some evidence from the magnetism of rocks indicates that it has reversed its direction completely in periods during the last several millions of years. The mixing of radiocarbon is so effective, however, that a change in direction in the earth's dipole would not affect radiocarbon dates.) There is a third possibility that the mixing of the ocean, which now takes about two thousand years on average, may have changed in times past. This seems quite unlikely, however, and it is probable that the cause of any deviations will have to be found in the cosmic-ray intensity, as the atmosphere of the earth records it, this change probably being due to

[7] M. Honda and J. R. Arnold, in *Science 143* (1964), p. 203; J. Geiss, H. Oeschger, and U. Schwartz, in *Space Sci. Rev. 1* (1962), p. 197.

[8] R. Ramaty, "Influence of Geomagnetism on Radiocarbon Production and Content," *Magnetism: The Cosmos* (Proc. NATO Conf. Planetary and Stellar Magnetism), ed. S. K. Runcorn (Edinburgh: Oliver and Boyd, 1966).

change in solar activity, or changes in the earth's magnetic field, or both.[9]

The techniques of measuring radiocarbon dates greatly improved with the introduction of the CO_2 proportional counting method of De Vries and Barendsen.[10] At present it is the most popular method. Other possibilities exist, and it is hoped that these will be investigated in practice, but on the whole, radiocarbon dates are probably measured now as accurately as is required in most cases. Further improvements to reduce the required sample size, as well as better techniques for the recognition of contaminants, would be helpful. On balance, the medieval scholar should find radiocarbon dating a most valuable method in his studies.

[9] W. F. Libby, "Radiocarbon and Paleomagnetism," *Magnetism: The Cosmos,* ed. S. K. Runcorn (Edinburgh: Oliver and Boyd, 1966), p. 13.

[10] H. De Vries and G. W. Barendsen, *Physica 18* (1952), p. 652, and *Space Sci. Rev. 19* (1953), p. 987.

II

THE POTENTIAL AND LIMITATIONS OF
RADIOCARBON DATING IN THE MIDDLE AGES:
THE ART HISTORIAN'S VIEW

W. Horn

Fig. 1. Cressing Temple, Essex, England. To the left: the barley barn; to the right:
the wheat barn (photo: John Tarlton).

*T*HE EXPERIMENT reviewed in this and the subsequent paper *
received its impetus from a radiocarbon measurement made in
1963 which seemed to be so out of line with historical probabilities, that
it threatened to shake the faith of architectural historians of the Middle

---

* After these two papers had been written, their authors made the interesting
discovery that French medieval oak in the Île de France and in Normandy can be
dated with the aid of the dendrochronological standard curves worked out for south

23

Ages in the reliability of radiocarbon dating for medieval archaeology. The disturbance was caused by a piece of timber that Cecil Hewett, an expert on medieval carpentry joints, had extracted from one of the principal roof-supporting posts of a remarkable medieval building, the barley barn of Cressing Temple in Essex, England (fig. 1), and forwarded through me to the Isotope Lab at the Institute of Geophysics and Planetary Physics of the University of California at Los Angeles for radiocarbon analysis. In the somewhat spotty and not truly professional literature which dealt with this building, it was ascribed to the year 1480.[1] Cecil A. Hewett, on the basis of an analysis of its carpentry joints, assigned it to the twelfth century (A.D. 1150–1200)—a view considered "out of line" by the more conservative students of the subject. The Isotope Lab at Los Angeles came forth with a radiocarbon age of 940 $\pm$ 70 years, corresponding to a historical date of A.D. 1010—a result which no one was willing to accept (UCLA-646).[2]

When Rainer Berger and I discussed the methodological implications of this event, it became clear to us that the measurement of the sample from Cressing Temple suffered from three defects:

1. The man who gathered the specimen did not inform the physicist who processed it whether the piece of wood removed for radiocarbon dating was extracted from a place deep in the interior of the tree out of which the post was hewn, or from somewhere closer to its outer rings. This fact alone could introduce a margin of error up to 200 or 300 years, whatever the age of the tree may have been (see legend to fig. 2);[3] and

---

German and West German oak. This fact was established by Veronika Giertz of the Forstbotanisches Institut of the University of Munich with wood samples gathered by us in a joint expedition undertaken in the summer of 1969. A full report on these findings will be published elsewhere. Some results bearing directly on the date of the buildings here discussed have been inserted at the galley stage of this publication (see under Méréville, Milly-la-Forêt, Arpajon below, pp. 31–37).

[1] For Cressing Temple see Cecil A. Hewett, "The Barns at Cressing Temple, Essex, and Their Significance in the History of English Carpentry," *J. Soc. Architect. Historians*, XXVI (1967), 48–70. A comprehensive study on the history of medieval carpentry joints by Cecil Hewett, based on buildings in the county of Essex, has been published under the title *The Development of Carpentry, 1200–1700, An Essex Study* (Newton Abbot, 1969).

[2] See G. J. Fergusson and W. F. Libby, "UCLA Radiocarbon Dates III," *Radiocarbon*, VI (1964), 337.

[3] The moment sapwood is converted into heartwood in the course of the growth of a tree, it is no longer subject to any further radiocarbon intake through the leaves of the tree and thus begins its C-14 decay cycle.

Fig. 2. Pencil rubbing of cross section through a post of one of the terminal trusses of the market hall of Milly (Seine-et-Oise), France, A.D. 1479, removed from the hall during a recent restoration and cut into pieces of three-foot length, now serving as benches in the garden of the chapel of the former leper hospital, St. Blaise-des-Simples. When prepared for construction in the Middle Ages, the tree was split in the center so that its pith came to lie close to the inner edge of one of the two posts formed in this manner. A sample of wood extracted from the center of the tree (point a) would yield a radiocarbon date about a hundred and fifty years earlier than a sample extracted from the waney edge (point b).

2. The physicist who processed the sample did not make allowance for the fact that it fell into a historical time span where the radiocarbon concentration of organic matter on earth was subject to deviations running in turn as high as 200 to 250 years—because the results of at least the most important of the experiments, by which this fact was established (Hans E. Suess), were as yet not published (see legend to fig. 3).[4]

[4] Hans E. Suess, "Secular Variations in the Cosmic-Ray Produced Carbon-14 in the Atmosphere and Their Interpretations," *J. Geophys. Res.,* LXX (1965), 5937–5952. For other studies on fluctuations of atmospheric C-14, made at about the same time by H. De Vries; E. H. Willis, M. Tauber, and K. D. Münnich; M. Stuiver; P. E. Damon, A. Long, and D. C. Grey; Kunihiko Kigoshi and Hiroichi Hasegawa, see Rainer Berger's remarks below, p. 95.

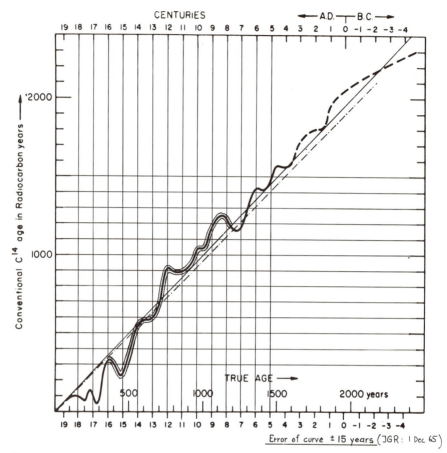

Fig. 3 Secular variations of cosmic ray-produced carbon-14 (after Hans E. Suess). The curve defines the fluctuations in the production of carbon-14 in the terrestrial biosphere from 400 B.C. to the present. Where the curve descends in a relatively straight line (as between A.D. 1200 and 1300), radiocarbon analysis will furnish a single date (such as "A.D. 1250"); where it flattens out into a plateau (as it does between A.D. 1300 and 1400), it can only furnish an indeterminable date in a time span (such as "any point in time between 1300 and 1400"). Where the curve doubles back by descending, rising, and falling (as it does between 1450 and 1650), a radio-carbon measurement will not bring a single date, but three alternate dates (such as "1460, 1550, or 1620"). Which one of these dates is the correct one can be established only by additional samples taken from a tree-depth position that is either earlier than 1450 or later than 1650.

3. No consideration was given for a possible nonconformity in the carbon-14 content of the measured sample with respect to the dating standard or time zero of the radiocarbon clock as disclosed by carbon-13 rather than carbon-12 isotope ratio measurements—which may have added to the other two margins of error a third one, rang-

ing anywhere from zero to about 30 years in the particular time span with which we are concerned.[5]

It was clear that disregard of any of these three factors and, in an even more significant manner, of their cumulative effect could introduce a margin of error of prohibitive magnitude.

Viewed from the perspective of the medieval archaeologist, this was distressing news. We had reached an impasse with our own traditional method of dating and were in need of outside help. Conditions were especially grave for those of us who were concerned with the history of vernacular architecture which abounds with undated and undatable buildings. We were clearly in need of a study that would enable us to judge the potential and limitations of radiocarbon dating for the Middle Ages more accurately and it was imperative that such a study would require a closer cooperation between the archaeologist and the physicist than was practiced in earlier attempts to settle this problem. Rainer Berger was interested in this problem, and Willard Libby, as I wish to acknowledge with particular gratitude, gave us the green light for the planning and the pursuit of such a study, and the use of the Isotope Lab at his Institute of Geophysics and Planetary Physics at the University of California at Los Angeles.

The subject of our investigation was some forty timbered medieval buildings of France and England with which I had been concerned from an architectural point of view for over a decade. Ten of these buildings could be dated by reliable historical sources; the remainder presented what appeared in moments of discouragement to be insuperable difficulties of dating. Samples from all of these buildings were collected by Berger and myself in the course of two trips, one to England in 1965, the other to France undertaken in 1967.[6]

Rainer Berger will report in detail the methods used in processing these samples and in calculating their probable historical dates. My own task is to evaluate these results from the point of view of the art historian. I shall report first on radiocarbon measurements obtained for specimens extracted from dated buildings, and shall then turn to the larger body of undated or undatable buildings, discussing the respective merits of the results derived from these measurements and of those obtained by traditional archaeological methods of dating.

---

[5] Cf. below, p. 93.

[6] I acknowledge with gratitude the support obtained for this work in 1965, by a travel grant from the American Philosophical Society and in 1967, by one from the Samuel S. Kress Foundation.

Fig. 4. Parçay-Meslay (Indre-et-Loire), France. Abbey grange, 1211–1227. Exterior from northeast (photo: Philip Spencer).

I. RADIOCARBON MEASUREMENTS OF HISTORICALLY DATED OR
DATABLE BUILDINGS (IN CHRONOLOGICAL SEQUENCE).

1. *The barn of the abbey grange of Parçay-Meslay (Indre-et-Loire), France.* This remarkable building, which has a clear length of 170 feet, a clear width of 80 feet, and a height to the bottom of the ridge piece of 44 feet, has its vast roof supported by four ranges of free-standing posts that divide the space internally into a nave and four accompanying aisles (figs. 4 and 5). It is, as far as I know, the only case of a surviving five-aisled medieval barn. There is good historical tradition which ascribes this building to Hugue de Rochecourbon, abbot of the monastery of Marmoutier from 1211 to 1227.[7] One sample taken from this building yielded as date the second quarter of the thirteen century (UCLA-570), another one, the date 1250 (UCLA-1313B).

2. *The abbey barn of the Cistercian monastery of Maubuisson (Seine-et-Oise), France.* The abbey of the Cistercian monastery of Maubuisson, commune de Saint-Ouen-l'Aumône, two kilometers southeast of the city of Pontoise (Seine-et-Oise), was founded in 1236 by Blanche de Castille, who wanted to be buried there.[8] The barn lies to the north of the conventual buildings, on slightly lower terrain (fig. 6). It is in fairly good condition, except for its south aisle which has been dismantled. The design of its roof with its fan-shaped longitudinal braces rising from the king posts to the purlins and to the ridge piece is unusual. The radio-

---

[7] For the dates of Parçay-Meslay, see Walter Horn, "On the Origins of the Medieval Bay-System," *J. Soc. Architect. Historians*, XVII (1958), 13.

[8] For the dates of the monastery of Maubuisson, see O. Verge du Taillis, *Chronique de l'Abbaye Royale de Maubuisson* (Paris, 1947), pp. 1236–1796.

FIG. 5. Parçay-Meslay (Indre-et-Loire), France. Abbey grange, 1211–1227. Interior looking northeast (photo: Philip Spencer).

Fig. 6. Maubuisson (Seine-et-Oise), France. Abbey barn of monastery founded in 1236. Northern range of arcades looking east (photo: James W. Roberts).

carbon age of a sample of wood taken from an arch brace reaching from the arcade spandrels to a tie beam (UCLA-1309) fell into a plateau of the secular variation curve where it could correspond to anything between 1050 and 1220. The terminal year of this span lies within a distance of 26 years from the earliest possible year of the historical target.

3. *The barn of the Cistercian abbey grange of Great Coxwell, Berkshire, England.* William Morris proclaimed this building to be "the greatest piece of architecture in England." It is without doubt the finest of the extant medieval barns of England and has its roof supported by a frame of timber of truly breathtaking proportions (figs. 7 and 8). The land on which this structure rises was given to the order of Citeaux by King John in 1204.[9] A structural detail (fig. 46) allows us to date it not

[9] For the construction dates of the barn of Great Coxwell, see Walter Horn and Ernest Born, *The Barns of the Abbey of Beaulieu at Great Coxwell and Beaulieu-St. Leonard's* (Berkeley and Los Angeles: University of California Press, 1965), pp. 17 ff.

later than 1250;[10] some would like to extend this to 1275.[11] We have two controlled radiocarbon measurements from different tree-depth positions, one yielding the date 1250 (UCLA-1048), the second one the date 1245 (UCLA-1049). Both dates are fully within the historical probability span.[12]

4. *The cruck-built barn of Church Enstone, Oxfordshire, England.* The barn is dated to the year 1382[13] by an inscription engraved into stone (a case of fantastic rarity!) which reads:

> *Ista Grangia facta et fundata fuit A.D. M CCC LXXXII per Walterum de Wynforton abbatem de Wynchecumbe ad exorationem Roberti Mason ballivi loci istius.*
> This barn was founded and built in the year 1382 by Walter of Wynforton abbot of Winchcombe at the petition of Robert Mason, bailiff of this place.

A bark sample (UCLA-1316) taken from the foot of the northern blade of the easternmost cruck of this building fell on a plateau of the Suess correction curve, yielding a date that could not be more accurately defined than lying within the range A.D. 1300–1400. To obtain a more precise date would require a sample taken about 100 tree rings inside the cambium layer of the tree from which this cruck blade was fashioned.

5. *The market hall of Méréville (Seine-et-Oise), France.* Together with the two market halls which follow this building (figs. 9 and 10), it is an excellent example of the tradition of medieval market halls of the Paris region and gives a good idea of what the famous thirteenth-century halls of the great market of Paris must have looked like. The early historians of the old duchy of Etampes to which Méréville belonged assigned the

[10] Ibid., pp. 19 ff.

[11] Stewart S. Rigold, "Some Major Kentish Timber Barns," *Archaeologia Cantiana,* LXXXI (1966), 3; John Fletcher, "Crucks in the West Berkshire and Oxford Region," *Oxoniensia,* XXXIII (1968), 78, takes the same position. Neither Rigold nor Fletcher support their date with any references to securely dated or securely datable parallels, and thus deprive me of the pleasure of correcting my views in the light of new evidence or the privilege of refuting their argument should such evidence be wanting. Cf. my remarks on "expert knowledge" and "consensus of opinion" below, p. 76; *Antiquaries J.* XLVI (1966), 356–357.

[12] A heartwood sample of unknown tree-depth position collected two years earlier (UCLA-574*A*) brought the date 1145, which fits well into the chronology suggested by the other two samples.

[13] Church Enstone has been surveyed and described by Raymond B. Wood Jones, "The Rectorial Barn at Church Enstone," *Oxoniensia,* XXI (1956), 43–47.

Fig. 7. Great Coxwell, Berkshire, England. Barn of abbey grange, ca. 1250. Exterior from northwest (photo: Walter Horn).

construction of its hall to the year 1511.[14] This view was based on a patent letter of King Louis XII, dated 14 November 1511, and granting to Bertrand de Reilhac, seigneur and Vicomte of Méréville (1503–1522), the right to establish fairs and markets at Méréville. The letter does not make mention of the construction of a new hall.[15] The fairs and markets of Méréville, ravaged during the Hundred Years' War (1338–1453), had in fact already been reinstituted by Etienne le Fèvre, vicomte of Méréville from 1456 to 1472.[16] The hall is mentioned in an *aveu et dénombrement* of Pierre V de Reilhac, dated 27 June 1482, which specifies the taxes the vicomte was entitled to impose upon the merchants, displaying their goods in this structure: "Item tous les bouchers vendant chair à la halle

[14] Ernest Menault, *Essais Historiques sur les Villages de Beauce, Angerville* (Paris, 1859), p. 68, and Maxime Legrand, *Etampes Pittoresque, guide du promeneur dans la ville et l'arrondissement,* II (Etampes, 1904), 603–604.

[15] The full text of this patent letter, dated Blois, 14 Novembre 1511, is known to me through a copy in the Archives Departementales de Versailles (*Manuscrit de Instituteur Mulart, École Communale de Méréville,* dated Méréville 20 Septembre 1899). For a partial publication of this text, see Abbé C. Bernois, "Histoire de Méréville," *Annales de la Société Historique et Archéologique du Gatinais,* XX (1902), 339.

[16] Abbé C. Bernois, op. cit., pp. 337 ff.

FIG. 8. Great Coxwell, Berkshire, England. Barn of abbey grange, ca. 1250. Interior
looking south (photo: courtesy of National Building Record).

Figs. 9–10. Méréville (Seine-et-Oise), France. Market hall, built by Bertrand de Reilhac shortly after 1511. Above: exterior from northeast; below: interior looking east (photo: James W. Roberts).

doivent chascun un jambe de porc ou le poids qu'elle est prise, les autres vendent en ville trois mailles."[17] A first sample taken in 1962 from one of the outer posts of the hall (UCLA-572) yielded a radiocarbon date of about 1440 with unfortunately no carbon-13 correction.[18] A second sample, taken in 1967, from a center shake of the large axial post that supports the frame of the lean-to at the western end of the hall (UCLA-1304) located 30 tree rings inward from the cambium layer yielded the alternative dates 1460 and 1600. UCLA-572, which was nonambiguous, established the date 1460 as the correct one. In the light of these measurements I was inclined to ascribe the construction of the market hall of Méréville to Etienne le Fèvre (1456–1472). The dendrochronological analysis of the timbers of this hall by Veronika Giertz, however, did not confirm this conclusion, but disclosed that the trees from which the timber of the hall are shaped were felled in 1516±4. This established with finality that it was Bertrand de Reilhac and not Etienne le Fèvre who built the present hall. As the charter entitling the vicomte to "establish fairs and markets" in Méréville was issued on 14 November 1511, the summer of 1512 turns out to be the earliest possible time for the construction of the hall. Our radiocarbon dates 1440 (UCLA-572) and 1460 (UCLA-1304) thus appear to be 50 and 70 years too early.

6. *The market hall of Milly-la-Forêt (Seine-et-Oise), France.* The municipal archives of the city of Milly contain a patent letter, by Louis XI, dated 5 May 1479, which authorizes the king's cousin, Amiral Louis de Graville, to establish a market and to erect a market hall in this city. The charter, to the best of my knowledge, has never been published. I am quoting the pertinent passages only:

5 Mai 1479

LOUIS, Par la Grace de Dieu,
> *Roy de france scavoir faisons, à tous present et avenir. Nous avons reçu l'humble suplication de notre cher et féal Cousin Conᵉ et chambellan Louis de Graville seigr. de Montegu et de Milly en Gastinois, contenant qu'à l'occasion des guerres et divisions passées, ledit lieu de Milly qui, voulait estre un Beau Bourg bien Ediffié peuplé et habitue est a present*

---

[17] *Aveu et dénombrement de la baronnie de Méréville, rendu par Pierre Reilhac, échanson du roi, à Jean de Foix, Comte d'Etampes, 27 Juin 1482.* The full text of this document is known to me through a copy in the Archives Departementales de Versailles. Excerpts were published by Abbé C. Bernois, op. cit., pp. 337–338.

[18] UCLA-572 brought an uncorrected date of 1460, which, recalculated in the light of the Suess fluctuations, had to be changed to 1440.

FIG. 11. Milly-la-Forêt (Seine-et-Oise), France. Market hall, built by Amiral Louis
de Graville shortly after 1479 (photo: Rameau et Fils, Etampes).

*fort demoly decimé et en ruine . . . Il Nous Luy donner audit lieu de
Milly un Marché franc chacunes emaine et sur ce Benignement Luy
impartir Notre Grace et Provision. . . . Auquel lieu que ainsy sera
ordonné et Etably Voulons et Nous Plaist Que Notre dit Cousin et Sesd.
successeurs puissent faire et faire faire Bastir (halle) et construire et
Ediffier! halle; – Etaux et autres choses necessaires pour le detail des
Bleds, chare, mercerie, Epicerie, Draperie et toutes autres denrées et
Merchandises.*[19]

As the granting of a new market was a rare privilege, and one that was
available to very few, we have no reason to doubt that the construction
of the new hall was undertaken shortly after the issuance of the patent
letter, and that the building went up in the remaining months of 1479
or, at the latest, in 1480.

[19] Archives Municipales, Ville de Milly, *Registre des Titres de la Baronnie de
Milly,* D:I P:I. Here quoted after a transcript transmitted to me by Mr. Raymond
Geber, member of the Commission des Antiquités et des Arts de Seine-et-Oise, to
whom I am deeply indebted for this kindness. A brief description of the hall of
Milly will be found in a booklet by Georges Lasserre entitled *Les Rues de Milly*
(Etampes, 1925).

The terminal northern truss of this market hall (fig. 11) has been renewed in its entire height during a recent restoration. Some of the discarded original posts, cut into pieces of three-foot lengths, are now being used as benches in the garden of St. Blaise-des-Simples, the twelfth-century chapel of a former hospital for lepers, located on the outskirts of the town. We took two samples of this hall. One (UCLA-1312) brought the date 1450; the other one (UCLA-1311) the date 1290. The first measurement is within a margin of 30 years of the historical target. The second is so out of line with it that we must assume that the beam from which it was extracted belonged to an earlier building, parts of which were reused in the present hall.

7. *The market hall of Arpajon (Seine-et-Oise), France*. A local tradition, for which I have not been able to find any supporting documentary evidence, ascribes the construction of this hall to Louis Mallet Amiral de Graville, and assigns it to the period 1450–1470.[20] There is no doubt in my mind that this building, like the market halls of Méréville and Milly, is the product of the economic resurgence which followed the termination (1453) of the Hundred Years' War, during the last exhaustive phase of which the plain around Paris was badly ravaged. The design of the hall is so closely related to that of Milly-la-Forêt that one feels tempted to ascribe it to the same carpenter. A heartwood sample taken from one of the principal posts of the hall (UCLA-1307) yielded the date 1450.

Dendrochronological analysis of a number of core drillings taken from various timbers of the hall established that Arpajon was probably a few years later than Milly-la-Forêt, but surely not many. We could not obtain the outermost tree ring in any of the timbers of either hall, but the cambium layer of the trees used in the construction of the hall of Arpajon turned out to be a few years later than that of Milly. The radiocarbon date obtained from UCLA-1307 thus appears to be 30 years too early.

8. *A monastic barn in a farmstead called Troussures (Oise), France*. This barn (fig. 12), located in the commune de Saint-Eusoye, canton de Froissy, arrondissement de Clermont, has its roof supported by two fine ranges of mansonry arcades which, like those of the abbey barn of Maubuisson (fig. 6), are clearly of thirteenth-century design. The entire

---

[20] A plaque affixed to one of the principal posts of the hall reads: "Cette magnifique Halle aurait été realisé entre 1450 et 1470 par Louis Mallet, Seigneur de Graville et de Marcousis, Amiral de France. Elle fut acheté par la Ville d'Arpajon le 18 Avril 1821 à Philippe de Noailles, Duc de Monchy, Maréchal de France et Gouverneur de Versailles. Sa charpente a été réstauré en 1951 a l'identique . . . en chataignier. . . ."

fabric is in a state of collapse. The three westernmost arcades of this building were replaced by wooden supports in 1609, as can be inferred from a post that exhibits this date in bold letters together with the name of the carpenter who was in charge of this renovation: "fait par n coersset charpentier de noyers 1609" (fig. 13).[21] The date appears once more on the tie beam that rests above this post. A sapwood sample (UCLA-1380), extracted from one of the edges of the signed and dated post, fell into a reversal loop of the secular variation curve and for that reason yielded not one but two alternative dates, namely, the years 1450 or 1600. Obviously it is the last of these two dates that applies.

9. *The market hall of the city of Richelieu (Indre-et-Loire), France.* The city, with all of its appurtenances including the market hall (fig. 14) and a magnificent castle, was built by Cardinal Richelieu between 1631 and 1640.[22] An oak-bark sample extracted from one of the longitudinal rails of the hall yielded two alternative dates, 1480 or 1630. Again, only the last of these dates can apply.

10. *The market hall of Questembert (Morbihan), France.* The vast roof of this remarkable (fig. 15), which rests on an armature of seventeen heavily scantled trusses with unusually sturdy longitudinal bracing, displays on one of its tie beams the date 1679 (ninth truss counting from east). The name of the carpenter who was in charge of this work, "Estienne Charpentier," appears in the parochial register of the town for that same period.[23] A bark sample from one of the principal posts of

---

[21] The barn of Troussures, has never been properly examined. A summary description of this building will be found in an article by chanoine Eugene Müller, entitled "Cours Archéologique à travers les Cantons de Clermont. Saint-Just, Maignelay, Froissy, Grevecoeur et Ressous-sur-Matz," *Société Académique, Sciences et Arts du Department de l'Oise,* XVI, 2ᵉ partie (1896), 280–326; see esp. pp. 296–297. The land on which the building stands was given to the Cistercian monastery of Chaalis in 1160, and formally established as a grange in 1176 (see Charles Higounet, "La Grange de Vaulerent, Structure et exploitation d'un terroir cistercien de la pleine de France," *Les Hommes et la Terre,* X [Paris, 1965], p. 18, n. 2).

[22] For Richelieu see Henriette de Chizeray, *Le Cardinal Richelieu et son Duché-Pairie* (Paris, 1961); Gabriel Hanotaux, *Histoire du Cardinal de Richelieu,* VI (Paris, 1947), 327–382 ("Le chateau et la ville de Richelieu"); and L. A. Bosseboeuf, "Histoire de Richelieu et des environs au point de vue civil, religieux et artistique," *Memoires de la Société archéologique de Touraine,* XXXV (1890), 266–290 ("Creation et organization de la ville, duché," etc.).

[23] For Questembert see Walter Horn, "Les Halles de Questembert," *Bulletin de la Société Polymathique du Morbihan* (1963), pp. 1–16; and M. E. Marquer, publishing under the pseudonym of Bleiguen, *Au Coeur du Haut-Vannetais, Questembert* (Rennes, 1958), pp. 113–115.

FIG. 12. Troussures (Oise), France. Thirteenth-century barn, formerly in the possession of the Monastery of Chaalis, partly renewed in 1609, now in state of collapse.
View of northern range of arcades (photo: Walter Horn).

the hall brought two alternative dates (because of the same reversal in
the curve for secular variations that brought similar alternatives for the
two preceding halls), about 1500 or between 1625 and 1670. Here too, of
course, only the later date makes sense.

fp N coev ſſef cħpfieR ðc нoiꝛPS   1609

FIG. 13. Troussures (Oise), France. Inscription of 1609 incised vertically into one of the wooden posts replacing the two westernmost arches of the southern row of arcades of the original barn constructed in the thirteenth century (after free-hand sketch by author). The village of Noyers mentioned in this inscription lies a few kilometers east of Troussures on Route D-151.

FIG. 14. Richelieu (Indre-et-Loire), France. Market hall, built by Cardinal Richelieu between 1631 and 1640. Detail of southern row of posts (photo: Walter Horn).

Fɪɢ. 15. Questembert (Morbihan), France. Market hall. Interior looking west, 1675 (photo: James W. Roberts).

Conclusions

What is my reaction as art historian to these findings? A glance at the chart in which the results of this series of measurements are summarized (table 1) shows that the radiocarbon measurements of five of the historically dated or datable monuments, from which our samples were taken, were found to be either right on the target or within a span of ten years around it (Parçay-Meslay, Great Coxwell, Méréville, Troussures, and Richelieu). One was between 5 and 50 years early (Questembert), one was 20 to 30 years late (Parçay-Meslay), and two were 30 to 40 years early (Maubuisson and Milly-la-Forêt). The historical date of Arpajon is not certain, but if it was constructed between 1450 and 1470 as local tradition claims, it would also be almost on top of the target. Church Enstone is unspecific, because it falls on a plateau of the Suess fluctuation curve and, like everything else on the plateau, can only be defined as falling into the time range 1300–1400.

If these results suggest that radiocarbon analysis brings us either straight on the target or to within a range of 30 to 40 years from the target (provided full allowance is made for all of the correction factors,

TABLE I

Comparative chart of historically dated or datable buildings and
corresponding radiocarbon dates

Building	Historical Date	Radiocarbon Date	Margin of Error
Parçay-Meslay	1211–1227	1225–1250	on target
		1250	20–30 yrs. late
Maubuisson	founded in 1236	1050–1220	at least 20 yrs. early
Great Coxwell	ca. 1250	1250	on target
		1245	on target
Church Enstone	1382	1300–1400	historical date within C-14 range
Méréville	1512	1440	70 yrs. early
		1460	50 yrs. early
Milly-la-Forêt	1480	1450	30 yrs. early
Arpajon	shortly after 1480	1450	30 yrs. early
Troussures	1609	1600	on target
Richelieu	1631–1640	1630	on target
Questembert	1675	1625–1670	5–50 yrs early

discussed in the introductory paragraph of this paper), we would be in command of a dating method highly superior to what, in the case of the buildings that form the subject of this study, can be obtained through traditional archaeological methods of dating.

Let us turn then to our second concern:

II. RADIOCARBON MEASUREMENTS OF UNDATED BUILDINGS AND THE RELATIONSHIP OF THESE MEASUREMENTS TO TRADITIONAL ARCHAEOLOGICAL METHODS OF DATING.

The most important criteria used traditionally in the dating of the particular type of building with which we are concerned are, in sequence of importance:

1. Written historical sources.
2. The design of the roof and the roof-supporting trusses.
3. The design of carpentry joints.
4. The masonry technique used in the fabric of these buildings.
5. The design of special members such as corbels or the profiles of moldings.
6. "Expert" knowledge acquired intuitively through a lifelong professional contact with buildings.

I shall discuss these individually, *but only and very specifically with regard to the buildings with which we are concerned in this study.*

1. *Written historical sources and their archaeological dating value.* Unless a written historical source is unequivocably clear about the identity of the building to which it refers, it may be very deceptive. A most illuminating case in point is a barn of unusual beauty in the county of Middlesex.

The Great Tithe Barn of Harmondsworth. This barn, 192 feet long, 37½ feet wide, and 37½ feet high (figs. 16 and 17), not more than a couple of miles from the International Airport of London, lies on the site of a Benedictine priory, which was founded during the reign of William the Conqueror, as a dependency of the abbey of the Holy Trinity at Rouen.[24] It is mentioned in the list of alien priories seized by the crown from 1288

---

[24] The barn of Harmondsworth has been surveyed and described by Albert Hartshorne, "The Great Barn at Harmondsworth," *Trans. London and Middlesex Archaeol. Soc.,* IV (1875), 417 ff.; it has also been dealt with by Francis B. Andrews, in "Medieval or 'Tithe' Barns," *Trans. Birmingham Archaeol. Soc.,* XXVI (1901), 25–26, and in the *Royal Commission on Historical Monuments in England* (Middlesex, 1937), pp. 61–62.

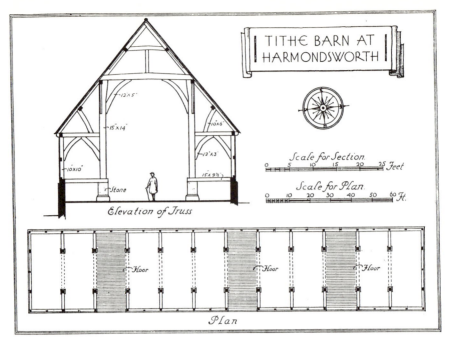

FIG. 16. Harmondsworth, Middlesex, England. Tithe barn. Plan and section (photo: courtesy of Royal Commission on Historical Monuments).

FIG. 17. Harmondsworth, Middlesex, England. Tithe barn. Interior looking south (photo: courtesy of Her Majesty's Stationery Office).

onward, in an entry which refers to the twenty-second year of the reign of Edward I, that is, 1293–94, in the following manner:

> *Item in granario ij quarti dimidium / frumenti xv s. precio quarti vi s. Item vi quarti ij busselli mixture xxxj. s. iij d. precio quarti v s. Item xxij quarti brasei under gall iij li. viij s. precio quarti iiij s*[25]

which I translate as follows:

> Likewise in the granary 2½ quarters of summerwheat 15 shillings, 6 shillings per quarter. Likewise 6 quarters and two bushels of mixed (cereals?), 31 shillings and threepence, 5 shillings per quarter. Likewise 22 quarters of malt, 4 pounds and 8 shillings, 4 shillings per quarter.

There is clear historical evidence, then, of the existence of a grain barn in 1293–94, on the grounds of the present barn. But is the present barn identical with this structure? The situation is complicated by the fact that there are two other good historical sources referring to barns in the parish of Harmondsworth.

The Winchester College Muniments, Computus Roll, *sub annis* 1423–24, records a payment of 6 pounds to William Kypping, Carpenter, for his work at Downton and a journey to Surrey and Middlesex to view the timber with one John atte Oke "next Kyngston" (upon Thames) for a new barn at Harmondsworth, Middlesex.[26] This barn was built in August 1427. Another entry in that same register records *sub annis* 1434–35 the visit of a carpenter of Uxbridge to Winchester College to make a contract for building a new barn at Harmondsworth.[27]

The barn had been associated with each and every one of these dates, and it had in addition also been dated independently in the "second half of the 14th century."[28] Without radiocarbon analysis of its timbers we

---

[25] Public Record Office, 22 Ed. I assis. rot. 90; I am most grateful to my colleague Robert Brentano for his assistance in transcribing this passage. The text is quoted by Hartshorne, op. cit., p. 417, but there wrongly ascribed to the year 1296.

[26] See John Harvey, *English Mediaeval Architects* (London, 1954), p. 156.

[27] Harvey, loc. cit.

[28] Hartshorne, who was the first to draw attention to the document of 1293-94, did not date the barn in the 13th century, but assigned it on the basis of its roof design to the "second half of the 14th century . . . not later than 1375". This date was also adopted by the *Royal Commission,* op. cit., pp. 61–62: "Built very likely in the 14th century, certainly not later than the 15th," and Nikolaus Pevsner, *The Buildings of England,* III (Middlesex, Harmondsworth, 1951), p. 95: "The manor went from the King to William of Wykeham in 1391, and he made it part of the

could not have settled this problem. We took three specimens (UCLA-575, 1050, 1051). All of them pointed to the turn from the thirteenth to the fourteenth century, which makes the first of the three available documentary sources the acceptable one and suggests that the extant barn of Harmondsworth was built after the confiscation of the manor by the Crown of England in 1288, but probably not later than the beginning of the fourteenth century.

Of no lesser interest, in this context, were two other English barns, one in the county of Gloucester, the other in Worcestershire.

The Great Monastic Barn of Frocester, Gloucestershire. For Frocester we had an excellent source suggesting a construction date of 1298–1306. A passage in the *History and Cartulary of the Abbey Church of St. Peter's in Gloucester* records the erection of the barn (figs. 18 and 19) as one of the accomplishments of John de Gamages, abbot of this monastery from 1284 to 1306:

> *Similiter manerium de Uptona per emptionem terrae Roberti le Hunte et variis aedificiis ibidem constructis multum emendavit, et tamen ibi quam alibi super communam multa aedificia sue tempore fuerant constructa, ut cameram abbatis de Hardpyrie cum aliis domibus novis apud Upledena erectis, et magna grangia de Froucestre et multis aliis.*[29]

> Likewise, after the release of the land by Robert le Hunte he greatly improved the manor of Upton by erecting many buildings, and there as well as on other holdings of the monastery many buildings were constructed at this time, such as the abbot's chamber at Hartpury, together with other new houses near Upleadon, and the great grange of Frocester as well as many others.

This date was accepted in print by R. A. Cordingley,[30] and after a careful study of the building, in the first draft of an unpublished manuscript by Fred Charles and myself. The radiocarbon samples taken from this building showed that the present roof of the barn is not the medieval

---

endowment of Winchester College. The barn probably belongs to this period in the history of the manor." Clearly in favor of a 15th-century date was John Harvey, loc. cit.

[29] On Frocester see *Victoria History of the Counties of England, Gloucestershire,* II (London, 1907), p. 56. The document here quoted is to be found in the *Historia et Cartularium Monasterii S. Petri Gloucestriae,* in *Rerum Britannicarum Medii Aevi, Scriptores* (Rolls Series), XXXIII: 1 (London, 1863), p. 40.

[30] R. A. Cordingley, "British Historical Roof-Types and their Members: A Classification," *Trans. Ancient Monuments Soc.,* n.s., IX (1961), caption to pl. 11.

Fig. 18. Frocester, Gloucestershire, England. Barn of abbey grange, formerly belonging to St. Peter's abbey at Gloucestershire. Exterior from south (photo: *Country Life*).

Fig. 19. Frocester, Gloucestershire, England. Barn of abbey grange, formerly belonging to St. Peter's abbey at Gloucestershire. Interior looking east (photo: James W. Roberts).

roof but a rebuilt one undertaken in the second half of the fifteenth century (UCLA-567B, UCLA-567C, UCLA-950, UCLA-951, UCLA-1002, UCLA-1003, UCLA-1001).[31]

The cruck-built barn of Middle Littleton, Worcestershire. Another barn at Middle Littleton in Worcestershire (figs. 20 and 21)[32] had been universally associated with what appeared to be a reliable data recorded in the Chronicle of the Monastery of Evesham assigning the construction of this barn to Abbot John Ombersley (1367–79): *Item ampud North-Luttletone aedificavit unam grangiam decimalem.*[33] "Likewise in North-Littleton he built a tithe barn."

Radiocarbon measurements taken of this building (UCLA-953, 954, 1004, 1005, 1006A, 1006B) pointed to a construction period of around 1250.[34] The fourteenth-century source just mentioned must have been related to another building.

In all the cases here discussed the sources were reliable and good. The connection of the source with the monument turned out to be faulty. It was radiocarbon analysis, not archaeological methods of dating, that taught us this lesson.

2. *The design of the roof and its archaeological dating value.* I have not been able to establish the date of a single building through the particulars of its roof design. And nothing has puzzled me more than the incompatibility of prevailing concepts about the typology and development of certain roof designs with many of our radiocarbon dates.

There was almost unanimous agreement among British archaeologists that the purlin roof came into use in England toward the middle of the fourteenth century, and all buildings with purlin roofs, on the basis of this assumption, were categorically dated in the "second half" of the fourteenth century or later. Most notable among these were the barns of Great Coxwell (figs. 7 and 8), Harmondsworth (figs. 16 and 17), and Bredon (figs. 22 and 23). Great Coxwell and Harmondsworth, as already men-

---

[31] Published in "UCLA Radiocarbon Dates," IV, *Radiocarbon,* VII (1965), 349, and UCLA Radiocarbon dates, V, *Radiocarbon,* VII (1966), 480.

[32] For a full description of the remarkable building, see Walter Horn and F. W. B. Charles, "The Cruck-built Barn of Middle Littleton, Worcestershire, England," with radiocarbon measurements by Rainer Berger, *J. Soc. Architect. Historians,* XXV (1966), 221–239.

[33] See *Chronicle Abbatiae de Evesham,* ed. William Dunn Macray, *Rerum Britannicarum Medii Aevi, Scriptores,* XXIX (London, 1863), 301.

[34] For a full discussion of these measurements, see Horn and Charles, op. cit., pp. 238–239.

FIG. 20. Middle Littleton, Worcestershire, England. Barn formerly belonging to the abbey of Evesham. Exterior from east (photo: Walter Horn).

FIG. 21. Middle Littleton, Worcestershire, England. Barn formerly belonging to the abbey of Evesham. Interior looking west (photo: Walter Horn).

FIG. 22. Bredon, Worcestershire, England. Barn formerly belonging to the abbey of Tewkesbury. Exterior from south (photo: Walter Horn).

FIG. 23. Bredon, Worcestershire, England. Barn formerly belonging to the abbey of Tewkesbury, in process of reroofing (1952). Interior looking north (photo: *The London Illustrated News*).

tioned, brought radiocarbon dates of "around 1250" and "around 1300," respectively.[35]

Three samples taken from Bredon yielded: one the time range 1135–1310 (UCLA-577A), the two others the alternative 1175 or 1250 (UCLA-1061) and 1490–1555 or 1640 (UCLA-1060). The first two samples suggest as the most probable date of construction the middle of the thirteenth century.[36] The third sample is puzzling, since the post from which it was taken has good original carpentry marks, which seems to preclude that it was a late replacement. We count with the possibility that this sample was contaminated.

The barn of the manor of Nettlestead, Kent. The barn of the manor of Nettlestead, Kent, was dated in the sixteenth century, because of the design of its trusses, by two men who knew the architecture of this region well, Arthur Oswald and S. E. Rigold.[37] The postmedieval outshots of this building, one of the finest pieces of rural architecture in the county of Kent (figs. 24 and 25) that perished in a hideous fire in 1962, gave it the appearance of an aisled structure. By origin it was a single-span barn, whose timbered walls and trusses derived their rigidity from a magnificent series of curved wall braces.

Three samples gathered from a charred post that survived the conflagration brought a very closely spaced cluster of dates, namely, the alternative 1455 or 1605 (UCLA-1085A), the date 1460 (UCLA-1085B), and the date 1440 (UCLA-1083). The measurements suggest as the most probable date of construction the middle of the fifteenth century.

Two barns in the parish of Lenham, Kent. In the parish of Lenham, Kent, there existed until very recently two handsome medieval barns, next to the church: one, Lenham "minor" (fig. 26, in background parallel to the picture plane), situated from east to west; the other, Lenham "major" (fig. 26, to the right and at right angles to the former), situated from north to south.[38] The barns cannot be older than 1298, because a

[35] For Great Coxwell and Harmondsworth see above, pp. 30 and 43.

[36] For Bredon see *Victoria History of the Counties of England, Worcestershire,* III (London, 1913), 279; Andrews, op. cit., pp. 16–17, and *Illustrated London News* 26 July 1952), p. 151 (restoration by National Trust); also an article by S. P. B. Mais in *Country Life* 21 June 1946), p. 1125.

[37] For Nettlestead see Arthur Oswald, "Nettlestead Place, Kent, the Home of Mr. and Mrs. Ronald Vinson," *Country Life* (16 Oct. 1958), Pt. I, 832–835; Pt. II (23 Oct. 1958), 886–889; and S. E. Rigold, "Some Major Kentish Timber Barns," *Archaeologia Cantiana,* LXXXI (1966), 28 ff.

[38] The barns of Lenham were first brought to my attention in 1960 by S. E. Rigold.

Fig. 24. Nettlestead Place, Nettlestead, Kent, England. Manor barn, destroyed by fire in the spring of 1962. Exterior from southwest (photo: Walter Horn).

Fig. 25. Nettlestead Place, Nettlestead, Kent, England. Manor barn, destroyed by fire in the spring of 1962. Interior view of roof looking east (photo: James W. Roberts).

FIG. 26. Lenham, Kent, England. Two barns, formerly in the possession of the Abbey of St. Augustine in Canterbury: Lenham "minor" in background, parallel to picture plane; Lenham "major" to the right and at right angles to the former (photo: courtesy of National Buildings Record).

directive issued by the archdeacon at Canterbury dated 27 February 1298, informs us that the church as well as "the houses in which the grain and other goods were stored were burned to the ground by arsonists" . . . "with premeditated malice."[39] There is a good historical likelihood that the two barns which are shown in figure 26 are the replacement of the buildings destroyed in 1298, and therefore might date from shortly after that fateful event. Since the photos reproduced in figures 26 and 27 were taken, the "minor" of the two barns at Lenham has disappeared—by a

[39] The archives of the dean and chapter of Canterbury Cathedral contain a mandate, dated 27 February 1298, which directs the official of the archdeacon of Canterbury to promulgate the sentence of excommunication against "those sons of iniquity who, unmindful of their welfare and kindled by the torch of hate and anger, with premeditated malice, acting in the spirit of the devil . . . burned down the church of Lenham, as well as the other buildings pertaining thereto after throwing them secretly into the chasm of fire, and in this manner laid to waste the grain and whatever other goods were stored in these houses" (*quod quidam iniquitatis filii sue salutis inmemores odii et iracundi facibus succensi in inferendis injuriis secumdum*

peculiar stroke of historical irony again in a fire set by arsonists.[40] Both barns have been described by Rigold in a competent study published in 1966.[41] He assigned the "major" barn of Lenham, on the basis of its design, to the "fifteenth century," the "minor" barn, "to the later fifteenth or early sixteenth century."[42]

Three radiocarbon samples taken in 1965 brought for Lenham "major" a date of about 1330–1340 (UCLA-1091) and for Lenham "minor" a range of 1280–1345 (UCLA-1089 and 1090). These dates not only appeared to reverse the relative sequence of construction, as claimed by Rigold, but also antedated the barns by a span of more than 200 years over the dates assigned by him. Rigold proposed to reconcile this conflict by assuming that the beams of Lenham "minor" from which our samples were cut were reused members salvaged from a building erected shortly after the fire of 1298.[43] In the summer of 1967, in order to inquire further into this problem, we collected additional samples from charred timbers left over from the fire of Lenham "minor," both from that part of the barn which Rigold considered genuine and old; we also collected a heartwood sample from one of the principal posts of Lenham "major." The two samples of Lenham "minor," extracted from different beams and different tree-depth positions, brought each the date range fourteenth century (UCLA-1345 and 1347); the sample from Lenham "major" brought the date 1310. These results are in complete agreement with the dates obtained by our earlier samples. UCLA-1346 was of particular in-

---

maliciam preconceptam . . . spiritu diabolico exercentes ecclesiam de Lenham . . . et domos suas pertinentes ad eandem ignis clanculo inmissi voragine combusserunt, bladaque sua et alia quamplurima bona in eisdem domibus ecclesie reposita penitus consumpserunt). For the full text of this document, see *The Canterbury and York Society, Diocese of Canterbury, Registrum Roberti Winchelsey, Cantuarensis Archiepiscopi*, A.D. 1294–1313, I, transcribed and edited by Rose Graham (Oxford, 1952), pt. 3, pp. 233–234. For guidance in tracing this document to its original source, I am most grateful to Dr. William Ury of the Archives of the Dean and Chapter in the Cathedral Library of Canterbury. The document became known to me through an excerpt in a local report on St. Mary's Church at Lenham, which was in the files of the Women's Institute of the parish.

[40] The barn was set afire on 15 September 1964 by two eleven-year-old boys who dropped a lighted match through a hole to see what the effect would be. Together with the barn, two hundred tons of hay and straw were destroyed. The flames shot forty feet high and threatened cottages and the church. See the account of the fire in the *Kent Messenger*, of Friday, 18 September 1964.

[41] Rigold, op. cit., pp. 14–15 (major barn), and pp. 17–18 (minor barn).

[42] Ibid.

[43] Ibid.

FIG. 27. Lenham, Kent, England, Lenham "minor," formerly in the possession of the Abbey of St. Augustine in Canterbury. Interior looking east. Destroyed by fire in 1964 (photo: courtesy of National Buildings Record).

terest. In order to bypass the ambiguities of the fourteenth-century plateau of the secular variation curve, we went as deep into the heartwood as conditions permitted. The 30 years gained in this manner took us indeed beyond the lower boundary of the plateau and thus enabled us to obtain a single date rather than the ambiguous fourteenth-century range.

The radiocarbon dates for the two Lenham barns are probably too close to each other to establish conclusively that Lenham "minor" is earlier than Lenham "major," but they establish with full finality that the design criteria used in assigning these buildings to the fifteenth and sixteenth centuries are untenable.

Lenham is not a unique case. I have already made reference to the distressing case of Frocester (figs. 18 and 19).[44] Neither R. A. Cordingly nor Fred Charles nor I could discover anything in the design of this roof that was incompatible with a late thirteenth-century date. And when our radiocarbon measurements made it clear that the roof was a postmedieval rebuild, Fred Charles and I could only focus upon a *minor detail* as a criterion that might have disclosed its postmedieval date, namely, the small square cleats that are wedged under the foot and next to the head of the arch braces to tighten the tenons (visible in fig. 19). We had not encountered this in any genuine medieval buildings.

The roof of the hall of the Castle of Leicester. The worst of all cases is that of the hall of the Castle of Leicester. This building, which serves as quarters for the court of the County of Leicester, incorporates in its present fabric the remains of the masonry walls and parts of the timbered frame of a Norman feudal hall of around 1150.[45] Up to the year 1821 the hall retained in essence its spacious medieval openness—and in this form it was seen and portrayed by a distinguished local architect and archaeologist Henry Goddard, the author of the engraving which is shown in figure 28.[46] Goddard's engraving shows that the medieval roof of the hall was supported by two rows of free-standing wooden posts, each of which is provided, a little over halfway up, with a scalloped Norman capital, and three feet above, at the springing level of the arch braces, with a simple Norman abacus.

In 1821 the hall was subdivided crosswise in its entire height by two

---

[44] Above, p. 46.

[45] On Leicester Hall see Levi Fox, "Leicester Castle," *Leicester Archaeol. Soc., Trans.* XXI, pt. 2 (1942/43), 127–170, and James Thompson, *An Account of Leicester Castle* (Leicester, 1859).

[46] Reproduced as frontispiece in Thompson, op. cit.

FIG. 28. Leicester, Leicestershire, England. Castle hall. Interior looking south by
Henry Goddard, showing condition prior to restoration undertaken in 1821.

internal masonry walls, dividing the space internally into a criminal
court and a civil court, separated from each other by a central entrance
hall with a jury room overhead (fig. 30).[47] At the same time the western

[47] For a plan showing the present condition of the Hall, see Fox, op. cit., p. 34.

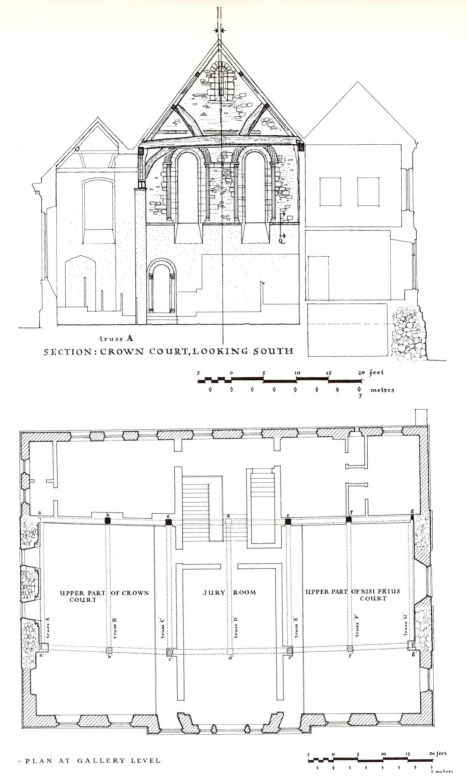

truss **A**

SECTION: CROWN COURT, LOOKING SOUTH

PLAN AT GALLERY LEVEL

FIGS. 29–30. Leicester Hall, Leicestershire, England. Castle hall. Plan of hall at tie-beam level (below); transverse section between trusses A and B (above). Drawing by Ernest Born (after measurements by Walter Horn and Ernest Born).

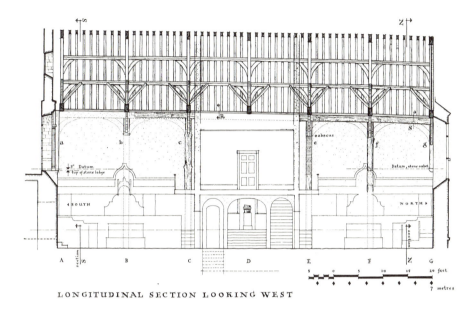

LONGITUDINAL SECTION LOOKING WEST

LONGITUDINAL SECTION LOOKING EAST

FIGS. 31–32. Leicester, Leicestershire, England. Castle hall. Longitudinal section looking west (above); longitudinal section looking east (below). Drawing by Ernest Born (after measurements by Walter Horn and Ernest Born).

aisle was sealed off by a longitudinal wall partition which concealed in its masonry the entire western row of wooden posts leaving parts of the nave face of these posts exposed in the surface of the masonry (fig. 31). Simultaneously, the entire eastern row of posts was amputated at the springing of the curved arch braces, and what was left above this level was placed upon a new underpinning of horizontal shoring beams upheld by newly constructed piers of brick (fig. 32). One of the scalloped Norman capitals of the eliminated lower portions of the posts survived this architectural surgery and is now on display on one of the landings of the stairwell which leads from the lobby to the conference and withdrawing rooms of the judges and barristers created in 1821 over the entrance room and in the original western aisle of the castle hall (fig. 33).

All the other capitals had disappeared, at least those of the amputated eastern row of posts of the hall; but there was a possibility that some of the capitals of the western row of posts might still be encased in the masonry in which these posts were submerged in 1821. In order to settle this problem, once and for all, I petitioned the county council of Leicester that the submerged timbers be exposed, wherever this was possible and compatible with the present use of the hall. The council graciously acceded to this request and the work was undertaken in two successive phases, in the summer of 1962 and 1964.[48] Of the two posts exposed in the course of this operation, one revealed, on precisely the level on which they would have to be found in the light of Goddard's engraving (fig. 28), the remains of a scalloped Norman capital and of the original Norman abacus (fig. 31, post c of truss C). The other post showed the remains of the Norman abacus, but the portion where the capital would have been found had been amputated (fig. 31, post e of truss E). There was no doubt that we were faced with the original Norman posts of the castle hall; and the remains of an abacus at the head of one of the amputated posts on the opposite side of the hall (fig. 32, post e' of truss E) suggested that what is left of the amputated eastern row of posts was also part of the original Norman frame of timber.

The question still to be settled was: How much of the superincumbent roof was Norman? Here the ways parted. John T. Smith was of the opinion that the design of the present roof precluded the assumption that

[48] I feel no limits of gratitude for the generous support received in this endeavor by County Architect T. A. Collins of Leicester.

FIG. 33. Leicester, Leicestershire, England. Castle hall. Scalloped Norman capital of one of principal roof-supporting posts, ca. A.D. 1150; (*a*) front view; (*b*) side view.

it is the original Norman roof.[49] It is a purlin roof resting on heavy trusses, with thin arched braces connecting its principal members, lengthwise and crosswise, as well as in the plane of the roof itself—a type of roof which in the mind of Smith as well as several other British archaeologists was associated with the fifteenth and later centuries.[50] I maintained, primarily on the basis of experiences gathered in connection with Continental and Scandinavian architecture, that there are good historical criteria in favor of the assumption that the Norman roof was a purlin

[49] J. T. Smith, "Medieval Aisled Halls and their Derivatives," *Archaeol. J.* CXII (1956), 87: "Of the 12th-century roofs at Hereford, Leicester and Oakham scarcely anything survives. All were completely rebuilt in the 15th century or later."

[50] That the present roof of the Hall of Leicester Castle is not the original Norman roof is a supposition first expressed by C. A. R. Radford, who observed that the tie beam of the roof-supporting truss that lies contiguous to the southern gable wall (fig. 30) cuts across the cornice of the Norman windows of this wall, and hence could not have been part of the original work (opinion expressed in a footnote to C. A. R. Radford's report on "Oakham Castle," publishied in *Archaeol. J.,* CXII [1956], 181–184; cf. n. 1, p. 183). Mr. Radford's observation is correct, but I cannot follow his conclusion. The timber frame of the Hall of Leicester Castle, while originally keyed firmly into the gable walls by means of half beams resting on masonry brackets, had simply sunk away from its original level over the centuries, and most significantly so presumably in 1821, when the wooden Norman pillars were cropped three feet below the tie beams and shored by modern timbers resting on modern piers of brick (cf. Walter Horn, "On the Origins of the Mediaeval Bay System," *J. Soc. Architect. Historians,* XVII [1958], 9).

roof, and that I saw no reason to question the Norman date of the roof
of Leicester Castle hall on general theoretical grounds. I added to this an
observation of a more technical nature, pointing out that if the upper
portions of the roof were rebuilt in conformity with a design that differed
from the original design, this changeover must be visible in the fabric
of the present roof. A change in the design of timbered frames requires
the cutting out of new mortices in the old timbers to serve as takeoff for
the new members and it also means the abandonment or readjustment of
old mortices which served as takeoff for the original beams. Yet, as the
eye moved from the Norman posts upward through every connecting
link into the ramification of the superincumbent trusses, one could not
detect even the smallest break in continuity (fig. 34).

The design—and this was a point on which everyone agreed—was
homogeneous throughout the entire width and length of the roof, and
the joinery was as tight and snug as one could possibly have wished it to
be. John Smith, although acknowledging the logic of this argument,
never wavered from his original position[51] and Rainer Berger and I, in
an attempt to settle the puzzling aspects of this controversy, decided to
make the roof of the castle hall of Leicester a test case for a high intensity
radiocarbon study. In the pursuance of this task (again supported by the
generous cooperation of the county council of Leicester and county architect T. A. Collins), we collected some twenty different samples from
various parts of this frame of timber. The experiment, unfortunately, was
hampered by two factors which, seen in restrospect, make Leicester Castle
hall not an ideal choice for this sort of experiment. One of these is that
the roof timbers of the hall have been heavily sprayed by preservative substances, which raises the question of chemical contamination; the other
is that in the majority of cases, because of the physical danger involved in

[51] The difficulties of this problem have haunted J. T. Smith and myself for over a
decade and were verbalized *in situ* by an exchange so puzzling in its implications
that both of us, some 14 years later, remember it word by word. Horn to Smith:
"You agree there is no break in the continuity of carpentry and jointing between the
demonstrably Norman parts of the timber frame and those which you claim to be
of post-Norman date?" Smith: "I agree." Horn: "Then I feel compelled to conclude
that the entire roof is Norman." Smith: "I cannot controvert your argument." Horn:
"Yet you continue to maintain that the roof above the level of the post is not of
Norman date." Smith: "I do." I am reporting this argument verbatim because it
illustrates the difficulties in which one can get involved in the analysis of vernacular
roof construction. Today I am inclined to think that J. T. Smith came closer to the
truth than I, despite the perplexing logic of his position.

Fig. 34. Leicester, Leicestershire, England. Castle hall. Roof over Crown Court Room, looking south. In foreground: tie beam of truss B, which yielded a radiocarbon date of A.D. 1450 (photo: James W. Roberts).

collecting them, and the conditions under which they had to be collected (in intervals between court sessions), the samples did not allow us to come to any firm conclusions about their relative tree-depth position. The experiment, although probably not of compelling conclusiveness, is nevertheless interesting enough to be reviewed as a test case.

The measurements are listed by their UCLA numbers in table 2 of Rainer Berger's paper (below, p. 129) and graphically illustrated in an isometric drawing of the roof of the hall, here shown in figure 35. They can be summarized as follows:

All samples taken from the posts of demonstrably Norman date, including the important but detached capital, brought unequivocal Norman dates (UCLA-566A, 94k, 942, and 1262). Of the higher-lying timbers, only one brought a Norman date, the tie beam of truss D (UCLA-566D, 566F; both taken from the same beam). Everything else brought thirteenth- and fifteenth-century dates. There was a group of seven samples that clustered around the year 1250 (UCLA-943, 1264, 1267, and 1269) or fell into the time range 1300–1400 (UCLA-566E, 945, and 949) and there

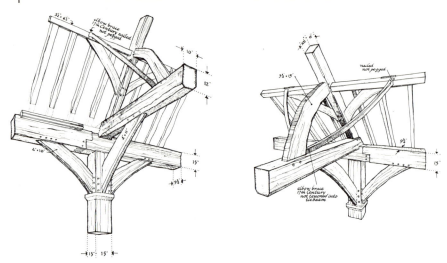

LEICESTER HALL · ASSEMBLY OF PRINCIPAL MEMBERS

Fɪɢ. 35. Leicester, Leicestershire, England. Castle hall. Assembly of principal roof-supporting members at tie-beam level. Drawing by Ernest Born (after measurements by Walter Horn and Ernest Born).

was another group of ten samples that clustered around 1450 (UCLA-566C, 566G, 944, 946, 947, 948, 1261, 1263, 1265, and 1286).[52]

The results tend to confirm Smith's view rather than mine. The roof of the hall of Leicester Castle will nevertheless remain a puzzle, until two disturbing features have been explained. One of these is that the tie beam of truss D brought a Norman date (two samples were taken, one from the middle, UCLA-566D, one from one of the ends of the beam, UCLA-566F). The other one is the fact that if the design that was used in the thirteenth- and fifteenth-century renovation is not identical with that of the original roof, then somewhere in the assemblage of the timbers there should be a line of demarcation disclosing the changeover from one design to the other; yet the timbers themselves—all contestants agreed on this point—show not the slightest trace of such a changeover.

Until these two anomalies are resolved we shall not cease to be haunted by the fear that the thirteenth- and fifteenth-century renovations of the roof involved the renewal of the individual beams and trusses only, and

[52] The samples in the 500 and 900 series (first published in "UCLA Radiocarbon Dates IV and V"; see *Radiocarbon*, VII (1965), 348 ff., and op. cit., VIII (1966), 481 ff., were analyzed and evaluated without reference to the secular variations ascertained by Hans Suess, since these were as yet not published. The dates here listed are based on a reinterpretation of the original measurements in the light of Suess' findings.

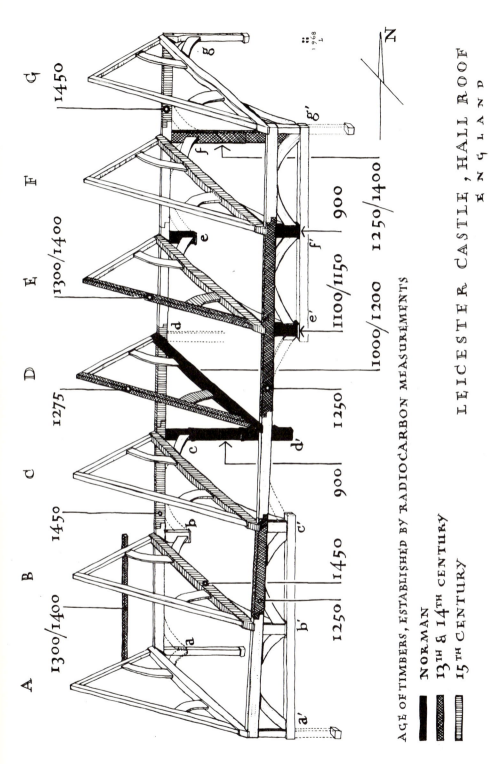

ACE OF TIMBERS, ESTABLISHED BY RADIOCARBON MEASUREMENTS

NORMAN

13TH & 14TH CENTURY

15TH CENTURY

LEICESTER CASTLE, HALL ROOF
ENGLAND

Fig. 36. Leicester, Leicestershire, England. Castle hall. Isometric view of present frame of roof and what is left of its supporting members, with radiocarbon dates of its respective timbers (drawing by Ernest Born).

not a change in the roof design. In any case we shall have to advance the supposed age of the design of the present roof from the fifteenth to the thirteenth or fourteenth century, since two of the principal rafters (trusses D and E), three arcade plates, and one of the longitudinal braces connecting the Norman posts with a thirteenth-century plate yielded such dates as 1250, 1275, and 1300–1400.

For the time being, perhaps, we ought to let the case of Leicester rest, until new and more conclusive evidence helps us to settle this difficult question. As far as our present objective is concerned, namely, the assessment of our ability to date buildings by virtue of their roof design, I would say that Leicester teaches us that we do not, at this juncture, possess sufficient historical knowledge about the nature and development of Norman roof designs to either establish or deny the Norman date of the surviving frame of timber. We have to establish its date by other means in order to gain firm ground in the shaping of our theories about the nature and development of the Norman roof design. This brings me to my next point.

3. *The design of carpentry joints and the archaeological dating value.* I personally have no confidence that with our present state of knowledge about medieval timber architecture we can attain any accuracy of dating through a comparative analysis of carpentry joints; for at least three reasons:

a) We do not have a sufficient amount of dated buildings to establish with certainty the chronological range or topographical spread of distinctive carpentry joints, not to speak of local or regional variations, developmental lag, or overlapping.

b) We will never attain this knowledge, because of a disastrous gap of historical evidence. I have made some calculations on this subject. Toward the end of the fifteenth century the total number of barns maintained by the monasteries of the order of Citeaux alone, in their home base and on their outlying states, ranged between two thousand and two thousand nine hundred.[53] To the best of my knowledge only two of these survive, one in magnificent condition at Great Coxwell and another on the Isle of Wight which was only recently brought to my attention. Let us make allowance for a colossal margin of error by assuming (1) that there are actually

---

[53] See Walter Horn and Ernest Born, *The Barns of the Abbey of Beaulieu* (Berkeley and Los Angeles, 1965), pp. 58 ff.

ten surviving Cistercian barns in England (i.e., five times as many as are known to me) and (2) that instead of two thousand or two thousand nine hundred there existed only a thousand Cistercian barns in medieval England (½-⅓ of my estimated total). The ratio 10:1000 is still a disastrous ratio for the historical evaluation of the spread in time and space of particular carpentry joints.

c) A third difficulty is that even the extant medieval material is at present very poorly surveyed. This has as one of its primary reason a deplorable prejudice against the study of vernacular architecture that has haunted our profession for nearly a century. In England and Germany this trend, fortunately, is beginning to be offset by the appearance of vigorous vernacular study groups; but in France, in the course of ten to fifteen years of work in this field, I have not encountered a single architectural historian, apart from myself, to preoccupy himself with this subject.

There is one instance, however, where the knowledge about the chronological limits of a particular carpentry joint has helped to offset an untenable traditional view about the date of a building in which these features occurred and thus to arrive at a historically more convincing date. This is the case of the barley barn at Cressing Temple, Essex, which gave the impetus to this study.[54]

The barley barn lies at right angles to another equally remarkable building which is known as the wheat barn (both of these are visible in fig. 1). The land on which these buildings stand belonged to an old Saxon manor which, after the Norman conquest, passed from Harold to Count Eustice of Bologna and from him to his daughter Maud, who married King Stephen. In 1136, by a charter dated at Evreux, Queen Maud granted the whole manor of *Cressynge* to the Knights Templars and it appears to have been the earliest English settlement of that order. In 1312, after the suppression of the order, the manor went to the Hospitallers in whose possession it remained until 1540 when the Hospital was dissolved.[55]

The literature available on the barns of Cressing Temple prior to Cecil Hewett's recent article on this subject [56] consisted of an anonymous article

---

[54] See above, p. 23.

[55] For further details see *The Victoria History of the Counties of England,* Essex, II (London, 1907), 177–178, and Philip Morant, *The History and Antiquities of the County of Essex* (London, 1768), pp. 113 ff.

[56] Quoted above, n. 1.

FIG. 37. Cressing Temple, Essex, England. Barley barn. Exterior showing its great south porch (photo: John Tarlton).

in *Country Life* published in the July 20 issue of 1940;[57] a brief description by their present owner, F. J. Cullen, published in the September 1949 issue of the *Seed Trade Review*;[58] and three articles by Cecil Hewett, one on "Timber-Building in Essex," published in 1961; another, entitled "Giant Barns in Essex," published in 1963; and a third one on "Structural Carpentry in Medieval Essex," published in 1962–63.[59]

[57] Anonymous author, "Harvest Homes, The Barns at Cressing Temple, An Historic Essex Farm," *Country Life* (20 July 1940), pp. 48–49, with photographs by John Tarlton.

[58] F. J. Cullen, "Cressing Temple, An Essex Manor," *Seed Trade Rev.* (September 1949); also available as a separate pamphlet privately published by Mr. Cullen, to whom we wish to express our gratitude for the friendly reception accorded us while working on his two barns.

The barns are also briefly discussed in the Essex volume of Nicolaus Pevsner's *Buildings of England* (Harmondsworth, 1954), p. 138, where it is stated that "The weatherboard Barley Barn is dated by experts ca. 1450, the brick built Wheat Barn about 1530."

[59] Cecil A. Hewett, "Timber Building in Essex, some Evidence for the possible Origins of the Lap-Dovetail," *Trans. Ancient Monuments Soc.,* n.s., IX (1961),

In the anonymous article in *Country Life*, the barley barn is dated "about 1480," the wheat barn "about the year 1530." Cullen accepts the date of 1480 for the barley barn but dates the wheat barn to around 1500. The date for the barley barn is probably derived from an inscription in its porch which bears the numeral 1480 in twentieth-century plaster with a twentieth-century style of figure. The reason for the dates of 1500 or 1530 for the wheat barn is wholly mysterious. Like those of most other medieval buildings of this construction type, these dates are based on "expert guesses" which lack the support of any further historical substantiation or comparative archaeological documentation. Hewett, who knows the barns more intimately than any other student of these two structures, was always convinced that they were of a considerably earlier date. In his *Country Life* article of 1962, he assigned the barley barn to "around 1300 A.D.,"[60] the wheat barn to "around 1500."[61] Encouraged by the early date of the first radiocarbon sample which brought the uncorrected date of A.D. 1010,[62] as well as the fact that the notched lap joints used in the barley barn (fig. 39) had good continental twelfth- and thirteenth-century parallels, he suggested a date of "between 1150 and 1200" for this building in his study of 1967, and expressed the view that the mortise-and-tenon jointing with its end-to-face or end-to-edge assembly as well as the full lap dovetail joints with extrant shoulders (fig. 40) which are found in the wheat barn would make it possible to ascribe the latter to "ca. 1275."[63]

The uncorrected radiocarbon measurement taken in 1963, as has already been mentioned, yielded the confusing and unacceptable date of 1010 ± 80. In the summer of 1965, Rainer Berger and I, in Cecil Hewett's presence, took three additional samples from several principal posts of the barley barn (UCLA-1075, 1076, 1077), and another one from a principal post of the wheat barn (UCLA-1078). The evidence thus obtained suggests that the barley barn of Cressing Temple was raised around A.D. 1200, the wheat barn around A.D. 1255. This supports Cecil Hewett's views to the extent of proving that the two barns are considerably earlier than

---

33–56; same author: "Giant Barns of an Essex Farm," *Country Life Annual* (1962), pp. 147–150; and "Structural Carpentry in Medieval Essex," *Medieval Archaeol.*, VI–VII (1962–63), pp. 240–271.

[60] Hewett, op. cit., p. 148.

[61] Ibid., p. 150.

[62] See above, p. 24.

[63] Cecil Hewett, "The Barns at Cressing Temple," *J. Soc. Architect. Historians*, XXVI (1967), 66 ff.

was previously believed. Hewett feels that "the difference in carpentry
and in the patination of the timbers would have postulated . . . a longer
lapse of time between the construction of the two buildings than is suggested by the radiocarbon dates." [64] In the summer of 1969, with the expert knowledge of Veronika Giertz, a very peremptory examination of
the two barns of Cressing Temple disclosed that their timbers were cut
from some young trees, whose wood does not encompass the necessary
number of tree rings for successful synchronization with the dendrochronological standard curve for German oak.

It is possible that Cecil Hewett's forthcoming book on the carpentry
joints in Essex will demonstrate that chronological sequences can be
established within the context of a study of regional types of joints and
their development; but whether these results can be automatically transferred to other counties—as they were in a recent article by S. E. Rigold [65]
—or from England to the Continent and vice versa remains another question. A glance at the joinery of two contemporary barns, one at Great
Coxwell in Berkshire (fig. 42) and the other at Middle Littleton in
Worcestershire (fig. 41), and their comparison with the joinery of the
two barns at Cressing Temple (figs. 39 and 40), makes one wonder
whether findings obtained in one area may ever be applicable to another.
Neither in Great Coxwell nor in Middle Littleton (both built in the
middle of the thirteenth century) can one detect even the slightest trace
of the notched lap-joint assemblage of the barley barn of Cressing
Temple (fig. 39). One cannot automatically presume that the development is uniform, nor that it is logical. In such matters as the design of
joinery, in a special sense, the inertia of custom and other professional
idiosyncracies may have acted as a powerful deterrent to developmental
logic and uniformity. Rigold ascribed the Court Lodge Barn at Brook
and the Great Manor Barn at Frindsbury (both in Kent) to the fourteenth century, because of their "splayed and tabled scarf-joints" (the
comparison with Great Coxwell and Cressing Temple should actually
have induced him to ascribe them to the middle of the thirteenth century). Radiocarbon analysis confirmed the fourteenth-century date for
Frindsbury (UCLA-1340; see below, p. 122) but suggested for Brook the
middle of the fifteenth century as the probable historical date of construction (UCLA-1341; see below, p. 117).

[64] Ibid., p. 68.
[65] S. E. Rigold, "Some Major Kentish Timber Barns," *Archaeologia Cantiana,*
LXXXI (1966), 1–30.

Fig. 38. Cressing Temple, Essex, England. Barley barn. Interior looking west (photo: John Tarlton).

4. *Masonry and its archaeological dating value.* This is a sad state of affairs. One should think that with the wealth of work that has been done on medieval masonry architecture we should be able to distinguish a thirteenth-century building from a fourteenth-century building by the different character of their masonry. Yet neither in the case of Great Coxwell (figs. 7 and 8) nor in the case of Bredon (figs. 22 and 23) nor that of Middle Littleton (figs. 20 and 21), all of which yielded radiocarbon dates clustered around the middle of the thirteenth century, has the masonry raised any doubts in the minds of those who date these barns

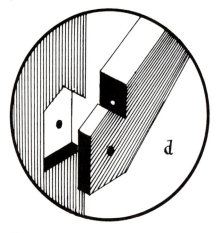

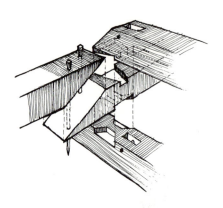

FIG. 39. Cressing Temple, Essex, England. Barley barn. Squint-notched lap joint with "retrousse" soffit, used in original collar beam (after Hewett, 1967, p. 55, fig. 8d).

FIG. 41. Middle Littleton, Worcestershire, England. Barn formerly belonging to the abbey of Evesham. Exploded collar-roof plate joint of base cruck, seen from "lower" side of barn (after Horn and Charles, 1966, p. 235, fig. 17).

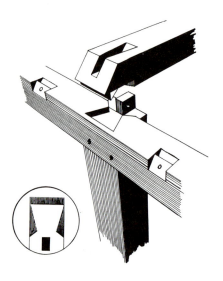

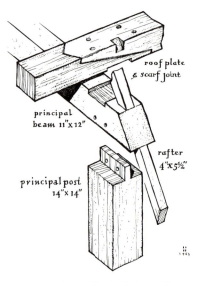

FIG. 40. Cressing Temple, Essex, England. Wheat barn. Main span tie-beam assemblage with plate and principal roof-supporting posts: a lap dovetail with entrant shoulders (after Hewett, 1967, p. 64, fig. 23).

FIG. 42. Great Coxwell, Berkshire, England. Barn of abbey grange, formerly in the possession of the Cistercian abbey of Beaulieu, Hampshire, ca. A.D. 1250. Assemblage of main post, tie beam, and arcade plate (by Walter Horn and Ernest Born).

into the "second half of the 14th century." Reason for this: a deplorable lack of good comparative masonry studies.

Buildings such as the magnificent barn of the Cistercian abbey of Ter Doest in Maritime Flanders, Belgium (figs. 43–44), are rare occurrences. The masonry of this barn, wholly of brick, can be dated with a fair degree of accuracy through a stylistic comparison of the blind relief of arches decorating its two magnificent gable walls with similar motifs found in the clearstory of the nave and the upper stories of the brick-built tower of the nearby church of Lisseweghe. The latter have been assigned, on relatively sound historical grounds, to the period 1250–1275.[66] Our radiocarbon measurements are not in contradiction with this date; yet neither are they precise enough to fully confirm it.

A heartwood sample taken from one of the principal posts of the barn brought the date 1230 (UCLA-568A); a sapwood sample from one of the aisle ties, the date 1250 (UCLA-568B).[67] A heartwood and a sapwood sample, subsequently taken from one of the horizontal base blocks of one of the principal posts of the barn, yielded the dates 1370 (UCLA-1036) and 1315–1415 (UCLA-1038),[68] and a further sample taken during a third visit from different timbers higher up in the frame, and from a different tree-depth position, yielded the date range 1270–1400 (Horn-1967, 1, UCLA-1315).

Rainer Berger concludes his analysis of these measurements with the remark that they may well suggest "the year A.D. 1300" for the erection of the barn, "with an error of some 40 years or so symmetrically about this date." [69] When we visited the barn in the summer of 1969 for dendro-

---

[66] Walter Horn and Ernest Born, *The Barns of the Abbey of Beaulieu* (Berkeley and Los Angeles, 1965), pp. 33 ff. Also to be consulted are: for Ter Doest, V. Fris and A. Heins, *Les Granges Monumentales des Anciennes Abbayes des Dunes et de Ter Doest dans la Flandre Maritime, XIIIᵉ siècle* (Gand, 1905), pp. 39–44, and Lucien Dendooven, *L'Abbaye de Ter Doest à Lissewege*, 2d ed. (Lissewege, 1957); for Lissewege see Luc Devliegher, "De Opkomst van de Kerkelijke Gotische Bouwkunst in West-Vlaanderen gedurende de XIIIᵉ Eeuw," *Bull. de la Commission Royale des Monuments et des Sites*, IV (1953), 265–273.

[67] The dates as originally published in "UCLA Radiocarbon Dates IV," *Radiocarbon*, VII (1965), 349, were A.D. 1135 (UCLA-568) and A.D. 1260 (UCLA-568B). Recalculated in the light of the Suess fluctuations these had to be converted into 1230 and 1250 respectively.

[68] For both samples we count with the possibility of contamination through modern manure, which, as we learned from a subsequent visit, was on occasion heaped up to a level where it could be absorbed in the open fibres of the base block from which these samples were taken.

[69] See below, p. 132.

FIG. 43. Ter Doest, Maritime Flanders, Belgium. Abbey barn, western gable wall
(photo: James W. Roberts).

FIG. 44. Ter Doest, Maritime Flanders, Belgium. Abbey barn. Interior looking north
(photo: James W. Roberts).

chronological analysis, Veronika Giertz observed immediately that its timbers were made of "meadow oak," on the average not more than 60 years of age, and for that reason would not furnish us with tree-ring sequences of sufficient length to permit synchronization with the standard curve for German oak. Conditions were very much like those which we had encountered a few days earlier in Cressing Temple, Essex.[70]

5. *Certain distinctive masonry details such as the design of corbels and profiles of moldings.* Here conditions are a little more favorable, but unfortunately there are so few details of this sort—at least in the type of building with which we are here concerned—that this criterion can almost be overlooked. I made use of it in the case of Great Coxwell, which displays a masonry corbel (fig. 42), all datable parallels for which fall into the first half of the thirteenth century. Some of these have recently been claimed to be a little later, unfortunately without submission of any substantiating evidence.[71] Radiocarbon analysis, as has already been mentioned, yielded the dates 1250, 1245, and 1250.

Conditions are better in many of the smaller or larger English palace and manor halls, where timbers are often molded, such as the scalloped Norman capitals at Leicester (fig. 33) or the beautifully molded arch braces of the Manor Hall of Nurstead Court, Kent (fig. 45). The former are typical for the middle of the twelfth, the latter for the middle of the fourteenth, century.[72] The same can be said of the molded arch braces of the small Manor Hall of Black Notley, Essex,[73] or the capital of a crown post of the hall of the manor of Tiptofts, Essex.[74]

Unfortunately, moldings of this kind are almost totally lacking in the large monastic barns or the great market halls with which this study is primarily concerned.

---

[70] See above, p. 70.

[71] S. E. Rigold in a review published in the *Antiquaries J.*, XLVI (1966), 356–357, of *The Barns of the Abbey of Beaulieu* (Berkeley and Los Angeles, 1965).

[72] For Nurstead Court, Kent, see article signed E. I. C. in *Gentleman's Magazine* (1837), pp. 364–367; John Henry Parker, *Domestic Architecture* in England, 2d ed. (London, 1882), pp. 281–282; Arthur Oswald, *Country Houses of Kent* (London, 1933), pp. 14–15; and J. T. Smith, "Medieval Aisled Halls and their Derivatives," *Archaeol. J.*, CXII (1956), 84–86.

[73] For Stanton's Farm, Black Notley, Essex, see *Royal Commission on Ancient and Historical Monuments, Essex,* I (London, 1921), 19–20; J. T. Smith, op. cit., pp. 81–82; and idem, "Medieval Roofs: A Classification," *Archaeol. J.*, CXV (1960), 111–112.

[74] For Tiptofts Manor, Essex, see J. Henry Middleton, "On a thirteenth-century

6. *"Expert" knowledge acquired intuitively through a lifelong professional contact with buildings.* Authority is not a substitute for documentation. When buildings are dated in the light of such details as the design of "bilobed carinate corbels," the form of "dripstone terminals," the profiles of "scrollhood molds," or the shape of "two-cusped shouldered lintels," such a procedure is acceptable only if the comparative material is properly identified, and can be pinpointed chronologically by unequivocable historical or archaeological evidence. Failure to comply with this method seems to have become a compulsive trait of review writing[75] It deprives the reader of the opportunity to judge the soundness of the reviewer's argument, and divests the proponent of the challenged view of the possibility to correct himself in the light of new or more convincing evidence. It is obvious that the temptation to establish dates intuitively rather than by the more rigid methods of historical demonstration is especially great in the case of buildings where historical documentation is almost totally wanting.

Even "consensus of opinion" cannot be taken as a substitute for demonstration. Prior to 1965 it was generally agreed among students of vernacular architecture that the "Tithe" Barn of Great Coxwell in Berkshire was built in the fourteenth century. In 1965 I drew attention to the fact that the closest parallels to certain decorative details in the barn of Great Coxwell were found in buildings dating from the first half of the thirteenth century, and radiocarbon measurements subsequently taken yielded the dates 1245 (UCLA-1049) and 1250 (UCLA-1048). At the spring meeting of 1967, I am told, it was the "general consensus" that the Great Coxwell was built "around 1275." It is quite possible, in my opinion, that Great Coxwell Barn was built around 1275, but it is not "consensus of opinion," not even that of such an experienced and highly sophisticated body as the Vernacular Architecture Group, that established this assumption as a fact. To prove that Great Coxwell dates from "around 1275," it would have to be demonstrated by comparison with securely datable

---

Oak Hall at Tiptofts Manor, in Essex," *Archaeologia*, LII (1890), 647–650; *Royal Commission on Historical Monuments,* op. cit., pp. 351–352; J. T. Smith, op. cit. (1956), p. 90, and J. M. Fletcher and P. S. Spokes, "The Origin and Development of Crown-Post Roofs," *Medieval Archaeol.,* VIII (1964), 171 ff.

[75] While my remarks are motivated by a particular review, I find it useless to blame an individual for shortcomings that have become an accepted standard of this entire genus of writing.

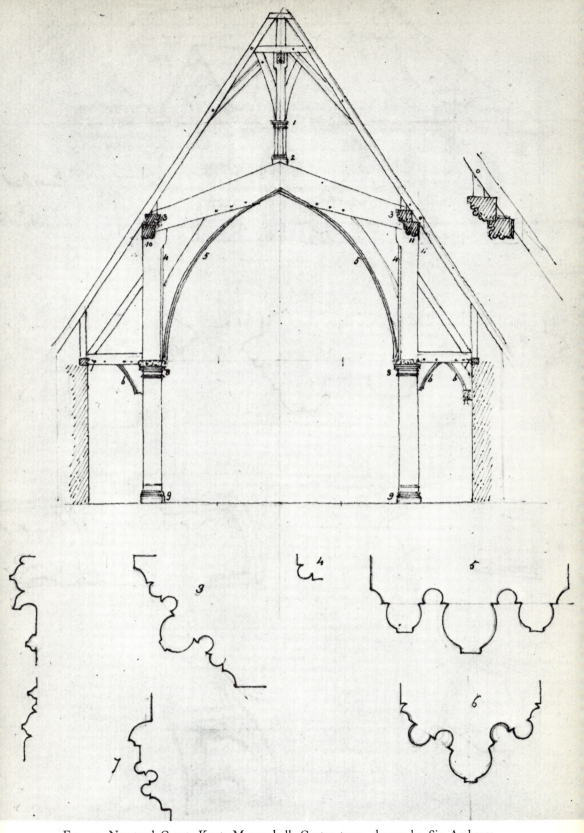

FIG. 45. Nurstead Court, Kent. Manor hall. Center truss, drawn by Sir Ambrose Poynter. Sketchbook, now at The Royal Institute of British Architects, in London, Sir Banister Fletcher Library, Drawings Collection (photo: courtesy of Royal Institute of British Architects).

examples (1) that the "bilobed carinate corbels" that serve as base for the great intermediate cruck blades of the barn were as common around 1275 as they were in the first half of the century, and (2) that the corbels of Great Coxwell are more closely related to those that date from around 1275 than to those that can be reliably ascribed to the first half of the thirteenth century. The same would have to be ascertained for the "drip-stone terminals," the "scrollhood molds," and the "two-cusped shouldered lintels" found in the building. In cases of this kind, I fear, "intuition" has tended to outdistance "proof." Even radiocarbon analysis may not be accurate enough to settle such relatively small discrepancies of dating. The ultimate answer may only be found in a dendrochronological analysis of the timbers of Great Coxwell.

FIG. 46. Great Coxwell, Berkshire, England. Barn of abbey grange, ca. 1250. Bilobed carinate corbel (photo: Walter Horn).

Conclusions

It can be said that medieval archaeology, with its own inherent dating methods, is doing very poorly with the type of buildings with which we are here concerned. This leaves as our last concern the question: How well are we doing with radiocarbon analysis?

The authoritative answer to this question, of course, must come from Rainer Berger. It is part of my assignment, nevertheless, to say a few words about what it looks like from the art historian's point of view. I would answer this question as follows:

If an archaeological date and a radiocarbon date are in disagreement, I would give the higher degree of credence to the radiocarbon date, provided that proper allowance is made for such factors as the original tree-depth position of a given sample, carbon-13 correction, and most of all the fluctuation in terrestrial radiocarbon intake as established by Hans Suess and others.

However, even if all of these factors are accounted for, there still remain some lingering doubts. One of them is: What happened to the former margins of error of ± 80 or ± 60? Are these absorbed in the interaction of the three correction factors named above? To be specific: Does the date 1250 as it emerges from this interaction mean 1250, does it mean 1220, does it mean 1280, or does it mean any point on the line that connects 1220 and 1280 with the highest possibility near 1250? What can we learn, in search for an answer to this question, (*a*) from radiocarbon dates obtained from historically dated buildings; and (*b*) from our measurements of multiple samples taken from the same beam at different tree-depth positions?

Another major and perhaps even more festering doubt is: Just how reliable are the assessments of the secular fluctuations in terrestrial radio-carbon intake made by Hans Suess? One observation that puzzled me more than anything else in this study is: Why are some of our radio-carbon measurements so unexpectedly accurate (e.g. Troussures, Richelieu), while others are so disconcertingly erratic (Ter Doest)? In observing the procedures used in translating quantity measurements of C-14 into historical dates, one feels awed by the multitude and magnitude of the required correction factors. An incorrect assessment of the tree-depth position of a given sample may have fatal consequences (as the samples of Cressing Temple and of the abbey grange of Canteloup have shown); yet it is not inordinately disconcerting, because such a mistake

can be easily checked, with the aid of drill cores, and satisfactorily corrected. But the errors that may be caused by insufficient knowledge of
the precise nature of the secular fluctuations of a given period are of a
different order, because we are not, at this juncture, in possession of
sufficient data to judge with the desired precision the limits of accuracy
obtainable in measuring these fluctuations. To have to make all of these
delicate adjustments on a fluctuation assessment obtained through one
single experiment based on dendrochronologically dated samples spaced
30 years apart struck me as an unsatisfactory condition. Is this experiment
not in need of confirmation by the running of a second series of radiocarbon measurements, preferably at ten-year intervals, over a historically
confined period, such as, for instance, the span between A.D. 1100 and
1500, for which dendrochronologically and historically dated samples are
available in abundance? If the fluctuation curve that emerges from this
second experiment confirms the fluctuation curve established by Hans E.
Suess, then we art historians could feel safer in our application of radiocarbon dating to medieval archaeology.

An experiment of this type is the more imperative, since at the present
time there exists not only one but two interpretations of the medieval
and postmedieval fluctuations in terrestrian radiocarbon intake measured
by Suess, namely (a) the original system published by Suess in 1965[76]
and (b) a modification of this interpretation worked out jointly by M.
Stuiver and Suess in 1966.[77] In checking the radiocarbon measurements of
historically dated or datable samples of medieval timber collected by us
against both of these systems, Rainer Berger found that he obtained
more coherent results from Suess' original correction curve than from
the Stuiver-Suess modification, intended to supersede it. This is bound
to leave uncertainties concerning the preferability of one over the other
system, that might be resolved by a new series of fluctuation measurements undertaken with a more closely spaced series of dated samples.
As long as this is not done, we have no means of judging how much of
the now-existing inaccuracies of radiocarbon dating must be ascribed to
limitations inherent in measurement techniques, how much to shortcomings in our assessment of its secular fluctuations.

While we collected and processed our materials we were repeatedly
warned to stay away from sapwood, because of its susceptibility to contamination. We were told that "results obtained from sapwood may well

[76] See the article quoted above in n. 4.
[77] *Radiocarbon* 8 (1966), pp. 634 ff.

be useless, or even worse, treated as being significant, when they may be in error."[78] As far as we know, this view is speculative and not based on any actual radiocarbon measurements undertaken for the purpose of ascertaining experimentally the relative suitability of sapwood and heartwood for carbon-14 dating. The criticism may in fact have been generated by one of our own measurements of a specimen from one of the cruck blades of the barn of Middle Littleton, which was heavily contaminated.[79]

There can be no doubt in anybody's mind that sapwood is more susceptible to contamination than heartwood, because it is more permeable to passage of liquids; and sapwood samples, for that reason, have to be more carefully decontaminated or chemically pretreated. But to draw from such occurrence the categorical inference that sapwood is untrustworthy and should be discarded from radiocarbon studies would be a serious blunder. Rainer Berger and I have made it a special point, wherever conditions permitted, to collect and measure samples from different tree-depth positions of one and the same piece of timber, and found that in every case, except the one of Middle Littleton, sapwood and heartwood (after full allowance was made for tree-depth position and other pertinent correction factors) yielded the same historical date. We found this to be the case in Beaulieu-St. Leonard's (UCLA-1014, 1015, 1016), Great Coxwell (UCLA-1048, 1049), Harmondsworth (UCLA-1050, 1051), Lenham "minor" (UCLA-1085, 1090), Nettlestead (UCLA-1085A, 1083, 1085), Méréville (UCLA-572, 1304), and Parçay-Meslay (UCLA-1313B, 570).[80] In other cases, where sapwood samples were taken from timbers, securely dated either by inscription or by written historical sources, the sapwood samples yielded measurements that turned out to be in full accord with the known historical dates. I am referring to such cases as the market halls of Questembert (UCLA-1310) and Richelieu (UCLA-1303) and the seventeenth-century work of the monastic barn of Troussures in France (UCLA-1308).[81]

In the light of these findings we see no reason whatsoever to disenfranchise sapwood from radiocarbon measurement. To do so on no other grounds than the presumption that sapwood is more easily contaminated than heartwood would be rendering a bad service to medieval archae-

---

[78] John M. Fletcher, in repeated personal communication and in letters to friends and colleagues.

[79] See Rainer Berger's account of this measurement published in the article by Walter Horn, F. W. B. Charles, and R. Berger cited above in n. 32.

[80] See below, pp. 101–128.

[81] See Rainer Berger's discussion of these measurements, below, pp. 112–113.

ology. In many buildings for which radiocarbon analysis is our only available method of dating, good heartwood samples cannot be obtained without the use of power tools and electricity—facilities that in general are not available in these places; not to speak of the difficulties of obtaining permission to use such equipment for the purpose of extracting heartwood cores from principal structural members. In other cases, where heartwood is available, but its correct tree-depth position cannot be ascertained, sapwood is clearly preferable, because it furnishes a more reliable tree-ring correction factor. One of our own measurements significantly illustrates this fact. A heartwood sample from one of the principal posts of the monastic barn of Canteloup (Eure), France, located about 30 tree rings from the pith of the tree, suggested as construction date the turn of the thirteenth to fourteenth century.[82] In calculating this date, we had proceeded on the assumption that the tree from which this post was hewn, was, at the time of felling, about 100 years old. After the barn had been dismantled, in the fall of 1967, to be reerected on the grounds of the nearby Abbey of St.-Wandrille (Fontanella), we obtained a cross section through the foot of one of the principal posts of this building. A tree-ring count of this section, undertaken at the Forest-botanical Institute of the University of Munich, disclosed that the trees used for the principal posts of the barn had grown to an age of 180 to 190 years before they were felled—which forced us to discard our original date and assign the building to the fifteenth century.

In the paper that follows, Rainer Berger arrives at the conclusion that in the best of cases in many of the medieval samples measured in the context of this study we appear to be moving within a margin of error of ± 20–30 years from the historical target. But there is a sufficient number of other cases to warn us against being overoptimistic on this score. A final assessment of the relative accuracy or inaccuracy of radiocarbon dating will require a great deal of further systematic studies. There can be no doubt that for ultimate precision we must turn to dendrochronology. For North America, south and west Germany, as we have learned from this symposium, tree-ring analysis is capable of spectacular accomplishments.[83] In the plains of north Germany, where the trees have constant access to ground water, conditions have been found to be considerably more difficult. In England dendrochronology was at the time of our gathering

[82] See below, pp. 117–120.

[83] See the accounts by C. W. Ferguson, B. Huber, and V. Giertz; below, pp. 183 and 201.

still in its beginning stages. There is the exciting possibility, however, that the work carried on at Oxford by John Fletcher may bring a breakthrough. France was *terra incognita* until the experiments conducted by Rainer Berger, Veronika Giertz, and myself, while this publication was in process of issue, brought the unexpected result that medieval oak of Normandy and of the Paris region can be dated with the standard curves for south German and west German oak. An extension of this same experiment to a small group of widely scattered timber buildings in England disclosed that conditions in Great Britain are considerably more complex than on the Continent (an observation that did not come as a surprise to us) and perhaps comparable to those prevailing in north Germany. Individual curves obtained from several drill cores of one and the same building could be easily harmonized with one another, but the middle curve obtained in this manner for the entire building could not be synchronized with the middle curves obtained in like manner for other buildings. A high percentage of the buildings we inspected were made of timbers cut from very young trees (often not more than 60 years of age) with extremely broad rings, hence obviously grown in meadows or valleys where their roots had permanent access to ground water, which made them unsuited for dendrochronological analysis.

There was, nonetheless, one startling exception: the Bailiff's House in the city of Bewdley, in Worcestershire, which Fred Charles had brought to our attention. This handsome half-timber building carries on the lintel of its street entrance the date 1610. The middle curve obtained from a number of drill cores taken by Veronika Giertz from the building was found to be in complete harmony with the standard curve for south German oak, for the entire period A.D. 1370–1600. This opens up the prospect that other buildings of this area may be dated with the same curves—unless we were to presume that the Bailiff's House in Bewdley was built with timber shipped to Bewdley from Germany.[84]

The puzzle of Bewdley could easily be settled by a dendrochronological study of a few carefully selected buildings from the same general region. But our inability to synchronize the curves from a considerable number

---

[84] Veronika Giertz found that a curve obtained from the Priory House of Droitwich shows distinct similarities with the curve of the Bailiff's House of Bewdley. This would suggest that other buildings in Worcestershire might be datable with the standard curves for German oak. But the wood of the only available drill core on which this curve was based was partially rotten, which calls for further sample from this house, to confirm or disprove this observation.

of other buildings in widely scattered areas of England (3 in Worcestershire, 1 in Warwickshire, 1 in Gloucestershire, 1 in Berkshire, 1 in
Middlesex, and 2 in Kent) would suggest that a considerable amount of
highly specialized regional work might have to be undertaken before
dendrochronology can be reliably used in all of these districts. New discoveries in the analysis of the dendrochronological idiosyncracies of the
"meadow oak" may change this picture. Their youth and broad rings
have so far made them either entirely unsusceptible to dendrochronological interpretation or call for methods so complex and costly as to
make their use for archaeological purposes prohibitive. Even in Normandy and in the Paris region we ran into some buildings that could
not be related to the otherwise usable German standard curves because
their timbers were fashioned from young "meadow oaks" with indis-
criminately broad rings. For these buildings radiocarbon analysis is today
and may be, for some time to come, our only hope. As yet we are far from
being able to dispense with radiocarbon analysis as an auxiliary method
of dating, in favor of dendrochronology. As long as this is the case the
question of the potential and limitations of radiocarbon analysis will
remain for art historians and archaeologists a matter of vital concern.

✠   ✠   ✠   ✠

In the foregoing exposition I have not shown any reluctance to bear
heavily on the weaknesses of our profession, when involved in the subtle
task of dating. In focusing so harshly upon the shortcomings of traditional dating methods, I do not wish to convey the impression that I
consider myself, as an individual, exempt from the pitfalls by which this
endeavor is haunted. The cases of Leicester and Frocester alone give cause
for humility. Beaulieu-St. Leonard's is another.

If there is one single piece of timber of which I would have assumed
without any sense of qualification that it was a leftover of one of the
most remarkable barns of England, it was a beam that now serves as
lintel over one of the wagon doors of a barn of relatively small dimensions, built at an unknown time within the floor area of the great barn
of Beaulieu-St. Leonard's in Hampshire. The barn is now in ruins, but
what is left of its masonry (as well as the general historical context of
the monastery to which it belonged) leaves no doubt that the original
structure was built during the first half of the thirteenth century. The
notches of the beam in question disclose that in its original architectural

setting it served as a wall plate.[85] The dimensions of this beam, 9½ by
11 inches, suggest that it served as footing for the rafters of a roof of
unusual dimensions.[86] It was reasonable to assume that it was a surviving
timber of the roof of the great thirteenth-century barn, the largest
medieval barn of England known in our days, and one of the largest in
the whole of England, with walls rising up to a height of 14 feet
6 inches.

In the summer of 1967 Rainer Berger extracted three samples of wood
from this beam at countable tree-ring intervals (UCLA-1014, 1015, and
1016). The radiocarbon measurements obtained from these samples reflected the tree-depth positions of the chosen specimens with an unexpected accuracy, but brought the archaeologically perplexing result that
the beam itself was shaped from a tree that was felled around 1650. "It
follows," as Berger puts it succinctly, "that the lintel is not composed of
timber used in the original structure; but it could, of course, have been
a seventeenth-century replacement of one of the wall plates of the original
barn."[87] If this is what it was, then it follows further that the thirteenth-
century barn of Beaulieu-St. Leonard's must still have been in place in
1650 and in sufficiently good condition to be considered worthy of being
repaired at that time.

In a study published in 1965 in which I discussed the barn of Beaulieu-
St. Leonard's at some length,[88] I pointed out that a careful examination
of the roof timbers of the smaller substitute barn in which this wall plate
was incorporated might disclose the presence of other "reused" timbers
of the original building. I myself could not examine these timbers in any
detail; first, because during the three visits which I paid to Beaulieu-St.
Leonard's, the trusses of the substitute barn were almost completely
buried in hay stacked from the floor clear up to the ridge of the roof,
and second, because the few trusses that were visible from the unob-
structed wagon bay contained a detail, an arch-shaped contact brace
filling the entire angle between rafter and collar beam (cf. above, p. 48),
which in those days appeared to me to be a sure mark of the fifteenth
century.

[85] When reused to serve as lintel for the wagon door of the present barn it was
turned around, so that its notches now face downward rather than up.
[86] For a photo and dimensional drawing of the beam, see Horn and Born, op. cit.,
pp. 44–45, figs. 39–40.
[87] See below, p. 117.
[88] Horn and Born, op. cit., p. 47.

When Fred Charles visited Beaulieu-St. Leonard's in the spring of 1968, at a time when the barn was sufficiently empty to enable him to measure its timbers, he found that the dimensions of the trusses of the new barn were, to the inch, identical with the dimensions of the trusses that once supported the roof over the nave of the original structure. He inferred from this coincidence that the roof of the present barn was built with timbers from the original roof of the barn.[89] Fred Charles incorporated these views in a reconstruction drawing of the thirteenth-century barn (fig. 18 below, p. 229), which differed greatly from one that Ernest Born and I had worked out in our book on the Barns of Beaulieu-St. Leonard's.[90] Charles's argument and observations appeared to me to be clear and convincing, and I was ready to jettison my original thoughts on this subject. But radiocarbon measurements of a small group of samples from the timbers of the substitute barn, collected by Fred Charles and myself in the summer of 1968, brought the surprising result that the trusses of the substitute barn were made from trees felled in the middle of the fifteenth century. It now looks as though Ernest Born and I might still be on solid ground with our reconstruction of the original barn— that this barn was rebuilt in the fifteenth century in the manner suggested by Fred Charles and that in the seventeenth century it was still in sufficiently good condition to warrant replacement of one of its massive wall plates.

Beaulieu-St. Leonard's is only one of a considerable number of other buildings that could be cited to show what tricky problems this type of timber architecture poses to our efforts of dating. It is easy for even an experienced eye to be by two or three or four, if not more, centuries off the truth in this game of dating. I shall never forget the experience made in 1960, when Ernest Born and I studied the market hall of Questembert in Morbihan, France.[91] Before we became aware of the fact that one of its tie beams carried the inscription 1675 my guesses ranged all the way from the thirteenth to the sixteenth century. Even today I could not point my finger on any detail or stylistic feature that would preclude a thirteenth-, fourteenth-, or fifteenth-century date for this building. Radiocarbon analysis yielded the date 1625–1670, which is a minimum of only five and a maximum of only 50 years off its actual date of construction;

---

[89] See Fred Charles's account below, p. 225.

[90] Horn and Born, op. cit., p. 43.

[91] See Walter Horn, "Les Halles de Questembert," *Bull. Soc. Polymathique du Morbihan* (1963), pp. 1–16.

while our own estimate encompassed a margin of error of nearly five centuries. We owe Willard Libby an enormous debt for his spectacular discovery of radiocarbon dating; and we should also express our gratitude to Hans Suess, whose fluctuation assessments have made this great discovery more applicable to our specific needs.

III

THE POTENTIAL AND LIMITATIONS OF RADIOCARBON DATING IN THE MIDDLE AGES: THE RADIOCHRONOLOGIST'S VIEW

R. Berger

A FUNDAMENTAL QUANTITY to be determined in any mechanism of change is time. Radiocarbon dating is one of the most important absolute dating methods capable of defining an age range closely surrounding an event in history or prehistory with an effective limit of approximately a hundred to more than fifty thousand years ago. The method applies the principle of a known immutable radioactive decay rate to the measurement of elapsed time.

Radiocarbon dating was conceived theoretically shortly after World War II and vigorously developed by Willard Libby and his co-workers.[1] The technique has proved to be of such value that many other investigators entered into the new area of radiocarbon dating, while the discoverer in recognition of his achievement was awarded the 1960 Nobel Prize in Chemistry. Since those early days, radiocarbon dating has been advanced to increasingly higher levels of perfection. The pertinent literature itself is published or referred to in a special journal: *Radiocarbon.*[2]

General Theory of Radiocarbon Dating

The earth is being bombarded constantly by cosmic rays with such intensity that atoms composing the top layer of our atmosphere are disintegrated. During this breakup, neutrons are generated which collide with the two main constituents of air: oxygen and nitrogen. It is, however,

---

[1] W. F. Libby, *Radiocarbon Dating* (Chicago: University of Chicago Press, 1955 and 1965).

[2] For literature prior to 1959, see compilation of pertinent publications in *Radiocarbon* (New Haven, Conn.: Yale University, 1959), vol. 1.

essentially only nitrogen which due to its larger cross section or target area undergoes a nuclear transformation to carbon-14 or radiocarbon:

$$N^{14} + neutron \longrightarrow C^{14} + proton.$$

The freshly produced radiocarbon is then rapidly attacked by oxygen and converted to carbon dioxide which in turn mingles with all the other 0.03 percent of carbon dioxide in our atmosphere. Equal worldwide distribution in the atmosphere is assured by the winds which cause relatively rapid mixing of the lower levels of the global-air envelope within the span of a year. The oceans in turn take part in establishing global equilibrium conditions by exchanging carbon dioxide with the atmosphere.

The next step involves the fact that all plant life is dependent on the process of photosynthesis in which carbon dioxide and water are combined in leaves to form plant matter with the aid of chlorophyll and sunlight. Thus plants continuously incorporate radiocarbon as they grow and indirectly animals and men do so as well. The introduction of radiocarbon stops, however, upon the death of an organism. From that moment the content of radioactive carbon will decrease with the characteristic speed of its decay in an immutable manner not affected by any known physical process.

What is known about the constancy of radiocarbon production throughout the last 50,000 years or so permits the conclusion that organic material many thousands of years old had at the time of its death essentially the same radiocarbon content as can be found today in modern living species. As a consequence, the date of death of an ancient sample can be calculated by comparing the intensity or quantity of radiocarbon left in it with that in a present-day standard. The only other prerequisite is a good knowledge of the rate of decay of carbon-14, or its decay constant, which is related to either the mean life or the half-life in the standard manner.[3]

$$① \quad \frac{\text{Time of death}}{\text{(in years)}} = \text{Mean life of } C^{14} \times \ln \frac{\text{Intensity of } C^{14} \text{ in standard}}{\text{Intensity of } C^{14} \text{ in sample}}.$$

---

[3] Half-life is the time interval required for the original radioactivity to decline to one-half that value. Half-life $(t_{1/2}) = \dfrac{\ln 2}{\text{decay constant } (\lambda)}$; Mean life = half-life $\times \dfrac{1}{\ln 2}$ ($\ln 2 = 0.69315$).

The Refinements in Radiocarbon Dating

Even though experience with radiocarbon dating has shown that the basic theoretical assumptions are by and large correct or even have been strengthened in the light of newer geophysical data, several amendments have been developed from the inception of the method which take into account individual significant features that were not immediately apparent.[4] Some of these have a marked effect on our ability to obtain more accurate radiocarbon dates.

Production of radiocarbon. The most recent estimate of the average production rate of neutrons by cosmic rays in the earth's atmosphere is some 2.5 ± 0.5 per cm^2 of the earth's surface per second,[5] at an optimum altitude of about 50,000 feet.[6] This is equivalent to knowing the rate of formation of carbon-14 to an accuracy of within 20 percent. In reality the neutron intensity varies with the latitude. Due to the properties of the geomagnetic field, the rate near the poles is four to five times greater than at the equator as shown in figure 1.[7] Initial proof for rapid mixing of the atmosphere was obtained by measuring the radiocarbon content of modern wood samples from locations throughout the world. All had remarkably similar concentrations or specific activities.[8]

Equilibrium of radiocarbon among the exchange reservoirs. The amount of radiocarbon available to plants from the atmosphere is not only controlled by the production rate in the stratosphere but also by the behavior of the natural reservoirs which store radiocarbon and exchange it among one another as listed below:

Exchange reservoirs

(Carbon content in g/cm^2 averaged over earth's surface)

Ocean, bicarbonate or carbonate		7.25
Sediments	ca.	1.00
Ocean, dissolved organic matter		0.59
Biosphere		0.33
Atmosphere		0.12
	ca.	9.3

---

[4] W. F. Libby, in *Proc. Symposium on Radioactive Dating and Low Level Counting,* International Atomic Energy Agency, Monaco, 2–10 March 1967.

[5] R. E. Lingenfelter, in *Revs. Geophys. 1* (1963), 1.

[6] L. C. L. Yuan, in *Phys. Rev. 77* (1950), 728.

[7] J. A. Simpson, Jr., in *Phys. Rev. 73* (1948), 1389.

[8] W. F. Libby, E. C. Anderson, and J. R. Arnold, in *Science 109* (1949), 227.

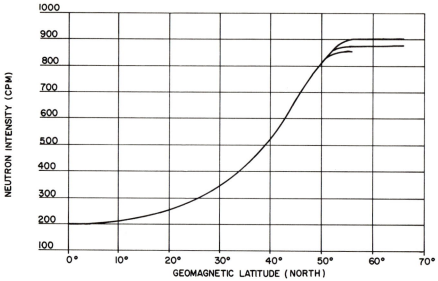

FIG. 1. Neutron intensity versus geomagnetic latitude at 30,000 feet [after J. A. Simpson, Jr., *Phys. Rev. 73* (1948), 1389].

Inspection of this table reveals the enormous buffering capacity of the oceans containing almost one hundred times more carbon than the atmosphere and resisting any changes in the contemporary specific activity.[9] In general, complete mixing requires considerably less time than the half-life of carbon-14 (5730 ± 30 years). Exchange processes between individual reservoirs vary from a few years between the stratosphere and troposphere to very long periods of time between sediments or rocks and other reservoirs. Ultimately, isotopic equilibrium is reached in which the addition of freshly formed stratospheric carbon-14 is balanced by radioactive decay and sedimentation. Models involving these dynamic processes have been discussed by Arnold and Anderson,[10] Broecker,[11] Broecker and Olson,[12] Craig,[13] De Vries,[14] Fergusson,[15] Fergusson and Rafter,[16] and

[9] L. Wood and W. F. Libby, in *Isotopic and Cosmic Chemistry,* H. Craig, S. L. Miller, and G. J. Wasserburg, eds. (Amsterdam: North Holland Publishing Company, 1964).

[10] J. R. Arnold and E. C. Anderson, in *Tellus 9* (1957), 28.

[11] W. S. Broecker, in *The Sea,* vol. 11, ed. M. N. Hill (New York: Interscience, 1963).

[12] W. S. Broecker and E. A. Olson, in *Science 132* (1960), 712.

[13] H. Craig, in *Tellus 9* (1957), 1.

[14] H. L. De Vries, in *Proc. Koninkl. Ned. Akad. Wetenschap, 61* (1958), no. 2, 1.

[15] G. J. Fergusson, preprint (1963), and in *Proc. Roy. Soc. A234* (1958), 561.

[16] T. A. Rafter and G. J. Fergusson, in *Proc. 11, U.N. Internat. Conf. Peaceful Uses Atomic Energy 18* (1958), 526.

Revelle and Suess.[17] As a result of all these complicated interactions, the most recent determination of the specific activity of radiocarbon in living matter is 13.56 ± 0.07 atoms/minute/gram of all other carbon.[18]

Isotope fractionation and standards. The element carbon as found in nature is composed of three different isotopes: the two stable species carbon-12 and carbon-13 and radioactive carbon-14. Their relative abundancies are respectively $1:10^{-2}:10^{-12}$. Many chemical reactions occur in natural processes in which one isotope is used preferentially rather than another of the same chemical element, resulting in a selection leading to isotopic fractionation. This phenomenon has been extensively explored for the relations between the stable carbon isotopes carbon-12 and carbon-13 by many carbon-13/carbon-12 isotope ratio measurements, notably by Craig.[19] He observed a lack of 1.84 percent of carbon-13 in wood when compared with atmospheric carbon dioxide. For the even heavier isotope carbon-14, a depletion of nearly twice 1.84 percent was predicted and subsequently confirmed by several independent investigators.

Plants have a tendency of not always fractionating carbon-14 to the very same extent, possibly due to differing microenvironmental conditions. Therefore, a radiocarbon sample may possess a slightly different specific activity at its instant of death or metabolic isolation than the accepted contemporary standard. These varying handicaps from the starting line of radioactive decay can produce inaccurate dates when measuring in the range of a few hundred to a few thousand years.

However, mass spectrometric determinations of carbon-13 can assist in determining what the original carbon-14 deviation from the norm was. In fact, carbon-13/carbon-12 isotope ratio measurements have become virtually mandatory for precise radiocarbon determinations. The accepted way of expressing the difference between the carbon-13/carbon-12 ratio of an unknown sample to the Chicago or PDB standard of Craig is:

$$② \quad \delta C^{13} = \left(\frac{C^{13}/C^{12} \text{ sample} - C^{13}/C^{12} \text{ standard}}{C^{13}/C^{12} \text{ standard}} \right) \times 1000.$$

Actually today a Solnhofen limestone furnished by the U.S. National Bureau of Standards has supplanted the PDB (a belemnite from the Peedee formation) in the laboratory; in the interest of conformity, how-

[17] R. Revelle and H. E. Suess, in *Tellus* 9 (1957), 18.

[18] I. Karlen, I. U. Olsson, P. Kallberg, and S. Kilicci, in *Arkiv Geofysik* 4 (1964), no. 22, 465.

[19] H. Craig, in *Geochim. et Cosmochim. Acta* 3 (1953), 53.

ever, data are still published with respect to the PDB standard. The conversion factor has been well determined, and the difference is only 1.1 per mil.[20]

Laboratory preparation of specimens or standards for dating always involves chemical reactions which, if not allowed to proceed to completion, will introduce isotopic fractionation. Depending on the types and number of reactions involved, significant errors may be caused.

In order to avoid variations in the contemporary standards for carbon-14 measurement among the world's dating facilities, the National Bureau of Standards made available a special preparation of oxalic acid for radiocarbon laboratories. When this compound was prepared, it already contained some radiocarbon excess due to nuclear-weapons testing, so that only 95 percent of the count rate is taken as being equivalent to the average activity of wood samples of the year 1890. This is the contemporary, mutually agreed standard, because it represents the natural radiocarbon content in wood growing just before the Industrial Revolution which changed the isotopic composition of atmospheric carbon dioxide.

The oxalic acid standard may also be fractionated in the laboratory. Experience has shown that the average carbon-13/carbon-12 deviation is about -19.0 per mil.[21] A corrected activity of the oxalic acid standard is by convention:[22]

$$\text{③ } \begin{matrix} \text{0.95 activity of} \\ \text{oxalic acid} \\ \text{corrected} \end{matrix} = \begin{matrix} \text{0.95 activity of} \\ \text{oxalic acid} \\ \text{observed} \end{matrix} \left(\frac{1 - 2(19.0 + \delta C^{13})\begin{Bmatrix} \text{of} \\ \text{oxalic} \\ \text{acid} \end{Bmatrix}}{1000} \right).$$

For very accurate radiocarbon determinations, both the observed per mil deviations from the carbon-13 and carbon-14 standards have to be considered, that is, δC^{13} ② and δC^{14} ④.

The deviation of carbon-14 activity of an unknown sample from the corrected contemporary standard ③ is given by:

$$\text{④ } \delta C^{14} = \left(\frac{\text{activity of sample} - 0.95 \text{ activity of oxalic acid}}{0.95 \text{ activity of oxalic acid}} \right) 1000.$$

[20] Ibid., *12* (1957), 133.
[21] H. Craig, in *Radiocarbon 3* (1961), 1.
[22] Editorial Statement, *Radiocarbon 3* (1961).

When combining the separate fractionation effects, the final deviation is denoted by:

$$\text{⑤} \quad \Delta = \delta C^{14} - \left(2\ \delta C^{13} + 50\right)\left(1 + \frac{C^{14}}{1000}\right).$$

The age of the unknown sample corrected for all isotopic fractionation effects combined is:

$$\text{⑥} \quad \text{age (years)} = \text{mean life of } C^{14} \times \ln\left(\frac{\Delta + 1000}{1000}\right).$$

Secular variations of radiocarbon levels. The apparent existence of secular variations in the carbon-14 level of atmospheric carbon dioxide has been the research object of many investigators such as Berger and Libby,[23] Damon, Long, and Grey,[24] De Vries,[25] Kigoshi and Hasegawa,[26] Libby,[27] Lingenfelter,[28] Stuiver,[29] Stuiver and Suess,[30] Suess,[31] Willis, Tauber, and Münnich,[32] and Wood and Libby.[33] The first observations were made by De Vries, who found an inconsistency in ages between dendrochronologically dated wood samples and their radiocarbon ages.

Present research indicates that the isotopic concentration of radiocarbon in wood fluctuates somewhat in time due to at least two separate effects. These can be recognized upon inspection of the empirical relationship between radiocarbon and tree-ring ages as illustrated in figure 2 based on the extensive study of Suess.[34]

The chart is the result of radiocarbon measurements of dated wood

[23] R. Berger and W. F. Libby, in *Radiocarbon 9* (1967), 477.

[24] P. E. Damon, A. Long, and D. C. Grey, in *J. Geophys. Res. 71* (1966), 1055.

[25] H. L. De Vries in *Koninkl. Ned. Akad. Wetenschap. Prodc. B61* (1958), 94.

[26] K. Kigoshi and H. Hasegawa, in *J. Geophys. Res. 71* (1965), 1065.

[27] W. F. Libby, in *Science 140* (1963), 278.

[28] R. E. Lingenfelter, in *Revs. Geophys. 1* (1963), 1.

[29] M. Stuiver, in *Science 149* (1965), 533.

[30] M. Stuiver and H. E. Suess, in *Radiocarbon 8* (1966), 534.

[31] H. E. Suess, in *J. Geophys. Res., 70* (1965), 5937.

[32] E. H. Willis, T. Tauber, and K. O. Münnich, in *Radiocarbon 2* (1960), 1.

[33] L. Wood and W. F. Libby, in *Isotopic and Cosmic Chemistry,* H. Craig, S. L. Miller, and G. J. Wasserburg, eds. (Amsterdam: North Holland Publishing Company, 1964).

[34] H. E. Suess, in *J. Geophys. Res., 70* (1965), 5937, and in *Proc. Symposium on Radioactive Dating and Low-Level Counting,* International Atomic Energy Commission, Monaco, 2–10 March 1967.

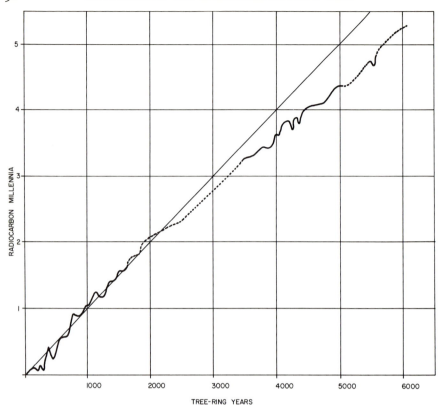

FIG. 2. Relationship between radiocarbon and tree-ring ages modified after Suess and including Schell, Fairhall, and Harp. The period from 2500 to 3500 years ago is as yet not extensively defined by measurements.

specimens, the younger being a mixture of European and North American trees while the older ones are practically all bristlecone pine (*Pinus aristata*) secured and tree ring-dated by Ferguson as discussed in an earlier paper.[35]

First, there appears to exist a long-range effect in operation caused perhaps by geomagnetic oscillations with a period close to 10,000 years of the type discussed by Bucha.[36] This has been interpreted as having resulted in a progressively higher radiocarbon content of the atmosphere, and the biosphere coupled to it, prior to about 2,000 years ago. It is thought that as a consequence radiocarbon dates between 2,000 and 10,000 years ago yield too recent ages if not corrected.

[35] C. W. Ferguson, in *Science 159* (1968), 839.
[36] V. Bucha, in *Nature 213* (1967), 1005.

The second short-range effect involves variations oscillating about the trend of the long-term deviation. It may be caused by changes in solar magnetic activity as revealed by sunspots and at the same time by climatic changes ultimately also controlled by the sun. This phenomenon has been discussed by Suess in another paper (pp. 159–166). The short-range effect has a profound influence on the accuracy of medieval dates as discussed below [37] and in the following paper by John Fletcher.

There remains, however, the question of the long-term isotopic integrity of the macromolecules in dendrochronologically dated wood, especially that of great age. It involves particularly the transport of carbon isotopes across tree rings which conceivably might induce radiometric age changes. A number of experiments in the past have led investigators to believe that tree-sap contamination of older rings is at best a minor problem. At present the entire question of whether an old tree ring truly reflects the isotopic concentration of the atmosphere of the year in which it was laid down is the object of a carefully controlled study.[38]

The industrial or Suess effect. With speedy industrialization, fossil-fuel combustion increased rapidly since the end of the last century. This brought about a dilution of the atmosphere with carbon-12, whereas the radioactive isotope of carbon had already decayed in geologic time in the coal or oil deposits. The biosphere responded to this disturbance of the isotopic equilibrium, as has been observed in wood grown after ca. 1890.[39] Due to the exchange of atmospheric with oceanic carbon dioxide, the dilution in air has not exceeded 3 percent. The effect in the ocean is almost negligible, being on the order of several tenths of one percent.[40] The industrial effect need not be of great concern to the medieval archaeologist, however; there is the chance of mistaking only approximately 300-year-old samples for modern, or vice versa.

The bomb effect. During the testing of nuclear weapons, both of fission and fusion designs, neutrons were released which behaved in the same manner as those produced naturally by cosmic rays. During the mid-

[37] W. Horn, F. W. D. Charles, and R. Berger, in *J. Soc. Architect. Historians* 25 no. 4 (1966), 221.

[38] Involves use of higher level C^{14} tracer.

[39] H. Suess, in *Science 120* (1954), 5.

[40] H. R. Brannon, Jr., A. C. Daughtry, D. Perry, W. W. Whitaker, and M. Williams, *Radiocarbon Dating Conference*, Andover, Mass., 1–4 Oct. 1956; W. S. Broecker, "Nuclear Geophysics," *Natl. Acad. Sci–Natl. Res. Council,* Publ. 1075 (1963), p. 138.

1950s a slow rise was observed in the carbon-14 activity of the atmosphere as discussed in a review by Libby [41] based on the early data of De Vries,[42] Münnich,[43] Rafter,[44] Fergusson,[45] and Williams.[46] As the intensity of testing increased, an accelerated rise in the level of carbon-14 in the atmosphere ensued, reaching a maximum in 1963–64 (fig. 3). Some of the most recent measurements are due to Berger and Libby,[47] Hagemann, Gray, and Machta,[48] Hardy and Rivera,[49] Olsson, Karlen, and Stenberg,[50] Nydal,[51] and Rafter.[52] From then onward the activity has been declining as it disappears into the oceans and biosphere and is no longer replenished as a consequence of the Test Ban Treaty in great quantities.

The rapid change in the radiocarbon inventory can be of some archaeological benefit, because very recent materials can be distinguished. For example, despite their "old" appearance, roots in an archaeological site may be intrusive and belong to a modern tree.

The half-life of radiocarbon. Considerable progress has been made to determine accurately the half-life of carbon-14. In the interest of international scientific cooperation, a committee composed of Paul E. Damon, Frederick Johnson, Johann C. Vogel, and Eric H. Willis drafted the following resolution which was unanimously approved by the participants of the last international radiocarbon conference:[53]

> The Sixth radiocarbon conference meeting at Pullman, Washington, on June 9, 1965, under the general title "International Carbon-14 and Tritium Dating Conference," reconsidered in some detail the question concerning the half-life that would be most useful in expressing radiocarbon dates. The consensus of opinion favored the retention of the previously used half-life of 5568 years.[54] The reasons for this decision were based in the

[41] W. F. Libby, in *Proc. Natl. Acad. Sci.* (U.S.), *44* (1958), 800.

[42] H. L. De Vries, in *Science 128* (1958), 250.

[43] K. O. Münnich, in *Naturwissenschaften 50,* no. 6 (1963), 211.

[44] T. A. Rafter, in New Zealand *J. Sci. Technol. 38B* (1957), 871.

[45] T. A. Rafter and G. J. Fergusson, in *Science 126* (1957), 557.

[46] M. Williams, Humble Oil and Refining Company.

[47] R. Berger and W. F. Libby, in *Radiocarbon 10* (1968).

[48] F. T. Hagemann, J. Gray, Jr., and L. Machta, in *U.S. Atomic Energy Comm. Report* HASL–159, 1965.

[49] E. P. Hardy, Jr., and J. Rivera, in *AEC Report* HASL–158, 1965.

[50] I. U. Olsson, I. Karlen, and A. Stenberg, in *Tellus 18* (1966), 294.

[51] R. Nydal, in *Tellus 18* (1966), 271.

[52] T. A. Rafter, in New Zealand *J. Sci. 8* (1965), 472.

[53] Statement in *Proc. Sixth Internat. Conf. Radiocarbon and Tritium Dating, Pullman, Wash., 1965,* U.S. Dept. of Commerce, CONF–650652, 1966.

[54] H. Godwin, in *Nature 195* (1962), 984.

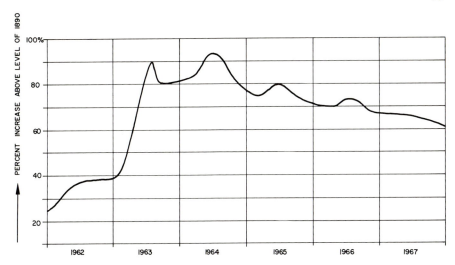

FIG. 3. The level of radiocarbon in atmospheric carbon dioxide measured at ground level at Chain Lake, California, due to worldwide nuclear weapons testing.

main on the desire to avoid the confusion which would arise should the many thousands of published dates require revision. It was also recognized that there are discrepancies between the radiocarbon chronology and other chronologies which would not be corrected by a change in half-life.

It was recognized that the value 5730 remains the best available half-life for the decay of radiocarbon. Those who wish to do so may continue to convert the published dates by multiplying by the factor 1.03.[55]

While this is the accepted position by all radiocarbon laboratories, changes in the half-life of carbon-14 are still possible. A longer half-life of 5833 ± 127 years has been advocated by Schell, Fairhall, and Harp.[56] Any general changes will be adopted by a future international conference.

Counting Methods

Radiocarbon occurs in extremely minute concentration (10^{-12}) in nature. The first sample of natural radiocarbon was obtained by concentrating biologically produced methane gas in a thermal diffusion column at a cost prohibitively high for routine dating.[57] Mass spec-

[55] F. Johnson, in *Science 149* (1965), 1326.

[56] W. R. Schell, A. W. Fairhall, and G. D. Harp, in *Proc. Sixth Internat. Conf. Radiocarbon and Tritium Dating at Pullman, Wash., 1965,* U.S. Dept. of Commerce, CONF–650652 (1966), 397.

[57] E. C. Anderson, W. F. Libby, S. Weinhouse, A. F. Reid, A. D. Kirshenbaum, and A. V. Grosse, in *Science 105* (1947), 576, and in *Phys. Rev. 72* (1947), 931.

trometric analyses are not possible, as such instruments are not sensitive enough for carbon-14 dating purposes.

Libby's original solid-carbon counting method was the only practical way at the time: [58] the substance to be dated was burnt to CO_2 which was reduced with magnesium to carbon black. This carbon was spread as thinly and evenly as possible over the surface of a brass cylinder. It was then inserted in a special Geiger-type screen wall counter. The man-hours needed for this process were relatively high. Due to lower counting efficiency, the counting errors were larger than in today's methods. Experience with contamination by natural and artificial radioactivities, the requirement for large samples, and a cutoff at about 20,000 years pointed to a need for improved counting methods.

An obvious approach to measure low-level quantities of carbon-14 with high efficiency is the use of a counter filled with a suitable gas derived from the specimen. Crane developed a Geiger counter filled with a mixture of carbon dioxide and carbon disulphide,[59] a method still used at the Michigan laboratory.

A similarly convenient technique was that first devised by De Vries and Barendsen [60] in which the sample is converted to a very pure form of carbon dioxide and assayed in a proportional counter. The secret of this method, perhaps having the lowest man-hour requirements of all, lies in sufficiently stringent removal of electronegative impurities which can easily affect counter operation as pointed out by Fergusson.[61]

In order to circumvent the early problems associated with the purification of carbon dioxide, a number of methods were devised to convert carbon dioxide into a less sensitive counting gas such as acetylene, by Barker, Crathorne, and Suess,[62] or methane, by Burke and Meinschein, and Moljk, Drever, and Curran.[63] Additional chemical reactions are necessary to convert CO_2 into the respective hydrocarbon gas with poten-

---

[58] W. F. Libby, in *Radiocarbon Dating* (University of Chicago Press, 1955 and 1965).

[59] H. Crane, in *Radiocarbon 3* (1961), 46.

[60] H. L. De Vries and E. Barendsen, *Physica 19* (1953), 987 and in *Nature 174* (1954), 1138.

[61] G. J. Fergusson, in *Nucleonics 13* (1955), 18.

[62] H. Barker, in *Nature 172* (1953), 631; A. R. Crathorne, in *Nature 172* (1953), 534; H. E. Suess, in *Science 120* (1954), 5.

[63] W. H. Burke, Jr., and W. G. Meinschein, in *Rev. Sci. Instr. 26* (1955), 1137; A. Moljk, R. W. P. Drever, and S. C. Curran, in *Proc. Roy. Soc.* (London) *A, 239* (1955), 433.

tial isotopic fractionation possible. Improvements, however, make hydro-carbon proportional counting just as reliable as other methods.

Finally, there is liquid scintillation counting of carbon-14, a technique advanced to good reliability by Noakes, Kim, and Stipp,[64] as well as Tamers.[65] Samples are converted to CO_2 from which is synthesized benzene. It is dissolved in a liquid scintillation solution which emits light pulses proportional to the amount of radiocarbon in solution. These are recognized in an arrangement of photomultiplier tubes and counted.

Dating Medieval Samples

Introduction. The UCLA radiocarbon laboratory has investigated since 1962 ages of medieval timber [66] in conjunction with studies in medieval architectural history by Fred Charles, John Fletcher, Cecil Hewett, Walter Horn, and John Smith. Several of these studies are discussed elsewhere in this volume. While the greater number of the radiocarbon dates appeared acceptable to our collaborators, some were clearly amiss and left doubt as to whether the radiocarbon dating of medieval timber was really understood. Notable discrepancies were encountered when the barley barn at Cressing Temple, Essex, and Leicester Hall, Leicester, were dated yielding ages which on firm historical grounds were much too early.

A breakthrough was accomplished with the dating of the medieval barn at Middle Littleton near Worcester in England. In the summer of 1965, Fred Charles, Walter Horn, and I collected several timber samples from various structural members of the Middle Littleton barn. The samples were then assayed for their radiocarbon content in Los Angeles. The age of the oak sapwood or heartwood specimens, however, ranged from about A.D. 610 to 935. Moreover, one of the samples appeared to be modern based on its high content of carbon-14. At first there occurred to us the interpretation that extensive replacement had taken place, but this explanation was not at all satisfactory, as the original numbering system of the master carpenter was found on virtually all important timbers

[64] J. E. Noakes, S. M. Kim, and J. J. Stipp, in *Proc. Sixth Internat. Conf. Radiocarbon and Tritium Dating, Pullman, Wash., 1965,* U.S. Dept. of Commerce CONF–650652 (1966), 68.

[65] M. A. Tamers, ibid. (1966), 53.

[66] R. Berger and W. F. Libby, in *Radiocarbon 9* (1967), 477; G. J. Fergusson and W. F. Libby, in *Radiocarbon 5* (1963), 1; in ibid. *6* (1964), 318; R. Berger, G. J. Fergusson, and W. F. Libby, in *Radiocarbon 7* (1965), 336; R. Berger and W. F. Libby, in ibid. *8* (1966), 467; in ibid. *9* (1967), 477; in ibid. *10,* (1968), 1; in ibid. *10,* (1968), 2; in ibid. *11,* (1969), 1.

comprising the structure. It was just before Christmas 1965 that the *Journal of Geophysical Research* published an article by Hans Suess in which was contained a curve correlating in an empirical manner radiocarbon with tree-ring ages, the latter thought to be representative of true calendar age.[67]

When the raw radiocarbon dates were interpreted in the light of Suess' curve, their age adjusted to a new range from ca. A.D. 680 to 750. A further step in narrowing this range was to apply an additional correction by introducing the tree-ring allowance which expresses in years (tree rings) how deep the specimen selected for radiocarbon dating was located in the original tree.[68] Subsequently, the historical date for each of the samples was calculated to be A.D. 1265, 1255, 1265, 1240, and 1270. In other words, a short floating chronology was matched to the master correlation. Finally, the dates were averaged into a composite historical date of about A.D. 1260. The error associated with this date is in all likelihood not much larger than about 20 years or so on each side. In essence, it appears to be safe to consider the barn as having been constructed in the mid-thirteenth century.[69]

An additional two aspects entered into the analysis of the Middle Littleton date. A carbon-13/carbon-12 isotopic correction was so small as not to be of any consequence. Moreover, the sapwood sample which had yielded a modern date in the end turned out to fit very well into the corrected dating range. During the collection it had been cut wet from its location. Presumably rainwater containing organic decay products from the lichen and moss growth on the roof had introduced a quantity of bomb-produced carbon-14. This was removed in the laboratory by extended treatment with hydrochloric acid, then some diluted sodium hydroxide, and last distilled water.

In the summer of 1965 many other wood samples from a number of medieval buildings of known and unknown historical age were collected and subsequently analyzed in an analogous manner. It soon became clear, however, that the only reliable assessment of radiocarbon dating in the Middle Ages could be based on more extensive dating of structures with historically well known ages.

[67] H. E. Suess, in *J. Geophys. Res.* 70 (1965), 5937.

[68] See also paper by J. Flecher in this volume.

[69] W. Horn, F. W. B. Charles, and R. Berger, in *J. Soc. Architect. Historians* 25 (1966), 221.

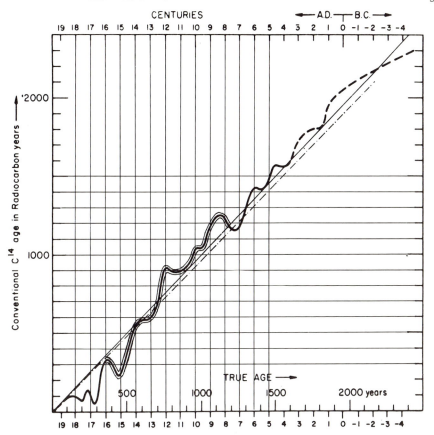

FIG. 4. Relationship between radiocarbon and tree-ring ages as reported by Suess. This curve is of particular interest to the medieval archaeologist. Its error is estimated to be about 15 years on either side of the curve.

Samples of known age

The following year, in a project conducted with Walter Horn, wood samples were collected in England, France, and the Low Countries from as precisely dated buildings as could be found and from which sample material could be conveniently removed. The procedure followed for collection and radiocarbon dating involved the following steps, which we would like to recommend for future applications.

Usually the best location for securing a wood specimen is one of the major interior roof-supporting structural timbers that are least likely to have been replaced. The beam or post location should be removed from direct animal or fertilizer contact and should not bear signs of preservation treatments such as paint, etc. Moreover, a vertical or downward face of a free-standing member will reduce the accumulation of dust and spiderwebs. Normally, if the sample were dark heartwood or lighter worm-eaten sapwood, no difference could be found in its suitability for radiocarbon dating provided all foreign matter and wood meal had been removed.

At the same time, it is necessary to determine the position of the sample selected with respect to the last living ring in the original tree. The age of European oak trees used for conversion into larger timbers usually ranges from 80 to 120 years. Consequently, for the final assessment of a date, it is important to know the inherent age of the wood sample extracted prior to the felling of the tree for construction purposes.

Sometimes a waney edge composed of sapwood or a mortise or tenon cut into the heartwood may provide the best sample. In large oak trees the sapwood-heartwood interface almost always occurs roughly 20 to 25 tree rings inside the cambium. It can thus provide a convenient time marker. Often bark can be found, especially on timber surfaces on the opposite side to the discriminating viewer inspecting a structure. In the living tree, however, bark is formed at a much slower rate than tree rings. Therefore, a given thickness of bark will reveal under magnification many more growth increments than an equal thickness of oakwood will show tree rings. In some cases a "rubbing" can be made from a wood surface on paper which will copy the tree-ring pattern including the number of rings and provide a lasting field record.

After the samples have passed the agricultural inspection station safely, they are cleaned mechanically in the laboratory in order to remove gross contamination. This is followed by treatment with hydrochloric acid and washing with distilled water to exclude carbonate dust and soluble contaminants.

Then about 10 to 15 grams of dry wood are converted to pure carbon dioxide and this is assayed for at least 1000 minutes overnight in a proportional counter for its radiocarbon content. The UCLA counter will reproduce results in the time span of the Middle Ages to within $\pm$ 30 years upon repeated counts of the same gas sample. Normally, in the journal *Radiocarbon,* such samples are conventionally quoted with statistical errors of about 1 percent equal to $\pm$ 80 years or $\pm$ 60 years if the sample gas has been counted twice.[70] This error may be considered generous and can be narrowed by using very pure carbon dioxide freed

[70] 1-sigma standard deviation or better.

FIG. 5. Combination combustion and purification high vacuum line in the UCLA
Isotope Laboratory.

from electronegative impurities in conjunction with very stable electronics.
The operation of the counter itself is monitored at intervals by introducing
standard samples of known age, the oxalic acid standard for the contemporary biosphere, and a background sample composed of radioactively
inert carbon dioxide derived from marble.

Concurrently, a small aliquot of the gas counted is analyzed in a

FIG. 6. Counter for radiocarbon dating inside steel shield surrounded by anti-coincidence counters. Electronic console at left registers all pertinent data.

double-beam mass spectrometer for carbon-13/carbon-12 isotopic fractionation.[71]

This measurement provides for the correction discussed earlier in this paper. Usually changes from zero to several tens of years are necessary.

[71] Nuclide dual collection mass spectrometer (McNier-Kenney, 60°).

FIG. 7. Close-up view of UCLA radiocarbon counter surrounded by anticoincidence arrangement to eliminate mesons.

Now the radiocarbon date refined by the carbon-13/carbon-12 isotopic correction is matched against the empirical correlation of Suess [72] for secular variations in the radiocarbon content of tree rings. This curve has an error of approximately ± 15 years and is suitable for the Middle Ages even though a more recent modification for the last few hundred years has appeared in print.[73]

Last, the tree-ring allowance is introduced into the calculation of the final date. For sapwood samples it may be essentially zero, while for a heartwood specimen from the center of the tree, up to a hundred years or so may have to be subtracted from the refined and tree ring–calibrated radiocarbon age.

After these analytical procedures and calculations, the ultimate age of the original sample is obtained. We have termed the result the probably historical date of construction of the building in question.

The samples discussed on the pages that follow were extracted from the

[72] E. H. Willis, T. Tauber, and K. O. Münnich, in *Radiocarbon 2* (1960), 1.
[73] M. Stuiver and H. E. Suess, in *Radiocarbon 8* (1966), 534.

timbers of an important, yet controversial, castle hall, several market halls, and many monastic barns. They are listed in straight alphabetical order. The historical evidence available for these buildings is fully discussed in the preceding paper by Walter Horn.

Arpajon (UCLA-1307). Oak heartwood from the market hall at Arpajon, south of Paris (approx. 48°35′N latitude, 2°15′E longitude), built in A.D. 1450–1470 by Louis Mallet. The radiocarbon age of 515 ± 30 years includes δC^{13} of — 23.83. The sample originated from one of the outer posts and the tree-ring correction was determined to be about 40 years. Taking into account the adjustment for secular variations, the calculated historical date for construction is ca. A.D. 1450.

Church Enstone (UCLA-1316). Bark from oak timber located in Church Enstone, Oxfordshire (approx. 51°55′N latitude, 1°27′W longitude). This church is dated by inscription to A.D. 1382. The bark sample was taken from the foot of the northern cruck blade of truss 5; growth increment correction of some 40 years is in order. The radiocarbon age of 630 ± 50 years is adjusted for a C^{13}/C^{12} ratio of — 24.61. During the fourteenth century the curve for secular variations of the radiocarbon content of tree rings follows a plateau. The present date falls within that range at its outer edge, but just barely so. Therefore, the calculated historical age is estimated to be certainly the fourteenth century, if not by closer

TABLE I

Known Age Measurements

UCLA no.	Site	Historic age (A.D.)	Experimental age (A.D.)
1307	Arpajon	1450–1470	1450
1316	Enstone	1382	14th century (1390)
1048	Gt. Coxwell	1250± 20	1250
1049	Gt. Coxwell	1250± 20	1245
1309	Maubuisson	1236	1050–1220
572	Méréville	1456–1472	1440
1304	Méréville	1456–1472	1460 or 1600
1311	Milly	1479	1290
1312	Milly	1479	1450
1313B	Parçay-Meslay	1211–1227	1250
570	Parçay-Meslay	1211–1227	1225–1250
1310	Questembert	1675	1500, 1625–1670
1303	Richelieu	1631–1640	1480 or 1630
1306	Sully	1363	ca. 1300
1308	Troussures	1609	1450 or 1600
1214	Bhudda statue	early 13th cent.	early 13th cent.

FIG. 8. Arpajon (Seine-et-Oise), France. Market hall; by local tradition alleged to have been erected between 1450 and 1470 by Louis Mallet, Amiral de Graville. Interior looking east (photo: Rameau et Fils).

evaluation ca. A.D. 1390. The dating of Church Enstone illustrates the point that one can sometimes obtain a more definitive date by collecting timber whose corrected radiocarbon date lies on a more vertical trend of the curve for secular variations by moving further back in time into the heartwood, which in turn can give a more precise date. Similarly, at the other end of such a plateau a heartwood sample may yield a dating range, while its sapwood will provide the needed accuracy.

Great Coxwell (UCLA-1048). Oak heartwood from the great tithe barn at Great Coxwell, near Faringdon, Berkshire (approx. 51°36'N latitude, 1°34'W longitude). The building has been described in complete detail by Horn and Born,[74] who date this barn in the second quarter of the thirteenth century. The radiocarbon age amounts to 870 ± 40 years with an inconsequential correction for C^{13}. Origin of the sample dated is post g of truss G at a depth of about 40 tree rings. From these data and correlation to secular variations of radiocarbon, the calculated historical date for the construction of Great Coxwell is ca. A.D. 1250.

[74] W. Horn and E. Born, *The Barns of the Abbey of Beaulieu at Its Granges of Great Coxwell and Beaulieu-St. Leonard's* (Berkeley and Los Angeles, 1965).

Great Coxwell (UCLA-1049). Oak sapwood from the waney edge of the same timber described in the preceding example (UCLA-1048). The radiocarbon age was determined to be 750 ± 30 years with a practically nonexistent δC^{13} correction based on — 25.2. The wood analyzed was located about 15 tree rings inside the last growth layer or cambium. The final calculated historical date of construction after consideration of all relevant factors is ca. A.D. 1245. We have found that in the case of buildings of unknown but suspected age a precautionary measure is to collect both a sapwood and a heartwood sample. Laboratory analysis may later indicate that only one sample need be dated. But the other one can be considered as insurance for situations discussed in UCLA-1316.

Maubuisson (UCLA-1309). Sapwood from waney edge of barn of the Abbey of Maubuisson, north of Paris (approx. 48°54′N latitude, 2°21′E longitude) founded A.D. 1236. The radiocarbon age of 860 ± 40 years takes into account a C^{13}/C^{12} ratio of — 22.58. The wood sample was obtained from a position about 10 tree rings inside the cambium of a curved brace with carpenter mark 9 of truss 9 on opposite sides of the main barn door. Since the correlation curve for secular variations essentially follows a plateau during the time span of ca. A.D. 1050–1220, and the present calibrated date falls within that range, no date with greater precision is possible. However, the outer limit of the range (1220) and the historical date of 1236 are commensurate even though this does not constitute rigorous proof.

Méréville (UCLA-572). Oakwood from one of the outer posts of the market hall of Méréville (Seine-et-Oise) (approx. 48°17′N latitude, 2°13′E longitude). The erection of the building is attributed to Etienne le Fevre, Vicomte de Méréville (1456–1472). The radiocarbon age of 490 ± 40 years is in agreement with a standard C^{13} isotopic ratio. We have used a tree-ring correction of about 20 years for this specimen which originates from one of the smaller outer posts. These were usually cut from trees not much larger than the desired thickness of the construction element. Taking all data into consideration, the calculated historical date is A.D. 1440.

During 1967 another oak heartwood sample (UCLA-1304) was obtained from the central shake in post j. The specimen was extracted at a depth of some 30 tree rings. Its corrected radiocarbon age (δC^{13} = — 24.69) was found to be 400 ± 50 years, which after correlation with the curve for secular variations corresponds to either ca. A.D. 1460 or 1600. The previous sample (UCLA-572), however, resolves this ambiguity and causes the date for the erection of the hall to be placed near A.D. 1440–1460—in good agreement with the historical date.

Milly (UCLA-1311). Oakwood sample from about 30–40 tree-rings depth in the center of post e′ under the crossrail of the market hall at Milly-la-Forêt (Seine-et-Oise, near Fontainebleau). The radiocarbon age of the sample was measured to be 730 ± 50 years, corrected for $\delta C^{13} = - 24.72$. Assessment of all the pertinent factors would suggest a date of ca. A.D. 1290 for the cutting of the tree from which the timber was made. This suggests that this post was not used initially in the present market hall, which dates from near A.D. 1479, as discussed in the previous paper and in the following sample. We were able to obtain another specimen, however, which dates this market hall more satisfactorily.

In order to obtain the second specimen, it was necessary to drive to St. Blaise-des-Simples outside Milly-la-Forêt, where wood from the original hall was found to be available in the garden of the chapel.

Milly (UCLA-1312). The sample was taken from an oakwood peg found *in situ* in a section cut from one of the original posts of the market hall of Milly (located west of Fontainebleau, approx. 48°24′N latitude, 2°28′E longitude). The section of the post had been fashioned into a solid bench set into the garden of St. Blaise-des-Simples, now used as the burial chapel of Jean Cocteau. The market hall itself was built shortly after A.D. 1479 by Louis Mallet de Graville. Radiocarbon dating yields an age of 420 ± 45 years which includes a C^{13} correction based on a value of − 22.80 with respect to the PDB standard. Since a peg would appear to have been shaped from young growth, no correction was applied. This is difficult to evaluate, however, at present. The most likely historical age for the erection of the hall can be reasonably assumed to be mid-fifteenth century or more specifically some date ca. A.D. 1450 ± 15 years.

Parçay-Meslay (UCLA-1313B). Oak sapwood from a waney edge of post 4 (counted from the western end in the southern row of posts) inside the barn of Parçay-Meslay, near Tours (approx. 47°28′N latitude, 0°21′W longitude). The barn was built in the time of Abbot Hugue de Rochecourbon, A.D. 1211–1227. Isotopic analyses give a corrected radiocarbon age of 655 ± 30 years in conjunction with a C^{13}/C^{12} ratio of − 24.52. When the only minor tree-ring correction is taken into account, a historical date of ca. A.D. 1250 is the final answer. The same barn had been dated earlier in the next example.

Parçay-Meslay (UCLA-570). A better age estimate of the construction of this barn is possible on the basis of another sample which was secured

from one of the other main posts. This sapwood sample yields a radiocarbon date (uncorrected) of 735 ± 50 years, which translates into a
calculated historical date of about the second quarter of the thirteenth
century—in good agreement with the historical date reported. This sample
illustrates how closely sophisticated radiocarbon dating can be made to
work if the correlation curve of the secular variations has the characteristics of a sharp vertical rise as in the thirteenth century.

Questembert (UCLA-1310). Bark sample from post nearest the center
aisle of truss 4 of the market hall at Questembert, near Vannes, Morbihan
(approx. 47°40′N latitude, 2°36′W longitude). A tie beam in the middle
of the hall bears the inscription A.D. 1675. The radiocarbon age has been
measured to be 330 ± 30 years, corrected for a fractionation in C^{13} of
− 26.02. A bark growth increment allowance of some 40 years is applicable. A reversal in the curve for secular variations permits in this instance
two dates: one lies about the year A.D. 1500 and the other in the range
1625–1670 or so. Obviously the latter range is applicable to this known
date. However, if the true historical age had not been available, an erroneous interpretation might have been attempted unless some other
independent evidence would have eased the choice.

FIG. 9. Richelieu (Indre-et-Loire), France. Market hall, built by Cardinal Richelieu
between 1631 and 1640. Interior looking west (photo: Combier Imp., Macon).

Richelieu (UCLA-1303). Oak bark from the market hall of Richelieu southwest of Tours (approx. 47° 1′N latitude, 0° 20′E longitude). Cardinal Richelieu built the village named after him as a model between A.D. 1631 and ca. 1640. It is located directly adjacent to the palace gardens, the palace having been used as a stone quarry later on. The bark sample with a growth increment correction of 30 years was removed from the lowest longitudinal rail marked VII between posts 6 and 7 on the southern side of the central aisle. A radiocarbon age of 380 ± 50 years was obtained after correction for δC^{13} of — 24.54. Final analysis provides for two alternate dates: A.D. 1480 or 1630. Therefore, a similar situation exists as in the case of Questembert preceding this illustration of dating.

Sully (UCLA-1306). Oakwood sample from curved long ashlar piece rising from the floor to the rafters in the upper hall of the chateau Sully-sur-Loire (approx. 47° 46′N latitude, 2° 22′E longtitude). The chateau was built in A.D. 1363 [75] as best as can be ascertained today. We obtained a radiocarbon date of 930 ± 30 years, which has been adjusted for a C^{13}/C^{12} ratio of — 23.04. Apparently it is necessary to apply a large tree-ring correction. In all likelihood the timbers in question were produced by splitting a larger oak beam.[76] Normally it is more efficient to quarter a tree rather than to half if for a cross section, as observed in the roof of Sully. If this is the case, then the tree-ring correction may have to be in excess of 100 years. This would leave the calculated historical date still short of its goal by about 50 years. During the collection of the sample it was not possible to inspect the face of the end of the ashlar piece. Therefore, a critical evaluation of the tree-ring pattern could not be carried out, which would have revealed whether the timber was indeed one quarter of a tree. In the future such a study may be possible on old rejected timbers after replacement by modern lumber.

It is known that medieval carpenters used wood preservatives such as salt (NaCl) and alum ($KAl(SO_4)_2 \cdot 12\ H_2O$).[77] Due to their inorganic nature, these compounds would not interfere in radiocarbon dating. However, the removal of traces of coal-based preservatives applied in modern times cannot always be guaranteed. Such radiometric contamination would tend to increase the age as observed.

[75] L. Martin, *Sully-sur-Loire: Des Origines à nos jours* (Sully-sur-Loire: Editions A. Pornin, 1962), p. 88.

[76] M. Violet-le-Duc, *Dictionnaire raisonné de l'architecture* (Paris: B. Bance, 1854), vol. III.

[77] Ibid., vol. II, 212.

Fig. 10. Troussures (Oise), France. Thirteenth century barn, formerly in the possession of the monastery of Chaalis; partly renewed in 1609. The second wooden post to the left exhibits the date 1609 and the name of the carpenter who repaired this section of the barn after the last two arches of the southern range of arcades had collapsed or had been removed for reasons unknown (photo: Walter Horn).

Troussures (UCLA-1308). Chestnut sapwood from a post in the position of a broken stone arcade pillar in the thirteenth-century abbey barn of Troussures (Oise). The post has been inscribed by the carpenter: "1609–fr N coevllet chptier de Noi?ps." The radiocarbon age was determined to be 400 ± 45 years after consideration of a δC^{13} of — 24.42. No tree-ring correction appeared justified. The calculated historical date in its final analysis permits two interpretations: either A.D. 1450 or 1600.

Buddha statue (UCLA-1214). Although this example does not fit geographically into the medieval European series of dates, it is contemporaneous. From a dating standpoint there should be no difference whether a sample originates in Europe or the Far East. As a matter of fact, this Amida buddha stands 2 m in height, exquisitely carved in wood and poised upon an octagonal lotus stand. The statue, now in a private collection in Los Angeles, was dated in Japan and placed on stylistic grounds into the Kamakura Era (13th century). The corrected radiocarbon age is 820 ± 50 years, which after tree-ring calibration indeed places the buddha into the thirteenth century.

Assessment of Accuracy of Dating

It is now possible to evaluate more clearly the potential and the limitations of radiocarbon dating for the period of the Middle Ages based on our measurements of structures of known age. The following procedures were found to give the best results for dating timber samples:

1. Select sample for least likely contamination.
2. Remove mechanically gross contamination.
3. Treat with HCl and distilled water.
4. Determine carbon-14 content of sample.
5. Measure carbon-13/carbon-12 ratio for isotopic fractionation.
6. Compare resulting age with curve for secular variations of radiocarbon in dendrochronologically dated wood.
7. Consider any necessary tree-ring allowance.

The resulting age determination has been called the calculated historical age of the sample. Thus, when all the pertinent correction factors are taken into account, much more precise dating is feasible for those periods in which the curve for secular variations has a near vertical trend. This is especially true for the thirteenth and fifteenth centuries. On the other hand, where the secular variation curve flattens out into a plateau—as it does during the eleventh, twelfth, and fourteenth centuries—only a general date range can be obtained, extending over as much as a hundred or even a hundred and fifty years. In the sixteenth and seventeenth centuries, where the secular variation curve rises and falls in rapid succession, we have to take our choice between two and on occasion even three alternative dates. Which of these is the correct one must be decided by independent evidence or special sample selection.

It goes without saying that additional closer-spaced and independent calibration measurements for the curve are desirable in order to understand its entire nature. We have found only minor deviations based on our historically dated samples; on the whole, the course of the curve is supported by our known dates. In fact, all our measurements of samples from different locations in the same timber yield radiocarbon dates in about the right order and spacing in time according to the course of the curve for secular variations.

In addition to the analysis of more dendrochronologically dated wood, check measurements based on well-dated parchment charters are under way. The ultimate assessment of radiocarbon dating in the Middle Ages will be made in the future after many more precise measurements have been carried out. At present, however, our procedures allow much more accurate dating than has been hitherto possible.

Samples of Unknown Age

Beaulieu-St. Leonard's (UCLA-1014 to 1016). At Beaulieu-St. Leonard's there are located the ruins of a large abbey barn, which has been dated on architectural-historical grounds to the mid-thirteenth century. It was a grange of the Cistercian abbey of Beaulieu (approx. 50°49′N latitude, 1°27′W longitude) in Hampshire and has been extensively analyzed by Horn and Born.[78] Within the confines of the walls of the original barn a much smaller one of more recent date has been constructed. A large lintel over one of the wagon doors has the appearance of belonging to the sole plate system of the original thirteenth-century barn (see figs. 39–40, n. 78 above). In order to test this assumption, sapwood, bark, and heartwood samples were obtained from this timber. They yielded the following radiocarbon ages: 100, 155, and 220 years. Subsequently, each radiocarbon date was compared to the curve of secular variations. All indicate A.D.

---

[78] *Barns of the Abbey of Beaulieu* (Berkeley and Los Angeles, 1965).

1650 as the time at which the tree was cut from which the lintel was shaped. It follows that the lintel is not composed of timber used in the original barn. But it could, of course, have been a seventeenth-century replacement of one of the wall plates of the original barn. This would suggest that the original structure was still extant in 1650 and considered worthy of being repaired at this time.

Beaumont-en-Gatinais (UCLA-1317). Oak bark from Post h' directly under tie beam of Beaumont Hall (Seine-et-Marne) (approx. 48°8'N latitude, 2°29'E longitude). The radiocarbon age was measured to be 120 ± 50 years. From this a historical date of ca. A.D. 1650 or the first half of the eighteenth century can be calculated. A local tradition assigns the construction of this hall to the fourteenth century. Further samples are needed to ascertain whether the post, analyzed by us, was a postmedieval replacement.

Bredon. This tithe barn is located near Tewkesbury, Worcestershire (52°2'N latitude, 2°7'W longitude).

Three different radiocarbon dates were determined:

UCLA-577A—945 ± 50 years. Timber from one of the main posts located in the northern range to the left of the east transept. The calculated historical age is the range 1035–1210. No tree-depth correction available.

UCLA-1060—270 ± 50 years. Sapwood from truss 1, post i'. δC^{13} = — 24.7. Tree-ring allowance: 15 years. Due to the reversal of the calibration curve, the calculated historical age is either A.D. 1640 or 1555 to 1490.

UCLA-1061—845 ± 40 years. Sapwood next to heartwood from truss D, post d, at a depth of 25 years. δC^{13} = — 26.0. The calculated historical date of construction is A.D. 1250. On balance Bredon tithe barn is likely to be mid-thirteenth century but will require additional work.

Brook (UCLA-1341). Oak sapwood from waney edge from shoring beam, N aisle, easternmost truss, of Court Lodge Barn at Brook, near Wye (51°11'N latitude, 0°56'E longitude). δC^{13} = — 24.34. The corrected radiocarbon age is 450 ± 50 years. Therefore, the probable historical age can be estimated to be about 500 years or mid-fifteenth century. S. E. Rigold (p. 70) ascribes this barn to the fourteenth century, because of its "splayed and tabled scarf joints."

Canteloup-St. Wandrille. The barn at Canteloup is presently being dismantled and reerected as a church on the grounds of the Abbaye de Fontenelle, St. Wandrille (Seine-Maritime) (49°32'N latitude, 0°45'E longitude). This project was initiated by Abbot Ignace Dalle, and is

FIG. 11. Canteloup (Eure), France. Monastic barn formerly in the possession of Notre Dame Le Parc d'Harcourt, dismantled in 1967 and now in the process of being reerected as a church for the monks of the abbey of St. Wandrille (Seine-Maritime), France. Exterior from south (photo: Walter Horn).

carried out under the direction of Paris architect Marion Tournan-Branly. Abbot Dalle is in this manner converting into a church a medieval utilitarian structure that belongs to an aisled and bay-divided building type which in the Middle Ages was used for a variety of functions: as dwelling for a farmer and his cattle, as barn for his crops, as festal hall for kings, bishops, and noblemen, and also as church.[79] We secured an oak sapwood sample from a waney edge of post V (carpenter's mark) on the south side of the barn. This specimen (UCLA-1301) had a radiocarbon age of 580 ± 50 years which takes into account a $\delta C^{13} = -26.88$. In addition, a heartwood sample from the same post was secured (UCLA-1302A). The wood was located about 30 years from the center of the tree, which was felled at an age of about 180 years as determined by the Forest-botanical Institute of the University of Munich. The radiocarbon age was 650 ± 40 years, which includes $\delta C^{13} = -24.16$. When all correction factors are taken into account, Canteloup was erected most probably

[79] Ibid.

Fig. 12. Canteloup (Eure), France. Monastic barn. Northern range of posts looking east (photo: Walter Horn).

around the beginning of the fifteenth century. An early analysis (UCLA-1302) had placed Canteloup at the end of the thirteenth or beginning of the fourteenth century, based on too small an estimate for the age of the post dated as determined by the number of tree rings.

Cressing Temple. At Cressing Temple, Witham, Essex, there are located two medieval barns in close proximity: one is referred to as the barley barn and the other as the wheat barn (51°50'N latitude, 0°36'E longitude). Recently three radiocarbon dates were obtained for the barley barn, which is considered to be the older on architectural-technical grounds. UCLA-1075 is an oak heartwood specimen from the interior of a mortise in post a′ at a depth of some 50 years with a radiocarbon age of 830 ± 40 years, which corresponds to calculated historical dates of either A.D. 1270 or 1210. In addition, a sapwood and heartwood sample pair were collected from post e′. The sapwood sample (UCLA-1076) had a radiocarbon age of 920 ± 40 years, $\delta C^{13} = -23.0$, and a tree allowance of ten years. This translates into a historical date range from ca. A.D. 1025 until 1200. The corresponding heartwood sample originated within 2 inches of the center of the tree. Its radiocarbon age was 950 ± 40 years, which includes a $\delta C^{13} = -24.7$. Since the tree-ring allowance should be at least 90 years, the calculated historical age reaches from ca. A.D. 1115 to 1190 (UCLA-1077). The difficulty in dating the construction of the barley barn is due

FIG. 13. Cressing Temple, Essex, England. Wheat barn. Exterior from southwest (photo: Ron Bates; reproduced by courtesy of Essex Record Office).

FIG. 14. Cressing Temple, Essex, England. Wheat barn. Interior near hipped section of roof (photo: John Tarlton).

mainly to the plateau of the calibration curve which lasts through the eleventh and twelfth centuries. Conservatively dating, the barley barn was most probably raised around A.D. 1200. Thus it appears to be the oldest-known extant English barn. The wheat barn was dated through a piece of sapwood from post e' located at a depth of about 15 years. The associated radiocarbon age of 730 ± 50 years can be converted into a historical date of erection of ca. A.D. 1250.

Drayton-St. Leonard. Another tithe barn is located in Oxonshire at Drayton-St. Leonard, near Dorchester (approx. 51°39'N latitude, 1°10'W longitude). Three radiocarbon dates were obtained from this building, which together can be interpreted to mean that this building was erected

FIG. 15. Drayton-St. Leonard, Oxfordshire, England. Monastic barn. Exterior from southwest (photo: courtesy of National Buildings Record).

during the early part of the fourteenth century. The details are as follows: UCLA-578, C^{14} age 675 ± 50 years; UCLA-1055, heartwood, corrected radiocarbon age 610 ± 50 years, $\delta C^{13} = -22.7$, tree-ring allowance of 35 years; UCLA-1056, sapwood from same post as UCLA-1055, radiocarbon age 525 ± 50 years, $\delta C^{13} = -22.3$, tree-ring allowance of 10 years. It should be pointed out that the correlation of these data does not present a perfect fit in all respects.

Egreville (UCLA-1318). Oak sapwood from the central shake in post c′ in the market hall of Egreville (Seine-et-Marne) (approx. 48°10′N latitude, 2°53′E longitude) ascribed to Anne-de-Pisseleu, dutchess of Etampes (†1559). The hall was heavily restored in 1638 and has incorporated in its present fabric a heterogeneous motley of timbers of various ages. The post from which our sample was taken is obviously a reused beam from an earlier structure of the first half of the fifteenth century (C^{14} age 490 ± 40 years; $\delta C^{13} = -22.52$; tree-ring allowance 30–50 years).

Frindsbury (UCLA-1340). Oak sapwood sample from the second post of the western row counting from the north in the barn of Frindsbury, near Rochester, Kent (approx. 51°24′N latitude, 0°30′E longitude). The radiocarbon date of 550 ± 40 years falls on the plateau of the fourteenth

FIG. 16. Drayton-St. Leonard, Oxfordshire, England. Monastic barn. Interior looking west (photo: courtesy of National Buildings Record).

century, which therefore spells the time range of construction. Rigold (p. 70) assigns this building to a date "not long after, possibly even before 1300," because of its "splayed and keyed scarfing."

Frocester. This English tithe barn is situated 5 miles west of the city of Stroud, Gloucestershire (51°45′N latitude, 2°12′W longitude). A total of eight different radiocarbon dates was determined from various members of this cruck-built barn, which has been described by Fred Charles in his paper. Instead of listing all the data, which can be found in the UCLA

FIG. 17. Egreville (Seine-et-Oise), France. Market hall. By local tradition ascribed to Anne de Pisseleu, Duchess of Etampes (d. 1559). Exterior from southwest (photo: Walter Horn).

FIG. 18. Frindsbury, Kent, England. The Great Manor barn. Exterior from south-west (photo: Walter Horn).

radiocarbon datelists IV and V,[80] the following deductions can be made. Six dates range in terms of their radiocarbon age from 200 until 485 years. These dates can be accommodated by the calibration curve to indicate construction during the second half of the fifteenth century. One sample 660 ± 50 years old would date actually from ca. A.D. 1270. The last specimen gives a modern date which could mean a replacement since A.D. 1650 or contamination difficult to remove. In other words, the oldest timber may be a carryover from the barn at this general location ascribed to the period of Abbot John de Gamache (A.D. 1284–1306). The larger entity of the barn if not the entire building appears to be of late fifteenth-century origin. Therefore, the present roof of the barn cannot be the one attributed to the time of Abbot John; however, it may resemble the older one as the older timber fits into place. To what degree Forcester is a replica of thirteenth-century design is today a moot question; indeed, it may show the continuance of a tradition.

Harmondsworth. Virtually within view of London International Airport stands the great tithe barn of Harmondsworth, Middlesex (approx. 51°29′N latitude, 0°28′W longitude). Three samples were taken. All of these, after being checked against the secular variation curve, yielded as historical date of construction the turn of the thirteenth-fourteenth centuries. UCLA-1050 gives a radiocarbon age of 670 ± 40 years including a δC^{13} of − 26.0. Tree-ring allowance is about 40 years. Sapwood from the same post (UCLA-1051) is 555 ± 40 years old, with the same C^{13} correction and a tree-ring allowance of about 15 years (post k). An earlier measurement, UCLA-575, at 720 ± 50 years had suggested a thirteenth-century origin.[81]

Harwell. The dates pertaining to radiocarbon analyses are discussed in the following paper by John Fletcher and are omitted here.

Leigh Court (UCLA-1344). This appears to be the most beautiful cruck barn in England, discovered only recently by Charles. It is situated in the vicinity of Worcester (52°11′N latitude, 2°13′W longitude). The radiocarbon date was 570 ± 40 years, fitting in time into the fourteenth-century plateau of the calibration curve. The calculated historical date of erection of Leigh Court barn could be any time between 1300 and 1400. A more precise date could be obtained if deep-seated heartwood were selected for dating.

[80] R. Berger, G. J. Fergusson, and W. F. Libby, in *Radiocarbon 7* (1965), 336; R. Berger and W. F. Libby, in *Radiocarbon 8* (1966), 467.
[81] R. Berger, G. J. Fergusson, and W. F. Libby, in *Radiocarbon 7* (1965), 336.

Fig. 19. Lenham, Kent, England. Lenham "major," formerly in the possession of the abbey of St. Augustine's in Canterbury. Exterior from southwest (photo: courtesy of National Buildings Record).

Lenham. There are two barns located at Lenham, Kent (approx. 51°13′N latitude, 0°38′W longitude). The minor barn burnt in recent years, whereas the larger one still can be inspected in all detail. From the burnt timbers of Lenham minor four radiocarbon dates were obtained. All fall into close proximity of the year 1298 in which the church of Lenham and its auxiliary buildings were ravaged by fire. Since a barn would have to be built shortly after such a catastrophe to shelter the harvest, the year 1298 must lie closely near the construction of the building. The calculated historical ages of two of the four analyses differ by not more than 40 years from 1298. This appears to be about on the order of accuracy one can obtain for this particular position in time.

In particular the radiocarbon dates for the minor barn are as follows: UCLA-1089 was a heartwood sample from the sleeper beam below post C, giving a radiocarbon age of 845 ± 40 years. This corresponds to a tree ring–calibrated age of 725 years. If the timber was cut from a tree not much larger than the diagonal of the sleeper beam, then about 120 years have to be allowed for growth before cutting. Therefore, the calculated historical age is ca. A.D. 1345.

UCLA-1090 again was a heartwood sample but located 9 inches from the center of the same beam as used in UCLA-1089. The radiocarbon age of 670 ± 40 corrected for negligible C^{13}/C^{12} fractionation corresponds to a tree-ring age of 700 years. Since the specimen originated about 30 years inside the cambium, the calculated historical age of erection was ca. A.D. 1280.

UCLA-1345 is based on heartwood from one of the principal posts approximately 40 rings inward from the heartwood-sapwood interface,

FIG. 20. Lenham, Kent, England. Lenham "major." Interior looking south (photo: courtesy of National Buildings Record).

which implies a necessary correction of about 60 years. The radiocarbon age is 550 ± 40 years, which takes into account a $\delta C^{13} = -24.94$. The historical age can be calculated to be the range of the fourteenth century.

UCLA-1347 is still another heartwood sample which was secured in an attempt to evade the plateau in the correction curve. Its origin is a tenon of a fallen post. The radiocarbon age of 550 ± 40 years stands corrected for the greatest deviation in $\delta C^{13} = -20.77$ observed so far. The final calculated historical age is the same age range as in the previous case, that is, the fourteenth century.

The dating of Lenham major is based on two measurements: UCLA-1091 and 1346. The first gives a corrected radiocarbon age of 595 ± 40 years, including $\delta C^{13} = -26.9$ based on bark. Hence, allowing about 40 years, Lenham major appears to have been built during the period of A.D. 1330–1440. The other date is fortunately more definitive. It is based on heartwood 30 years inside the waney edge of a principal post in the western row, third truss from the north. The radiocarbon age is 640 ± 40 years corrected for δC^{13} of -24.12. This translates into a historical age of ca. A.D. 1310. Both dates are in good agreement, placing the erection of the building toward one end of the period calculated in UCLA-1091.

Leicester Castle. Clearly this paper cannot provide the detailed analyses of all the twenty-five radiocarbon dates obtained over a period of years for this famous Norman Castle which is still in use today as a courthouse. The dates have been assembled for convenience in the following table.

A few facts immediately stand out. First, of the Norman castle only the original posts remain, including one tie beam. There appear to have taken place three major episodes during which the structure was renovated: during the middle of the thirteenth, during the fourteenth, and during the middle of the fifteenth century. Inspection of the timber joints shows their astonishingly close fit, which may suggest that the basic Norman construction features were retained in later centuries. On the other hand, there is no guarantee that certain modifications feasible in the overall context were not introduced. In essence Leicester Castle reflects the basic parameters in the wider sense. Thus the aisled bay construction still impresses the visitor with its robust fundamental character.

Nettlestead. The manor barn at Nettlestead, Kent (approx. 51°11′N latitude, 0°26′E longitude) was recently the victim of fire. Among the partially charred large timbers stored among the nettles, one sleeper beam permitted us to isolate three samples. UCLA-1085A is sapwood, UCLA-1083 is oakwood from the sapwood-heartwood interface, and UCLA-

TABLE 2
Search for Norman Timber in Leicester Castle

UCLA no.	C^{14} age *	Calibrated age (A.D.)	Ref.
566A	1070	900	67
566C	400	1450 or 1600	67
566D	960	1000–1200	67
566F	980	1000–1100	67
566E	590	1300–1400	67
566G	450	1450	67
941	1245	800–900	68
942	1185	900	68
943	640	1250	68
944	505	1400	68
945	595	1300–1400	68
946	285	1450, 1550, 1650	68
947	410	1450, 1600	68
948	530	1400	68
949	605	1300–1400	68
1260	625	1250–1400	70
1261	415	1450, 1600	70
1262	1050	1100–1150	70
1263	280	1450	70
1264	645	1250	70
1265	320	1450 or 1600	70
1266	630	1275	70
1267	645	1250	70
1268	365	1450	70
1269	700	1250	70

* Statistical errors are between 40 and 50 years.

1085B is heartwood. The tree-ring depth positions are 5, 20, and 50 years, respectively. The δC^{13} corrections are only minor, based on — 24.0, —24.4, and — 24.2. Indeed, the raw radiocarbon ages fall into the right sequence of 350, 490, and 535 years, all associated with an error of ± 40 years. These ages translate into the following historical dates: ca. A.D. 1605 or 1455, ca. 1440, and ca. 1465. Therefore, it is reasonable to assume that Nettlestead barn was built ca. A.D. 1450.

The manor house itself yields an earlier date. UCLA-1084 based on heartwood from a ceiling shake at $\delta C^{13} = -$ 24.4 is 610 ± 50 years old. Permitting roughly 40 years for the tree-ring depth of the sample, the historical date can be calculated to be some time during the fourteenth century.

Fig. 21. Nurstead Court, Kent, England. Manor hall. Center truss of Great Aisled Hall at tie-beam and crown-post level, after removal of covering plaster wall (photo: courtesy of National Buildings Record).

Fig. 22. St. Pierre-sur-Dives (Calvados), France. Market hall. Exterior from north-west (photo: Walter Horn).

Nurstead Court (UCLA-1094). The manor house at Nurstead Court, Kent (51°23′N latitude, 0°32′E longitude), contains incorporated in its present fabric the roof-supporting trusses and most of the roof of an aisled medieval hall. A heartwood sample secured from an edge of the great central tie beam of the former hall yielded a radiocarbon age of 970 ± 40 years, corrected for $\delta C^{13} = -24.7$, which is equivalent to a range covering the eleventh and twelfth centuries. Since the tree-depth position is not known, nothing definite can be said now of the historical age of the hall.

FIG. 23. St. Pierre-sur-Dives (Calvados), France. Interior looking west. Original frame of timber before it was gutted by incendiary bombs in World War II (photo: Archives Photographiques).

The elaborate profiles of the tie beams and the great arched braces of this structure point to the middle of the fourteenth century as probable date of construction.

Middle Littleton. The dating of this barn has been discussed already on earlier pages. It provided us with our first opportunity to radiocarbon-date correctly in the Middle Ages, with the aid of the secular variation curve worked out by Hans Suess.

St. Pierre-sur-Dives (UCLA-1338). Oak heartwood from the market hall in St. Pierre-sur-Dives (Calvados) (49° 1′N latitude, 0° 2′W longitude). This hall has been extensively repaired after heavy damage sustained during World War II. Only four of the original posts of the hall are still in place. We removed a sample from the central shake under the aisle tie beam of post 1 in the northeast corner of the building. Its radiocarbon age was 890 ± 40 years corrected for $\delta C^{13} = -23.03$. After correlation to secular variations, the original hall reaches back into the twelfth to mid-thirteenth centuries and despite this antiquity is still in active use today.

Ter Doest. Barn of the abbey of Ter Doest, near Bruges, Belgium (approx. 51° 16′N latitude, 3° 12′E longitude). Stylistic analysis of decorations of its brick walls places the barn into the second half of the thirteenth century when compared to the design elements of a historically dated church nearby. The dating of this building by the radiocarbon method has presented some difficulties which lie mainly with attempts to date by a single specimen or maybe two specimens. This has led to differing interpretations. On balance, however, a short chronology can be drawn as shown in the illustration below. This then can be matched to the master correlation of secular variations. Ultimately the age of erection for the barn can be deduced to be around the year A.D. 1300 with an error of some 40 years symmetrically about this date.

Little Wymondley. The barn of Little Wymondley belonged to Wymondley Priory which was founded during the reign of Henry II by Richard B. de Argentein, Lord of the Manor at Great Wymondley, some time before A.D. 1218. It is located in Hereford (approx. 51° 44′N latitude, 0° 18′W longitude) and has incorporated in its present frame of timber a few beams that can be clearly recognized as repositioned structural members of an earlier building, presumably the original barn built prior to 1218 in the thirteenth century. A sapwood sample taken from one of these reused timbers (UCLA-1057) belonged to a building constructed around A.D. 1260, based on a radiocarbon age of 670 ± 40 years, cor-

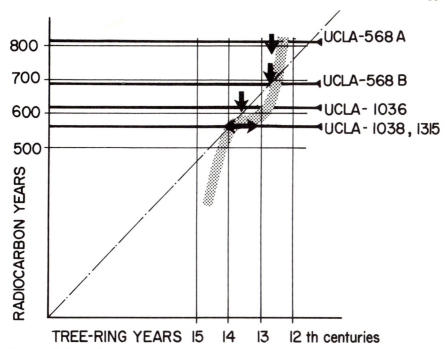

FIG. 24. Relationship of radiocarbon ages and tree-ring years for the dating of the barn at Ter Doest. The vertical arrows are offset from the shaded correlation curve by the number of years dictated by the tree-ring allowance. In the case of UCLA-568A it cannot be more than about 50 years, UCLA-1038 and 1315 give a non-specific date range. Most likely date for the erection of Ter Doest is ca. A.D. 1300 ± 40 years.

rected for $\delta C^{13} = -24.4$. Whether or not this timber is a remnant of the original barn cannot be determined with any certainty today. A second heartwood sample (UCLA-1058) obtained from about 30 tree rings inside one of the regular posts yielded two alternative dates when compared with the curve for secular variations, namely, ca. 1475 and 1625. This is determined from a radiocarbon age of 350 ± 40 years which takes into account $\delta C^{13} = -23.8$. The age determinations show that the present barn is not, as Horn believed, the original thirteenth-century barn of the priory of Little Wymondley, but rather a fifteenth-century replacement, judging from construction details.

Samples for Dating

Since the geochemistry and geophysics of radiocarbon dating permits its worldwide application, whatever holds true for dating during the

FIG. 25. Little Wymondley, Hertfordshire, England. Priory barn. Exterior from south (photo: James W. Roberts).

Middle Ages in the Old World may be used elsewhere equally well. Besides the dating of timbers which served as a general assesment, many other substances may be also placed in time.

A most important consideration in collecting samples for radiocarbon dating is the context in which they are found. Obviously a radiocarbon date can never be better than the degree of real association between the substance dated and the artifact thought to be contemporaneous. Inspection at the site must determine how good this criterion may be. Undisturbed stratigraphy, where it really exists, will make the selection by the excavator easier than at sites where mixing of hypothetical stratigraphic levels has occurred. The latter problem is encountered much more frequently than is generally thought.

Moreover, there remains the question of how closely spaced in time should radiocarbon samples be secured. Clearly, closer spacing than the statistical error associated with radiocarbon dates and the limitations that depend on the location of the specimen in time will not yield necessarily any more pertinent information. Yet, often only insufficient sample ma-

FIG. 26. Little Wymondley, Hertfordshire, England. Priory barn. Assembly of
principal structural members (photo: James W. Roberts).

terial is obtainable. Then the statistical error becomes larger, and the significance of a date must be reevaluated. It is for this reason that dating laboratories should be informed of the time estimates involved, because it may prove to be futile to attempt a worthwhile date.

The actual sample quantity is determined by the amount required to fill the dating counter. Dating counters are constructed of differing sizes, and it is best to inquire beforehand how much is needed by the respective laboratory. As a general guide, such materials as wood, charcoal, plant remains, textiles, leather, or hair should be submitted in ½-1–ounce quantities, shells and bones in several ounces, and soils and tufa in pound amounts. In special cases, however, extremely small samples in milligram size can be dated.[82]

Specimens are best wrapped in either aluminum foil, which is self-closing, or in plastic bags. Touching the sample materials by hand has not generally a contaminating effect. The best location to remove coarse extraneous material is right at the find, where rootlets, stone, and excessive dirt can be left behind. Before packing, specimens must be properly labeled and identified. It is desirable to detail the significance of a sample, since crucial specimens can be counted longer for a smaller statistical error.

1. *Wood*. When wood samples are collected the precautions discussed earlier apply. If one cannot be sure of the original nature of the piece of wood dated, allowances should be made beyond the error of the radiocarbon date for uncertainty in space-time.

2. *Charcoal*. The chemical properties of charcoal are such that it is one of the most indestructible organic substances found in nature. Structured charcoal is recognized by the presence of tree-ring pattern as opposed to the completely amorphous appearance of naturally occurring asphalts. In some cases it is difficult to distinguish between finely powdered charcoal and small dark inorganic grains usually of volcanic origin. A simple ignition test will provide the answer. The nature of charcoal excavated at archaeological sites has been discussed by Cook.[83] Prior to radiocarbon dating, removal of rootlets and other extraneous matter is necessary before treatments are begun with hydrochloric acid to destroy inorganic carbonates and dilute sodium hydroxide for extraction of humic acids.

3. *Plant remains*. Remains of plants like grass, reed, and leaves should be treated just as wood or charcoal. Seeds possess sometimes an abnormally

---

[82] H. Oeschger, B. Alder, H. Lodski, C. C. Langway, Jr., and A. Renaud, *Earth and Planetary Science Letters* 1 (1966), 49.
[83] S. F. Cook, in *Amer. Antiquity* 29 (1964), 514.

high content of carbon-14 and may yield unreliable dates. The nature of this problem is at present not entirely understood.

4. *Textiles.* All such materials whether of botanical or zoological origin are datable with the proper precautions toward contamination.

5. *Hair, skin, and leather.* Mummified tissues can be dated as well as bones.[84]

6. *Bones.* These can be dated based either on the carbonate, collagen,[85] or amino acid[86] content. Carbonate-based determinations are, however, suspect if groundwater had access to the bones, as exchange reactions between groundwater and bone carbonates may produce an erroneous date.[87] In combination with the correct pretreatments, especially humic acid extraction, human remains can be directly dated, obviating problems of association. It must be remembered, however, that the collagen content of bones varies widely, depending on the environment in which they were deposited. A preliminary test to determine whether sufficient bone protein is present is to analyze about 100 mg of bone for its nitrogen content, which is a quantitative indicator for collagen.

7. *Soils.* In many soils dark organic-rich bands can be distinguished. Dates based on carbonate-freed soils can be used to interpret the depositional history at a site. Such studies can then be conveniently coupled with palynological investigations.

8. *Marine shells.* They can be dated fairly reliably if a number of factors are considered. The isotopic content of shells is a reflection of the surrounding seawater[88] and in most cases will yield an apparent age of anywhere from zero to several hundred years. Since the carbon-14 content of seawater decreases with depth, variations in the contemporary specific activity of shells is possible as the seawater participates in mixing with deeper ocean layers or sweet-water additions. Only open beaches without special oceanographic conditions like upwelling, strong currents, or admixture of other waters will yield consistent dates. As Craig has pointed out,[89] shell dates should be either compared with contemporary land plants or recent shells from the same location as applied by Berger, Taylor, and

[84] P. C. Orr and R. Berger, in *Science 148* (1965), 1466.

[85] R. Berger, A. G. Horney, and W. F. Libby, in *Science 144* (1964), 999; M. A. Tamers and F. J. Pearson, jr., in *Nature 208* (1965), 1053.

[86] Modified procedure after T.-Y. Ho, in *Proc. Natl. Acad. Sci.* (U.S.) *54* (1965), 26 reported by R. Berger and W. F. Libby in *Radiocarbon 10*, 2 (1968).

[87] W. S. Broecker and A. Walton, in *Geochim. et Cosmochim. Acta 16* (1959), 15.

[88] W. G. Mook and J. C. Vogel, in *Science 159* (1968), 874.

[89] H. Craig, in *J. Geol. 62* (1954), 115.

Libby,[90] or Suess.[91] Postdepositional exchange of shell with groundwater carbonate can be estimated by dating shell protein, conchiolin.[92]

9. *Nonmarine shells*. Shells having grown in hard-water lakes may show carbon-14 deficiencies up to about 25 percent, equivalent to nearly 2000 years. The effect is most pronounced in recent shells but diminishes in importance in those several tens of thousands of years old. Similarly affected are land-snail shells. It is best to avoid nonmarine shells altogether, because the inherent uncertainties cannot be compensated against in a reliable manner as pointed out by several investigators.[93]

10. *Shards*. Potsherds can be radiocarbon-dated if their texture is very coarse and carbon from the cooking fires or for that matter from burnt food has accumulated in the sherd. The quantity of sherds required is on the order of several pounds due to the low carbon content. Procedures are presently being worked out to test the reliability of this approach.[94]

11. *Wattle-and-daub*. In house construction using adobe or loam-type soil, straw and twigs may have been used by the builders to increase the strength of the walls. This organic material can be suitably extracted and dated with the proper precautions against contamination.[95]

12. *Plaster*. Common mortars are very often based on calcium oxide which in the process of hardening via calcium hydroxide reacts with atmospheric carbon dioxide to form a calcium carbonate matrix surrounding and cementing sand particles. A procedure to date houses by this method has been proposed by Delibrias and Labeyrie.[96] Cements and concretes cannot be dated due to the content of clay-containing lime.

13. *Special substances*. Among these may be mentioned tar-impregnated wood or bones from tar pits such as those in California. Continuous extraction with suitable organic solvents can extract most of the tar. In bones, however, the complete separation of tar and protein may be

---

[90] R. Berger, R. E. Taylor and W. F. Libby, in *Science 153* (1966), 864.

[91] H. E. Suess, in *Science 120* (1954), 467.

[92] R. Berger, A. G. Horney, and W. F. Libby, in *Science 144* (1964), 999.

[93] M. L. Keith and G. M. Anderson, in *Science 141* (1963), 634; W. S. Broecker, in *Science 143* (1964), 596; M. Rubin, R. C. Litkins, and E. G. Berry, in *J. Geol. 71* (1963), 84.

[94] R. E. Taylor and R. Berger, in *Amer. Antiquity 33* (1968), 363.

[95] Suggested by C. W. Meighan, UCLA.

[96] G. Delibrias and J. Labeyrie, in *Proc. Sixth Internat. Conf. Radiocarbon and Tritium Dating, Pullman, Wash., 1965*. U.S. Dept. of Commerce, CONF-650652 (1966), 344.

difficult. Then an isolation procedure involving the fraction collection of specific amino acids native to bone is necessary.[97]

In studies involving human coprolites, the dietary pattern of ancient populations can be ascertained, as discussed by Callen and a recent University of California publication.[98] In addition, studies involving the longevity of microorganisms in these coprolites are feasible.[99]

Finally, the radiocarbon dating of iron might be mentioned. It involves the isolation of carbon used in iron manufacture when this carbon was derived from charcoal.[100]

Radiocarbon and Other Dating Methods

The accuracy of radiocarbon dating is superseded only by two other methods: (1) firm historical dating and (2) dendrochronology. The latter can be extremely precise with virtually no error for well–cross-checked time ranges.

There are a number of materials that cannot be dated by carbon-14 such as most ceramics, obsidian, and metals. Thermoluminescence dating offers a way out of this dilemma for ceramics, and obsidian-hydration dating can measure the age of such volcanic glass. The first of these techniques is discussed in other papers in this volume. Obsidian-hydration dating may not have application in medieval studies in the Old World; however, its use in similar time ranges in other regions is of considerable importance.[101]

In summary, radiocarbon dating properly applied in conjunction with other historical and physical time-measuring techniques can provide the solution to many research problems in the time span of the Middle Ages.

[97] T.-Y. Ho, L. Marcus, and R. Berger in *Science 164* (1969), 1051.

[98] E. O. Callen, in *Science in Archaeology*, D. Brothwell and E. Higgs, eds. (New York: Basic Books, 1963); also *University of California Archaeological Survey Report* no. 70, Berkeley, 1967.

[99] R. Berger and D. Y. Tubbs, ibid., paper no. 5.

[100] M. Stuiver and N. J. van der Merwe, in *Current Anthropol. 9* (1968), 48.

[101] J. W. Michels, in *Science 158* (1967), 211; C. W. Meighan, L. J. Foote, and P. V. Aiello, in *Science 160* (1968), 1069.

IV

RADIOCARBON DATING OF MEDIEVAL, TIMBER-FRAMED CRUCK COTTAGES

J. M. Fletcher

$\mathcal{S}$CIENTISTS ARE used to the challenge presented by the need to make sophisticated measurements from which accurate values, for example, of the velocity of light or of the dimensions of crystals, can be obtained. This paper deals with a similar challenge, that of providing reasonably accurate constructional dates for a form of vernacular dwelling of historical and archaeological interest. But dates are not ends in themselves; rather, they are facts which help to place events in their correct order or to trace evolutionary trends.

In a collaborative program with the University of California at Los Angeles, initiated in 1962 by G. J. Fergusson, Willard Libby, and myself, radiocarbon measurements [1] have been made on oak taken from some of the cruck cottages of North Berkshire that lie within a few miles of the Thames and some ten to fifteen miles south of Oxford (fig. 1). These houses, still in use after various postmedieval modifications, form a class of timber-framed dwellings to which the term "cruck" is applied from the presence of curved blades which reach from the low plinth almost to the apex (see fig. 4 for an example). Other examples of this class have survived in counties in the south, west, and Midlands of England [2] (fig. 2), but none in East Anglia or the extreme southeast of England or in northwestern Continental Europe.

The dating of the cruck houses typified by those surviving in North Berkshire is desirable, because they are probably the only form of truly vernacular dwelling which has survived in England from the Middle Ages: they pose a number of questions to economic and architectural

---

[1] G. J. Fergusson and W. F. Libby, in *Radiocarbon* 5 (1963), 19; J. M. Fletcher, trans., in *Newbury District Field Club* 11 (1963), 94.

[2] J. T. Smith, in *Arch. J.* 105 (1960), 111, and in *Med. Arch.* 8 (1964), 119.

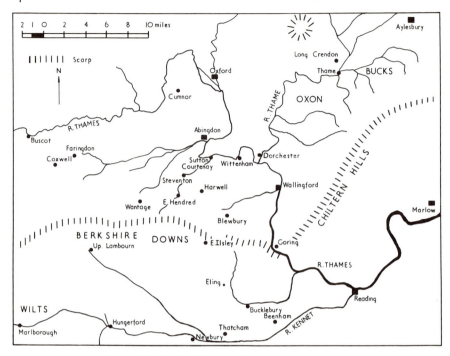

FIG. 1. North Berkshire and surrounding region.

historians. Were these dwellings a product of the change in the labor market which resulted from the Black Death of 1349, or were many of them built before that event? How are they related to the monastic barns such as those at Great Coxwell [3] and Littleton [4] to the west (fig. 2)? Or to the many open-hearth manorial halls (situated locally, for example, at Harwell, Steventon, Sutton Courtenay, and North Moreton) which have similar curved blades? And why are cruck dwellings absent in some of the villages (such as East Hendred and Sutton Courtenay) which lie only a few miles from the two villages from which samples have been taken in this work? To answer such questions, one would like to know their construction dates to a precision of, say, fifty years, rather than one hundred or one hundred and fifty years.

Cruck Houses Samples

The houses that have been examined for their radiocarbon activity show no clearly datable features such as moldings, but the carpenters'

[3] W. Horn and E. Born, *The Barns of the Abbey of Beaulieu and its Granges of Great Coxwell and Beaulieu-St. Leonard's* (University of California Press, 1965).
[4] W. Horn, F. W. B. Charles, and R. Berger, in *J. Soc. Architect. Historians* 25 (1966), 221.

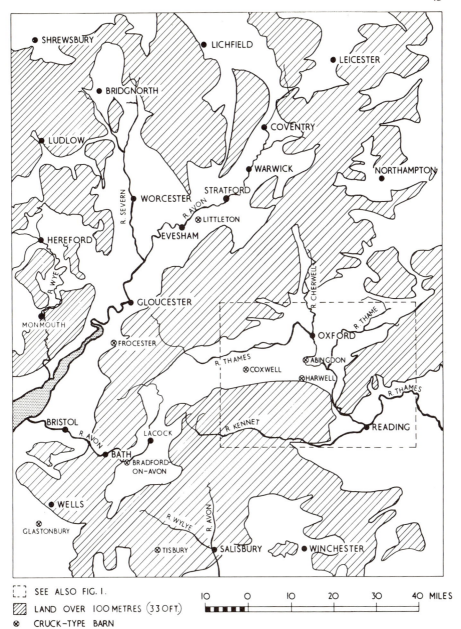

SEE ALSO FIG. I.
LAND OVER 100 METRES (330 FT.)
CRUCK-TYPE BARN

10   0   10   20   30   40 MILES

FIG. 2. Regions with fourteenth- and fifteenth-century cruck barns and houses.

joints and the type of assembly marks indicate that they are of medieval origin and rather earlier than the Up Lambourn cruck house (also in Berkshire: see fig. 1) which is likely to be mid-sixteenth century.[5]

[5] J. M. Fletcher, trans., in *Newbury District Field Club 11* (1967), 5.

TABLE I
Details of the Cruck Houses Sampled for Radiocarbon Measurements

		Bays			Remarks
	No.	Breadth (feet)	Length (feet)	Height (feet)	
At Long Wittenham					
Church Farm house	–	–	–	–	Evidence absent
Church Farm tractor shed	2+?	15	13	15½	Collar extended across blades. First floor probably original.
At Harwell					
Dell Cottage	3	17½	13⅓	19)	First floor absent originally
Le Carillon (fig. 4)	2+?2	19	2×12 2×?	20)	
School House	?	16	1×10½	23	Only 1 bay survives
For Comparison					
Cruck outhouse, Middle Farm, Harwell ca. 1370 (fig. 5)	3	17	2×14 1×?	23	
Cruck cottage Up-Lambourn, ca. 1550	2+2	19	2×12 2×10	22	Collar extended across blades. First floor is original

Long Wittenham. Two of the five dwellings examined form part of Church Farm, Long Wittenham, and have been described and illustrated by Portman.[6] The farmhouse itself lies some one hundred and fifty yards south of the church, but is no longer recognizable externally as a cruck house: there is now a two-storied and jettied range, probably sixteenth century, to the north and a Victorian façade on the south. The other structure (now a tractor shed) lies within a hundred yards of the farmhouse and runs parallel and adjacent to the village street: at one time it served as two cottages but is now used to house farm implements and so was given its current name by Portman.

[6] D. Portman, in *Berks. Arch. J.* 56 (1958), 35.

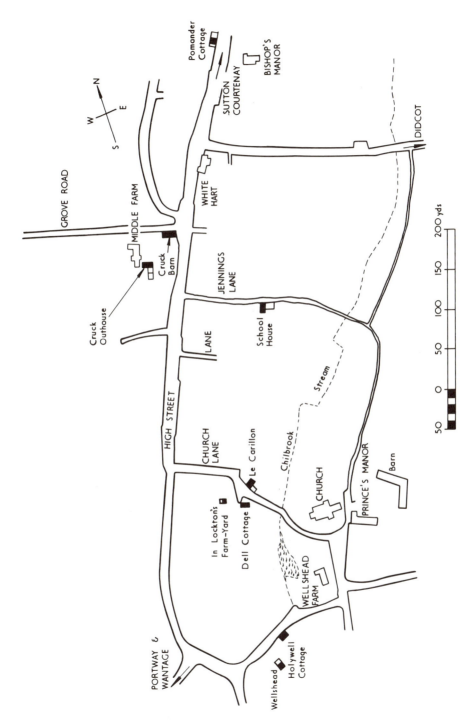

Fig. 3. Harwell, Berks. Location of crucks.

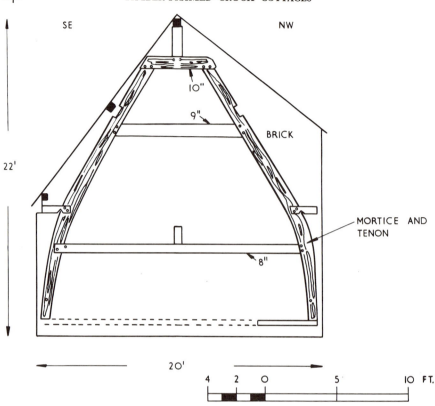

FIG. 4. Le Carillon, Harwell.

Harwell. The other three dwellings that have been samples are in the village of Harwell, where cruck blades survive in eight houses (fig. 3). Some (figs. 5 and 6) are seen from the outside to be cruck structures, but with others it is only the presence internally of one or two blades that provides the evidence for their former structure.

Four of the known cruck houses lies within two hundred yards of the church in the areas known as Wellshead and Church Lane (fig. 3), for which there are deeds relating to several houses in the early part of the fourteenth century. Details of one of these four (Dell Cottage, fig. 5) have been published:[7] samples have been taken from it and from Le Carillon, which is adjacent but on the other side of Church Lane and rather larger. One of its two surviving trusses is illustrated in figures 4 and 6. As these trusses are 24 feet apart, there was presumably a truss between them, the whole forming perhaps the central two bays of a four-bay range.

[7] J. M. Fletcher, in *Oxoniensia 36/37* (1961–62), 207.

Fig. 5. Dell Cottage, Harwell, from the northwest.

The third Harwell cruck house (School House) has a large cruck truss at right angles to Jenning's Lane. On its east side there is a box-framed addition, identified by the fillet on its chimney as being ca. 1600. Internally there is seen to have been a bay of ca. 1500 design at right angles to the cruck range, perhaps contemporary with it, perhaps later.[8]

In Harwell, besides the eight cruck houses there is a three-bay cruck outhouse and a seven-bay cruck barn, which form part of the farmstead (fig. 3) now known as Middle Farm. In the Middle Ages, it was a knight's fee which was acquired in 1355 by one of the village's ten freeholders named Richard Brounz, who held the office of Sheriff of Berkshire and Oxfordshire in 1381–82. He was one of the two knights of the shire to represent Berkshire in most of the parliaments from 1379 to 1387. The carpentry and dimensions of the cruck outhouses (fig. 7) resemble those of the cruck houses tested for carbon-14. The arched form of its open truss suggests that it is contemporary with the adjacent porch and open hall (fig. 7) which Richard Brounz added ca. 1370 to the manor house itself.

[8] J. M. Fletcher, in *Berks. Arch. J.* 62 (1965–66), 45.

FIG. 6. Le Carillon, Harwell. Present external truss (as in fig. 4), from the northeast.

Sampling

Although others have often taken samples for radiocarbon dating from the outermost rings or other parts of the sapwood, this was avoided, even when feasible. Such samples are often contaminated by preservatives, bacteria, woodworm, etc., and occasionally give spurious results in the absence of special precautions.

Small blocks (about 2 in. wide and deep, weighing 3 to 7 ozs., and covering 10 to 30 rings) were cut from one of the cruck blades at a height of 4 to 7 feet from the plinth and for preference on the inside of the house. Surface contamination (by paint, etc.) was removed by planing.

The "growth allowance," that is, the number of rings from the sample to the bark, can be as high as 120 years, as mature oaks in the part of

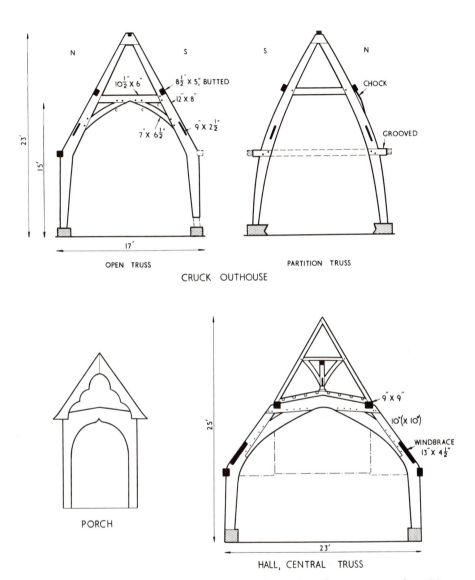

FIG. 7. Brounz's Manor (Middle Farm), Harwell: cruck outhouse, open and partition truss porch, hall, central truss.

England concerned were usually felled when 100 to 120 years old. In assessing the growth allowance, it was helpful to know that the two blades of a truss form were obtained by dividing, longitudinally, a roughly square balk of timber; and also that we had some complete cross sections

TABLE 2

Construction Dates Derived from Samples from Different Blades in the
Tractor Shed, Long Wittenham

Truss	Blade	UCLA no.	Growth allowance (years)	Age		Construction date	
				C^{14}	True (1966)	From C^{14} age	True age
I	N	237B	20	438	498	A.D. 1532	A.D. 1472
II	N	265	20	425	492	1545	1478
I	S	266	20	410	486	1560	1484
			Average	425	490	A.D. 1545	A.D. 1480

of oak beams of medieval origin from the same locality that had been
set aside for dendrochronology.

In the first place, the agreement or otherwise of construction dates
derived from samples taken from three *separate* blades of the tractor shed
at Long Wittenham was determined (table 2). The construction date,
ca. A.D. 1545, derived in 1963 with no correction for the De Vries effect,
seemed late, as there is good evidence that the box-frame form of construction had largely superseded earlier forms in this locality by that
time. However, with the corrections (derived from the Stuiver-Suess
curve [9] which is based on tree-ring dates and was published in 1966) for
the variations in the carbon-14 level of the atmosphere, the construction
date (table 2) becomes ca. A.D. 1480, that is, 65 years earlier.

Results

The samples covered wood which ranged from near sapwood to near
heartwood so that the growth allowance varies from about 20 to 60 years.
The *apparent* construction dates first calculated from the radiocarbon
measurements after they were made in 1962 spanned 175 years (table 3).
The latest of the five dates—A.D. 1600, for the School House, Harwell—
was clearly not consistent with the presence of an added range identifiable
as being of about that date.

The corrected dates (table 3) obtainable in 1966 using the Stuiver-Suess
curve [10] remove this anomaly as the construction date for the School
House becomes 75 years earlier. The five dates, for which the experimental

[9] M. Stuiver and H. E. Suess, in *Radiocarbon 8* (1966), 534.
[10] Ibid.

TABLE 3
Construction Dates for Berkshire Cruck Dwellings

Dwelling	UCLA no.	Growth allowance (years)	C¹⁴	True	Calc. 1963	1966
			\multicolumn{2}{Age}	\multicolumn{2}{Construction date}	

Dwelling	UCLA no.	Growth allowance (years)	C^{14}	True	Calc. 1963	1966
Long Wittenham						
Church farm	238	50*	560	555	1440	A.D. 1445
Tractor shed	237, 265 and 266	20	425	490	1545	1480
Harwell						
Le Carillon	235	40	565	560	1425	1430
Dell Cottage	267	20	575 570) 480 520)	570) 545 520)	1445	1425
School House	236	60	410	485	1600	1525

* Very approximate as circumstances prevented a reliable estimate being made.

standard deviation has been given as $\pm$ 60 years, span the period from A.D. 1425 to 1525. Thus the radiocarbon results mean that there is a relatively high probability both that all five cruck dwellings were built after 1350 and that all (except the School House) were built before 1550: the probability for the School House being built before 1550 is rather less high from the radiocarbon work, but here the associated evidence mentioned above increases this probability.

Although carbon-13/carbon-12 ratios were not run on these samples, subsequent results (appendix, p. 157) on various portions of the oak tie beam recently removed from Harwell Church indicated that the deviations of the fractionation from the accepted mean value ($-25‰$) were of a minor nature ($1‰$ deviation in the C^{13}/C^{12} ratio introduces an error of 16 years).

Historical Implications

Assignment of these cruck houses to post A.D. 1350 is consistent with the economic situation, occasioned by the Black Death, which prevailed in the North Berkshire and other regions toward the end of the fourteenth century. The buyers' market enabled a few of the peasants to become relatively prosperous by acquiring land. This upper strata of peasantry was no longer content with the unframed hovels of the villeins and when circumstances so permitted built for themselves well-framed cruck houses. These, at least in Harwell, were in the same style as was adopted about the same time or slightly earlier for a house in connection with the local manor.

The building of cruck houses in the late fourteenth and fifteenth centuries has also been reported from the recent study of documentary sources for Worcestershire carried out by R. K. Field.[11] He has extracted much information from the court rolls about the houses that the peasants agreed with their lords to build—the ash or oak "couples," that is, the blades, often being provided by the lord of the manor. The tendency for such houses to be large, namely three- to four-bay structures, had gained momentum in Worcestershire by the fifteenth century, though the total recorded as being built (56 houses in 40 villages for the period 1375–1500) is trivial. Rich peasants were few in number!

Opportunities for acquiring a moderate degree of wealth (usually through land to the extent of 50–100 acres) must have varied considerably from village to village in the abnormal postplague conditions. Where the lords were distant noblemen or ecclesiastical bodies, the chances for renting demesne lands were usually greater than when there were residential lords of the manor. Thus the presence of several cruck houses in Harwell may be related to the lords of its two manors: the Bishop of Winchester for one; and the Earl of Cornwall, and after 1361, the College of St. Nicholas at Wallingford Castle, for the other. But in the adjacent village of East Hendred, where there was a manorial lord who was resident and relatively important, few cruck houses have been found.

The sites of surviving cruck houses of the fourteenth and fifteenth centuries are usually villages, but occasionally they are small market towns such as Thame (fig. 1), in the middle and upper reaches of valleys in the western end of the southern and central counties of England (fig. 2). The region is very approximately bounded by the Vale of Aylesbury and the valley of the Thame on the east; by the Vale of Pewsey and the valley of the Wiltshire Avon on the south; by the Severn Valley and its tributaries on the west; and by the undulating country around Leicester on the north.

Several factors—geographical and economic—must have contributed to the first timber-framed cruck houses being limited to this region. Its

---

[11] R. K. Field, in *Md. Arch.* 9 (1965), 105.

rainfall is moderate and the valleys have the fertile land which encouraged the change from agriculture to grazing, which needed less labor. Some parts of the region, such as the Aylesbury-Thame district, were well placed for access to the London meat market, while other parts were adjacent to areas where cloth production was increasing. The fourteenth century saw the cloth trade migrating from towns to villages, for example, in Northern Berkshire from Oxford and Abingdon to East Hendred and Steventon (fig. 1). The villages favored had streams from the adjacent hills or downs and these streams were being harnessed,[12] well before 1400, to provide fulling mills.[13] Additionally, of course, cruck houses could not be built without there being locally available[14] the oak (or ash) suitable for providing 20–25-feet-long blades, and the permission to make such timber available.

It seems that most of the cruck cottages in the more hilly parts of northern and western England and in Wales (e.g., the 31 examples recorded[15] for Monmouthshire) are of later date than those in northern Berkshire, implying that this form of vernacular architecture spread, over a period of decades, into areas beyond the north and west fringes of the originating region.

Archaeological Conclusions

The framed cruck houses that have been samples represent only a small fraction of those surviving, but they are in an area of England which was relatively prosperous toward the end of the Middle Ages. With the historical evidence provided by Salzman[16] and Field,[17] the results suggest

[12] R. D. Pelham, Society for the Protection of Ancient Buildings, Publication no. 5, London.

[13] In the process of fulling, raw cloth was scoured, cleansed, and thickened by beating it in water. This was done originally by 'walkers' who tramped on the cloth in a trough. With water power and fulling mills, the beating was done by a wooden bar (L. F. Salzman, *Mediaeval English Industries,* 1923, p. 221).

[14] Although oak trees were few in the immediate vicinity of Harwell, there would have been many then, as now, in the hamlet of Eling, which from Norman times onward had been part of the Upper Manor of Harwell. Eling (fig. 1) lies some 9 miles south of Harwell and is now in the parish of Hampstead Norris. It is possible that the attachment of this hamlet to a Harwell manor was specifically to give a balanced economy by providing a source of timber.

[15] Sir C. Fox and Lord Raglan, *Monmouthshire Houses,* Pt. I (Cardiff: Medieval, 1951).

[16] L. F. Salzman, *Buildings in England down to 1540* (Oxford, 1952).

[17] R. K. Field, in *Med. Arch.* 9 (1965), 105.

that framed cruck houses were rare (or even perhaps nonexistent) before the fourteenth century.

It is now quite a few years since the hypothesis [18] that this form of house was primarily associated with the *highland* zone of Britain has been suspect. Numerous survivals, for example, those in Leicestershire and in Berkshire, show that altitude is of no significance, although it is true that they are absent in the southeastern counties where the Wealden house, which is roughly contemporary, occurs.

The absence of cruck houses in certain regions of England has also given rise to theories [19] seeking to show that they were part of the heritage of the Celts or one of the post-Roman invaders of Britain, suggesting that this style emerged from some ancient tradition after lying dormant for centuries. At the moment, however, these aspects are not yet entirely clear.

Charles [20] has drawn attention to the great skill of the medieval carpenter and to his ability to design and frame timber buildings appropriate to the materials available and the needs of the time. The prosperous peasant's cruck house of the fifteenth century can be regarded as a vernacular adaption of the fourteenth-century timber framing used in many manor houses and barns (fig. 2) in the same regions of England. The curved blades used ca. 1370 in the hall (fig. 7) of Brounz's manor in Harwell were the basis for the cruck houses built in the same village at the same time or a generation or so later. Indeed, the sequence (table 4) was from the so-called base-cruck to the true cruck, not vice versa.[21]

Requirements for Radiocarbon Dating in the Late Medieval Period

To achieve the accuracy desirable for this period, it is suggested that particular attention be paid to three points:

(*a*) The growth allowance must be assessable: this may make tenons unsuitable as samples.

(*b*) Contamination by younger or older carbon must be rigorously

[18] J. T. Smith, in *Arch. J. 105* (1960), 111, and in *Med. Arch. 8* (1964), 119; Sir C. Fox and Lord Raglan, *Monmouthshire Houses,* Pt. I (Cardiff: Medieval, 1951).

[19] J. T. Smith, in *Arch. J. 105* (1960), 111, and in *Med. Arch. 8* (1964), 119.

[20] F. W. B. Charles, *Medieval Cruck-Building and Its Derivatives,* Soc. Medieval Archaeology, Monograph no. 2, 1967.

[21] It is unfortunate that this term has been applied to the curved blades or posts in timber-framed medieval halls as this nomenclature confuses the chronological sequence in the post-Romanesque period.

TABLE 4

Sequence prior to Cruck Houses

Period	
Romanesque	Framing in Flanders, Northwest France, and England used straight timber almost exclusively.
1225–1275	Curved timbers used in some Cistercian buildings (Abbaye de Noirlac,* Coxwell barn †) and in Flanders (St. Jacobs Church, Bruges).
1275–1375	Curved timbers widely used in Flanders and various parts of England for braces in churches, etc., for curved posts (blades) in the open halls of manor houses. ‡ But rare in Southeast and East England.
1375 onward	General use of curved timber over the whole of England. Blades of the previous period adopted to the building of cruck houses.

* Sir C. Fox and Lord Raglan, Monmouthshire Houses, Pt. I (Cardiff: Medieval, 1951).
† W. Horn, F. W. B. Charles, and R. Berger, in *J. Soc. Arch. Historians* 25 (1966), 221.
‡ W. Horn and E. Born, *The Barns of the Abbey of Beaulieu and its Granges of Great Coxwell and Beaulieu-St. Leonard's* (University of California Press, 1965). Although oak trees were few in the immediate vicinity of Harwell, there would have been many then, as now, in the hamlet of Eling, which from Norman times onward had been part of the Upper Manor of Harwell. Eling (fig. 1) lies some 9 miles south of Harwell and is now in the parish of Hampstead Norris. It is possible that the attachment of this hamlet to a Harwell manor was specifically to give a balanced economy by providing a source of timber.

avoided. The laboratory problem of removing such contamination can be eased by providing high-quality heartwood.

(c) The shape of the Stuiver-Suess curve (fig. 8) is such that ambiguities are introduced for wood that was growing either from ca. A.D. 1100 to 1210, or from ca. A.D. 1500 to 1650.

Where there is the likelihood that the date of the sample itself (not necessarily the construction date) will fall in one of these ranges, two samples differing by 50 or more annual rings should be counted.

It happens that none of the cruck samples in the present series gave a radiocarbon age to which this ambiguity applied. But there was also a sample from a large tie beam removed in 1962 from Harwell Church on account of the presence of deathwatch beetle. This tie beam is one of the three now in the north transept from a reroofing in late medieval times, this roof being quite different from the origina scissor-brace roof [22] of ca.

[22] J. M. Fletcher and P. S. Spokes, in *Med. Arch. 8* (1964), 152.

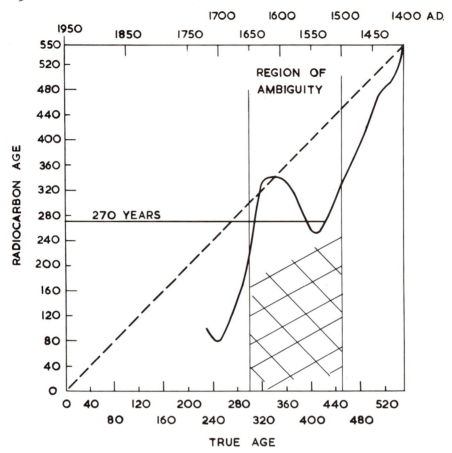

FIG. 8. Stuiver-Suess curve for true ages 230–550 years (i.e., for A.D. 1720 to 1400).

1250 in the south transept. Two determinations (UCLA-1250) on the same sample (for which the growth allowance was 40 years) gave radiocarbon ages of 260 and 280 years ($C^{13}/C^{12} = -26.23\permil$).[23] Converted by the Stuiver-Suess curve (fig. 8), there are three possible true ages corresponding to the mean radiocarbon age of 270 years: these are 310, 390, and 420 years. The corresponding three possible dates of use are A.D. 1570, 1600, and 1680.

The style suggests the earliest of the three possibilities and indeed would be consistent with a date even earlier in the sixteenth century. With the cooperation of Rainer Berger, another sample from the same piece of wood but separated by about 60 annual rings was recently measured: the radiocarbon age (UCLA-1257 which became available the day before this

[23] R. Berger and W. F. Libby, in *Radiocarbon 10*, 1, (1968), 14a.

paper was presented) was 390 ± 60 years.[24] The Stuiver-Suess curve for such an age gives only one true age, 480 years, and with the growth allowance (100 years) the date derived for the use of the tie beam is ca. A.D. 1570, that is, the earliest of the three possible dates indicated by UCLA-1250.[25]

APPENDIX

C^{13}/C^{12} Values of Parts of the Oak Tie Beam
(with about 120 annual rings)
used in the North Transept of Harwell Church,
ca. A.D. 1570

Sample	Ring No. (from center)	Growth	Ring	C^{13}/C^{12}
1	22	Summer	Wide	—24.8‰
				—24.6
2	)	Spring	–	—24.7
	)			—25.1
	30)			
3	)	Summer	Wide	—24.4
	)			—25.4
4	)	Spring	–	—27.5
	)			—26.2
	42)			
5	)	Summer	Wide	—26.6
	)			—27.5
6	78–80	Spring–summer	Very narrow	—25.4
				—25.5
7	94–96	Spring–summer	Narrow	—25.7
				—25.7

These measurements were made by S. R. Silverman of the California Research Corporation at La Habra for which I express my gratitude. The duplicates (on separate shavings from the same ring) showed a variation considerably greater than that (± 0.1%) usually obtained from homogenized samples.

[24] R. Berger and W. F. Libby, in *Radiocarbon 10*, 2 (1968).

[25] I am grateful to the many in England who have helped me obtain and prepare samples and to Rainer Berger, G. J. Fergusson, and W. F. Libby of UCLA for making the radiocarbon measurements.

V

CLIMATE AND RADIOCARBON DURING THE

MIDDLE AGES

H. E. Suess

*T*HE METHOD of radiocarbon dating is based on the assumption that the radiocarbon level, that is, the ratio of carbon-12 to carbon-14 in the atmospheric carbon dioxide, has always remained constant. As we know now, this is not quite true. There is no longer any question that there have been changes of the carbon-14 level in the atmospheric carbon dioxide over the past centuries. This has been shown, primarily, by comparing the dendrochronologically determined ages with the carbon-14 ages of wood samples. The first person to notice these deviations was H. De Vries, in Holland.[1] De Vries found that several of his wood samples showed a radiocarbon content up to two percent higher than that calculated from their dendrochronologically determined ages. The few results of the measurements that De Vries had published, however, were barely outside the limits of error which, at that time, were about one percent. For this reason many scientists did not, for a long time, believe in the existence of these fluctuations until they were confirmed by several other laboratories—in Europe by a joint investigation at Copenhagen, Heidelberg, and Cambridge, and in this country by the laboratories in New Haven, Philadelphia, Tucson, and La Jolla. The observed fluctuations are certainly worldwide phenomena, because the atmosphere of the earth is well mixed. A gas released into the atmosphere at one particular point of the earth's surface becomes evenly distributed throughout the troposphere of the entire global surface within a time on the order of a few years. Therefore, the errors in the conventional radiocarbon ages are the same for all the plant material of a given age and are independent from its geographic origin. It is, therefore, possible to correct

[1] H. De Vries, "Variation in concentration of radiocarbon with time and location on earth," *Koninkl. Ned. Akad. Wetenschap. Proc. B61* (1958), 94–102.

for these errors by using a calibration curve or a conversion table. A calibration curve for the period from A.D. 800 to the present is shown in figure 1.[2]

In order to explain the existence of variations in the carbon-14 level of the atmospheric carbon dioxide, one has to bear in mind that the total amount of carbon-14 on the surface of the earth is much larger than that contained in atmospheric CO_2. Carbon-14 is present, not only in the atmosphere and in the terrestrial biosphere, but also in all the bicarbonates dissolved in the oceans. Obviously, the carbon-14 level, that is, the carbon-12–carbon-14 ratio, depends on the size of the total carbon-14 reservoir on the surface of the earth and on the production rate of carbon-14 by the cosmic radiation. Carbon-14 has a half-life of 5730 years and, therefore, in order to change the carbon-14 level by one percent in 100 years, for example, either the cosmic-ray production rate or the amount of the total carbon reservoir on the surface of the earth into which the carbon-14 becomes distributed has to change by a factor 5700/100 = 57 times larger than the one percent change in the carbon-14 level. No one believes that such large changes can actually occur. The reason why we do observe variations of the carbon-14 level in the atmosphere at all is because the atmosphere is not in complete equilibrium with the large carbon reservoir of the oceans. As has been discussed by R. Revelle and H. E. Suess,[3] the carbon-14 atoms, produced in the atmosphere by cosmic-ray neutrons, take an average time on the order of 30 years before they become absorbed in the ocean. The oceans themselves cannot be considered well-mixed reservoirs; in fact, the radiocarbon content of the bicarbonate in deep Pacific Ocean water is about 15 percent, that of deep Atlantic Ocean water about 6 percent, below that of surface ocean water.[4] One can easily show that this delay in the distribution of the cosmic ray–produced radiocarbon into the oceans causes the atmospheric carbon-14 level to fluctuate to a much larger degree than the average carbon-14 of the surface of the earth as a whole.

[2] H. E. Suess, "Secular variations of the cosmic ray–produced carbon-14 in the atmosphere and their interpretations," *J. Geophys. Res. 70* (1965), 5937.

[3] R. Revelle and H. E. Suess, "Carbon dioxide exchange between atmosphere and ocean," *Tellus 9* (1957), 18.

[4] G. Bien, N. W. Rakestraw, and H. E. Suess, "Radiocarbon dating of the deep water of the Pacific and Indian Oceans," *Radioactive Dating,* Proc. of the Athens, Greece, Symposium 159–173, IAEA, Vienna (1963); *Bull. Inst. Ocean., Monaco 61* (1963).

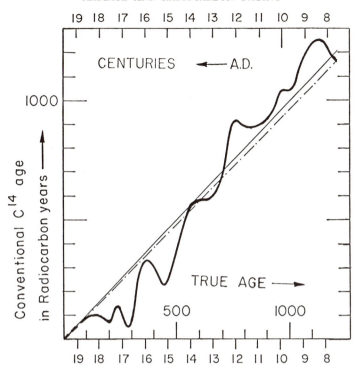

FIG. 1. Empirical relationship between conventional radiocarbon dates (assuming $t_{1/2} = 5568$ years), as derived from La Jolla measurements, and dendrochronologically determined wood ages. The diagonal broken line refers to data calculated with a C^{14} half-life of 5730 years.

One possible reason for variations in the atmospheric carbon-14 level can be recognized immediately. Through some change in conditions, the distribution of radiocarbon between atmospheric carbon dioxide and the bicarbonates of the ocean may be changed. This, for example, could be a consequence of more rapid mixing in the oceans, but even if the oceans would mix infinitely fast, the carbon-14 level in the atmosphere would drop by only 15 percent at the most. Or, the carbon dioxide partial pressure in the atmosphere could change and that, of course, would also change the carbon-14 level in the atmospheric carbon dioxide. However, with the delayed time of 30 years for the equilibrium between atmosphere and surface ocean water, the carbon dioxide would have to change by quite a large factor—a factor on the order of two—in order to produce changes in the carbon-14 on the order of 2 or 3 percent within 100 years. A change in the average temperature would, of course, affect the partial pressure of carbon dioxide in the atmosphere. In order to lower the carbon dioxide content by a factor of two, the average surface temperature of the ocean would have to drop by more than 20° C. No such sudden drop in ocean temperature can occur within one century.

It, therefore, does not seem possible that changes in the geochemical condition have led to variations in the level of carbon-14 in the atmosphere of the observed magnitude. It seems now fairly well established that the cause for at least the more rapid fluctuations, that is, those occurring on a time scale on the order of 100 years, are changes in the cosmic-ray production rate of the carbon-14. It was shown by John Simpson and his co-workers [5] that the cosmic-ray intensity is strongly modulated by solar activity and that the cosmic-ray flux reflects the sunspot cycle of 11 years. During maximal solar activity the cosmic-ray intensity is strongly attenuated relative to periods of low sunspot activity. The difference in the cosmic-ray flux between periods of high solar and low solar activity depends on the energy range of the cosmic rays under consideration, and therefore the functional dependence of the cosmic-ray production rate of carbon-14 on the sunspot numbers is quite complicated. This functional dependence, however, has been calculated by R. E. Lingenfelter,[6] who estimated the difference in the production rate of carbon-14 between periods of sunspot maximum and sunspot minimum to be about 30 percent. Varitions of 30 percent in the production rate, however, are quite adequate to explain the variations in the carbon-14 level that are observed.

In order to investigate, in a quantitative way, the question of how much change is necessary in the cosmic-ray intensity to produce a certain change in the carbon-14 level, it is convenient to consider variations in the form of harmonic oscillations. If we do this, we can calculate the change in the production rate $\overline{Q}$ as a function of the period of the variations. The results of such calculations show (Houtermans [7]) that the system atmosphere–ocean behaves as a "low-pass" filter; in other words, variations of a long period of thousands of years affect the carbon-14 level in the atmosphere to a much greater degree than variations of a short period on the order of tens or hundreds of years. Variations with a time constant

[5] J. A. Simpson, "Recent investigations of the low energy cosmic and solar particle radiations," *Pontificiae Acad. Sci. Scripta Varia. 25,* Civit. Vaticana (1963); "The primary cosmic ray spectrum and the transition region between interplanetary and interstellar space," Proc. Int. Conf. on Cosmic Rays, *Jaipus 2* (1963), 155–169.

[6] R. E. Lingenfelter, "Production of carbon-14 by cosmic ray neutrons," *Revs. Geophys. 1* (1963), 1.

[7] J. C. H. Houtermans, "Oh the quantitative relationships between geophysical parameters and the natural C-14 inventory," *Z. Physik 193* (1966), 1–12.

of the 11-year solar cycle are attenuated by a factor of 100, whereas variations occurring on a time scale 10 times longer are attenuated by only a factor on the order of ten. A quantitative calculation of the relationships between production rate and carbon-14 level also gives the phase lag between input oscillations and those of the carbon-14 level.

Figures 2 and 3 show the observed carbon-14 level according to measurements of the La Jolla Radiocarbon Laboratory. In figure 2 these variations are compared with the sunspot numbers, and in figure 3 with data for the climate, as given by the British meteorologist, H. H. Lamb.[8] The most remarkable feature in the carbon-14 variations are the two humps, on the order of 2 percent, in the fifteenth and seventeenth centuries. Indications for these two humps were already published by De Vries in 1956. Another remarkable feature is the sharp minimum in the carbon-14 level around 1200, discovered in La Jolla. It does not require much imagination to see that a correlation between carbon-14 level and sunspot numbers can be recognized in figure 2, and with climatic data in figure 3. It is, of course, possible that these variations of the radiocarbon level, on a time scale of some 100 years, are caused by two independent effects, one correlated with sunspots and the other independently with the climate. It seems, however, more probable that the sun affects both the carbon-14 production as well as the weather. The question of a correlation between sunspots and climatic changes has, as yet, apparently not been resolved in an unambiguous way, but the evidence from radiocarbon is definitely an indication that such correlation exists.

The modulation of the cosmic-ray production rate of carbon-14 by the sun leads to a rise in the carbon-14 level during periods of low sunspot numbers and to a drop during periods of high sunspot numbers. In other words, the derivative of the carbon-14 level as a function of time is approximately proportional to the deviation from an average value of the sunspot numbers. This is, of course, only a very crude approximation because of the period dependence of the attenuation coefficients involved. Accurate calculations leading to integral equations have been made by J. C. H. Houtermans.[9] Undoubtedly, an unbiased observer will be able to recognize such a correlation in figure 2. However, subjective impressions of this kind may be misleading and, therefore, a rigorous evaluation

[8] H. H. Lamb, "Climatic changes within historical time," *Ann. New York Acad. Sci. 95* (1961), 124–161.

[9] J. C. H. Houtermans, "On the quantitative relationships between geophysical parameters and the natural C-14 inventory," *Z. Physik 193* (1966), 1–12.

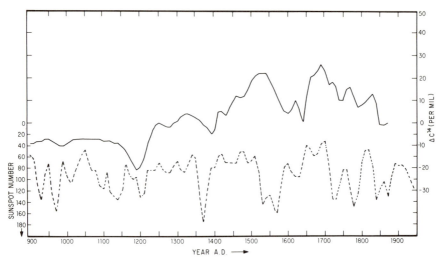

FIG. 2. Upper curve shows $\triangle C^{14}$ in per mil, lower broken curve gives the sunspot numbers per year (at maxima) on an inverted scale. Both curves show computer-interpolated points at 10-year intervals from A.D. 900 to 1900. The derivative of the upper C^{14} curve is expected to show some correlation with the lower curve for the sunspots.

of correlation coefficients between the two functions was made by Houtermans, Suess, and Walter Munk.[10] These showed that a significant probability exists for coherences in the 200-year and the 50-year bands of the two time series. At other frequencies there does not seem to be any significant coherence.

In order to investigate the possibility of the correlation of a time series such as the carbon-14 level in the atmosphere or sunspot numbers with the climate, one needs quantitative data as a measure for the climate. Until recently it was impossible to find such data in the literature, but Lamb has now published estimates for the average temperature in England and also winter severity indices for Europe and some areas in Japan.[11] These indices, represented by actual number, had been published by Lamb long before variations in the carbon-14 level were known, and the data shown in the upper and lower parts of figure 3 have been derived completely independently in England and the United States, respectively.

---

[10] J. C. H. Houtermans, Hans E. Suess, and Walter Munk, "The effect of industrial fuel combustion on the carbon-14 level of atmospheric CO_2," *Proc. Monaco Symposium on Radioactive Dating and Methods of Low-Level Counting*, IAEA, Vienna (1967), 57–68.

[11] H. H. Lamb, "Climatic changes within historical time," *Ann. New York Acad. Sci.* 95 (1961), 124–161.

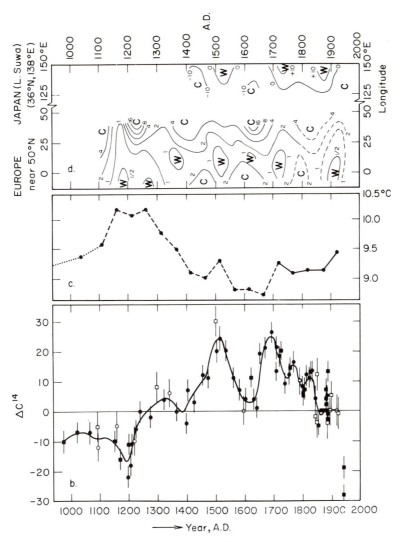

FIG. 3. Lower Part: Variations in the C^{14} level (cf. fig. 2). A smooth line is drawn through the measured points, which are C^{13}-corrected and calculated with a C^{14} half-life of 5730 years. Middle Part: Fifty-year mean temperatures for England according to Lamb [8]. Upper Part: Winter severity indices for Europe and a lake in Japan, as a function of latitude according to Lamb.

According to Lamb, the early medieval time until A.D. 1200 was a rela-tively warm period. In the thirteenth century, however, the weather changed to a more continental type, with extremely severe winters in eastern Europe. But the fourteenth century, showed a milder, more oceanic climate. The severe winters that signify the so-called Little Ice

Age were particularly pronounced in the fifteenth and seventeenth centuries. It appears, therefore, that periods of low solar activity, during which the carbon-14 level in the atmosphere was rising, were characterized in Europe by a distinct continental climate with its characteristically severe winters.

VI

SUNSPOTS AND RADIOCARBON DATING

IN THE MIDDLE AGES

D. C. Grey and P. E. Damon

*T*HE RATIONALE of radiocarbon dating is too well known to belabor at length here, but it is perhaps worthwhile to emphasize two important points essential to the dating process. First, it is essential that there be a defined point in time at which the sample became isolated from its environment, so that the only process which can affect the radiocarbon concentration in the sample is that of radioactive decay. It is from this moment that the radiocarbon clock measures the age of the sample. Second, it is necessary to know the initial concentration of radiocarbon in the sample at the time of its isolation.

Libby used samples of tree ring–dated wood and historically dated samples from Egypt to show that, within the limit of experimental error at the time, the initial radiocarbon concentration of wood samples appeared to be very nearly constant.[1] By 1958 De Vries had developed improved instrumentation and was able to show that there had been significant variations in the initial carbon-14 content of wood samples.[2] Since 1958, a number of laboratories, utilizing dendrochronologically dated wood, developed a large body of information about these variations. The agreement between laboratories is excellent and there can be no doubt about the reality of the variations.

Figure 1 represents a compilation of data pertaining to radiocarbon fluctuations in wood samples. The data are taken from Ralph et al.;[3]

---

[1] W. F. Libby, *Radiocarbon Dating,* 1st ed. (Chicago: University of Chicago Press, 1952), 2d ed., 1955.

[2] Hessel De Vries, "Variation in concentration of radiocarbon with time and location on earth," *Proc. Konikl. Ned. Akad. Wetenschap. B61* (1958), 94–102.

[3] E. K. Ralph, H. N. Michael, and J. Gruninger, Jr., "University of Pennsylvania Dates VII," *Radiocarbon 7* (1965), 179–186.

Suess,[4] corrected to oxalic-acid standard according to Stuiver and Suess;[5] Stuiver;[6] Suess,[7] with an estimated correction to oxalic-acid standard; Damon and Grey,[8] including corrected data from Damon et al.;[9] and Haynes et al.[10]

Figure 2 represents the same data in the form of a direct comparison of radiocarbon age with dendrochronological age for the same samples. Two Egyptian check samples are included, one from the reign of Sesostris III, which is the earliest astronomically fixed reign in the Egyptian chronology, and one from the earlier reign of Zoser. These show the same variations as the tree ring–dated wood when one allows for the finite age of the wood at the time it was incorporated into the archaeologically dated structure or site.

It is perhaps not entirely out of order to pause to pay particular tribute to the workers at the Laboratory for Tree-Ring Research at the University of Arizona for their invaluable contributions to the carbon-14 fluctuation studies. Several of these professors deserve special mention: the late E. Schulman, whose search for paleoclimatic records brought to light the incredibly old bristlecone pine; H. C. Fritts, whose studies of forest profiles put the classical dendrochronological methods on a firm theoretical basis; and C. W. Ferguson, who has extended the bristlecone pine chronology to over 7100 years and has provided virtually all the dendrochronologically dated samples upon which carbon-14 fluctuation studies are based.[11]

---

[4] H. E. Suess, "Secular variations of cosmic ray–produced carbon-14 in the atmosphere and their interpretations," *J. Geophys. Res. 70* (1965), 5937–5952.

[5] M. Stuiver and H. E. Suess, "On the relationship between radiocarbon dates and true sample ages," *Radiocarbon 8* (1966), 534–540.

[6] M. Stuiver, "Carbon-14 content of 18th- and 19th-century wood; variations correlated with sunspot activity," *Science 149* (1965), 533–534.

[7] H. E. Suess, "Bristlecone pine calibration of the radiocarbon time scale from 4100 B.C. to 1500 B.C.," *Symposium on Radioactive Dating and Methods of Low-Level Counting at Monaco, 2–10 March 1967.*

[8] Paul E. Damon, "Climatic vs. Magnetic Perturbation of the Atmospheric Carbon-14 Reservoir," Proceedings XII Nobel Symposium: *Radiocarbon Variations and Absolute Chronology, Uppsala 11–15 Aug. 1969* (Stockholm: Almquist and Wiksell, in press).

[9] Paul E. Damon, A. Long, and D. C. Grey, "Fluctuation of atmospheric C^{14} during the last six millennia," *J. Geophys. Res. 71* (1966), 1055–1063.

[10] C. V. Haynes, D. C. Grey, P. E. Damon, and R. Bennett, Arizona radiocarbon dates VII," *Radiocarbon 9* (1967), 1–14.

[11] References to their work is found in the paper by C. W. Ferguson in this volume.

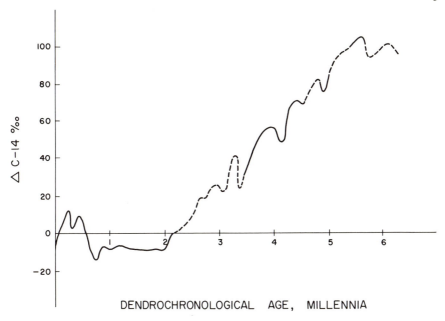

FIG. 1. Per-mil variations in initial C¹⁴ content of wood samples as a function of dendrochronological age. The data were first smoothed by a 500-year smoothing function. Then a 50-year smoothing function was applied and any significant departures from the first curve were considered real and were plotted.

It can be seen from figure 2 that carbon-14 dating errors in the A.D. period are perhaps not more than about 200 years, but that in the period from 5000 to 7000 years ago, the errors amount to almost 1000 years. It might be noted in passing that if the "Archaeological Age" used by M. J. Aitken in calibrating thermoluminescence dates (see his paper in this volume, p. 271) is taken to be "radiocarbon age" and corrected according to figure 2, the agreement is greatly improved.

In the light of the large number of dating techniques that may be employed, and because of the fact that all have limitations which may give rise to disagreement between the techniques, it would seem highly desirable to append to each date in the literature some notation as to how that date was derived, such as, for example, a letter suffix appended to the numerical value which would indicate the method employed: perhaps Rc for radiocarbon, KA for potassium argon, D for dendrochronological, Th for thermoluminescence, etc.

So far many investigators, including publishers of radiocarbon date lists, have followed the conventionally agreed-upon practice of subtracting radiocarbon ages from the A.D. 1950 reference datum and expressing the

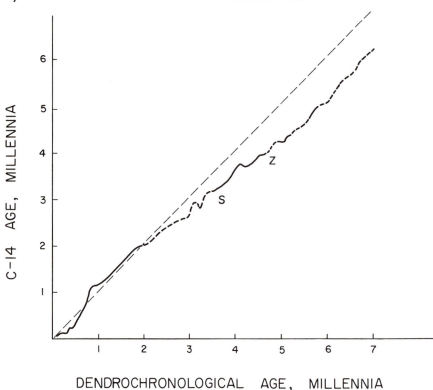

FIG. 2. A direct comparison of radiocarbon and dendrochronological dates during the last seven millennia. Two Egyptian historically dated samples are included for comparison. S indicates samples from the reign of Sesostris III; Z indicates samples from the time of Zoser.

resulting differences as a B.C. or A.D. date. Such a practice implies to the unwary reader that a calendar date can actually be directly obtained from a radiocarbon age which is often not the case. Note in figure 2 that a radiocarbon age of 5000 Rc corresponds to a dendrochronological age of about 5800 D, which in turn implies a calendar date of about 3850 B.C., whereas subtracting 5000 Rc from A.D. 1950 gives a value of 3050 Rc B.C. if one can accept such a notation.

Figure 3 compares radiocarbon ages with tree-ring ages for the A.D. period. The curve is considerably smoothed in places, because the fine detail cannot be shown on such a scale. It must be pointed out that the wood samples measured in the series often consisted of five to ten or more growth rings per specimen, and hence the carbon-14 measurements represent averages over these short periods of time. It must also be mentioned that the limit of precision of individual radiocarbon measurements (one standard deviation) during the A.D. period is about 30 years, so that there is some uncertainty in portions of the curve where replicate samples have not been run. Nevertheless, the general features of the curve are correct, as indicated by agreement between several laboratories, and the fine structure of the curve is certainly indicative of the nature of the variations which do occur. Eventually, it is to be hoped that single-ring samples can be measured in replicate for each year through critical time periods.

Figure 3 clearly indicates that the precision with which wood samples can be dated varies considerably from one portion of the record to another. Note that a radiocarbon date of A.D. 1620 Rc corresponds to at least three dendrochronological dates, ranging from about A.D. 1480 to 1650. (Hereafter, in this report, dendrochronological dates and calendar

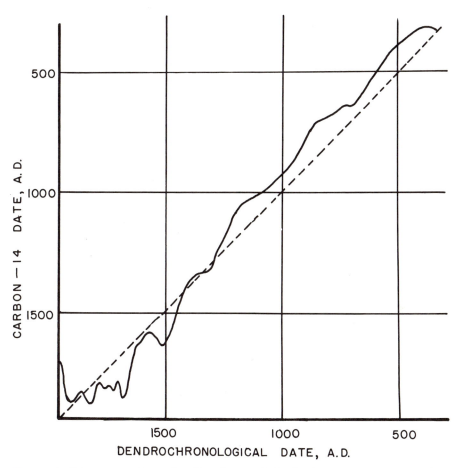

FIG. 3. A direct comparison of radiocarbon and dendrochronological ages for the A.D. time period. The curve is smoothed by a 22-year Gaussian smoothing function.

dates will be equated.) A radiocarbon date of A.D. 1750 Rc, on the other hand, appears to be rather precisely determined at about A.D. 1650. A radiocarbon date of A.D. 1850 Rc might represent almost any true date from A.D. 1650 to modern times.

In brief, those regions of the curve of figure 3 which are nearly parallel to the abscissa or are recurved, such as from A.D. 1650 to about 1900, A.D. 1490 to 1650, A.D. 1300 to 1400, A.D. 1100 to 1220, and A.D. 680 to 900 (dendrochronological dates, actually), correspond to time periods for which dating by radiocarbon is limited in precision. On the other hand, where the curve is nearly vertical, the precision can be very good, as would be the case for radiocarbon dates lying in the range A.D. 1400 Rc to 1570 Rc, A.D. 1200 Rc to 1300 Rc, etc. Figure 4 shows how the imprecision of carbon-14 dates varies in the A.D. time period, assuming that all radiocarbon dates in this time period have a standard deviation of 50 years. Two curves are shown: the upper one establishes the earliest true date corresponding to the given radiocarbon date, while the lower curve establishes the later limit. The large variation of the lower curve between

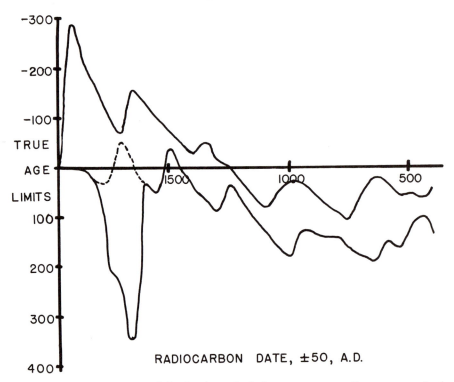

FIG. 4. The effective range of dendrochronological years corresponding to a standard deviation of 50 years in radiocarbon dates; A.D. time period.

about A.D. 1600 Rc and 1800 Rc is due to the Suess (fossil-fuel or industrial) effect with its depressed carbon-14 level from 1890 until ca. 1945. The lower carbon-14 content in this period (1890–1945) may be erroneously interpreted as indicating an age of up to several hundred years. If the sample can be placed in preindustrial times on independent grounds, the dotted branch of the lower curve may be used.

Figure 5 shows an even more detailed version of the comparison of radiocarbon and dendrochronological dates for the last 260 years. As can be seen from figures 3 and 4, this is one of the worst portions of the A.D. record from the point of view of radiocarbon dating precision. It is this portion of the curve, however, that has permitted a degree of insight into the causes of the carbon-14 variations, as will soon be seen.

Before discussing the causes of the carbon-14 fluctuations, it is necessary to clarify one important point. The limitations in precision described

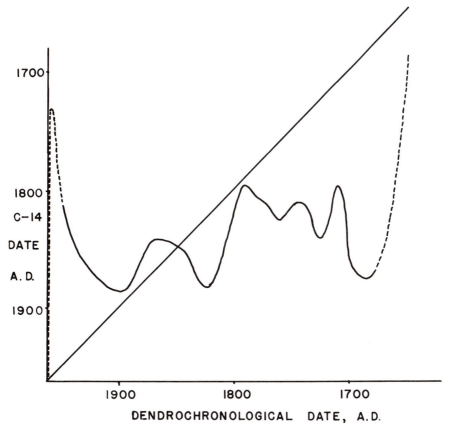

FIG. 5. A direct comparison of radiocarbon and dendrochronological dates from A.D. 1700 to A.D. 1930. The curve is smoothed by a 22-year Gaussian smoothing function.

above are applicable to the typical case of a radiocarbon date derived from a single measurement of a wood sample. Should the original sample be large enough so that a series of samples, each consisting of only a few annual growth layers, can be obtained from it, then the carbon-14 variations within the sample can be determined, and these variations can then be compared with those of the dendrochronologically dated specimens. If the patterns match within the time range indicated by the radiocarbon age of the sample, then a date which is accurate and precise to within a few years may be possible. Indeed, Ferguson, Huber, and Suess have applied this method to Swiss lake dwellings with fair results, even though they were hampered by the lack of detail in both the sample and the standard-fluctuation curves.[12]

Radiocarbon Variations

Table 1 outlines the a priori possibilities for causing variations in radiocarbon concentration in the atmosphere and hence in wood samples that derive their carbon from the atmosphere. Most of these will be passed over with little more than a comment.

Since radiocarbon is produced in the earth's atmosphere by the action of cosmic rays, it follows that any variation in the cosmic-ray flux reaching the earth's atmosphere will result in a variation in the rate of radiocarbon production. There seems to be no very good reason to assume that the cosmic-ray flux in the vicinity of the solar system should be entirely constant. Supernovae inject large pulses of cosmic rays into space, and these pulses might be preserved through considerable reaches of time and space. An attempt to correlate variations of radiocarbon with recorded observations of novae and supernovae gathered from Chinese and Korean records, by Xi-Ze-zong and Po Shu-jen revealed no corresponding increases in atmospheric carbon-14 within the anticipated time of arrival of particulate matter.[13] It is difficult to calculate arrival times for cosmic-ray particles from such events, even in those cases where distances are known, because interstellar fields will cause large deviations from straight-line paths. Hence no conclusive statements about such events are possible at this time.

Broxon first suggested that cosmic rays arriving at the earth vary with

[12] C. W. Ferguson, B. Huber, and H. E. Suess, "Determination of the age of Swiss lake dwellings as example of dendrochronologically calibrated radiocarbon dating," *Zeit. für Naturforschung 21a,* Heft 7 (1966), 1173–1177.

[13] Xi-Ze-zong and Po Shu-jen, "Ancient oriental records of novae and supernovae," *Science 150* (1967), 1–7.

TABLE I

The a priori Causes of Radiocarbon Variations.

I. Variations in the rate of radiocarbon production in the atmosphere.
    1.   Variations in the cosmic-ray flux through the solar system.
        a.   Cosmic-ray bursts from supernovae, etc.
        b.   Interstellar modulation of the cosmic-ray flux.
    2.   Modulation of the cosmic-ray flux by the solar wind.
    3.   Modulation of the cosmic-ray flux by the geomagnetic field.
    4.   Production by nuclear weapons testing.
    5.   Production by antimatter meteorite collisions with earth.

II. Variations in the rate of exchange of radiocarbon between various geochemical reservoirs such as atmosphere, oceans, and biosphere.
    1.   Temperature variations control CO_2 solubility and rate of circulation.
    2.   Sea-level variations affect ocean circulation and capacity.
    3. CO_2 assimilation by the terrestrial biosphere is proportional to biomass, CO_2 concentration, and depends on temperature and humidity.
    4.   Certain reservoirs (subarctic soil organics, ocean sediments, etc.) do not return radiocarbon. Variation in the size or rate of intake of these reservoirs constitutes a variable "sink" in the C^{14} system.

III. Dilution of the atmospheric radiocarbon by stable-carbon injections.
    1.   Volcanic and hydrothermal injections.
    2.   Combustion of fossil fuels by man.

solar-flare activity,[14] and by 1954 Forbush had established that there was a long-term variation in cosmic-ray flux associated with the sunspot cycle.[15] This mechanism will be discussed in some detail later.

There is no question that a variation in the earth's magnetic-field strength would have an effect on radiocarbon production, because the earth's field serves as a shield against low-energy cosmic rays. Kigoshi and Hasegawa have tried to establish that the geomagnetic field has changed by appreciable amounts in historic times, but the radiocarbon record does not show the result of such a change.[16] Athavale has pointed out that there is a very real possibility that most of the paleomagnetic studies to date reflect largely local changes in the magnetic field, and that

[14] James W. Broxon, "Relation of the cosmic radiation to geomagnetic and heliophysical activity," *Phys. Rev. 62* (1942), 508.

[15] S. E. Forbush, "Worldwide cosmic-ray variations 1937–1952," *J. Geophys. Res. 59* (1954), 525–545.

[16] K. Kigoshi and H. Hasegawa, "Secular variation of atmospheric radiocarbon and its dependence on geomagnetism," *J. Geophys. Res. 71* (1966), 1065–1071.

the overall magnetic moment of the earth has not changed appreciably.[17] It is known that the earth's field has undergone complete reversals at many times in the geologic past, the most recent having occurred around 700,000 years ago, but the case for significant changes during the times reached by radiocarbon dating has yet to be proven.

Nuclear weapon testing doubled the atmospheric inventory of radiocarbon, but the amounts from this source are known, and, in any case, they have no bearing on radiocarbon dating of earlier events.

Cowan, Atluri, and Libby speculated that an antimatter meteorite in collision with the earth would release large amounts of radiation and might produce significant amounts of radiocarbon.[18] The 1908 Tunguska meteorite possessed certain peculiar properties according to witnesses, and it was considered that this might represent an antimatter test case. No variation in radiocarbon large enough which could be clearly linked to a massive nuclear reaction was detected by these workers.

Variation in exchange rate between geochemical reservoirs has been shown to be significant in the long-term radiocarbon variations like those between 5000 and 7000 years ago.[19] Since these variations are long-term in nature, they do not affect the precision of radiocarbon dating appreciably, and the use of dendrochronological calibration, where possible, removes inaccuracies from that source.

Dilution of atmospheric radiocarbon by volcanic hydrothermal emanations is insignificant except on a local basis. Sites near volcanoes or geysers are suspect, but no worldwide effects are likely. The use of fossil fuels by man has added great quantities of inert carbon to the atmosphere, but this effect is only important since 1890.

The correlation between cosmic-ray bombardment rates in the earth's atmosphere and sunspots is explained by magnetohydrodynamicists as a result of the action of the solar wind, that is, the supersonic streaming of electrically charged particles fleeing from the million-degree temperatures of the sun's upper atmosphere.[20] The particles interact with magnetic

---

[17] R. N. Athavale, "Intensity of the geomagnetic field in India over the past 4000 years," *Nature 210* (1966), 1310–1312, 5043.

[18] C. Cowan, C. R. Atluri, and W. F. Libby, "Possible antimatter content of the Tunguska Meteorite of 1908," *Nature 206* (1965), 861–865.

[19] Paul E. Damon, "Climatic vs. Magnetic Perturbation of the Atmospheric Carbon-14 Reservoir," Proceedings XII Nobel Symposium: *Radiocarbon Variations and Absolute Chronology, Uppsala 11–15 Aug. 1969* (in press).

[20] E. N. Parker, Interplanetary Dynamical Processes (New York: John Wiley & Sons, 1963).

fields. The solar wind tends to carry with it any weak magnetic fields which it encounters, but is, on the other hand, forced to avoid regions of strong magnetic fields.

The geomagnetic field tends to ward off the streaming particles of the solar wind, but, since the field becomes weaker with increasing distance from the earth, a bounding surface may be found which marks the closest approach of the solar wind. This surface is called the geomagnetopause, and it encloses the geomagnetosphere, which is far from spherical but is instead compressed on the upwind side and dragged out to great distances on the downwind side.

Near the sun the flow of the solar wind is supersonic and laminar, and it carries with it the weak field of the sun and any weak field it encounters in interplanetary space. As the solar wind moves away from the sun it is spread over an ever-growing surface and diminishes in intensity. Eventually the flow undergoes a sudden transition from laminar or streamlined flow to turbulent flow with an abrupt decrease in speed. This boundary occurs at a distance from the sun which may be on the order of 100 times the radius of the earth's orbit, and it marks the surface of what might be called the heliomagnetosphere.

Both the geomagnetosphere and the heliomagnetosphere react to changes in the solar wind. An increase in the solar wind will tend to expand the heliomagnetosphere, compress the upwind side of the geomagnetosphere, and drag out the downwind tail of the geomagnetosphere.

Cosmic rays are charged particles, like those of the solar wind, which react with magnetic fields. As cosmic rays approach the region near the sun, they are deflected slightly by the weak fields of the heliomagnetosphere. Weaker cosmic rays may be deflected strongly enough so that they never reach the central regions near the sun and earth. More energetic cosmic rays may reach the geomagnetosphere and be deflected by the stronger fields there.

When the geomagnetosphere and heliomagnetosphere vary in response to the changing solar wind, the cosmic-ray flux reaching the earth's atmosphere also changes, and hence the rate of production of radiocarbon also changes. The solar wind depends on solar-flare (sunspot) activity, and so one concludes that radiocarbon production must be related somehow to sunspot activity.

While the *rate* of radiocarbon production depends on sunspot number, the *amount* of radiocarbon in the atmosphere depends not only on the instantaneous rate but also the rates of production at past times, the lengths of time these rates persisted, and the way in which the atmosphere stores the radiocarbon and exchanges it with other geochemical reservoirs. The mathematician would say that there is an integrodifferential relationship between radiocarbon content of the atmosphere and sunspot number. Atmospheric radiocarbon is related to the integral of the sunspot number, while the sunspot number is related to the derivative of the radiocarbon function. While either way of stating the relationship is equally correct in the mathematical sense, there is a practical difference between the two from the point of view of numerical calculations. Finding the derivative of the radiocarbon function is much less precise than finding the integral of the sunspot data.

Stuiver attempted to use an electrical analog model of the terrestrial carbon system proposed by De Vries to integrate a radiocarbon production function based on sunspot numbers.[21] Stuiver did not state the production function used. The results were suggestive but far from conclusive. In a second attempt, Stuiver simply summed the sunspot numbers over a solar cycle (thus effecting an integration), summing each cycle independently, and compared the resultant histogram, inverted, with the radiocarbon variation curve.[22] The correlation was quite good. The model, though very simple, provided the two essential ingredients of integration (by summing the sunspot numbers) and exchange with other reservoirs (by dropping the previous accumulation at the end of each solar cycle).

In 1963, Lingenfelter used the extant data on direct measurements of atmospheric neutrons produced by cosmic rays to calculate the rate of production of carbon-14 at sunspot maximum and sunspot minimum.[23] The difference was about 25 percent. Lingenfelter assumed a linear relationship between carbon-14 production and sunspot number and wrote a simple equation relating the two quantities.

Grey, Damon, and Long used the Lingenfelter production equation to describe the input to a simple mathematical model (see table 2 for mathematical details).[24] Figure 6 shows the comparison of the resultant

[21] M. Stuiver, "Variations in radiocarbon concentration and sunspot activity," *J. Geophys. Res. 66* (1961), 273–276.

[22] M. Stuiver, "Carbon-14 content of 18th- and 19th-century wood; variations correlated with sunspot activity," *Science 149* (1965), 533–534.

[23] R. E. Lingenfelter, "Production of carbon-14 by cosmic-ray neutrons," *Rev. Geophys. 1* (1963), 35–55.

[24] D. C. Grey, P. E. Damon, and A. Long, "Variations in atmospheric C¹⁴," paper presented at Sixth Western National Meeting of the American Geophysical Union, University of California, Los Angeles, 7–9 September 1966.

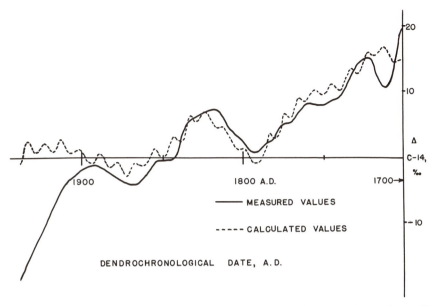

1900   1800 A.D.   1700→

———— MEASURED VALUES

----- CALCULATED VALUES

DENDROCHRONOLOGICAL   DATE, A.D.

FIG. 6. A comparison of per-mil radiocarbon variations as determined experimentally (solid curve) and as calculated from the simple solar-modulation model (dashed curve); after Grey, Damon, and Long (22).

calculated variations in radiocarbon content of wood samples with the variations which are actually measured. The agreement is quite good and suggests that the model is basically correct.

D. J. Schove attempted to reconstruct sunspot numbers for times prior to 1610 by utilizing historical accounts of aurorae, which are closely related to solar-flare activity.[25] Using the model of Grey, Damon, and Long and his own estimated sunspot data, Schove calculated the radiocarbon variations from A.D. 1200 to the present time. Figure 7 shows the results. The agreement is good enough to indicate that Schove has succeeded rather well in his attempt.

Sunspots were known to the Chinese as early as 500 B.C., and are mentioned in the European literature at the time of Charlemagne. Certainly, sunspots were well known at the time of Galileo. It was Galileo who first, around 1610, established that sunspots were squarely on the face of the sun and not due to bodies interposed between the sun and earth as others had hypothesized. From this time until 1700, the Zürich observatory kept records of sunspot maxima and minima. From 1700 to the present time,

[25] D. J. Schove, "The sunspot cycle 649 B.C. to A.D. 2000, *J. Geophys. Res.* 60 (1955), 127–146.

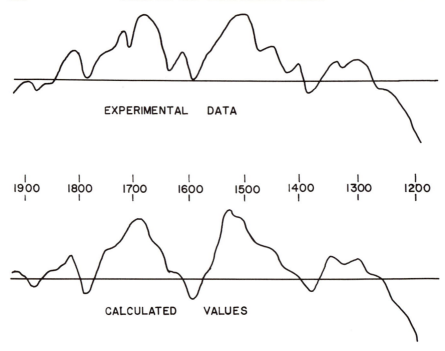

EXPERIMENTAL DATA

1900	1800	1700	1600	1500	1400	1300	1200

CALCULATED VALUES

FIG. 7. A comparison of the curve of experimentally determined radiocarbon fluctuations in wood samples with the fluctuations calculated from the model of Grey, Damon, and Long (22), using Schove's estimated sunspot data (23).

the same observatory has kept records of daily sunspot observations. The compiled Zürich data have been reported by Waldmeier.[26]

Since sunspots are known to have existed from ancient times, it seems likely that radiocarbon fluctuations on the order of 2–3 percent may have existed throughout the time for which carbon-14 dating is usable. Imprecisions comparable to those of figures 3 and 4 would therefore have existed throughout the record.

No one has yet devised a successful scheme for predicting the time of occurrence of the intensity of maximum sunspot activity. Although there is an approximate 11-year cycle in sunspot activity, the cycle ranges from 5 to 17 years in actual length between maxima. The spacing between minima tends to be more nearly constant. Some have postulated the existence of longer, say, 80-year, cycles in solar behavior, but the record is too short to provide a meaningful analysis of such longer period variations.

[26] M. Waldmeier, *The Sunspot Activity in the Years 1610–1960* (Zürich: Schulthess, 1961).

Suda [27] and more recently Head cited in Pay [28] have attempted to relate solar-flare activity to the effect of gravitational forces exerted on the sun by the planets, but without complete success. Should some such mechanism be established, the radiocarbon clock could be partly compensated for the solar-wind effect for almost any desirable length of time because of the extreme precision with which planetary motions can be calculated. The result would be an improved knowledge of the precision to be expected from radiocarbon dating in certain time periods.

As mentioned previously, the process of calculating sunspot numbers from known radiocarbon fluctuations is an imprecise one, but one could thus provide approximate values for checking long-term models of solar variations.

It is now pretty well known that the atmospheric neutron flux does not vary linearly with sunspot number as Lingenfelter assumed. Modeling is continuing at the University of Arizona with more accurate representations. In any case, it is an oversimplification to assume that sunspot numbers are the best indicator of the properties of the solar wind which govern cosmic-ray flux. Only a first-order approximation is obtained from such calculations.

It is rather surprising that not more sunspot data are not available prior to A.D. 1700. Even a casual perusal of the literature of Galileo's time makes it quite clear that sunspots were a topic of wide interest at the time. While the contemporaneous invention of the telescope greatly facilitated sunspot observations, the previous use of the camera obscura had yielded much information. The fact that the Zürich observatory kept records of the maxima and minima of solar activity during the seventeenth century indicated that there has been sufficient previous study to establish the quasi-cyclic behavior of sunspots. Galileo's observations of the rotation of the sun, and the advent of the heliocentric Copernican theory, should have combined, one imagines, to make solar observations a widespread study. Perhaps there are records which have not yet come to light. It would also be of interest to know when some observer first noted the relation between aurorae and sunspots.

In summary, it can be said that the solar-induced variations in radio-

---

[27] T. Suda, "Some statistical aspects of solar activity indices," *Met. Soc. Jap. Tokyo J. ser. 2, 40* (5) (1962), 287–299.

[28] R. Pay, "Position of planets linked to solar flare prediction," *Technology Week,* 15 May 1967, pp. 35–58.

carbon production have probably always been present to the extent of perhaps about 3 percent of the atmospheric concentration. These variations impose limitations upon the precision of routine radiocarbon dating for certain time periods while permitting good precision in others. The calibration of radiocarbon dates against tree-ring dates provides good accuracy throughout the last 7000 years. For those samples which permit determination of the radiocarbon fluctuations over a number of years, precise dating is possible in any part of the record. Ultimately, for ideal samples, precision on the order of a decade may become possible, if the necessary effort is justified.[29]

[29] This research was supported by grant number GA-1379 from the National Science Foundation and by the State of Arizona. Contribution no. 169 of the program in Geochronology at the University of Arizona.

TABLE 2

Equations Governing the Sunspot-Radiocarbon Model (22)

R_j The amount of radiocarbon in the atmosphere at the end of year j.

Q_j The rate of radiocarbon production during year j.

S_j Mean annual sunspot number during year j.

R_s Standard value of R, related to the international oxalic acid dating standard.

T   A time constant, related to the net of exchange of radiocarbon from atmosphere to other geochemical reservoirs.

$\triangle_j$ 1000 $(R_j - R_s)/R_s$. A measure of the departure of R_j from the standard reference value. Can be determined experimentally or calculated from the model.

– A bar superior indicates an average over the years A.D. 1700 to 1900.

EXPERIMENTALLY,
$$R_s = 8.10^9 \text{ atom/cm}^2$$

LINGENFELTER GIVES
$$Q_j = (2.637 - .00297 \ S_j) \cdot 32 \cdot 10^6 \text{ atom/cm}^2/\text{yr}$$

THE MODEL EQUATIONS ARE
$$R_j = R_{j-1} \exp(-1/T) + Q_j \cdot 1$$
$$\overline{R} = \overline{Q}/ \ [1 - \exp(-1/T)] \doteq \overline{Q}T$$

Values of T ranging from 1 to 100 were used, and the calculated R values compared with the experimentally determined R values by means of a simple product-moment correlation coefficient. Various phase lags between the calculated and experimental values were also tried. Maximum correlation occurred for zero phase lag and T = 100 years. The model is not very sensitive to values of T, but the 100-year value compares well with results from other studies. Calculations were done on an IBM 7092 computer at the University of Arizona Numerical Analysis Laboratory.

VII

CONCEPTS AND TECHNIQUES OF
DENDROCHRONOLOGY

C. W. Ferguson

*D*ENDROCHRONOLOGY may be defined as the study of the chronological sequence of annual growth rings in trees. The concepts and techniques of the science, as presented here, reflect the work and practice of the Laboratory of Tree-Ring Research at the University of Arizona in Tuscon. Development of the science of dendrochronology—as opposed to the simple counting of tree rings in a stump—began in 1901 with an observation on aridity in relation to elevation by Andrew Ellicott Douglass,[1] an astronomer interested in sunspots, and continues up to our strongly computer-oriented age. The objective of this paper will be to acquaint the reader with some of the fundamentals so that he may better understand the tree-ring studies done on living trees[2] as well as in archaeological material.

In the southwestern United States most of the tree-ring studies have been conducted on four major species: Douglas fir (*Pseudotsuga menziesii*), ponderosa pine (*Pinus ponderosa*), pinyon pine (*Pinus edulis*), and Rocky Mountain juniper (*Juniperus scopulorum*). Much work also has been done on the giant sequoia (*Sequoia gigantea*). Although it reaches an age of about 3200 years, it is not a good dendrochronological species. In recent years, attention has been focused upon two species of the upper timberline: limber pine (*Pinus flexilis*) and bristlecone pine (*Pinus aristata*).

---

[1] A résumé of the work of Douglass and a complete list of his publications is contained in a memorial article in the *Tree-Ring Bulletin 24*, 3–4 (May 1962), 2–10.

[2] B. Bannister, "Dendrochronology," in *Science in Archaeology*, Brothwell and Higgs, eds. (New York: Basic Books, 1963), pp. 161–176.

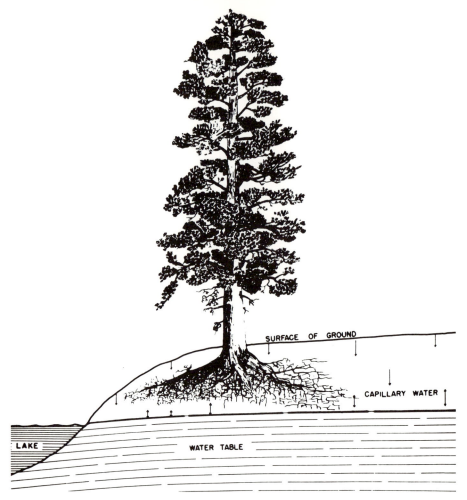

SURFACE OF GROUND

CAPILLARY WATER

LAKE   WATER TABLE

Fig. 1. A complacent site, with ample moisture, which would produce a tree that would have rings of uniform width.

Sampling Living Trees

In dendrochronological studies, criteria for sampling include trees that (1) are not too close to other trees, as competition may overshadow climatic response; (2) have no subsurface supply of water, for example, an adjacent spring or perennial stream (figs. 1 and 2); and (3) have no outward appearance of injury or disease.

Sampling may be done by taking a cross section or, more conveniently, by using a Swedish increment borer, a precision tool designed to remove a small core 3/16 inch in diameter, without causing the living tree any harm. The tip of the borer has a razor-sharp cutting edge with external

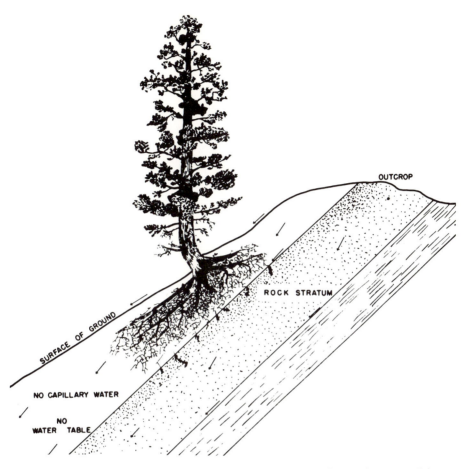

FIG. 2. A sensitive site where soil moisture drains or seeps off, and the tree will have annual rings that will vary in width in response to year-to-year changes in precipitation.

screw threads that draws the borer into the tree as the handle is turned. A sixteen-inch borer is a common size, but they can be obtained up to forty-eight inches in length.

Before the core is removed from the extractor spoon, it should be numbered. All data are handled with the bark (recent) at the right; hence, the core should be in this position. The reason is solely one of tradition; there is no reason the reverse could not be practiced. Comparison is facilitated, however, when preparation is standardized, and we do have what is by far the largest collection of tree-ring data. The somewhat fragile increment cores must be handled with care. If they are sound when removed, they may be carried loose in a large tubular container. If they are not in one piece, however, they must be stabilized individually. Soda straws, into which a core fits, or corrugated cardboard sections are good containers for individual specimens. Cores may be laid down between the corrugations and taped in place.

Various site and specimen data are recorded. These usually include: exact geographic location, such as township, range, and section; slope (the steepness expressed in percent, and relative position on the slope, as mid, upper, and lower) and exposure (aspect) according to compass points; soil conditions (type and depth); associated plant growth (species and areal density); relation to other trees; physical characteristics of the tree, such as diameter of stem, height of crown, and general overall appearance; and any natural or man-made disturbance, such as lightning or fire damage, excessive grazing, lumbering, etc.

The Laboratory now uses two standard forms, on 5 × 8 inch cards, to record data for the site and for the individual specimens. Thus the general description, map references, etc., do not have to be repeated for each tree sampled. A map, sketched as the collecting progresses, locates the individual trees. An embossed aluminum label, bearing either a field number or a permanent Laboratory designation, is attached to each tree. The procedure encompassing maps, labels, pictures, and notes serves not only to identify the tree, but is designated to permit resampling of individual trees at periodic intervals by a succession of field crews. In this way, the record can be kept up to date and perhaps strengthened by additional collecting in prime areas.

Preparation of Cores

Cores are mounted in a grooved stick to facilitate handling and storage. The mount, specially milled from a piece of clear wood, is ⅜ inch wide by ½ inch high, and of sufficient length to accommodate the core. One of the narrow sides is grooved to hold half of the core, and the shoulders are sloped. Cores should be air-dried prior to mounting so that they will not shrink and crack after they are glued in place. When cores break in the field, sequential numbering of fragments will aid in reconstructing the core for mounting.

The specimen number and such notes as the species, site, and collection data are written on the mount in pencil. These data should agree with those on site and specimen cards and with the permanent Laboratory system of identification.

A thin stream of permanent glue (a plastic glue is preferred because it will not crystallize) is spread evenly in the groove, and the core is inserted with the bark end to the observer's right. The original vertical cell structure is placed in the groove tilted toward the observer at an angle of 30° to 45° above the horizontal. The cell alignment can be detected by examining the cell structure at either end and by the sheen on the sides of the core caused by the shearing action of the borer. The core is pressed firmly into the groove and wrapped tightly and evenly with string to hold the core firm while the glue is drying.

A surface may be prepared by either a microtome or a sanding technique. A razor blade, preferably a larger-than-average size, used in a sliding, drawing action will provide a smooth cut. A blade holder, especially one that will allow a little flexibility in the outer portion of the blade, will facilitate the operation. Some species and particularly specimens with heavy latewood may be more easily cut if the cores are moistened by immersing them in water for a few seconds. In specimens having fairly large, distinct rings, a surface may be prepared by sanding with a small belt sander, utilizing a series of grits from about 100 to 400. If this is to be the procedure, the cores should be mounted with the cells vertically aligned.

Discussion up to this point has been concerned solely with cores. In the case of hardwoods, however, which do not lend themselves to the coring technique, or of the occasional conifer sampled by sectioning, a cross section constitutes the study specimen. As with the cores that are sanded, a small belt sander is the best tool for preparing a surface on the cross sections.[3] Handling and examination of the specimen is made easier by removing dirt and dust with a jet of compressed air.

Examination of Cores

The dark color of the latewood cells (fig. 3) may be deepened by a light coat of kerosene applied with a small cotton swab. Frontal light will be reflected by the concavity of the large-diameter earlywood cells exposed in the angle cut. The absorption of light by the thick-walled, smaller-diameter latewood cells will further sharpen the contrast between the two ring components and thus easily delineate the ring boundaries.

[3] C. W. Ferguson, *Annual Rings in Big Sagebrush, Artemisia tridentata,* University of Arizona Press, Papers of the Laboratory of Tree-Ring Research, no. 1 (1964), 12, 13.

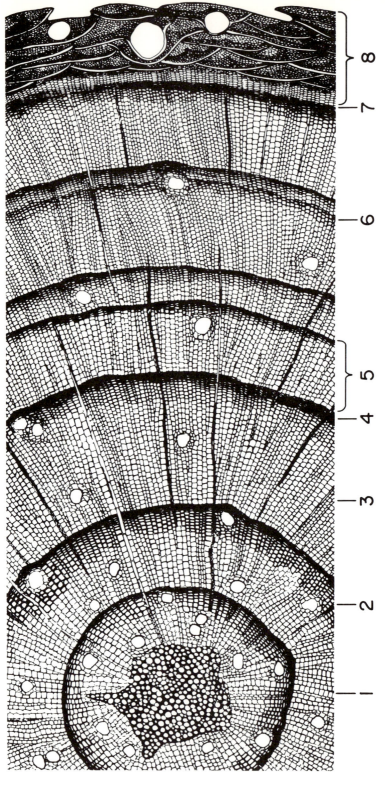

Fig. 3: Cross section of a typical conifer stem showing: (1) pith, (2) resin duct, (3) earlywood cells (light), (4) latewood cells (dark), (5) annual ring, (6) false interannular ring, (7) cambium, and (8) bark.

For all but the most difficult specimens, a 10-power hand lens is adequate. For cores showing smaller average ring widths or in instances of prolonged examination, a binocular microscope with a zoom lens is ideal.

The dating is marked on the core by making a pinhole on each decade ring, two on the half centuries, and three on the centuries. For convenience in reexamining, the centuries are labeled, 19 for 1900, etc., on the near shoulder of the mount. The innermost ring year is labeled on the far shoulder. Critical rings are noted on the near wall of the mount, as "1904 ab," "1934 m," for absent or micro rings. A summary of the work done should be noted on the mount, as "dtd. 1763 on 5–29–66, CWF," or "msd. 1800 on 5–30–66, PSM," when the specimen is dated or measured.

Chronology Building

Basic to a tree-ring chronology is the fact that each consecutive annual growth ring is assigned to the calendar year in which it was formed. Thus cores taken through living tissue have the chronology control provided by an outermost ring with a precisely known date. Inward from this so-called bark ring, successive annual growth layers are assigned to sequentially earlier years. A pattern of wide and narrow rings, common to all radii and to different specimens due to the dominance of a single climatic factor, forms the basis for cross-dating among specimens (fig. 4). The master chronology is unique in its year-by-year pattern; nowhere throughout time is precisely the same long-term sequence (of 100-plus years) of wide and narrow rings repeated, because year-to-year variations in climate are never exactly the same.

When the quality of cross-dating [4] has been established and a modern chronology developed for a given area, it is possible to date tree-ring material, either wood or charcoal, from earlier periods. These records can be incorporated into the master chronology and thus extended further into the past (fig. 5). In the southwestern United States, this type of record, based upon archaeological material, now extends to 59 B.C. [5] In the same manner, wood of the millennia-old bristlecone pine, especially from remnants that predate the 4000-year-old living trees, has enabled us to

[4] Terms relating to, or derived from, the study of tree rings are defined in a glossary, compiled from many sources, at the end of this article.

[5] E. Schulman, *Dendroclimatic Changes in Semiarid America* (Tucson: University of Arizona Press, 1956), 142 pp.

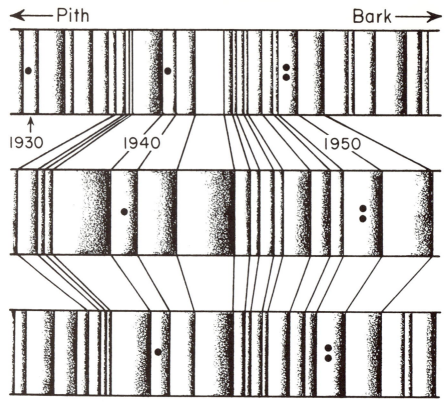

Fig. 4. Cross-dated ring patterns from three different trees. Rings vary in absolute width between specimens, but the relative widths are the same. Decade years are marked with a single pinhole, mid-century rings with two pinholes.

extend the chronology for the White Mountains in east-central California back to 5150 B.C., thus providing a continuous chronology of 7485 years.[6]

Statistical Analysis

We have developed routine computer programs for calculating certain statistical measurements from tree-ring series.[7] The entire set of rings from the lower trunk of a mature tree can be related to yearly climatic variation

[6] C. W. Ferguson, "Bristlecone Pine: Science and Esthetics," *Science* *159* (1968), 839–846. C. W. Ferguson, "A 7104-year annual tree-ring chronology for bristlecone pine, *Pinus aristata*, from the White Mountains, California," *Tree-Ring Bulletin*, 29, nos. 3–4 (1969), 3–29. C. W. Ferguson, "Dendrochronology of bristlecone pine, *Pinus aristata*," XII Nobel Symposium: *Radiocarbon Variations and Absolute Chronology* (Stockholm: Almquist and Wiksell, in press).

[7] H. C. Fritts, "Computer Programs for Tree-Ring Research," *Tree-Ring Bulletin* 25, 3–4 (1963), 2–7.

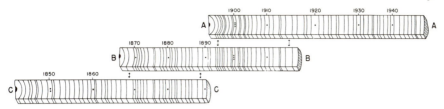

Fig. 5. A series of cross-dated specimens illustrates, in foreshortened form, the process of chronology building. Series A represents a specimen from a living tree with a known outside date. An archaeological specimen (B) is cross-dated with an early portion of the modern specimen and is identified as of intermediate age. An earlier archaeological specimen (C), when dated, extends the chronology further into the past.

by removing, statistically, the gradual changes associated with the age of the tree. An exponential curve is fitted to each series of ring-width values, and measured ring widths are divided by yearly values of the fitted curve. This process transforms the ring-width values to tree-ring indices which exhibit a mean of 1.00 and a variance that is independent of tree age, position within the trunk, and mean growth of the tree. Additional programs include (1) correlation coefficients, which give a measure of common relative variability of indices for pairs of cores from one tree or for different trees; (2) mean sensitivity, which expresses the relative year-to-year variation in the ring-index values; (3) first-order serial correlation, which measures the degree of dependence of a single growth-ring index upon the index of the preceding ring; and (4) standard deviation, which measures the variation about the sample mean.

From application of these statistical measurements to a particular site, one can infer how certain ecological conditions have limited ring growth.[8] An understanding of these relationships facilitates the search for sites and trees that contain sensitive records.

Mean sensitivity, defined as the average ratio of the absolute difference between each two successive widths divided by their mean,[9] is used as an index of the limiting effects of climate on tree-ring growth.[10] Standard deviation, which measures variability about the sample mean, resembles the mean sensitivity when the serial correlation is low and where, as in the more complacent series, there are few very narrow rings. The mean

[8] H. C. Fritts, D. G. Smith, J. W. Cardis, and C. A. Budelsky, in *Ecology 46* (1965), 393.
[9] A. E. Douglass, *Climatic Cycles and Tree Growth,* Carnegie Institution, Washington, D.C., pub. 289, no. 1 (1919); 289, no. 2 (1938).
[10] Schulman, op. cit.

sensitivity values become relatively greater in a sensitive series, especially when rings are missing (missing rings are expressed as zero values for single years).

The quality of sensitivity is illustrated for two types of trees by photographs of cross sections (fig. 6). The "complacent" record exhibits little or no variation in ring width from year to year and is typical of trees on sites with characteristics favoring optimum growth. The fairly "sensitive" record shows variability in ring width from year to year.

As sensitivity increases, so, too, does the probability that rings will be missing. A tree-ring sequence exhibiting extreme sensitivity, having almost the appearance of erratic growth, may contain less than 90 percent of the annual rings along a single radius and thus be too difficult to use initially in chronology building, but ultimately it may provide an excellent climatic record. The relationship of chronology sensitivity and site factors is more fully discussed by Fritts.[11]

Dating of either modern specimens or archaeological materials [12] may be achieved by visual inspection (sliding coincidence or memory methods), by the use of skeleton plots (fig. 7), or by the use of plotted ring measurements (fig. 8). In instances where ring series cannot conclusively be dated by visual or plot techniques, a computer-programmed correlation routine may be used to measure all possible matches between two series of indices.[13] Correlation coefficients exhibit a normal random fluctuation within narrow limits around "zero" except at the match point, where a highly significant positive correlation may be obtainable. The correlation coefficients obtained by Scott [14] have a probability of less than one in 10,000 of occurring by chance alone.

[11] Fritts et al., op. cit.

[12] A more complete description may be found in A. E. Douglass, "Cross-dating in Dendrochronology," *J. Forestry 39,* 10 (1941), 825–831; R. D. Roughton, "A Review of Literature on Dendrochronology and Age Determination of Woody Plants," *State of Colorado Department of Game and Fish, Technical Bull. no. 15* (1962), 99 pp.; W. G. McGinnies, "Dendrochronology," *J. Forestry 61,* 1 (1963, 5–11. M. A. Stokes and T. L. Smiley, *An Introduction to Tree-Ring Dating* (Chicago: University of Chicago Press, 1968).

[13] A computer program was developed to provide a quantitative expression of the similarity between two tree-ring chronologies. This technique, providing evidence of cross-dating in instances too subtle for the eye to see, has been effectively used twice by Ferguson and Wright (1963, *Tree-Rings in The Western Great Basin,* in 1962 Great Basin Anthropological Conference, Carson City, The Nevada State Museum, Anthropological Papers, no. 1, pp. 10–16) and by Scott (see n. 14).

[14] S. D. Scott, *Dendrochronology in Mexico,* University of Arizona Press, Papers of the Laboratory of Tree-Ring Research, no. 2 (1966), 71, 72.

Fɪɢ. 6. A complacent ring sequence (top) compared with a sensitive pattern (bottom).

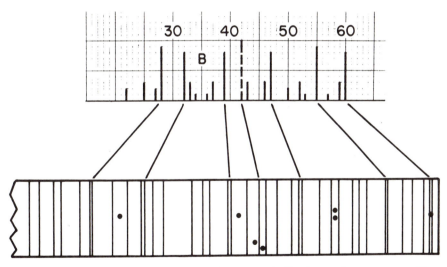

Fɪɢ. 7. Construction of a skeleton plot from an idealized tree-ring sequence. Ring widths are represented on the plot by vertical lines in an inverse proportion; that is, tall lines represent narrow rings. An exceptionally wide ring is designated by a "B" (big), and the location of a missing ring, marked on the specimen by offset pinholes, is identified on the plot by a full two-centimeter line in red (dashed). Horizontal scale is 1 year per 2 mm.

Archaeological Dating

Four conditions permit the dating of prehistoric material:[15]

1. There must be trees that produce clearly defined annual rings as a result of a definite growing season.
2. Tree growth must depend principally upon one controlling climatic factor.
3. There must have been an indigenous prehistoric population that made extensive use of wood.
4. The wood must be well enough preserved so that it still retains its cellular structure.

Determination of Cutting Dates

Identification of each growth ring by the year in which it was formed is the primary consideration of the dendrochronologist in the dating of archaeological tree-ring material. However, the correct interpretation of the dated ring sequence in terms of the cutting date for the specimen requires care on the part of the field archaeologist and some insight on the part of the dendrochronologist. Hence, bark or the indicated presence of bark on the outside would be the proof positive, and the outermost ring would represent the cutting date. In the case of eroded, rotted, burned, or shaped timber, however, an indeterminate number of ring years may be lost. Clues to the nearness to the bark may be present in the form of beetle galleries,[16] by scars formed on the log during transportation, and by the presence and amount of sapwood. The degree of certainty of the cutting (or bark) date can be classified, and this is used as an additional description to the tree-ring date. Discussions of this are given by Bannister and by Dean.[17]

[15] B. Bannister and T. L. Smiley, "Dendrochronology," in *Geochronology with Special Reference to Southwestern United States*, T. L. Smiley, ed., pp. 177–195, Univ. of Arizona Bull. 26, no. 2, Phys. Sci. Bull., no. 2 (1955).

[16] C. W. Ferguson and R. A. Wright, "Tree-Ring Dates for Cutting Activity at the Charcoal Kilns, Panamint Mountains, California," *Tree-Ring Bulletin 24*, nos. 1–2 (1962), 3–9.

[17] B. Bannister, *Tree-ring Dating of the Archaeological Sites in the Chaco Canyon Region, New Mexico*, Southwestern Monuments Association, Technical Series 6, Part 2 (1965); and J. S. Dean, *Chronological Analysis of Tsegi Phase Sites in Northwestern Arizona*, Ph.D. dissertation, Dept. of Anthropology, Univ. of Arizona, 1967. J. S. Dean, *Chronological Analysis of Tsegi Phase Sites in Northern Arizona*, University of Arizona Press, Papers of the Laboratory of Tree-Ring Research, no. 3 (1969).

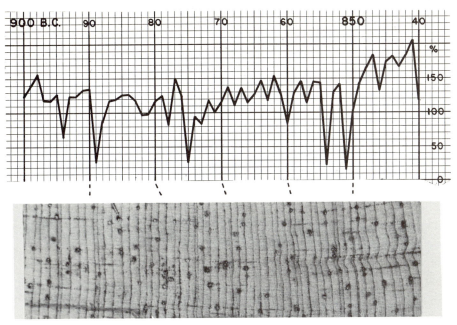

Fig. 8. A segment of the bristlecone pine master chronology, representing three trees from 900 to 840 B.C., used to date a fourth specimen, shown in cross section. The ring-width distribution is skewed, with a general complacency, but having a few rings that are noticeably smaller than average, such as the rings for the years of 894, 889, 875, 854, and 851 B.C. The ring for 851 becomes locally absent in the upper part of the photograph.

Interpretation

So far, the discussion has dealt solely with the tree-ring dating of the wood or charcoal itself. Because of inherent problems and their relation to the acceptance of the dates provided by the laboratory dendrochronologist, some mention must be made of the interpretation of the tree-ring material. Only the date is provided by the dendrochronologist; the interpretation is developed by the archaeologist, first through correct association in the field, and then through the development of the proper relationship to other dates, artifacts, and features within the site. The usual sources of error in interpretation that confront the archaeologist are grouped into four general categories:[18]

[18] The basic pitfalls in interpretation have been presented by Bannister in "Dendrochronology," chap. 17, in *Science in Archaeology*, Brothwell and Higgs, eds. (New York: Basic Books, 1963) and further developed by Dean (op. cit.) and W. S. Robinson, *Tree-ring Materials as a Basis for Cultural Interpretations*, Ph.D. dissertation, Dept. of Anthropology, Univ. of Arizona, 1967.

1. The association between the dated tree-ring specimen and the archaeological manifestation being dated is direct, but the specimen itself came from a tree that died or was cut prior to its use in the situation in question. In this category would be reused timber, snags that were dead when cut, driftwood logs, wooden artifacts that had assumed the status of family heirlooms, and stockpiled logs.

2. The association between the dated tree-ring specimen and the archaeological manifestation being dated is not direct, the specimen having been used prior to the feature being dated. Thus tree-ring dates for the construction of a room may be applied to the contents of the room only when the temporal relationship of the room and its contents is known. In small sites with a short-term occupation, this problem may be of only minor significance. In sites with a long occupation, however, the problem becomes more critical.

3. The association between the dated tree-ring specimen and the archaeological manifestation being dated is direct, but the specimen itself represents a later incorporation into an already existing feature. The most common forms are timbers used for remodeling or replacement, perhaps following reoccupation. This may turn a problem into a solution by indicating the time of remodeling or by helping to delimit an occupation period.

4. The association between the dated tree-ring specimen and the archaeological manifestation being dated is not direct, the specimen having been used later than the feature being dated. This is somewhat the reverse of the second type of error source. Here, dates from an artifact or from charcoal in a fire pit are associated with a room constructed somewhat earlier.

Application in a New Area

If a tree-ring study is to be initiated in a new area, the foregoing procedures may have to be modified. Even though the ultimate focus may be on a single species and in a more or less uniform ecological area, this would be learned only as the result of a systematic search of the existent complex of species through diverse geographic, topographic, and ecological areas.

In the broad initial survey, certain species may be ruled out because of poor ring structure, complacency, short life, or general scarcity of the species. Within a species, ring characteristics may be modified by elevation, latitude, or microenvironmental conditions. Because of these possible variations, the initial survey should take the form of a transect oriented at right angles to the suspected gradient.

Even when working with a species of established quality, often it is necessary to sample young trees which may be used to validate interpretations or to solve problems in the tree-ring chronology. Thus all age classes should be included within the species and site transects. For example, a younger tree or one on a better site may contain evidence of a ring of minimum width that may be locally absent or entirely missing in older, slower-growing specimens.

For a potentially usable species, correlations should be made between ring widths and various components of the climatic environment, not only to ascertain the climatic factors governing growth, but, more importantly, to verify the annual nature of the periodic growth increment.

In terms of possible tree-ring dating of archaeological materials, a thorough understanding of the species found in the area now is first necessary.[19] Obviously, if these are not interpretable, then there is nothing to be gained in attempting to date comparable specimens found in an archaeological context.

Potentially datable wood found in an archaeological context may provide a "floating" archaeological chronology, which, although it cannot be assigned a calendar date, would serve to relate various structures to one another. As the floating chronology is lengthened and gains depth in the number of specimens and geographic areas represented, it will become more valuable internally and as a potential extension to the chronology developed from living trees.

Relation to Radiocarbon

The production rate of radioactive carbon-14 in the atmosphere varies only slightly throughout the A.D. period.[20] The pattern derived from radiocarbon analysis of dated wood from a variety of archaeological sources is substantiated by the carbon-14 dates of bristlecone pine wood from com-

[19] C. W. Ferguson, "Growth Rings in Woody Shrubs as Potential Aids in Archaeological Interpretation," *The Kiva 25,* 2 (1959), 24–30.

[20] Various aspects of related radiocarbon studies are summarized in Hans E. Suess, *J. Geophys. Res. 70* (1965), 5937; Paul E. Damon, Austin Long, and Donald C. Grey, *J. Geophys. Res. 71* (1966), 1055; Froelich Rainey and Elizabeth K. Ralph, *Science 153* (1966), 1481; Minze Stuiver and Hans E. Suess, *Radiocarbon 8* (1966), 534; and various authors in the proceedings of the XII Nobel Symposium: *Radiocarbon Variations and Absolute Chronology* (Stockholm: Almquist and Wiksell, in press).

parable time periods. Dates derived from the radiocarbon analysis of tree ring–dated bristlecone pine wood have the advantage of being from a single species, from a long series, and from a single geographic area. With this consistency, a single radiocarbon laboratory, working under constant conditions and within a short space of time, could analyze precisely dated wood in five- or ten-year units throughout the total range of the medieval period. The resultant framework of dendrochronologically calibrated carbon-14 dates would permit a more accurate interpretation of carbon-14 dates derived from structures or artifacts associated with the medieval archaeology.

GLOSSARY

Age class. An arbitrary grouping of plants of essentially the same age.

Annual increment. The three-dimensional sheath of secondary xylem added to stems and roots each year. The annual increment has the appearance of a ring (*annual ring*) when a concentric stem is viewed in cross section. An annual ring, especially in conifers, may be reduced in width completely about the ring's circuit. It is then called a *microscopic ring*. Such a ring may be small to the point of being totally absent about some portion of its circuit. It is then referred to as being *locally absent*. When no growth layer was deposited in the visible portion of the specimen in a given year, the ring for this year is *absent* or *missing*. A growth ring showing two (or more) surges of growth in one year is a *double* (or *multiple*) *ring*. The second layer in the double ring is a *false ring*.

Annual ring. See Annual increment.

Bark. A general term for the tissues outside the vascular cambium in trunks and stems of woody plants.

Cambial activity. The process, in woody plants, by which cambial initials divide and form derivatives which differentiate into phloem cells toward the outside and xylem cells toward the inside.

Cambium. A tissue located in the woody stems and roots of many higher plants, including trees, in which cells divide and form new tissues, producing xylem (wood) toward the inside and phloem (inner bark) toward the outside. Cork cambium lies outside the phloem and produces layers of cork that constitute most of the outer bark.

Complacent. Descriptive of a ring series that does not vary appreciably in width from year to year. Also descriptive of the site producing such a ring series. Antithesis of "sensitive."

Conifer. Trees that produce naked seeds in cones, as opposed to fruits, and are typically needle-leaved evergreens.

Cross-dating. The systematic comparison of ring patterns, permitting the establishment of absolute dating for each growth ring as the calendar year in which it was formed, between radii of a single tree, between trees, between species, between age classes within a species, and between sites and major geographical areas in relation to one another and to climatic and historic data.

Crown. That part of a tree which has leaf-bearing branches, often supported by a branch-free trunk (stem) or multiple stems.

DBH. Diameter at breast height. Approximately 4½ feet above the ground is the standard height for diameter measurements of tree trunks.

Deciduous tree. A tree that normally produces new leaves every spring, loses them in the fall of the same year, and overwinters in a leafless condition.

Dendrograph. Instrument attached to a tree to obtain a continuous automatically recorded plot of radial stem growth.

Dendrometer. A nonrecording instrument used to obtain periodic measurements of change in a radius of a tree trunk.

Diffuse-porous wood. Nonconiferous wood having vessels of fairly uniform size evenly distributed throughout each annual increment.

Earlywood. The distinct inner component of an annual ring, formed during the first part of the growing season. Earlywood is recognized in diffuse-porous and nonporous woods by differences in density, cell size, cell-wall thickness, and color; and in ring-porous wood by the aligned vessels.

Evergreen trees. Trees, such as most conifers, that retain green leaves all winter.

Full bark. Descriptive of a tree having a trunk completely covered with bark, in contrast to one with lateral dieback of the stem cambium.

Growth increment. The amount of stem or tip material added as a result of periodic or annual growth. *See also* Annual increment.

Hardwood trees. A general term, used mostly in the lumber industry, referring to broad-leaved trees of nonconiferous species.

Latewood. The distinct outer component of an annual ring. *See also* Earlywood.

Lobe. The form, when seen in cross section, of the outer portion of the cleft and irregular stem that is characteristic of many shrubs and some trees, especially of the older plants. A lobe may terminate either in an area of living tissue or in one which died at some time in the past.

Nonporous wood. Wood of conifers, characterized by tracheids instead of vessels in the xylem.

Phloem. Food-conducting tissue formed by the vascular cambium and constituting the inner bark.

Pith. Tissue in the center of stems composed of a mass of parenchyma cells.

Radial growth. Increase in radius at a given height. Total radial-growth increment of the xylem for a given year is ring width of that year.

Rays. A layer of cells extending radially in the wood and inner bark of tree trunks.

Release. A change in the external environment of a tree that reduces competi-

tion with other trees, as would result if the surrounding trees were removed; a decrease in suppression.

Ring. Two-dimensional cross section of an annual stem increment. *See also*
Annual increment.

Ring-porous wood. Nonconiferous wood in which large-diameter vessels comprise the inner (earlywood) component of the annual stem increment.

Root. The underground parts of plants on which, as opposed to stems, there
are no buds, leaves, or leaf scars.

Sensitive. Descriptive of a ring series that varies greatly in width from year
to year, as, for example, in response to annual changes in precipitation.
Also descriptive of the site producing such a ring series. Antithesis of
"complacent."

Signature. A short, easily identifiable sequence of large and small rings.

Softwood trees. A general term, used mostly in the lumber industry, referring
to coniferous trees.

Stand. A group of trees growing in a continuous area.

Stem. Any of the above-ground parts of a tree which bear or have borne buds
and leaves. The trunk and all branches are stems.

Suppression. A condition of growth retardation usually associated with competition. *See also* Release.

Terminal growth increment. An annual increment of longitudinal growth of
the main stem.

Tracheid. A tubelike, water-conducting cell. Tracheids also serve for support,
and are especially characteristic of conifers.

Trunk. The main stem of a tree, generally the branch-free part below the
crown.

Vessel. Specialized water-conducting tissue in the xylem of nonconifers.

Xylem. Water-conducting tissue of most plants and supporting tissue (wood) of
trees; develops inward from the cambium.

VIII

CENTRAL EUROPEAN DENDROCHRONOLOGY
FOR THE MIDDLE AGES

B. Huber and V. Giertz[1]

*T*HIS PAPER is aimed at presenting the progress of research in dendrochronology for Central Europe. For obvious reasons it cannot claim validity for the whole of Europe, especially as there is research under way in Belgium, Denmark, Norway, and the USSR. In fact, we would like to describe our methods, showing the various differences in methodology with respect to the American technique, rather than to discuss the whole subject *in toto* including the general principles of tree-ring dating.[2]

Technically, the tree-ring width is measured in the Forest-botanical Institute in Munich with a microscope equipped with variable optics. The ocular contains a scale calibrated from 0 to 100 whereby 31 units represent 1 mm. The values obtained are directly reproduced on graph paper, the vertical division of which has a logarithmic scale. On the abscissa, 0.5 cm represents one year. The semilogarithmic paper has the advantage that curves measured by other values can be directly compared. Moreover, the emphasis throughout the graph is so placed that even minima and very delicate differences in the ring width are shown. Thus when tree-ring curves are compared they are matched by hand over an illuminated glass plate.

Accuracy of Dendrochronological Dating

First, it is important to point out that differing climatic conditions in Europe make accurate cross-dating impossible. A further handicap is that

[1] Paper was kindly presented for B. Huber by Mr. Siebenlist and Mrs. V. Giertz-Siebenlist.

[2] B. Huber, "Mikroskopische Untersuchungen von Hölzern," in *Handbuch der Mikroskopie in der Technik,* vol. 8, pt. 1, H. Freund, gen. ed. (Frankfurt: Umschau Verlag, 1951).

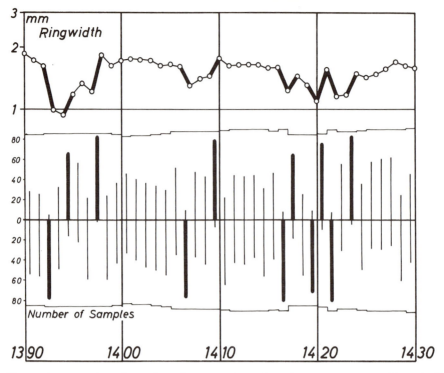

Fɪɢ. ɪ. A 40 years' cut from the oak master chronology from 1390 to 1430 (described in the text).

European trees normally do not grow very old compared with, say, bristlecone pines. Consequently, tree-ring curves are not of great length. The oldest tree examined by us is a Spessart oak with 586 rings. Unfortunately, most material available shows considerably shorter curves. So for the greatest degree of confidence in synchronization, the curve length is of particular importance.

Curves comprising not more than 25 years may present an identical up and down of the ring width, although dating from different periods. Concerning samples 50 years old, this becomes highly improbable and samples 100 and more years old exclude this possibility.

The following diagram illustrates schematically how accuracy in dating depends on the number of tree rings. The ordinate shows the percentage of agreement. This is found by comparing two ring curves— ring width as ordinate, age as abscissa—then counting how often the curves rise or fall together, or how often one curve rises while the other falls or vice versa. For nonsynchronous curves, agreement practically equals disagreement. The percentage of agreement or disagreement has

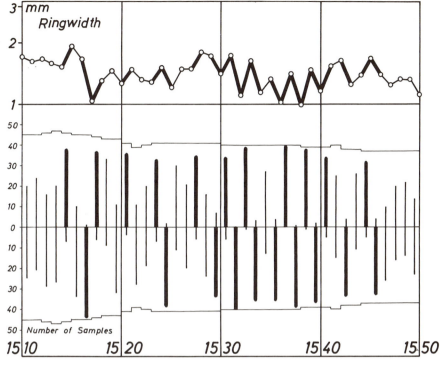

FIG. 2. A 40 years' cut from the oak master chronology from 1510 to 1550, including the saw signature from 1529 to 1541.

an average of 50. In reality this value varies with the number of years (a) corresponding to the formula:

$$\text{Percentage of agreement} \quad 50 \pm \frac{50}{\sqrt{a}}.$$

This formula is the result of thousands of countings during World War II when no new material was available. Curve pairs were compared in every possible situation. Wrongly placed, agreement was, as anticipated, 50 percent, with a standard deviation of $\frac{50}{\sqrt{a}}$, that is, ± 5 percent for 100 years, or, respectively, ± 7 percent for 50 years. Quite naturally, the standard deviation was sometimes higher, partly as high as three times the calculated value, that is, between 35 and 65 percent for 100 years, and between 50 and 70 percent for curves of about 50 years. Material with good cross-dating normally shows an agreement of 70 to 80 percent. The result is even better when comparing not only curves of a single specimen, but average curves of at least five samples.

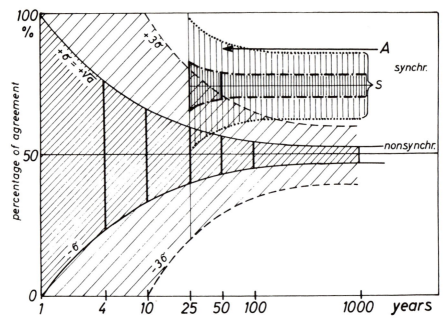

FIG. 3. Dependence of the confidence of dendrochronological dating upon the number of tree rings.

When applying more than 20 curves of a single specimen, the average curve hardly varies. Such curves are absolutely safe. We are trying to collect so many samples that we can base our master chronology exclusively on curves with such a high confidence level and can eliminate dubiously dated curves. A poor cross-dating and the resulting necessity of elimination consequently has a high quota of nonsynchronizable curves. It is sometimes up to 30 percent of the material.

A further handicap for our tree-ring evaluation is the fact that agreement diminishes with growing geographic distance.

Geographic Aspects

This brings us to the question of the basic geographic validity of ring curves. As a consequence of small, climatically different zones, the stem increment per year depends on various and always different factors.

The first geochronology was invented by the Swedish geologist de Geer in the eighties of the nineteenth century. In Scandinavia, glacial deposits can show annual layers of clay, called varves, which are darker in summer due to a higher organic content, and lighter in the winter. These layers allow an absolute dating of the retreat of glaciers in Scandinavia.

When de Geer was eighty years old, he believed that the fluctuations in the width of varves and in tree rings were regulated by a cosmic factor. Based on this belief, his wife and widow dated woods and varves from the Old and the New World and even from the northern to the southern hemispheres.

We now know that this type of "teleconnection" was wrong. But we found during special examinations a sometimes surprising similarity in tree-ring curves coming from similar geographic latitude.

In fact, the hill oaks (*Quercus petraea*) of southern Germany, on which we concentrated our examinations in Munich, correspond with those from the Danube region up to the Rhine. The chronology of Ernst Hollstein, in Trier, of material originating partly in France is almost identical with ours, when compared with samples from the Hessian or Franconian region.

However, the lowland oak of the northern German lowland shows quite another reaction. Even within single stands of trees, the percentage of agreement is rather low. This problem is especially to be dealt with by the recently founded dendrochronology center of Walter Liese in Hamburg-Reinbek. Due to the rather low rate of agreement, the percentage of material to be eliminated is partly much higher than 30 percent. The aim of Liese's work is a chronology of the lowland oak starting from our time back to the ninth century, in order to be able to date the samples from the Haithabu settlement in the Baltic Sea.

The main problem for the years to come will be the examination of samples from all European geographic regions with respect to their geographical deviations. A start has already been made in southern England, France, Switzerland, and Czechoslovakia.

Material

A further distinction between European and American dendrochronology can be made with respect to supply of material. As already indicated, modern European trees mostly date from the seventeenth century, with the exception of a few single trees such as the above-mentioned Spessart oak, the first ring of which appeared in 1370. Concerning periods prior to this time, we have to rely on construction timber in the roofs of medieval churches, castles, and other buildings. Older samples come from archaeologic excavations, as no buildings from this period are still existent.

Oak. Due to so-called bridging, our institute was able to create a master chronology of oak, covering more than 1000 years. This master chronology

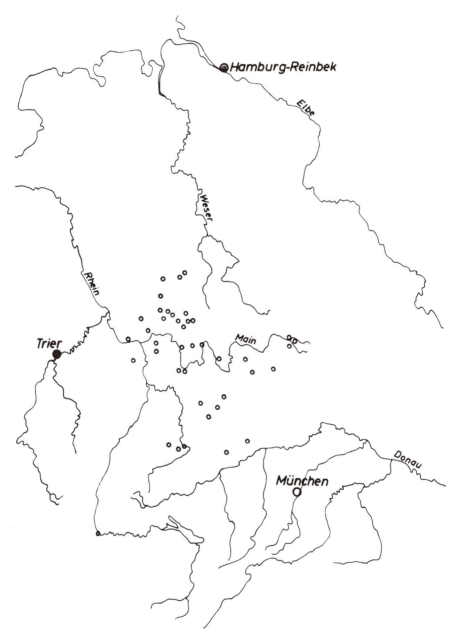

Fig. 4. The three centers of German tree-ring research and the places where the samples come from, which were examined by the Institute of Forest-botany of the University of Munich.

dates from the present back to the year 832. Independently, Ernst Hollstein in Trier was able to draw up an oak master chronology for the Celtic and Romanic period, dating from about 500 B.C. to A.D. 600. His work has advanced so far that the remaining missing period will soon be covered.

For prehistoric times, there exist a number of partial chronologies of the Bronze and the Neolithic Age, each covering a time of about 200 to 300 years. We hope to be able to interconnect these sections, thus creating a European oak master chronology covering the last 5000 years. This would form an adequate counterpart to the *Pinus aristata* chronology of California, covering now more than 7000 years.

As a result of the quantity of medieval material, our chronology has its greatest density of measurements for this period. It is based on 50 to 100 curves.

Illustrations 1 and 2 point out various characteristics of our standard curve. The upper part shows the average ring widths. The lower part is framed by two horizontal lines, stating the number of single curves for each separate year. The vertical lines above and below zero show the number of rising and falling curves. If more than 80 percent are synchronous, the line is thickly drawn.

Illustration 1 shows a period of 40 years from 1390 to 1430. From 1392 to 1393 the majority of curves falls, from 1397 to 1398 there is a rise. In German, these years are called *"Weiserjahre."* Like A. E. Douglass, the founder of dendrochronology, we call a sequence of those years a "signature." The "Early Pueblo Signature" of the ponderosa pine, found by Douglass in ancient Indian settlements and dated much later to fall between A.D. 423 and 431, is still the most famous of all. One of the best signatures we found is the sequence of wide and narrow rings between 1416 and 1422. It was initially observed in the oldest Spessart oak and later on in more than eighty historic beams.

Our so-called saw signature dating from 1529 to 1541 is shown in figure 5. Such an unusually long sequence of wide and narrow rings is unique and to our knowledge was never observed in any other time or with regard to any other species.

There are different reasons why oak examinations have been our principal aim. The first factor is the widespread use of oak timber for buildings in southern Germany. It was, and still is, especially appreciated for its hardness. Even in regions with a majority of conifer stands, oak beams were at least used for belfry constructions to support the bell weight. Moreover, oak is especially suited for dendrochronological examinations

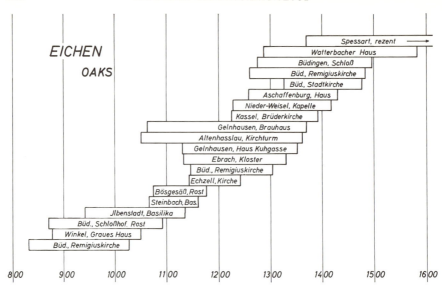

Fɪɢ. 5. Schematic representation of the oak master chronology. The single blocks show the length of the curves based on samples from the respective buildings.

as it, like all other ring-porous wood, shows no missing rings. This is due to a physiological peculiarity, described earlier,[3] which also explains why the oak chronology is one of the most favorite means to calibrate radiocarbon dating.

The only irregularity observed by us was a double ring, probably due to insect attack (*Tortrix viridana*). This double ring was, however, easily identified when enlarged and could not be mistaken for normal rings. We found it in a stake from the neolithic settlement of Auvernier in Switzerland.

Still another advantage of oak is the statistically well explored sapwood quota or thickness of about 20 years for 100- to 200-year-old oaks. This sapwood quota is easily identified: macroscopically by a somewhat lighter tint and hints of plant pest infection, microscopically by the fact that sapwood vessels in contrast to heartwood are not blocked by tylosis. As timber is normally treated, the last year ring is often missing and therefore the cutting year, whereas the sapwood limit frequently is still existent. Due to the statistically well known value of 20 years, the year of felling may be estimated quite accurately, which is the principal answer sought by historians and archaeologists.

[3] B. Huber, "The physiological importance of ring and diffuse porosity." Original article in *Ber. Dtsch. Botan. Ges.* 53 (1935), 711–719.

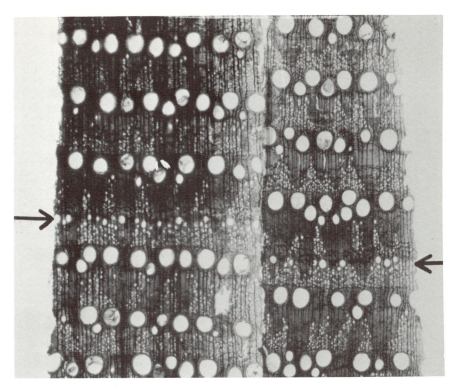

FIG. 6. The only double ring found in oaks.

Fir (Abies alba). In order to increase confidence in the oak chronology we are now trying to extend our work to other species of wood. Such an opportunity was presented by the fir (*Abies alba*). It was already known since 1951 that firs could be excellently synchronized, even over great geographic distances. Firs from the Baskides, the Bavarian Forest, the Bavarian Alps, the Black Forest, and the Vosges Mountains show a large measure of agreement.

The map below shows the origin of our samples. The present extent of our fir chronology is also illustrated—as with the oak—in a block diagram. Modern beams date back as far as A.D. 1541.

In 1963 a floating chronology from samples of the Constance and Freiburg cathedrals as well as the Maulbronn monastery was established. There exist detailed documents concerning the completion of this monastery, so that the total curve could at first be dated to within a standard error of ± 10 years. A little later, we found that the average fir curve could be synchronized with the average oak curve; in other words, the curve starts in 873 and ends in 1300. In the meantime, we tried to bridge

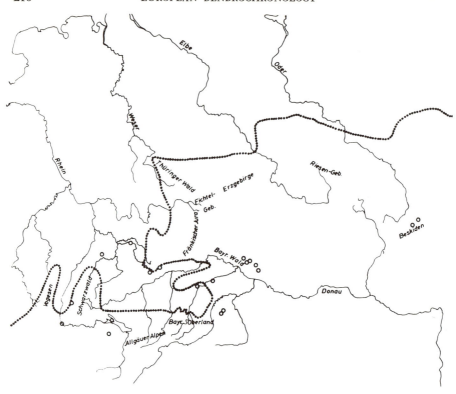

Fig. 7. Origin of fir samples. The dotted line shows the northern limit of the natural growth of fir.

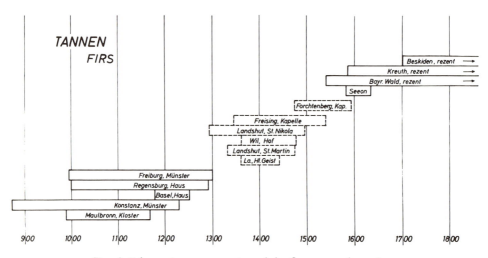

Fig. 8. Schematic representation of the fir master chronology.

the gap between our time and the year 1300. After examination of samples from church roof constructions in Lower Bavaria, this was almost completely accomplished. We were thus in a position to equal our oak master chronology with a fir master chronology.

Larch (Larix europaea). There is only one other type of conifer giving satisfactory dendrochronological results, and that is the larch (*Larix europaea*) of the Bavarian Alps. From samples of old and abandoned mountain sheds, we were able to draw up a curve going back to the fourteenth century. This chronology, however, cannot claim much importance, as the larch is a typical alpine plant and was normally not used as timber in populated areas.

Beech (Fagus silvatica). There is, however, quite a promising widely diffused porous deciduous tree, the beech (*Fagus silvatica*). Curves already exist from our time back to 1653. We have begun to receive a large amount of medieval material which is now awaiting examination.

Spruce (Picea excelsa). Our examinations have shown that a number of types of wood are not suitable for dendrochronological analysis. One example is the spruce (*Picea excelsa*). In order to obtain satisfactory results, it has to be dealt with like the lowland oak, as there are large deviations even within trees from the same stand. The quantity of wood for analysis must be unusually large to allow for the rejection of a correspondingly large amount of unsuitable material. In spite of this, the spruce will be the object of thorough examination in the coming years, as it is very frequent in southern Germany and was also often used as timber.

Alder (Alnus glutinosa). The black alder (*Alnus glutinosa*) has definitely proved to be unsatisfactory for analysis. The main factor is the large number of missing rings which make any synchronization impossible.

Comparative Studies of Different Wood Species

A field for further research will be comparative dendrochronology of different wood species. This field attracted attention some time ago when archaeologic finds were being examined. The fact that oak, ash (*Fraxinus excelsior*), and black alder were frequently found together made it only natural to compare the curves for these different wood species. All comparisons made from such samples to date are only speculative, however, as there exist no decisive common factors to prove these synchronizations.

Some four years ago, a dissertation written at the Institute of Forestbotany of the University of Munich was aimed at explaining differences

and agreement between these three wood species. The result was nega-
tive. The similarity of the curves is so small that the dating of ash or black
alder by means of the oak chronology is impossible.

However, a simliar comparison between fir and oak gave a positive
result. This study has not yet been fully published.[4] In fact, our fir chronology of the southern and eastern European region is largely based on our
oak master chronology. A probable explanation for this agreement may
be that both species are confined to certain favorable growth areas. This
applies also to beech trees. Curves drawn for beech show definite, although not quite complete, agreement with those for fir and oak.

Finally, permit me to point out that the future development of European dendrochronology has several promising aspects.[5] The principal aim
will be the further enlargement of the master chronologies. We are sure
that research in various adjoining geographic regions will bring new and
interesting knowledge to the question of the extent of applicability of
dating. A further plan is the examination of the possibility to synchronize
different wood species in order to use them interchangeably. Last but not
least, there is the field of climatology, where American scientists already
have shown great advances. In Europe we will still need many years until
a comprehensive assessment can be made.

[4] Manuscript in preparation.

[5] The most recent assessment of dendrochronological investigations of medieval
Germany, and advances in the establishment of master chronologies since the UCLA
conference of October 1967, is found in *Kunstchronik,* 21st year, no. 6, June 1968.
This publication contains relevant articles by J. Bauch, B. Becker, W. Elling, V.
Giertz-Siebenlist, L. H. Heydenreich, E. Hollstein, B. Huber, Th. Kempf, E. Kubach,
U. Lobbedey, and W. Niess.

IX

THE MEDIEVAL TIMBER-FRAME TRADITION

F. W. B. Charles

*T*HE SUBJECT of this paper is the study of timber-framed construction per se. I am concerned that the scientists now working on
dating problems of timber-framed buildings should know that all the implications do not involve the hidden properties of odd splinters of oak
which they are being asked to uncover, nor even the dates themselves of individual buildings. In fact, their solution of the central mystery of medieval carpentry—how and when it came into being—could transform the
whole present concept of the history of architecture of the Middle Ages.
For this aspect of the subject—the craft and products of the carpenter who
had to be contractor, forester, architect-engineer, and wood-carver as well
—is still neglected by most architectural historians, who tend to look on
it as a minor branch of serious building, while to the layman it remains
just pretty "black and white." Even for the experts, I believe that a
relatively few scientifically affirmed dates of selected buildings would
clarify the nature of the tradition as a whole—either confirming the viewpoint expressed in this paper or causing very serious rethinking. Fortunately, the first radiocarbon results seem to be leading in the right direction, and I am impatient for their extension over a much wider range of
building types and periods.

My own experience as a practicing architect consists primarily of field-
work rather than documentary research, and depends for its results on the
structural survey, which must take into account every aspect of construction as well as examination of how the building was erected; this is
followed by comparison with other buildings previously surveyed, often
involving a second or third visit to them to verify details. This methodical
approach eventually leads one to an intuitive response or introduction to
a building. A glance at its plan form, roof construction, size and shape of
timbers, wall-frame system, and general proportions immediately suggests

at least its historical period. Then must follow more rational analysis. So few buildings, however, conform as a whole to a specific ideal type that any attempt to compile a general classification or typological history from isolated features, such as roof trusses or wall framing, is doomed to failure. Moreover, the more intricate details of construction vary so much— different methods of fixing the purlins to the principals, for example, are found in buildings contemporary with each other and within the same ownership—that the idea of one form or joint evolving through time into another appears to be untenable. It seems clear on the contrary that the carpenter of the earliest timber-framed building yet discovered already knew the entire repertory of structural forms and jointing technique.

Indeed, I would submit that the technical history of timber framing is diametrically opposite to that of masonry as observed within the same period. The experimental phase of carpentry was over long before the Norman masons began to pile stone upon stone without science or regard (it seems) for stability. So stone architecture had to evolve with every building project, dependent incidentally on the experience of carpenters for each innovation. If "Gothic" was invented by masons, carpenters had been able to design their structures in no other way for centuries.

I intend to review a few buildings which seem to me to give the key to the identification of that phase in the total history of timber framing which we can study in buildings of the thirteenth and fourteenth centuries. I will then mention the earliest manifestations of *framed* cruck construction as pointing to the age and possible origin of one widely used roof structure—the "purlin" roof—if not of the framing technique itself. Lastly, I will indicate those buildings which most urgently call for scientific dating, before current neglect and demolition make it too late.

The drawings (all of the same scale) show the structural types represented by the buildings.[1] First, there is to be considered West Bromwich

---

[1] The terms adopted for at least two of the structural elements are different from those in current usage. The most important is "collar PLATE" for the commonly accepted term, "collar purlin." In building construction a plate is the uppermost wall member bearing joists or rafters or members of a superimposed structural unit, such as the next story or the roof. The plate must be laid so that in cross section its upper and lower face are horizontal. The purlin, on the other hand, is a component of the roof structure, spanning between trusses and jointed to the principal rafters. Therefore, it is laid with its cross section aligned to the roof slope. The different manner of positioning these two members makes distinction easy. Confusion also exists between tie beam and crossbeam. The purpose of the tie beam is to connect the wall plates and prevent their spread. It is also the base member of a triangulated truss whose other main components are the two principal rafters. The crossbeam holds together

Manor House in Staffordshire. Discovered in 1955 by Stanley Jones, co-worker of John Smith, this building was the first domestic base-cruck hall to demand serious attention.[2] In this context, its most important feature is that it combines a "rafter" roof—that almost certainly originated, as far as England is conerned, in Lowland England—with a base cruck which, like the simple cruck, is a typical Highland product.

The distinctive features of the upper roof are: (1) its coupled rafters each joined by a collar; (2) the collar plate giving support to each of the collars at their mid span and hence to the pairs of rafters; and (3) the crown post braced to the tie beam and supporting the collar plate. The lower structure consists of the cruck blades, crossbeam, and knee braces. The whole frame is designed for strength to resist the tension and stress it would have to withstand while being reared. This arch supports the roof plates, firmly braced to the cruck blades. The upper roof, it should be noted, is virtually a separate structure standing on the roof plates. The spere truss (fig. 4) is constructed as an aisled frame, although no example of wholly aisled halls has yet been found outside the Lowland region. The ancillary buildings, the solar and service cross wings, which there is no reason to doubt are contemporary with the hall, have purlin roofs entirely in character with Highland region idiom. The complete house not only thus combines Highland and Lowland features, but its design and construction are sophisticated and articulate to a degree. Its date if based on the vigorous ogee-arched doorheads as a single dating feature is ca. 1300.

Rectory Farm, discovered in Worcestershire a few years later, was of identical type but with marked differences in architectural and structural design.[3] These differences can be seen by comparing the drawings. For example, the crossbeam, instead of being jointed to the inner edge of the cruck blades, as at West Bromwich, is here mortised and tenoned to the top of the blades. But again the mixture of Highland and Lowland features is the more important point to bear in mind.

Amberley Court in Herefordshire, a county nearer to the true High-

the *vertical* supports of a structure—either posts or cruck blades. Its presence usually denotes that the transverse frame to which it belongs was *reared*, rather than assembled in the vertical, piece by piece.

[2] For West Bromwich, see J. T. Smith, "Medieval Roofs: A Classification," *Archaeol. J. CXV* (1960), 141.

[3] For Rectory Farm at Grafton Flyford, see F. W. B. Charles, "Medieval Cruck-Building and its Derivatives," The Society for Medieval Archaeology, Monograph Series (London, 1967), no. 2, pp. 33 and 38 ff.

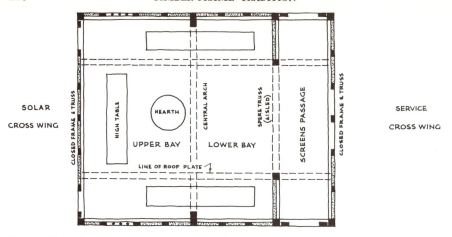

FIG. 1. Plan of a typical base-cruck hall showing position of central arch and spere truss.

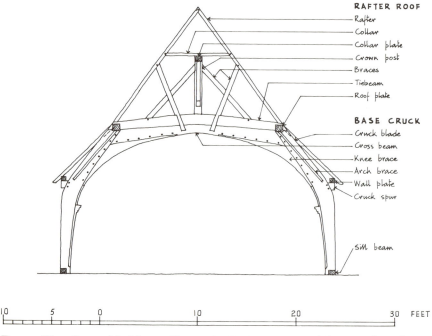

FIG. 2. West Bromwich Manor House, Staffordshire. Central base-cruck arch and superimposed rafter roof.

Fig. 3. West Bromwich Manor House, Staffordshire. The central arch with roof plate heavily braced to the cruck blades.

lands than either Staffordshire or Worcestershire, is of very different style.[4] It is also a base-cruck hall, but its upper roof is of purlin construction with a tie-beam truss between the bays—the tie beam of this truss being in fact the crossbeam of the cruck arch—and intermediate collar trusses at the center of each bay whose principal rafters rest directly on the roof plates. The existence of roof plates instead of purlins at this level could be attributed to Lowland influence. But significantly the roof plates are not continuous members. Instead they are jointed into the sides of the cruck blades exactly as purlins into principal rafters. It is this method that eliminated the need for a tie beam, since the plates thus jointed into the main structure could not spread. Thus the crossbeam, essential for rearing the cruck arch, also served as the tie beam for triangulating the upper truss.

Stoke Bliss Farm, in the extreme west of Worcestershire, is another hall

[4] For Amberley Court, see Charles, op. cit., pp. 39 ff.

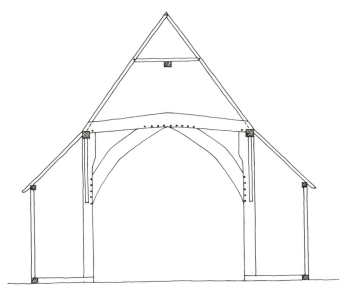

Fig. 4. West Bromwich Manor House, Staffordshire. Spere truss. Framing of aisles not shown.

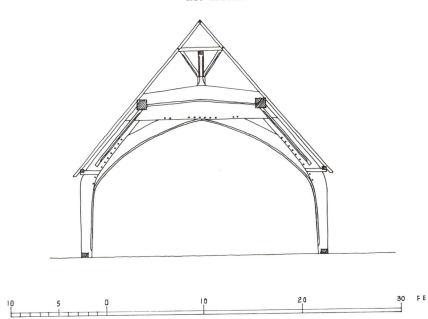

10   5   0   10   20   30 FEET

Fig. 5. Rectory Farm, Grafton Flyford, Worcestershire. A base-cruck hall of the same type as West Bromwich Manor House with upper rafter roof, but various architectural and structural differences.

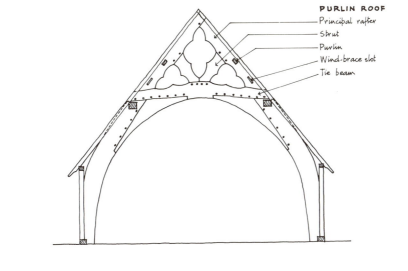

PURLIN ROOF
─Principal rafter
─Strut
─Purlin
─Wind-brace slot
─Tie beam

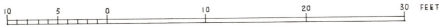

10   5   0   10   20   30   FEET

FIG. 6. Amberley Court, Herefordshire. Central base-cruck arch with superimposed
purlin roof.

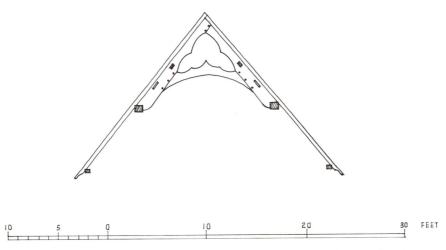

10   5   0   10   20   30   FEET

FIG. 7. Amberley Court, Herefordshire. Intermediate open collar-truss bearing on
roof plate—a typical feature of medieval purlin-roof halls.

of similar type and style.[5] The huge timbers of both of these houses, with
deep cusping and molding—the richness of Stoke Bliss in this respect is
exceptional—denote a date certainly not later than 1350, but I should not
be astonished if carbon-14 analysis were to place them fifty or even a

─────────

[5] For Stoke Bliss Farm, see ibid., p. 41.

F<small>IG</small>. 8. Stoke Bliss Farm, Worcestershire. The apex of the base-cruck central arch, now obstructed by the inserted first floor.

hundred years earlier. Lower Brockhampton, a few miles distant in the same county, has a wholly purlin-type roof—a true Highland product throughout.[6]

Other base-cruck halls have been found in Warwickshire, Berkshire, Sussex, and Hampshire. One of Berkshire's examples, Sanderville Manor [7] at South Moreton, has ornamental cusping more characteristic of Herefordshire. Even more remarkable, the base-cruck blades are also connected by purlins. Yet this building stands only a mile or two distant from Abbey Grange at Sutton Courtenay,[8] which has all the features of purely Lowland construction except for its base-cruck structure.

Thus these halls are surely evidence that the carpenter of the thirteenth and fourteenth centuries could work out his design in accordance with functional and architectural requirements—and, no doubt, his available

[6] For Lower Brockhampton, see ibid., p. 41.

[7] Sanderville Manor was first noted as a base-cruck hall at the Vernacular Architecture Group Conference held in Berkshire in 1966.

[8] For Sutton Courtenay, see J. T. Smith, op. cit., p. 121; J. M. Fletcher and P. S. Stokes, "The Origin and Development of the Crown-Post Roofs," *Medieval Archaeol. VIII* (1964), 173, *in* Charles, op. cit., pp. 41 ff.

Fig. 9. Lower Brockhampton, Herefordshire. A restored base-cruck hall with purlin jointed into the cruck blades.

timber resources—entirely unrestricted by lack of technical knowledge imposed by regional isolation or any other cause.

Medieval barns tell the same story. Middle Littleton barn in Worcestershire, surveyed by Walter Horn, Rainer Berger, and myself,[9] is another base-cruck structure incorporating aisled end bays as the speres of domestic halls. Previously presumed from documentary evidence to have been

[9] Walter Horn, F. W. B. Charles, and R. Berger, "The Cruck-built Barn of Middle Littleton in Worcestershire, England," *J. Soc. Architect. Historians XXV* (1966), 221–239.

Fig. 10. Sanderville Manor, South Moreton, Berkshire. A base-cruck hall similar to the Herefordshire examples.

built by John Ombersley, abbot of Evesham from 1367 to 1397, carbon-14 analysis has placed it at ca. 1250.[10] Bredon barn,[11] by contrast, is wholly aisled. Leigh Court barn, only recently brought to my attention by one of my assistants, who discovered it accidentally, is of simple cruck construction and, with its twelve cruck trusses each spanning more than thirty feet, must be the greatest cruck structure in existence.[12]

All the barns mentioned are located in Worcestershire. Thus within a single county there are three buildings of the same function, yet built in wholly different structural systems. A little further afield on the western border of Berkshire, Great Coxwell barn has aisled transverse frames alternating with intermediate trusses of cruck form.[13] But these are not true cruck construction, as the blades are not connected to form a continuous arch.

[10] Ibid., pp. 224 and 238–239.

[11] MS in prep. For historical references, see W. Horn's paper, n. 36.

[12] Leigh Court Barn lies five miles outside Worcester just off the main road to Hereford. This remarkable building has so far entirely escaped the attention of students of vernacular English architecture.

[13] For Great Coxwell, see Walter Horn and Ernest Born, *The Barns of the Abbey of Beaulieu at Its Granges of Great Coxwell and Beaulieu-St. Leonard's* (Berkeley and Los Angeles: University of California Press, 1965).

Fig. 11. Middle Littleton barn, Worcestershire. One of its eight base-cruck trusses.

Fig. 12. Middle Littleton barn. The aisled end bay.

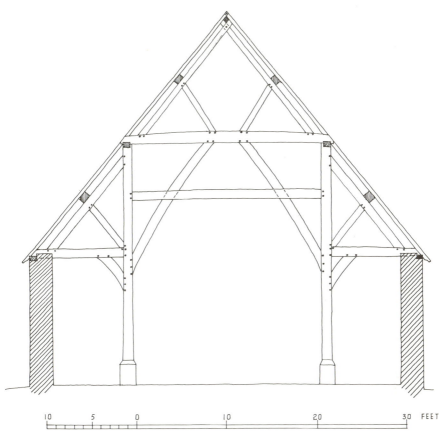

FIG. 13. Bredon barn, Worcestershire. A wholly aisled structure of which the transverse frames, as indicated by the existence of crossbeams, were reared.

Lastly, the now ruined barn of Beaulieu-St. Leonard's in Hampshire,[14] perhaps the largest ever built in England, had aisled frames thirty feet apart spanning thirty-four feet by means of huge but slender king-post trusses whose tie beams, owing to their great length, each consisted of two timbers jointed at mid span. Intermediately in each bay was an open double collar truss, and at either end, built against the stone gable wall, was a queen-post truss.

Assuming a time range of a hundred years from ca. 1250 to embrace all

[14] Ibid. I would like to express my gratitude to Walter Horn for the many opportunities for discoveries he has passed on to me by his insistence on reasoned explanation of every detail in a building's structure. In this instance he obliged me to visit the Beaulieu barn which resulted in my discovery of practically all the trusses and other timber work of the original barn which now form the roof structure of the smaller barn built within its walls.

FIG. 14. Bredon barn, Worcestershire. A wholly aisled structure.

of these barns, there is clearly little room for innovation or technical evolution beyond that period. Other structural types of comparable date have been investigated by Cecil Hewett.[15] It appears that none of such buildings could have been designed without centuries of experience and interchange of ideas beforehand. In other words, these halls and barns, rather than being formative of a tradition, are more acceptable as its final

[15] Cecil Hewitt, "Structural Carpentry in Medieval Essex," *Medieval Archaeol. VI–VII* (1962–63), and: "The Barns at Cressing Temple, Essex, and their Significance in the History of English Carpentry," *J. Soc. Architect. Historians XXVI* (1967), 48–70.

FIG. 15. Leigh Court barn, Worcestershire. A wholly cruck-built structure.

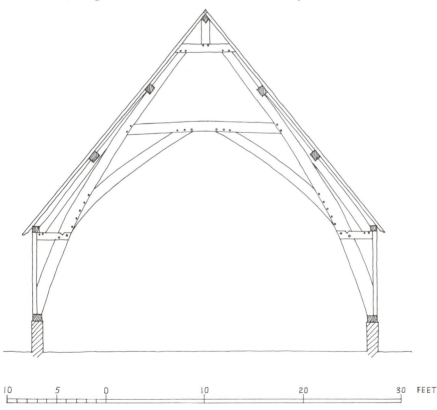

| 10 | 5 | 0 | | 10 | 20 | 30 | FEET |

FIG. 16. Leigh Court barn, Worcestershire. A wholly cruck-built structure of eleven bays in length with two wagon porches also cruck-built.

Fig. 17. Great Coxwell barn, Berkshire. A structure combining aisled and cruck forms.

culmination. For beyond 1350 timber framing loses the architectural quality and individuality which all these buildings possess, and becomes more and more the standard—though still a high standard—of the housebuilder.

The place of simple cruck construction [16] far from being an aberration, as believed until recently, or, as is now being suggested, a late development from base crucks,[17] is central to the main part of the timber-frame tradi-

---

[16] For a more detailed treatment, see F. W. B. Charles, "Medieval Cruck-Building and its Derivatives," The Society for Medieval Archaeology, Monograph Series (London, 1967), no. 2.

[17] See J. M. Fletcher's paper in this volume.

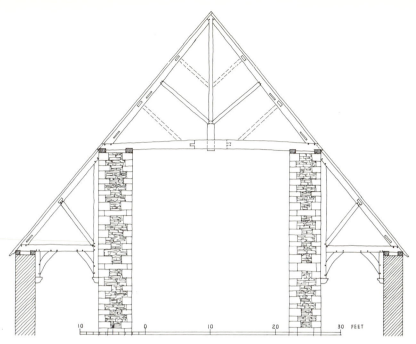

FIG. 18. The now ruined barn of Beaulieu-St. Leonard's, Hampshire. The king-post bay trusses of which all the original six have been reused in the smaller barn built within the walls of the original building. The aisled-roof construction is conjectured as this has been wholly lost.

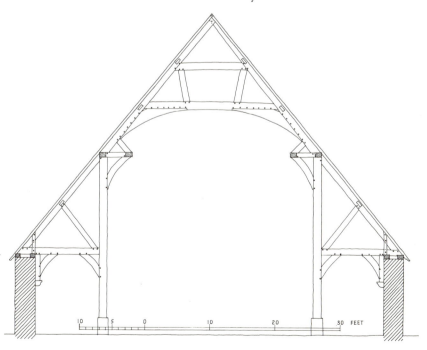

FIG. 19. The barn of Beaulieu-St. Leonard's, Hampshire. The intermediate bay trusses of which four of the original seven have been reused in the smaller barn.

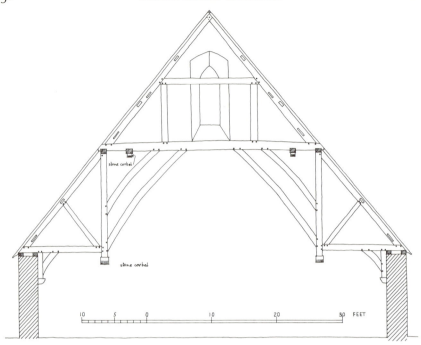

FIG. 20. The barn of Beaulieu-St. Leonard's, Hampshire. The terminal queen-post truss of which one of the original two has been reused in the smaller barn.

FIG. 21. Beaulieu-St. Leonard's barn, Hampshire. Some of the king-post trusses of the original barn as reused in the smaller barn built on its site.

FIG. 22. Beaulieu barn. One of the open collar trusses and other timbers of the original barn as reused in the smaller barn. The tie beam is a later addition.

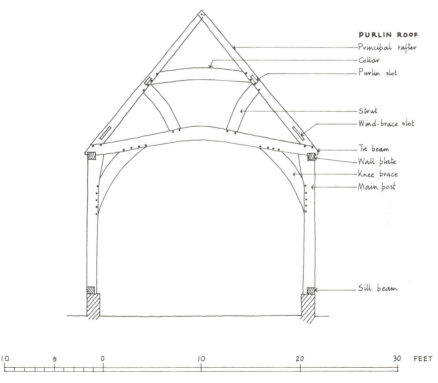

PURLIN ROOF
Principal rafter
Collar
Purlin slot
Strut
Wind-brace slot
Tie beam
Wall plate
Knee brace
Main post
Sill beam

10   5   0   10   20   30   FEET

FIG. 23. The central arch of a medieval hall of post-and-truss construction.

Fig. 24. Kilmalkedar Church, County Kerry, Ireland. The west front with its "reflection" in stone of cruck blades.

Fig. 25. Kilmalkedar Church. The interior of the side wall in which the mason has copied a carpentry joint of rail or wall plate into the post instead of setting his lintel on top of the column capital.

FIG. 26. Lower Norchard, Peopleton, Worcestershire. Exterior of typical four-bay cruck house.

tion—that is, the structural systems incorporating purlin roofs, as opposed to rafter roofs. The first characteristic of the cruck form of construction is that it was designed for framing on the ground and rearing. From this follows the prime purpose and possible origin of the structural elements of the purlin roof. The frame of course is rigid from sill beam to ridge, and as each successive frame is reared, the purlins are the distance pieces which locate and secure the frame in its vertical position. The wind braces triangulate the corners. This process also determines the numbering method and sequence of erection carried over into post-and-truss buildings, even though such buildings were not reared.

In striking contrast with this laborious, almost ritual process of construction, the roof of the Lowland tradition—the rafter roof—was simply a matter of erecting pairs of rafters on continuous wall plates, supported either by posts dug into the ground (post-hole construction), by framed timber walls, or by solid masonry walls. Could the framing technique have been first introduced into this tradition from cruck construction which by its nature *had* to be powerfully framed?

Whatever the answer, the earliest signs of cruck building are to be

F‍IG. 27. Lower Norchard. The wrecked cruck truss and other timbers after the hall's wanton destruction.

found in the stone churches of the west of Ireland. As a matter of fact, these buildings are cruck structures wrought in stone. Some contain many details derived directly from cruck carpentry besides the characteristic blades expressed on their west fronts.

The earliest surviving church may be ca. 700,[18] and cruck building must already have been well established. Six hundred years later the earliest cruck building, at least as so far dated, is Stokesay Castle in Shropshire, ca. 1280.[19] But this building is unusual, both structurally and architecturally, owing to the height above floor level at which the cruck blades are set. Repairs have exaggerated the effect, as the lower section of each blade has been cut off, but the hall's interior was always exceptionally lofty. More typical of cruck building as still found in the western Midlands and Wales today—and incidentally more similar in their proportions to their ancient forbears, the Irish churches—are the two-bay domestic halls with additional floored bays at each end under the same roof line.

[18] Geoffrey Webb, *Architecture in Britain in the Middle Ages* (Harmondsworth, 1956), pp. 1 and 12.

[19] For Stokesay Castle, see Reginald A. Cordingley, "Stokesay Castle, Shropshire: The Chronology of Its Buildings," *Art Bulletin XLV* (1963), 91–107.

Fig. 28. Plas Ucha, North Wales. A fourteenth-century nobleman's cruck hall, originally with timber walls.

Fig. 29. Plas Cadwgan, North Wales. Two huge cruck blades and other timbers awaiting preservation at the Avoncroft Museum of Buildings after the demolition of the hall.

Fig. 30. Pirton Church, Worcestershire. One of several timber-framed steeples which should be scientifically dated.

What was clearly a nobleman's house, despite its humble exterior, still stands, though ruined, at Plas Ucha in North Wales.[20] Another, in the same district, Plas Cadwgan,[21] now wholly destroyed, could still however be dated, as its great cruck arch and spere were salvaged. Both now await funds for their permanent preservation at England's first museum of timber-framed buildings, that at Bromsgrove in Worcestershire.

[20] See Peter Smith, in *Ancient Monuments Soc. Trans., XII* (1954), 97–106.
[21] Surveyed and drawn by Peter Smith whose account of this building awaits publication.

From these and a few other surviving examples, it appears that cruck construction remained practically unchanged through perhaps a thousand years, only descending the social ladder from the status of church to that of peasant house. It is surely among these buildings that the earliest framed structure of any style is most likely to be found.

Finally, England's almost forgotten treasures of ancient oak architecture do not reside only in the shape of great barns or her few timber churches, nor even in the apparently unnoticed timber steeples which might prove as ancient as the Norman churches to which some of them are attached, but perhaps in her least cared for houses and cottages. Thus the field is still wide open for scientists, engineers, and historians alike, but the bulldozers are approaching and the threat of fire becomes more menacing every year.

X

THE RELIABILITY OF TYPOLOGICAL DATING

OF MEDIEVAL ENGLISH ROOFS

J. T. Smith

*I*N THIS PAPER I would like to consider three things: first, I would like to review the existing means of dating timber roofs other than by typological means; then I shall consider the problems peculiar to their typology; and lastly I shall discuss the three main typological series of English roofs and assess their usefulness for dating.

It is only in recent years that the development of timber roofs and timber-framed houses has been studied systematically, so that it is not always obvious how the date of any particular example is arrived at. Inscribed dates, which are the surest evidence, do not exist before the sixteenth century. Dating evidence based on documents relating to the ownership of property is seldom conclusive, because the documents concern the site rather than any buildings on it, reference to which is incidental. Moreover, it is difficult to establish the precise location of the plot of land referred to and in those rare instances where the location is certain and a timber building still stands there, it is usually arguable whether the existing building is the one referred to or a later replacement. The simpler and older the structure, whether secular or ecclesiastical, the greater the difficulty of identification. Generally it is only in towns where large-scale corporate ownership of property has left long continuous series of records that sites can be identified at all easily; Oxford is one such case,[1] Salisbury probably another, but there will never be many more. Even in the most favorable circumstances when a site can be traced back for centuries, the probable date of the structure upon it, inferred from its architectural characteristics, is usually a factor in ascribing it to a particular owner, so that to refine its dating by his occupancy is really a circular argument. As

---

[1] H. E. Salter, *Survey of Oxford*, Oxford Historical Society, n.s., XIV (1960).

for that rare document, the building contract, in only a handful of cases can one be linked to a surviving timber structure through an unbroken site history.[2] It thus appears that documentary sources, though by no means fully explored, offer rather limited opportunities for dating timber buildings independently of architectural evidence.

Then there is the literary evidence of chronicles to the effect that a certain person, usually an abbot, built a church or part of one, or a house or a barn. Where such buildings are of stone, as they usually are, only their timber roofs are of interest for the present enquiry. Quite apart from the occasional difficulty of deciding to which building a document refers,[3] there is the much more serious problem arising from the fact that in stone buildings it is rarely possible to prove the roof to be contemporary with the walls. Only in the comparatively few instances where the walls incorporate posts that are linked to the roof timbers are the stone and timberwork demonstrably of the same date. Unfortunately, most roofs in this small category are of late elaborate church forms which do not present serious dating problems, such as the hammer-beam and arch-braced roofs of East Anglia.[4] Except for these it is impossible to show by superficial examination that a timber roof is contemporary with the stone building beneath it. If follows that chroniclers' statements provide few, if any, dates for roofs that can be accepted without critical evaluation of the roofs themselves.

It is generally thought that the roofs of timber buildings do not present the same problem as those of stone buildings, and that where the various supports and the roof are clearly jointed together the whole is of one date unless there is somewhere a change in the quality of workmanship or a bad fit of the parts. A recent clash of opinion has shown this notion to be false. The Great Hall of Leicester Castle has mid-twelfth-century posts (dated by carved capitals) which are tenoned into the arcade plates, into which in turn tie beams are dovetailed which stiffen the posts and beams, and jointed into both are braces. Among several competent observers who examined the roof without finding any discontinuity in

---

[2] See N. Drinkwater and E. Mercer, "The Blue Boar Inn, Salisbury," *Archaeol. J.* *CXX* (1963), 236–241; and Helen Bonney, "'Balle's Place,' Salisbury," *Wiltshire Archaeol. and Natur. Hist. Mag.* 59 (1964), 155–167 (continuous site history).

[3] See the case of the barn at Middle Littleton, Worcestershire: W. Horn and F. W. B. Charles, "The Cruck-built Barn of Middle Littleton . . ." *J. Soc. Architect. Historians XXV* (1966), 221–239. See also n. 45 below.

[4] Well illustrated in two books by H. Munro, *Suffolk Churches,* 3d ed. (London, 1954) and *Norfolk Churches* (Ipswich, 1949).

construction, there were on the one hand those who said the whole structure must be twelfth century and on the other those who argued on purely typological grounds that the roof was much later than the posts, either late fourteenth or fifteenth century. Carbon-14 dating indicates that the latter view may be right,[5] and study of empty mortises in the posts tends to confirm this view by suggesting an alternative form of roof; but the awkward fact remains that in principle the roof of a timber structure cannot be assumed to be of the same date as the plates and their supports.

Nevertheless, despite these problems of principle, a few roofs that have a bearing on the dating of the commoner types can be dated quite closely. Recent investigation in Westminster Abbey showed that the roofs of the presbytery and north transept are those put up between the start of re-building in 1245 and the completion of the eastern arm and transepts in 1259; the likelihood of this dating was established by the ample and continuous documentation of repairs available in the abbey muniments, and confirmed by the existence of similar roofs in other great thirteenth-century churches;[6] in other words, precise dating was achieved in the same way as it was for stone churches over a hundred years before by a combination of documentary and typological evidence, a method which may be called associative dating. It remains to exploit this step forward by examining such other great churches as still have medieval roofs.

Another key to the dating of wooden roofs is the moldings with which they are embellished. Almost as soon as the study of Gothic architecture began, the closely dated stone moldings in major churches were arranged into typological series and used to date other buildings, so that it used to be said of an older generation of antiquaries that they knew when a molding was just half an hour too late. Whether anyone is equally confident about stone moldings today is doubtful, and in any case it is difficult to say how closely moldings in wood parallel those in stone either in form or time. A useful broad distinction is that while much early timberwork is finished very plainly, such moldings as there are observed are usually of bold, distinctive forms datable by reference to those in stone. In contrast, the far commoner late medieval moldings are mostly of simple, persistent kinds. Thus the rare twelfth- and thirteenth-century capitals on the principal posts of aisled halls resemble those of stone buildings closely and are presumably of very similar date, whereas the smaller capitals (and

    [5] See W. Horn below.
    [6] R. W. McDowall, J. T. Smith, and C. F. Stell, "Westminster Abbey: The Timber Roof . . . ," *Archaeologia* C (1966), 155–174.

bases) of the later crown posts are hard to date, because they appear to be inconsequential series of rolls and hollows bearing only the most general resemblance to their stone counterparts of the late fourteenth and fifteenth centuries, which are themselves harder to date than their predecessors. Until molding profiles of all kinds have been assembled for comparative study, they will not themselves provide a very sure key to dating, nor will they serve to establish a roof chronology.

To sum up the situation, at present a handful of roofs are closely dated documentarily, a few have been fairly securely dated by carbon-14 analysis, some can be dated approximately by moldings, and the rest have to be dated typologically. But before attacking the subject of typology, it will be useful to consider how much material has to be covered.

England is rich in medieval timber structures of various kinds, most of them houses. The eight hundred and fifty houses dated before 1530 in a survey of Essex over forty years ago [7] could certainly be increased now; Kent, never systematically surveyed, may well have two thousand; Surrey, East Sussex, Herefordshire, Buckinghamshire, and parts of Suffolk have many medieval houses, the total running to perhaps another two thousand. Elsewhere in England, south of the river Trent, timber houses of this age are much rarer; east of the Pennines, between Humber and Tyne, they are rarer still; while in northwest England (including Lancashire) there exists only a handful. Wales has a considerable number of medieval timber houses, the best of them situated in the north of the country. A second smaller category of timber structures comprises the roofs of stone churches, monastic buildings, and a few special buildings such as timber belfries.[8] Whatever difficulties the typologist has to face, he will at any rate not be short of material. All these structures comprise two main typological groups, one covering roofs and the other wall framing, and there is also a typology of ground plans for houses.

Now I would like to consider the formation of typological series for roofs, which presents some problems hardly found with other kinds of artifacts. At any given time a great variety of roof constructions exists, varying greatly in size and complexity, so that even if adequate information were available the assembly of type series would still be difficult. But many important roofs stand twenty or thirty feet above the ground, so that merely to collect the data is more difficult than, say, examining

[7] Royal Commission on Historical Monuments, *Essex* (4 vols., 1916–1923).
[8] The first serious study of these was by C. A. Hewett, *Archaeol. J. CXIX* (1962), 225–244.

brooches. Moreover, among the roofs built at any given time there will be both old-fashioned types continuing to serve long-established purposes and types embodying innovations to meet new needs. Therefore, a simple type of roof covering a humble building may be exactly contemporary with a far more advanced type in a royal palace hall, so that a purely typological sequence based on surviving roofs will not correspond to the chronological order of the examples on which it is based. Furthermore, the earlier stages in the sequence have to be based on inferences drawn from excavations; and it is sometimes the case that a surviving roof that is typologically primitive cannot be paralleled in the archaeological record. This is a problem unknown to the student of portable objects.

Matters are further complicated by the existence of markedly different families of roof types which have different and largely complementary distributions, to account for which certain assumptions have to be made which are not necessary for objects distributed by trade or conquest. In fact, the researcher may make these assumptions in a state of profound ignorance about how ideas and techniques of any sort were diffused in the Middle Ages.

My own assumptions which relate to chronology may be summarized as follows. The first is that innovations occur first in buildings of the ruling class, which tend to be large and important buildings where new structural problems first arise, and appear only later in lesser ones. This is not to say that no changes occur in the smaller buildings and roofs which have not already occurred in larger ones, but they will tend to be less important and relate to different social needs. Naturally this notion is incapable of proof but it is one which is generally implied though never stated in studies of medieval architecture.

A second and equally unprovable assumption is that technical changes are likely to have come about by a long series of small steps rather than by big dramatic advances, with the possible exception of ideas transmitted by invasion. The kind of change brought about in English Romanesque architecture by the Norman Conquest illustrates the degree of change I have in mind, and it will be remembered that the effect even of this well-documented event is a matter of argument.

Closely related to this assumption is a third one, namely, that for the techniques of the building trades to travel from one country to another there must have been a substantial movement of craftsmen. For this to happen there must either have been conquest as in Norman England; or the two countries had to have similar social structures; or they may have shared institutions whose common needs permit a free flow of ideas, although this condition without similar social structures is very rare.[9]

My fourth and last assumption, which has particular bearing on the disputed dating of certain roofs, is that innovation is unlikely to have appeared in one building a long time before it appears in other buildings of the same type; like the first assumption, it relates technical progress to the class structure of medieval society and attempts to use broad social changes, however imperfectly they are known in detail, as the framework which alone makes sense of all other changes.

Let me now construct a typological model of medieval English roofs in order to show how far its components can be relied on for dating.

Typology of Medieval English Roofs

The oldest type of English roof—oldest in the sense that surviving examples are earlier than the earliest of either of the other two major types, but without prejudice to conclusions derived from excavations—is the rafter roof [10] and its derived forms. It appears to have originated on the European mainland, probably northern Germany, where it is associated with timber houses of the Roman Iron Age. On distributional as well as typological grounds [11] it can be argued that it was a Norman import into England in the eleventh century, although the earliest examples are not datable before ca. 1200. These, though, are highly developed forms of the rafter roof; for more primitive examples, we must go to certain late thirteenth-century roofs which are remarkable for having the plates placed above the tie beam instead of below it, as is normal. This technique is now called reversed assembly [12] and appears to be a relic of the time before the

[9] Thus in church architecture Cistercian planning was more widely disseminated throughout Europe than any specific structural feature; and the early development of a national Gothic in England and France argues strongly that structural ideas were not transmitted across the Channel after the middle of the 12th century.

[10] In using this term, which is a useful reformation of terminology and replaces "trussed rafter," I follow F. W. B. Charles, *Medieval Cruck Building and its Derivatives* (London, 1967), esp. pp. 6–7.

[11] J. T. Smith, "Medieval English Roofs: A Classification," *Archaeol. J. CXV* (1958), 111–149, esp. 116, 126; J. T. Smith, "Cruck Construction: A Survey of the Problems," *Medieval Archaeol. 8* (1964), 119–151.

[12] It occurs in barns at Belchamp St. Paul, Essex and Great Coxwell, Berks: C. A. Hewett, "Timber-Building in Essex," *Trans. Ancient Monuments Soc.* n.s., IX (1961), 33–56; and Walter Horn and Ernest Born, *The Barns . . . at . . . Great Coxwell and Beaulieu* (University of California Press, 1965).

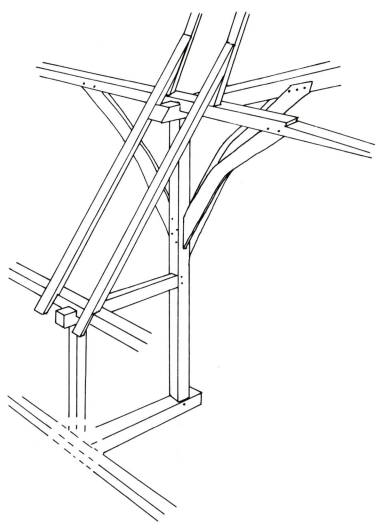

Fig. 1. Barn, Belchamp St. Paul, Essex; not to scale. Shows "reversed assembly," that is, the plate is above the tie beam, not, as in all other examples illustrated, below it. Based on Hewett, as note 12, figure 4.

timbers of aisled buildings were set, not on stylobates or ground sills, but into the ground. Where such buildings have been excavated the alignment of the posts is not sufficiently good to have permitted the normal assembly of the later Middle Ages, only the linking of each pair of posts directly by a tie beam, so that the plates carrying the common rafters had necessarily to sit above the ties. Evidently by the beginning of the thirteenth century reversed assembly was no longer used in the more advanced types of barns in Essex but persisted in the lesser ones, and in some houses.[13] But it also suggests that in even the biggest timber buildings posts had been set into the ground in the not very distant past, a point which is confirmed by the excavation of an aisled manor house with earthfast posts at Brome, Suffolk, whereas in the same county and in Essex by the late thirteenth century comparable timber-framed houses were built on ground sills. Evidently in eastern and southeastern England a major structural change had taken place by the end of the thirteenth century whereby, in the buildings of the feudal ruling class, stability could be achieved without setting the posts in the ground but rather by the use of braces across the angles formed by the timbers. This gives us a *terminus post quem*, so that however difficult dating may be we need not make matters worse by imagining an indefinite antiquity for these techniques. Lateral stability was the first consideration, with lengthwise stiffening to prevent the rafters racking from end to end, a quite secondary matter.[14] The first technique tried was the passing brace, running across three or more timbers by means of halved (lap) joints. As an example, thirteenth-century English barns such as those at Cressing Temple represent as high a level of achievement in this technique as can be found anywhere. Not that this feature was necessarily or even probably developed in barns; rather, it seems to have been taken over from church roofs, where its application was less spectacular because the churches had stone walls. This possibility is difficult to establish because, although suitably early passing-brace roofs exist in French churches such as the roof of the nave of Lisieux cathedral of ca. 1181,[15] there are none in English churches before the late thirteenth century,[16] in other words, later than the Cressing barns. Assuming that it is not subject to any major correction, the carbon-14 date is remarkably early; yet, typologically, this great barn shows the passing brace at its fullest development. That this could be so soon after the passing brace had

---

[13] A. P. Baggs, "Hook Farm, Lower Woodcott, Hampshire," *Trans. Newbury District Field Club XI*, no. 4 (1967).

[14] E.g., the Sextry Barn, Ely, and Fyfield Hall: R. Willis, in *Pub. Cambridge Antiquarian Soc. I* (1840–1846), 5–8, and J. T. Smith, "Medieval Aisled Halls . . . ," *Archaeol. J. CXII* (1955), 76–94, respectively.

[15] Drawings in *Charpentes* (Centre de Recherches des Monuments Historiques, Paris, n.d. but ca. 1960), and there said to have been built in ca. 1181 and repaired after a fire in 1226. The cathedral was certainly rebuilt between 1171 and 1181: F. Barlow, *Letters of Arnulf of Lisieux* (London, 1939), xlvii–l; and it appears that the fire affected only the upper parts of choir and transept: L. Serbat, *Lisieux* (Series Petites Monographies, Paris, 1926), 23, also 15.

[16] E.g., Beverley Minster.

been invented—and there is no reason to think either that the Cressing dating is seriously wrong or that much earlier examples remain to be discovered—is because the technique involved the use of such long timbers in a not very efficient way that better methods were soon evolved. Consequently, the typological series of passing braces is short and its use for dating correspondingly small, in the sense that it applies to comparatively few examples; yet it survived remarkably long in a secondary role, persisting well into the fifteenth century.[17]

Scissor-braced construction is another early English type of roof. It was used in several cathedrals in the first half of the thirteenth century—at Peterborough perhaps as early as ca. 1190—and in a few instances the main trusses in such roofs had, on the tie beams, a pair of long queen struts rising up to the collar beam.[18] Simple scissor-braced roofs cannot be dated closely by purely typological means, as they persist for a long time. Some in monastic buildings or parish churches are as early as the middle of the thirteenth century,[19] while others, such as the roof of St. George's Guildhall, King's Lynn, are of the early fifteenth century,[20] so that they have to be dated by the buildings they cover rather than typologically. Consequently, there is always some uncertainty whether the scissor-braced roof of a thirteenth-century building is original or a rebuilding of an earlier roof. Joints, the typology of which in Engand is now being studied by Hewett,[21] provide some help, since halved (lap) joints are earlier than mortise-and-tenon joints in work of comparable size and quality. This alone would place the roof of the Gloucester Blackfriars earlier than the King's Lynn roof.

Yet there are simpler rafter roofs than these. Typologically, the simplest English form has a collar beam below which, usually, are two straight

[17] Royal Commission on Historical Monuments, *Monuments Threatened and Destroyed* (London, 1963), pp. 42–43.

[18] R. W. McDowall et al. (as n. 6), pp. 167–168 (associative dating). For Peterborough see J. M. Fletcher and P. S. Spokes, "The Origin and Development of Crown-Post Roofs," *Medieval Archaeol. XIII* (1964), 152–183, esp. 182–183.

[19] E.g., those of the Blackfriars, Gloucester, of between 1241 and ca. 1265; A. D. Saunders, in *Archaeol. J. CXXII* (1965), 217–219; illustration in Smith (as n. 11), pl. XIV. On typological grounds I reject the ascription of the south transept roof of Harwell Church to 1220–1240; Fletcher and Spokes (as n. 17), pp. 160–161. It has a central purlin derived from the crown post which itself, in Berkshire, is unlikely to be that early. See below, pp. 000–000.

[20] Dated to 1425. I am indebted to Miss Vanessa Parker for this information.

[21] C. A. Hewett, "Structural Carpentry in Medieval Essex," *Medieval Archaeol. VI–VII* (1962–63), 240–271; C. A. Hewett (as n. 8), p. 12.

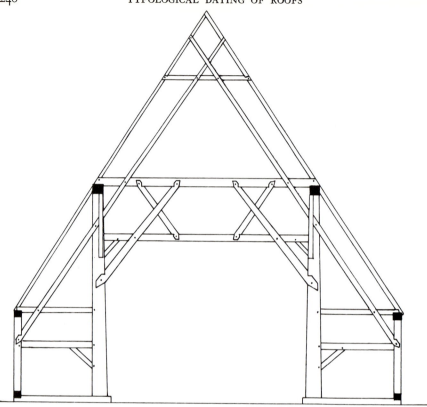

Fig. 2. Cressing Temple, Essex, Wheat Barn; Hewett, as note 55 (slightly modified).
Carbon-14 date of ca. 1200.

braces to the rafters. In addition, it may well have, near the feet of the
rafters, the short vertical timbers called ashlar pieces, resting on an inner
plate or cornice. Due to its simplicity, the collared-rafter roof was rarely
used in the securely dated major buildings, which, being larger, demanded
more complicated solutions to their roof problems. So the simplest type is
not the earliest surviving one, and, as with many a simple thing in
archaeology, it tends to be ignored or is thought not to need explanation.
In such ignorance the earliest roofs datable with reasonable certainty are
those of aisled timber halls dated to the late thirteenth or early fourteenth
century by molded capitals, for example, Stanton's Farm, Black Notley,
Essex, and Chennel's Brook Farm, Horsham, Sussex.[22] There may well
be earlier examples in stone churches, such as—to take a random example

[22] Stanton's Farm: R. C. H. M., *Essex II,* 19–20; Smith (as n. 11), p. 112;
Chennels Brook Farm: R. T. Mason, *Sussex Archaeological Collections CI* (1963),
40–47, and *Framed Buildings of the Weald* (Handcross, 1964), p. 34.

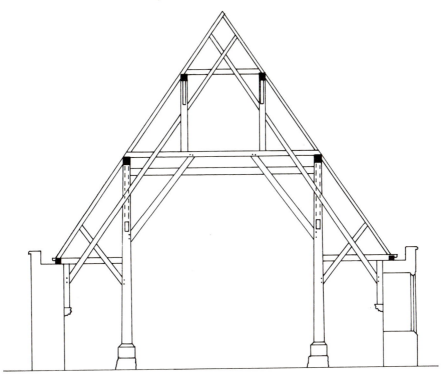

FIG. 3. Ely, Cambridgeshire, Sextry Barn; Willis, as note 14. Dated by moldings to mid-thirteenth century.

—the roof of the early thirteenth-century nave at Church Stretton,[23] but since in such cases the timberwork cannot be proved to be contemporary with the walls below, I am forced to omit them. A more serious difficulty arises from the long persistence of rafter roofs, both in their southeastern homeland and in the more remote parts of England where they are comparatively rare. The brick-built south chapel added to the church at Humsdon, Herts, about 1600 has a rafter roof; on the Welsh border the nave of Clifford church, Herefordshire, has another, dated by moldings to the early sixteenth century.[24] Equally late examples can be found in houses, such as Ewhurst Place, Ifield, Sussex, of ca. 1560.[25] Therefore, the collared-rafter roof, regarded purely as a type, cannot be dated more closely than over a span of three centuries. Although joints, moldings, or plan and type may narrow the date of the building itself, or the style of

[23] D. S. Cranage, *The Churches of Shropshire* (Shrewsbury, 1894–1912), p. 82.
[24] Humsdon: R. C. H. M., *Hertfordshire* (1910), p. 127; Clifford: R. C. H. M., *Herefordshire I* (1931), 38.
[25] Mason, *Framed Buildings* (as n. 22), pp. 89–90.

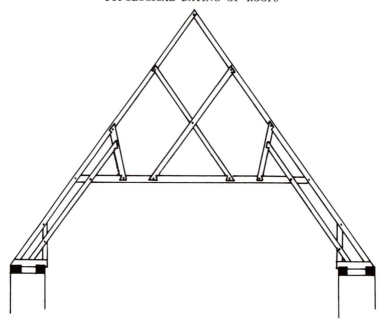

FIG. 4. Nave of Lisieux cathedral, Normandy, France; as note 15, q.v. for associative dating.

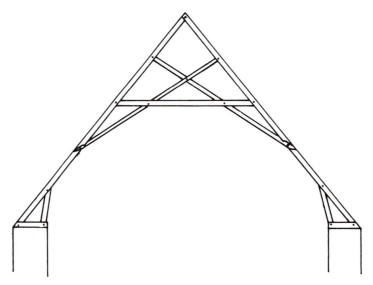

FIG. 5. Gloucester, Blackfriars, based on a drawing by J. Buckler, B. M. *Add. MS* 36437, fol. 74, which is captioned "roof of chapel at west end of dormitory." Completed by ca. 1265; Saunders, as note 19.

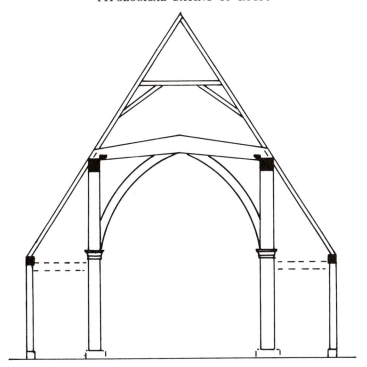

Fig. 6. Stanton's Farm, Black Notley, Essex; as note 22. Dated by moldings to early fourteenth century.

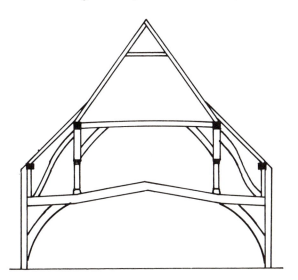

Fig. 7. Gate House Farm, Felstead, Essex; as note 28. Dated by R. C. H. M. to late fourteenth century on moldings, which, however, could be of the first half of the century.

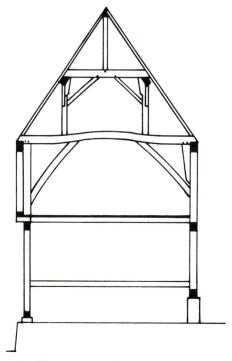

Fig. 8. Candle Court, Reepham, Norfolk; R. C. H. M.
MS. Probably late sixteenth century, based principally
on fireplace and window details.

its masonry, brickwork, and details may provide a *terminus post quem,*
this still leaves a considerable number of absolutely plain roofs for which
no closer date can be offered. Even the sectional dimensions (scantlings)
of the timber do not show any uniform tendency, whether from heavy to
lighter or from waney-edged to perfectly squared-up work. The rafter
roof like other simple persistent artifacts shows the typological approach
at its weakest as a guide to chronology.

Raised-aisled Construction and Derivatives

I have coined this straightforward term, because the description of roofs
of this type as queen-post roofs is, historically speaking, misleading.

RAISED-AISLED CONSTRUCTION WITH TIE BEAMS

Within those parts of England where both rafter roofs and aisled houses
are common [26]—a limitation that excludes remote outliers such as the

[26] For map see Smith (as n. 11), p. 133.

bishop's palace at Hereford as well as the important northern group—a considerable number of roofs have a structure identical with that of the aisled buildings themselves, save that it is raised up on a tie beam. Such a structure is essentially a somewhat complicated form of rafter roof, incorporating above the raised-aisled framework a collared-rafter or collar-purlin roof or some other derivative of the uniform scantling class of structures.

The earliest raised-roof was found in the Sextry Barn, Ely, dated by stone moldings to the middle of the thirteenth century,[27] which accords perfectly with its position in the passing-brace typology. At Gatehouse Farm, Felstead, Essex, a collared-rafter roof is associated with the raised-aisled structure and may be of the early fourteenth century.[28] An interesting feature is the existence above tie-beam level of an "aisle" wall, so that the main tie beam is tenoned into the posts forming the aisle walls and the wall plates are set a little way above the ties—in effect, a form of reversed assembly.[29]

The few fifteenth- and early sixteenth-century roofs of this type continue to reflect contemporary developments in such matters as the form of the post heads and other details. The latest example so far discovered, at Reepham, Norfolk, still maintained the aisled structure, but what started as plates were modified into purlins by being turned to correspond with the roof slope. With this development, by the late sixteenth century, the type can be presumed to have ended. The Reepham roof can be dated by the timber-framed house it covers, but to date individual examples by purely typological criteria is not easy, and will remain so until more is known of the general development of timberwork in East Anglia, where alone raised-aisled construction in its simplest form is found.

HAMMER-BEAM ROOFS

In wide buildings the inconvenience of the free-standing posts was early felt, and to dispense with them by means of a very low tie beam, as at Gatehouse Farm, did not much improve matters. Yet even before this improvement occurred in houses, perhaps already by the late thirteenth century, the special needs of the large kitchens required for feudal households impelled carpenters to provide a high pyramidal roof covering a

---

[27] Willis (as n. 14).
[28] R. C. H. M., *Essex II*, 76; reproduced in Smith (as n. 11), p. 121.
[29] Above, p. 244.

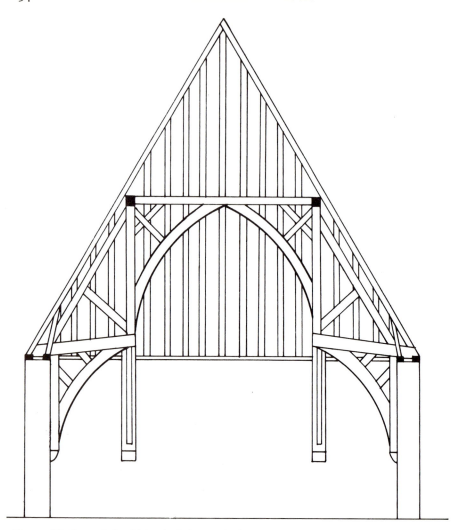

FIG. 9. Kitchen of the Bishop's Palace, Chichester, Sussex. After F. Ostendorf, *Die Geschichte des Dachwerks* (Leipzig and Berlin, 1908), Abb. 286*aa*. Ascribed to the early fifteenth century by W. H. Godfrey, *Victoria County History of Sussex, III* 148, but may be of the same date as the masonry, which is dated to the late thirteenth century by moldings and bracing.

quite large space without encumbering the floor with posts. In order to achieve this, a roof-supporting post near each corner was built up at wall-plate level by two beams that were at right angles to the walls, joined at their ends, and were themselves supported by brackets. This was the late thirteenth-century genesis of the medieval English carpenter's finest

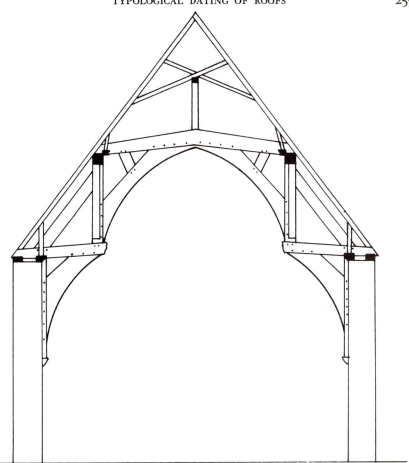

Fig. 10. Pilgrim's Hall, Winchester, Hants; *Proceedings of the Hampshire Field Club*, III (1894–1897), 71–77. Early fourteenth century, dated by carved details and moldings.

achievement, the hammer-beam roof, which, prior to the fifteenth century, was simply a sophisticated form of raised-aisled construction.[30] These early examples are clearly differentiated from those of the fifteenth century by their reproduction above the hammer beams of the roofs of aisled halls, the sequence of which they follow. Indeed, dating difficulties here have been largely caused by the perverse persistence of earlier antiquaries in regarding the most splendid of all hammer-beam roofs, the one put up over Westminster Hall in 1397–1399, as the first of its kind. So,

[30] It is not a development of the simple rafter roof with ashlar pieces, as claimed by J. H. Harvey, *Gothic England* (London, 1947), pp. 51–52.

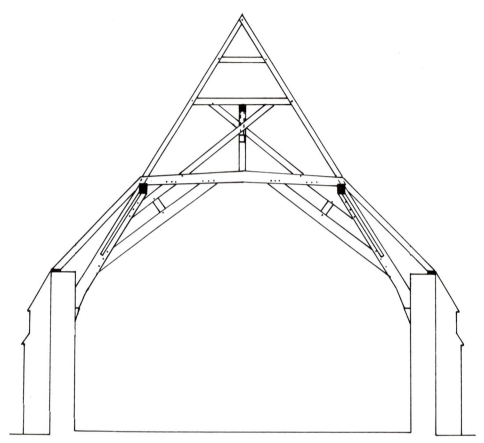

Fig. 11. The Old Deanery, Salisbury, Wilts; as note 35. The roof trusses are linked
structurally with the stone walls which can be dated between 1258 and 1274.

once this irrational belief is rejected, a typological and chronological
sequence based on such criteria as crown-post and brace forms, moldings,
etc., is not hard to produce.

The major change in hammer-beam roofs of the fifteenth century was
the development of a principal rafter into which side purlins could be
tenoned allowing the simple raised-aisled structure to disappear. Thereafter, East Anglian hammer beams and hammer posts become merely
forms of strutting designed to keep the principal rafter rigid, or, in some
cases, are purely decorative. This aspect of hammer-beam typology has
never been worked out, but dating is less of a problem, because these
roofs always have moldings and ornamentation.

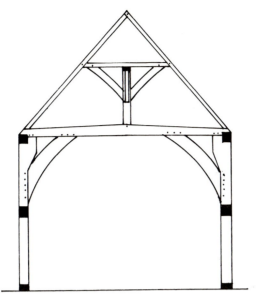

FIG. 12. Bramfieldbury, Bramfield, Herts; G. Bailey and B. Hutton, *Crown-post Roofs in Hertfordshire* (Hutchins, 1966), page 9. Dated to 1430 (ibid., pp. 6, 19).

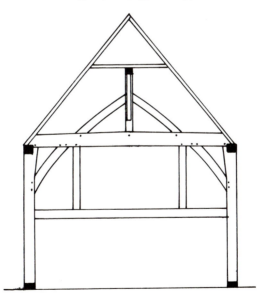

FIG. 13. Winkhurst Farm, near Chiddingstone, Kent; R. C. H. M. MS. Probably end of fifteenth or early sixteenth century, based on plan type and form of braces.

CROWN-POST ROOFS

A recent study [31] has made the dating of crown-post roofs the subject of controversy as opposed to mere disagreement about the date of particular examples. The claim there made, that the early roofs of southern England appear to be descended from those of northern France, is generally agreed to. However, whether French influence continued to be felt throughout the thirteenth century, as is now argued, is quite another matter, and since the way it is resolved will determine the dating and to some extent the form of the typological series, the matter must be discussed here.

The presumed connection between French roofs and the earlier surviving English roofs rests on structural likenesses. Yet, in roofs stiffened longitudinally by collar purlins or ridge pieces, there are important differences between the two countries. They are differences of degree rather than kind, so that the weight given to them depends on the researcher. In England the true crown-post roof numbers many hundreds in which a central post rises to some point lower than the apex of the roof and supports a purlin immediately beneath the collars. In a few roofs the post continues to the apex where the common rafters are tenoned into it. A mere handful of roofs [32] have, instead of a crown post, a king post rising to the apex of the roof to support a ridge piece. In France, on the other hand, crown posts are rare, and the commonest form of roof has a king post into which one or two collar purlins and perhaps a ridge purlin may be tenoned.[33] These are not the only differences: even more significant are the differences of detail between the two countries. In northern France the braces commonly occur both above and below the purlin, whereas in England they are always below. The few French crown-post roofs usually have the purlin tenoned into the post rather than in the English fashion of post into purlin. Also, in French king-post and collar-purlin roofs the purlin is as often as not positioned above the collar. I therefore conclude that although a few early French roofs present the features developed later in England, it is unlikely that "south-eastern England usually copied France until ca. 1270" [34] because the *characteristic* French forms do not appear. But if the comparison be confined to the greater churches, the contrast is still more remarkable, with Salisbury, Lincoln, and Westmin-

---

[31] Fletcher and Spokes (as n. 18).
[32] In southeastern England; see below, pp. 267–268, for northern king-post roofs.
[33] *Charpentes* (as n. 15), II, *passim*.
[34] Fletcher and Spokes (as n. 18), p. 182.

ster lagging far behind Paris, Meaux, and Rouen in the provision of any kind of axial purlin and bracing. Yet it is precisely in buildings of this quality and importance, and especially Westminster, that French influence might be expected.

If these arguments are accepted, French practice has little bearing on English chronology and the series of English crown posts does not begin much before the middle of the thirteenth century, with the Old Deanery, Salisbury, of the 1260s as one of the early examples.[35] The end of the series is marked for houses in southeastern England by the abandonment of the open hall in favor of storys throughout. When this change began in the early sixteenth century, the crown post went out of fashion. Within these chronological limits of ca. 1250–ca. 1540,[36] and within southeastern England, the crown post is certainly the most important roof type. To discuss chronology is difficult since few examples have been adequately recorded and fewer precisely dated, while even the criteria to establish a typology are at present doubtful.[37]

Elsewhere crown posts occur more rarely, and the principal problem is to decide their relation to the main line of development in the southeast. The southeastern region cannot at present be more precisely defined than by saying that in it all houses of whatever quality have rafter roofs or their derivatives and that it ends where cruck roofs and their derivatives begin. An area so defined cannot be bounded by a line on a map but rather by a zone where cruck and rafter roofs mingle and gradually give way to areas where there is a preponderance of cruck forms. Although the dating of particular examples outside the southeast is difficult, it is observable that the simple types are most common and that in comparison with them the number of crown-post roofs is fairly small, especially outside the areas fringing the southeast. Moreover, in such areas the crown-post roofs show little variety or development and their moldings are usually indicative of the fourteenth century rather than any later date, whereas other types of roof extend over a longer period and show marked development. This is consistent with the idea of an early penetration of the rafter roof over the whole of England, its development and extensive use in the southeast, and a decline elsewhere in favor of quite different roof designs.[38]

[35] N. Drinkwater, "The Old Deanery, Salisbury," *Antiquaries J. XLIV* (1964), 41–59.

[36] R. T. Mason, *Framed Buildings* (as n. 22), pp. 62–63.

[37] The importance which Fletcher and Spokes (as n. 18), attached to joweled heads is made doubtful by their own evidence, esp. figs. 54 and 55.

[38] Smith (as n. 11).

CRUCK-TRUSSED ROOFS

Outside southeastern England the most widespread roof type is the cruck truss, a deceptively simple construction which is correspondingly hard to date, with the result that both the chronology and the typology of crucks have been in dispute for a generation or more.

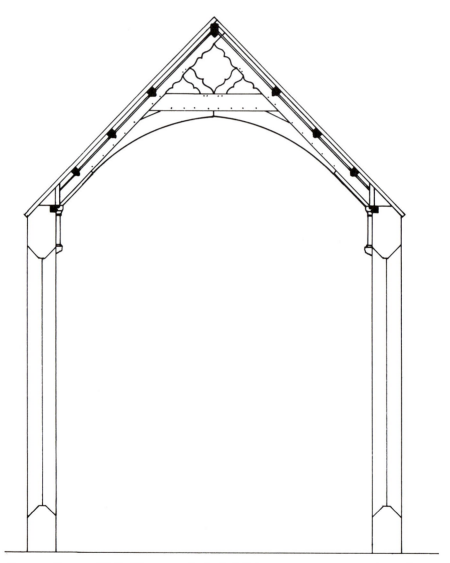

FIG. 14. Guesten Hall, Worcester Cathedral Priory; source as note 46, Dollman. Commonly dated to 1320, following a monastic chronicle; but see Brakspear, as note 46.

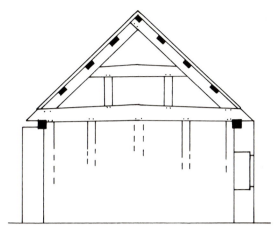

FIG. 15. Refectory of Great Malvern Priory, Worcester; sources as note 48. Probably third quarter of fourteenth century (moldings and window tracery). M. E. Wood gives ca. 1340 (p. 325).

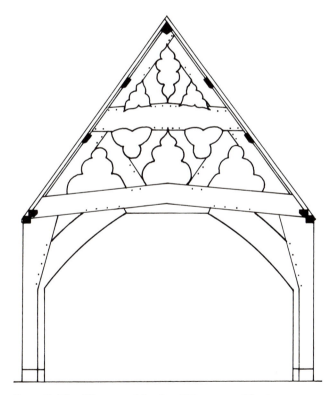

FIG. 16. The Vicarage, Martley, Worcester; Charles, as note 10, page 55, and there dated to ca. 1300, without reasons. A quarter-round molding suggests a later date, perhaps mid-fourteenth century.

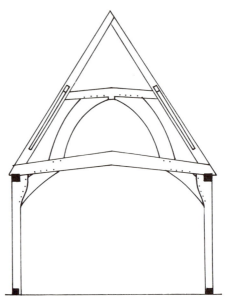

FIG. 17. Blaengavenny, Llantilio, Pertholey, Mon. Based on drawing by S. R. Jones, Sheffield. Probably early sixteenth century based on local roof typology; Fox and Raglan, as note 43, page 81.

Considering typology first, it has been generally assumed that there is a straightforward progression from simple to complex forms.[39] The treatment of the blades at the apex has been regarded as the key by some, starting with their crossing at the apex and finishing with their being truncated at various heights and joined by a horizontal member (collar or yoke). Observation suggests that the reverse sequence is true since most crucks found in houses known by other criteria to be medieval have complicated apex forms. It is the late derived forms of cruck found in postmedieval houses which invariably show a simple crossing of the blades. In this respect crucks conform to a generalization applicable to all medieval roofs of comparable size and purpose, namely, that the early examples display a complexity of component members fastened together by relatively simple joints, whereas later ones perform similar functions with fewer members and more complicated joints. The problem is compounded by the long history of cruck construction which, if German archaeologists are correct, can be traced back to the first four centuries of our era in the Ruhr district and the lower Rhineland, where it was used for important

[39] For the clearest statement of this view, see J. Walton, "The Development of the Cruck Framework," *Antiquity XXII* (1948), 179–189.

houses.[40] Very recently a small building of the fourth century A.D. associated with a Roman villa in Buckinghamshire has produced comparable evidence of pairs of inward-sloping posts.[41]

Now the proposition that earthfast timber buildings were designed to resist lateral wind pressure only can be more easily demonstrated in aisled buildings than others, but is probably true of all roofs.[42] If this is the case, the consequence of setting the feet of the blades on stones was a need to provide lengthwise stability, so that just as with rafter roofs the progressively more efficient means of achieving stability provide another evolutionary sequence. A third such sequence is provided by the form of the blades themselves in relation to the cross section of the building. The way this works provides a good illustration of the principle referred to above, in that roof structures for comparable purposes become simpler as joints (and other carpentry techniques) become more sophisticated. Early crucks have a form approximating the letter A, with the difference that the blades, instead of joining at the apex, are commonly tenoned into a collar or yoke upon which is set either a king post or ridge piece. Had the common rafter followed the line of the blades, this construction would have given an undesirably steep roof pitch and very low walls. But walls of reasonable height were provided, and they were joined to the crucks by short spur ties.[43] Then, to give a roof the required pitch, it was necessary to carry the purlins on principal rafters, the lower ends of which rested on the spur ties and the upper ends on the blades. By the end of the Middle Ages the blades themselves were being shaped in the cutting so as to receive the purlins directly, without the need for intermediate members. It is in this respect that the crucks of Worcestershire and Monmouthshire differ most markedly, the former being typologically earlier than the latter; whether they are chronologically earlier too is doubtful. The Monmouthshire crucks represent a simpler way of using timber to achieve the

[40] L. Banfer et al., "Eine germanische Siedlung in Westick bei Kamen, Kr. Unna," *Westfalen XXI* (1937), 410–453; R. von Uslar, "Die germanische Siedlung in Haldern bei Wesel," *Bonner Jahrbücher CXLIX* (1949), 105–145; and see W. A. van Es, *Wijster,* = *Palaeohistoria XI* (1967), 379–402.

[41] K. Branigan, "The Decline of a Romano-British Farm," *University of Birmingham Archaeological Society Bulletin,* no. 5 (1967), 40–42; fuller publication forthcoming in *Medieval Archaeol.*

[42] This matter will be dealt with more fully in an appendix to the report on the excavation of the 9th–13th-century palace site at Cheddar, Somerset, by Mr. P. Rahtz, of the University of Birmingham.

[43] A useful term coined by Sir C. Fox and Lord Raglan, *Monmouthshire Houses I* (Cardiff, 1951), 24.

twin aims of supporting the roof and providing an impressive internal appearance, whereas the Worcestershire crucks which are comparable in span tend to develop in that direction but never attain the same economy of means. This may be a manifestation of a common development, one which is hard to define closely in present circumstances but which seems to amount to this: within the wider framework of regional or almost countrywide tradition may be found a local propensity to develop a particular aspect of that tradition, apparently without regard to techniques developed elsewhere to the same end. It follows from this that the same typological forms in different parts of England and Wales should not be ascribed to the same date without regard to local development.

TRUSS ROOFS

I use this modification of Charles' term "post and truss roof"[44] to cover all roofs in which the common rafters rest on purlins slotted into the back of a supporting frame which is either triangular or A-shaped. The walls may be constructed either of timber or stone. On distributional grounds as well as structural similarities they are likely to be descended from cruck roofs,[45] but they have never been the subject of a satisfactory study.

The earliest truss-blade roofs appear to be of about the middle of the fourteenth century, perhaps a little earlier. The roof of the destroyed Guesten Hall at Worcester had seven close-spaced trusses forming eight bays; each truss had an arch-braced collar beam with cusped struts above it, and there were three purlins on each side and a ridge piece. The moldings and ornaments of the timberwork as well as those of the masonry were consistent with a date about the middle of the fourteenth century.[46] A secular building of much the same date is the timber-framed Martley Vicarage, Worcestershire, which has a quarter-round molding on several of the principal members indicating this date.[47] Another large roof of the same type, the refectory of Great Malvern Priory, Worcestershire, can be dated somewhat later in the fourteenth century by its moldings and

[44] Charles (as n. 10), pp. 43–64.

[45] Smith (as n. 11), p. 146; Charles (as n. 10), p. 43 and n. 57.

[46] F. T. Dollman and J. R. Jobbins, *An Analysis of Ancient Domestic Architecture I* (London, 1861). The plates of this work are not numbered. H. Brakspear rejected a chronicle date of 1320 on architectural grounds; *Victoria County History, Worcestershire IV*, 355.

[47] Charles (as n. 10), pp. 54–55, ascribes it to ca. 1300.

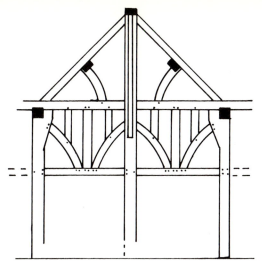

FIG. 18. The Ark, Tadcaster, Yorks; truss at north end of hall. Source as note 52. Dated to the second half of the fifteenth century (p. 6) by a comparison of two roof trusses in northwest wing with some of ca. 1490 in York, for which see J. S. Purvis and E. A. Gee, *St. Anthony's Hall, York* (London, 1953). A better comparison can now be made with the sources cited in note 53, from which it appears that the building may well be dated fully a hundred years earlier.

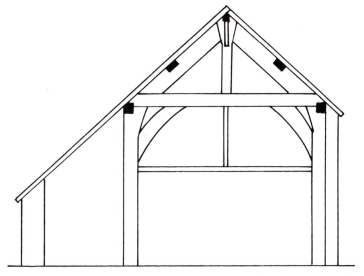

FIG. 19. High Bentley, Shelf, York (W. R.); Atkinson and McDowall, as note 53, figure 6. Dated to the late fourteenth century (p. 81) because a fifteenth-century cross wing is said to have destroyed the west end of the hall; but the evidence is not incompatible with rather later dates.

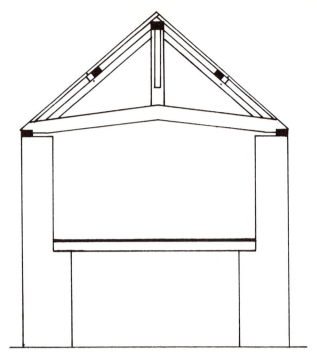

FIG. 20. East Wing, Preston Patrick Hall, Westmorland; based on
R. C. H. M. MS sketch. Dated to ca. 1500, R. C. H. M. *Westmorland* (1936), pp. 195–196.

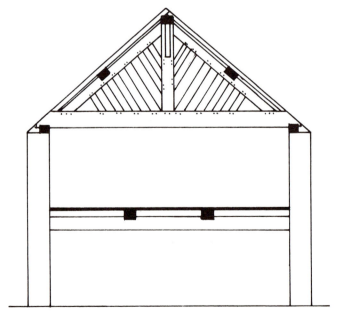

FIG. 21. Priestley Ing, Hebden Royd, Yorks (W. R.). Late sixteenth
century; Stell, note 53, page 14.

window heads,[48] and thereafter the series of truss roofs is unbroken to the end of the Middle Ages. Although the three earliest examples so far published are in Worcestershire, the type has a wide distribution, from Cornwall to Cheshire and as far east as Hampshire and Leicestershire. So far no significant development has been observed in the form of the blades, the number of purlins, or even the provision of wind-braces. Therefore, external criteria, such as moldings, datable features of the supporting walls, or the plan if it is a house, must be used to establish a date for which, at the moment, typology by itself gives hardly any clue.

KING-POST ROOFS

Compared with any of the preceding types, the king-post roof with ridge-piece and side purlins is relatively rare in the Middle Ages and seems to be the last major type to make its appearance. I distinguish king-post roofs of this type, which in northern England are found in churches and houses alike. First, there are those of midland and southern England, which are confined to late medieval churches [49] and are closely allied to cambered- and firred-beam roofs. Second, there are the king posts which are sometimes set upon the yoke or collar of a cruck truss.[50]

A terminus post quem for the origin of the northern king-post type is provided by the recent excavation at Chapel Haddlesey, Yorks, of a large manor house, which had on its long axis a series of shallow holes in which ridge posts stood.[51] This building was dated by pottery to the late twelfth or early thirteenth century. Some two hundred years later a ridge post was still used in the hall of a timber-framed house at Tadcaster, but was incorporated in the wall of a cross wing and stood on a stone base. The middle or open truss had an arch-braced collar beam upon which stood a short king post typical of the end of the Middle Ages.[52] At manorial level, therefore, the king-post roof probably evolved sometime in the thirteenth or fourteenth centuries and by the middle of the fifteenth century had reached the form it retained with only minor modifications

---

[48] Dollman and Jobbins, as n. 45; the building has long been destroyed.

[49] F. E. Howard, "On the Construction of Medieval Roofs," *Archaeol. J. LXXI* (1914), 293–352, esp. figs. 10, 23, 26; Smith (as n. 11), p. 130.

[50] E.g., C. F. Innocent, *The Development of English Building Construction* (Cambridge, 1916), fig. 9.

[51] H. E. Jean le Patourel, summary in *Medieval Archaeol. IX* (1965), 206–207.

[52] E. A. Gee and J. K. Keighley, *The Ark, Tadcaster* (Tadcaster, 1962), p. 11.

for about two hundred years.[53] In this form the king post is braced by principal rafters which carry purlins. The development and chronology of this roof type are expressed in the way the purlins are supported, and in their number. As a matter of fact, the sequence starts with various modes of support for the purlins, including clasping with braces and the use of cleats, until by about the middle of the sixteenth century (and perhaps earlier) when the method of trenching them into the backs of the principals had become standard. So far, however, the typology of these roofs has not been expounded in detail, so that their chronology has to be based on the detail of the buildings with which they are associated.

Conclusions

In the course of the conference Martin Aitken remarked: "I think when one is given a date by an archaeologist it is very difficult to unravel what it is based on." That certainly applies to the dating of medieval roofs, and to a large extent to all medieval buildings. Nevertheless, recent discussion of specific buildings suggests that the accepted chronological scheme may well be broadly correct, with no greater margin of error than that of, say, carbon-14 dating, and often less. This claim is not true of typology by itself, which has severe limitations where the simpler roofs are concerned, but fortunately the vast majority of medieval roofs are in houses where other elements help to refine the dating. The truth of Aitken's remark becomes apparent when it is realized that all these other elements for the most part lack a firmly based chronology, which in the last resort could only be provided by an adequate series of examples with inscribed dates. Lacking them, associative dating, dependent as it is on the critical assessment of the building or roof concerned, must form the foundation for all our typology and chronology. This approach, by the standards of the natural sciences, is perilously imprecise.

The present typological scheme—"system" is too grand a word for it— has been challenged. Sometimes its conclusions have been proved quite wrong, for example—at precisely its weakest point—the dating of barns, which provide hardly any possibility of cross-checking with other features.

The two great barns at Cressing Temple are the extreme case; originally ascribed to 1480 and 1510 respectively,[54] they have been shown by carbon-

---

[53] F. Atkinson and R. W. McDowall, "Aisled Houses in the Halifax Area," *Antiquaries J. XLVII* (1967), 77–94; C. F. Stell, "Pennine Houses. . . ," *Folk-Life 3* (1956), 5–24.
[54] As n. 7.

14 dating to be of ca. 1200 and 1250 respectively.[55] Yet even these errors show only that typology has never been systematized or properly used, for had Willis' dating of the Scxtry Barn [56] been better known, they would not have been made. What is needed now is the systematic study of roofs, especially those which can be dated by nontypological means, while at the same time a firm basis for the dating of moldings and other elements should be sought. The resulting firmer and more precise typology and chronology would probably not differ to a great extent from those used at present, but it is high time to see just how securely based our dating is.

[55] See the papers above by W. Horn and R. Berger.
[56] As n. 14.

XI

THERMOLUMINESCENCE DATING OF
ANCIENT POTTERY

M. J. Aitken

*T*HE BASIC CONCEPT of thermoluminescence dating involves the following facts, some of which are graphically represented in figure 1. The clay fabric of most pottery contains a few parts per million of uranium and thorium and a few percent of potassium. The presence of these natural radioisotopes means that any mineral inclusions in the pottery are subjected to a radiation dosage that is typically one roentgen per year. In the case of certain minerals (e. g., quartz), part of the energy absorbed from this radiation is stored in the crystal lattice by the trapping of electrons in defects. As time goes on the number of trapped electrons grows. An experimental measure of the number of trapped electrons is possible, because if the mineral is heated to several hundred degrees centigrade (about 380°C in the case of a commonly occurring quartz), the electrons are released from their traps (by thermal vibrations) and the energy is emitted in the form of light. This light emission is called *thermoluminescence* and it can be measured accurately by means of a sensitive photomultiplier. Since heating releases the trapped electrons, when ancient man fired raw clay into pottery he unwittingly drained out all the accumulation that had occurred during geological times and started off the growth of "stored thermoluminescence" from zero again. Obviously the amount of thermoluminescence will depend both on the concentrations of uranium, thorium, and potassium present and on the thermoluminescence properties of the mineral inclusions, but as will be seen, each potsherd can be calibrated in these respects and an *absolute* age deduced.

Thermoluminescence is quite distinct from "red-hot glow." The latter light continues to be emitted as long as the elevated temperature is maintained, whereas the former ceases as soon as all electrons have been

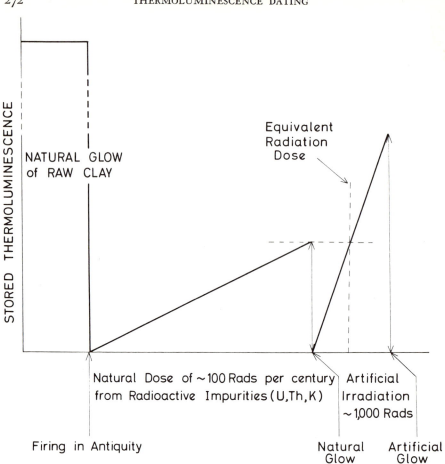

Fɪɢ. ɪ. Basis of T-L dating.

emptied from their traps. The phenomenon has been studied by scientists over the past few hundred years (see, for example, "About a Diamond that Shines in the Dark" by Sir Robert Boyle, 1664),[1] often being described as "cold light," because it can be emitted at a temperature very much below that at which red glow sets in. The color is in fact specific to the mineral and independent of the temperature of emission. The idea of using thermoluminescence for pottery dating was first suggested by Farington Daniels of Wisconsin in 1953 at about the same time as he was developing the application of thermoluminescence for radiation dosimetry—now used widely both in the fields of radiotherapy and radiation

[1] R. Boyle, "About a Diamond that Shines in the Dark," annexed to *Experiments and Considerations Touching Colours* (London: Henry Herringham, 1664).

protection.[2] The feasibility of dating pottery in this way has since been investigated at the universities of Bern, California, Kyoto,[3] Oxford,[4] Pennsylvania,[5] and Wisconsin.[6] The remainder of this article outlines the approach that has been developed at Oxford; this aims to determine absolute ages rather than rely on known-age samples for calibration.

Measurement

A simplified experimental setup for measuring thermoluminescence is shown in figure 2. After grinding up, a weighed portion (typically 15 mg) of the sample is evenly spread over the central area of a nichrome or stainless steel plate (about 0.25 mm thick). This plate is heated by a servo-controlled current of 100 or 200 amps, so that its temperature, which is measured by a thermocouple, rises at a constant, reproducible rate of, say, 20°C per second. The light emitted is detected by a sensitive, low-noise photomultiplier (e.g., E.M.I. Type 6255S) and the output from the photomultiplier is fed, after amplification, to the vertical axis of an X–Y recorder. The horizontal axis is driven by the thermocouple. The resulting plot of light output versus temperature is called a "glow curve."

The intensity of the natural thermoluminescence from pottery is very weak and in order to avoid it being swamped by thermal radiation (red-hot glow) when the temperature gets above 300°C, it is essential to have a heavy blue filter in front of the photomultiplier. Also, in order to suppress nonradiation-induced thermoluminescence (e.g., triboluminescence), it is vital to carry out the heating in an atmosphere of oxygen-free nitrogen. Also, it is important to avoid the exposure of the ground-up sample to light, particularly ultraviolet, as this may cause decay of the thermoluminescence.

It will be noted that in the glow curve shown (fig. 2) there is very little

[2] F. Daniels, D. A. Boyd, and D. F. Saunders, "Thermoluminescence as a Research Tool," *Science 117* (1953), 343–349.

[3] Y. Ichikawa, "Dating of Ancient Ceramics by Thermoluminescence," *Bull. Inst. Chem. Res., Kyoto Univ. 43, 1* (1965), 1–6.

[4] M. J. Aitken, "Thermoluminescence," *Sci. J. 1* (1965), 32–38. M. S. Tite, "Thermoluminescence Dating of Ancient Ceramics: A Reassessment," *Archaeometry 9* (1966), 155–169.

[5] E. K. Ralph and M. C. Han, Dating of Pottery by Thermoluminescence," *Nature 210* (1966), 245–247. See also this volume for more recent paper.

[6] R. B. Mazess and D. W. Zimmerman, "Pottery Dating from Thermoluminescence," *Science 152;* 347–348.

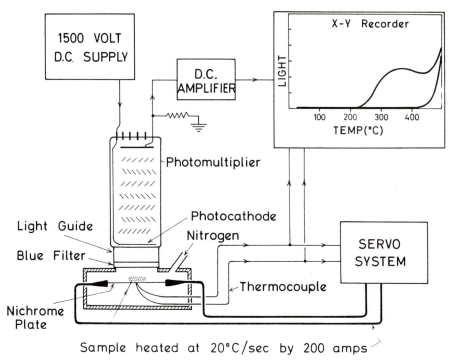

FIG. 2. Outline of apparatus for T-L measurement.

light emitted below about 250°C. This is because the traps that release
their electrons below that temperature are not deep enough to retain
electrons over the centuries of burial. However, the light emitted above,
say, 350°C is due to the release of electrons from traps that are deeper, and
the electrons in these are thought to be stable over time periods well in
excess of 10,000 years. In the preceding discussion of the accumulation of
thermoluminescence it was taken for granted that there were no decay
effects, and this is reasonable as long as it is implicitly understood that we
are talking about the light emitted in the 400°C region of the glow curve.
An experimental check of stability can in fact be made quite simply for
each sample measured. This is by comparing the shape of the "natural"
glow curve with that of the "artificial" glow curve obtained after recent
exposure of the sample to a dose of radiation from a radioisotope source
(see fig. 3). At any temperature the natural thermoluminescence can be
expressed in terms of an "equivalent radiation dose"—effectively the ratio
between the two glow curves with the artificial glow curve normalized to
unit dose. In case 1 of figure 3 the equivalent radiation dose rises to a
plateau above 300°C, and this is evidence that above that temperature de-

cay effects are negligible. In case 2, however, there is no plateau and such a sample must be discarded. The absence of a plateau may also be due to failure to suppress completely the nonradiation-induced thermoluminescence, but in either case there is no justification for accepting the measurement.

In figure 1 the artificial dose is shown as being applied to a sample from which the natural thermoluminescence had been drained. In practice it is found that the heating of a sample may cause changes in sensitivity (probably due to mineralogical changes), and it is more reliable to apply the artificial dose to a second, undrained portion of the material and obtain the "artificial" glow curve by subtraction of the "natural" glow curve observed from the first portion.

A variety of techniques are available for determination of the uranium, thorium, and potassium contents of the potsherd. The ones presently employed have the merit of simplicity: the radiation dose rate from uranium and thorium is calculated from a determination of the alpha activity using the technique described by Turner et al.[7] and the potassium content is determined by chemical analysis. Alpha counting is to be preferred for the uranium and thorium rather than chemical analysis in order to avoid gross errors due to possible disequilibrium of the uranium series in glacial and postglacial clays.

Radiation Attenuation Effects

A major part of the thermoluminescence observed from a ground-up sample of potsherd comes from mineral inclusions, and study so far has been concentrated on pottery in which these inclusions are quartz. The diameters of these inclusions may exceptionally be as much as several millimeters but are commonly in the range of several hundred microns. Since the uranium and thorium is carried in the clay matrix in which these inclusions are embedded rather than in the inclusions themselves, the alpha particles from these radioisotopes, having ranges between 20 and 50 microns, reach only a thin surface layer of the inclusions. Since 90 percent of the radiation dose from uranium and thorium is carried by alpha particles, the effective average dose received by an inclusion is very much less than that received by the fine grains of the clay matrix. Furthermore, the average dose is dependent on the size of the inclusion. This

[7] R. C. Turner, J. M. Radley, and W. V. Mayneord, *Brit. J. Radiology 368* (1958), 397–404.

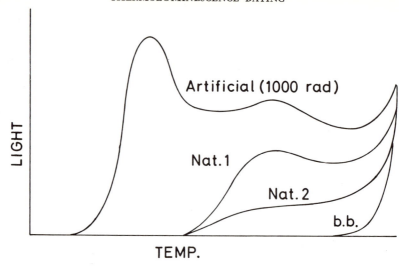

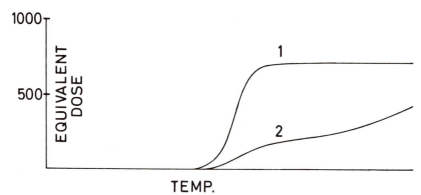

Fig. 3. The "plateau" test: (*a*) Glow curves, (*b*) ratio of ordinates in (*a*) for case 1—good plateau and case 2—no plateau.

difficulty is met in two ways (Fleming,[8] Zimmerman [9]). The first, which can be loosely called "inclusion dating," is by separating out the inclusions (using heavy liquid and magnetic separation techniques) and selecting (by sieving) only those grains in the size range 100 to 200 microns. Such grains are big enough for the average alpha-particle dose to be negligible but not big enough for attenuation of the beta-particle dose to be significant. The natural and artificial glow curves are measured for this selected fraction and the equivalent radiation dose obtained as illustrated

[8] S. J. Fleming, Study of Thermoluminescence of Crystalline Extracts from Pottery, *Archaeometry 9* (1966), 170–173.

[9] D. W. Zimmerman, "Thermoluminescence from Fine Grains from Ancient Pottery," *Archaeometry 10* (1967), 26.

in figure 3. The age is calculated by dividing the equivalent radiation dose by the beta- and gamma-radiation dose rate as determined by the uranium, thorium, and potassium measurements, the alpha contribution being ignored.

The second method is complementary to the first. Only grains fine enough for attenuation of the alpha contribution to be negligible are selected—in the range 1 to 5 microns diameter. The equivalent radiation dose is measured as before, but in calculating the age the alpha-particle contribution is included in the dose rate. It is important, however, to make allowance for reduced effectiveness of alpha particles relative to beta and gamma radiation in inducing thermoluminescence—by a factor of about 0.2 for the same amount of absorbed energy.

Environmental Radiation

Although the gamma rays are responsible for only a minor part of the total radiation dose rate, when as in "inclusion dating" the alpha-particle contribution is discarded, the gamma rays provide nearly half of the effective dose rate. Because gamma rays are highly penetrating, the gamma dose comes from the surrounding soil rather than the potsherd itself, and consequently it is necessary to assess the radioactive content of the environment in which the sherd has been buried. To some extent this is also the case for fine-grain dating because of the poor effectiveness of alpha particles in inducing thermoluminescence. In both cases, too, the cosmic-ray contribution may become significant. The situation for a typical pot in typical soil is shown in figure 4. This assumes that the radioactive content of the soil is the same as that of the potsherd. In practice this is not always the case, and it is necessary to obtain a sample of burial soil for analysis and assess the gamma-ray dose rate on this basis.

This is a satisfactory procedure as long as the potsherd has been buried in a uniform layer of soil which accumulated rapidly enough to have been a foot thick for the major part of the burial time (nearly all the gamma-ray dose is contributed by soil within a foot distance). However, actual archaeological situations are often much more complex. For a start there may be no certainty as to the length of time a foot-thick layer of soil has covered the sherd, and so the gamma dose rate is correspondingly indeterminate. Further, there may be several types of soil or rock within a foot of the sherd, or the sherd may have been partially buried in a heap of fallen rubble and brickwork. Unless all these have the same radioactive content, it is impossible to make an accurate calculation of the dose rate,

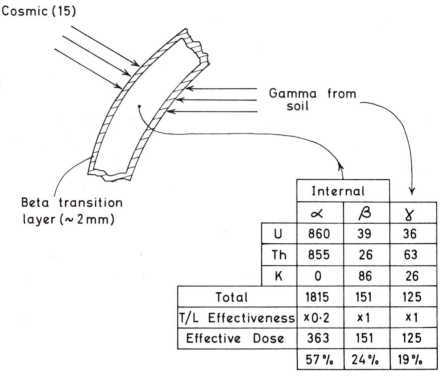

Annual Potsherd Dosage (millirads)

for pot and soil containing :–
U : 3 ppM, Th : 12 ppM, K : 1% .

Cosmic (15)

Gamma from soil

Beta transition layer (~ 2 mm)

	Internal		
	α	β	γ
U	860	39	36
Th	855	26	63
K	0	86	26
Total	1815	151	125
T/L Effectiveness	×0·2	×1	×1
Effective Dose	363	151	125
	57%	24%	19%

Fɪɢ. 4. Typical annual radiation dose (in millirads) for buried potsherd.

except in very simple situations. Consequently, scrutiny of the burial situation and firm rejection where appropriate are necessary if the best accuracy in dating is to be attained. On-site measurements of the radio-activity are very useful in this context: if these show that the radioactivities of the various materials surrounding a potsherd are all similar, then a complex situation is acceptable. Another technique used is to bury a thermoluminescence dosimeter (e.g., natural calcium fluoride in exactly the same situation as that from which the potsherd was taken; present-day dosimeter materials have a thermoluminescence sensitivity nearly a million times that of typical pottery), so that a precise determination of the gamma-ray dose can be obtained in a few weeks' burial.

The foregoing considerations automatically exclude already-excavated sherds from the possibility of accurate dating, but from experience it seems that a precision approaching ± 20 percent can be achieved despite uncertainty about the burial conditions. Of course, the uncertainty is worse with inclusion dating than with fine-grain dating, and also, as it is dependent on the radioactive content, it is difficult to make any hard and fast estimate of the uncertainty until the measurements have been carried out.

General Assessment of Method

A test of the two techniques is at present in progress, using a wide variety of fabric types of known-age pot from well-defined burial conditions in current excavations. Preliminary results suggest a precision of ± 10 percent may be attainable. For various reasons, mainly concerned with further uncertainties in the assessment of the radiation dose rate, it is not to be expected that either technique will give a better precision than ± 5 percent.

In comparison with the radiocarbon method, thermoluminescence has two advantages: first, it is applicable to a commoner archaeological material, and second, the measured signal is larger for older objects. On the other hand, because the information is stored at the atomic level rather than in the nucleus, one feels that it is inherently more vulnerable to outside influences.

XII

POTENTIAL OF THERMOLUMINESCENCE IN
SUPPLEMENTING RADIOCARBON FOR
DATING IN THE MIDDLE AGES

M. C. Han and E. K. Ralph

*T*HERE IS NO question of the importance of radiocarbon dating nor of its tremendous contribution to archaeology and geochronology. For dating in the Renaissance and medieval periods, however, one may point out a few weaknesses, among them the fact that the technique usually cannot date ceramics directly.

Furthermore, most dating techniques are least precise at the limits of their ranges. For carbon-14, with a range of more than 40,000 years, the period of interest to this conference covers only 700 years, or roughly 1.7 percent of this span. Therefore, in this comparatively modern period, in which maximum precision is desired, percentagewise, it is difficult to attain.

It has now been established from measurements of samples of known age that there may have been minor fluctuations in the inventory of carbon-14 in past times. These fluctuations and their possible causes have been published [1] and are being discussed in other papers presented at this conference. The most pronounced fluctuation is the long-term one which has been noted in the first millennium B.C. and continues back in time to the present limit of dendrochronologically dated samples, to the fifth millennium B.C. In addition to this long-period deviation from steady-state carbon-14 inventories, however, there appear to be some shorter-term fluctuations. One of the most pronounced of these occurs in the period of A.D. 1700 to 1500. As one may see in figure 1, these fluctuations are of

---

[1] References to these publications are contained in E. K. Ralph, H. N. Michael, and J. Gruninger, Jr., in *Radiocarbon 7* (1965), 179–186.

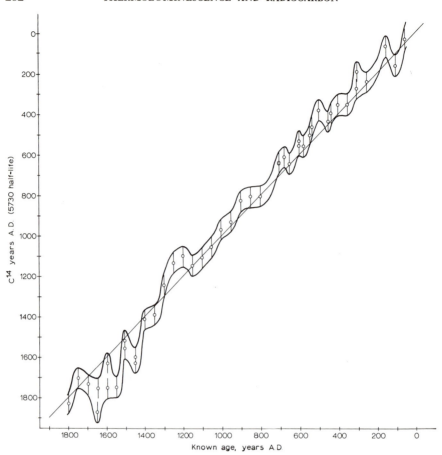

Fig. 1. Radiocarbon dates for tree-ring samples of known age (University of Pennsylvania Radiocarbon Laboratory).

sufficient magnitude to cause ambiguity for dating as large as up to 200 years. This and the next consideration may be observed more clearly in the regression curve seen in figure 2.[2]

Prior to A.D. 1300 the short-term fluctuations, if statistically significant, are much smaller, but on the *average,* from A.D. 1300 to the beginning of the Christian era, carbon-14 dates tend to be slightly earlier than known ages. The difference happens to be about 3 percent in "before present" ages, which is equal to the difference between ages calculated with the Libby half-life of 5568 years and the new value of 5730 years. Whether or not this is a coincidence or whether it reflects the uncertainty in the true

[2] We are indebted to R. Stuckenrath for his contribution in the preparation of the regression curve.

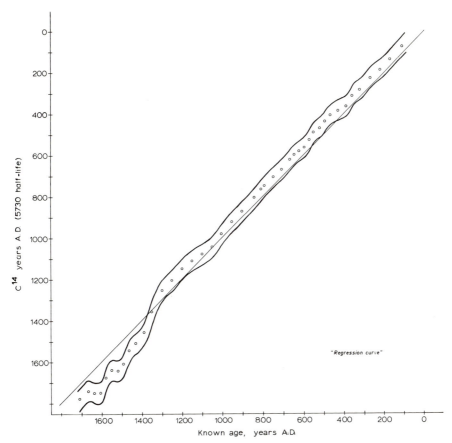

FIG. 2. Regression-smoothed plot of radiocarbon dates for tree-ring samples of known age (University of Pennsylvania Radiocarbon Laboratory).

value of the half-life cannot be resolved by natural radiocarbon dating alone, since this measurement is dependent also upon the constancy of the carbon-14 inventory. But, at the moment, we can say that for the time span of A.D. 1300 to the beginning of the Christian era, carbon-14 ages calculated with the 5568 half-life value are in better agreement with known ages.

One of the most serious handicaps encountered in radiocarbon dating can be the fact that the sample is related to the age of the artifact or occupation of interest by association only. The accuracy of the association is therefore mainly dependent upon the skill and attention of the excavator. This accuracy is especially important for the comparatively recent Renaissance and medieval periods for which the evidence tends to be buried less deeply. An error of a few centimeters in stratigraphic inter-

pretation could cause a significant error in the precise relationship of associated materials. It is in this category that thermoluminescence dating
of pottery has one obvious advantage—the artifact itself is dated.

Another fortunate circumstance for the application of thermoluminescence is that pottery was used universally throughout the ages back to
about 7000 B.C. A minor point that might be mentioned, too, is that pottery
is fragile so that there is less likelihood that the sample to be dated was
used for many centuries prior to its final deposition. In contrast, in carbon-
14 dating, when it is possible to date the artifact itself, it may be a piece of
a large beam of a structure, plank of a ship, or similar material. Not only
may there be the danger that the beam was reused, but it may have been
originally a very large beam from which the outer growth layers, the ones
contemporaneous with the time of construction, have disappeared.

Thermoluminescence dating, now in its infancy, has also inherent weaknesses and difficulties. Its potential is based upon the fact that it provides
an entirely independent means of dating, and that it is applicable to
pottery and other fired ceramics—objects found commonly by archaeologists and inherently most of the time unsuitable for direct radiocarbon
dating.

Development of the Method

The suggestion that thermoluminescence might provide a means of
dating pottery was made by Farrington Daniels[3] and also by F. G.
Houtermans[4] some years ago. The technique was investigated further by
George Kennedy[5] and is now being engaged in actively at the Applied
Science Center for Archaeology at the University Museum, University of
Pennsylvania, the University of California at Los Angeles, and Oxford
University.

Thermoluminescence in pottery is due to the fact that radiations from
the traces of radioactive elements in pottery bombard the other constituents of the clays and raise electrons to metastable levels. When the pottery
is heated, such as in firing, each electron falls back to its stable position
and emits a photon of light. On being reheated, the amount of thermoluminescence observed is, therefore, representative of the accumulated radia-

---

[3] F. Daniels, C. A. Boyd, and D. F. Saunders, in *Science 117* (1953), 349.
[4] F. G. Houtermans, E. Jager, M. Schon, and H. Stauffer, in *Ann. d. Physik 20*
(1957), 283.
[5] G. Kennedy and L. Knopff, in *Archaeology 13* (1960), 147.

tion damage and hence of the time elapsed since the original firing of the pottery.

$$\text{Age} = k \, \frac{(\text{N-TL})}{(a) \, (\text{A-TL})} \qquad (\text{Eq. 1}),$$

where

    N-TL = natural thermoluminescence,

        a = relative radioactive content in pottery, determined by counting the rate of alpha disintegration,

    A-TL = artificial thermoluminescence or the susceptibility of pottery to radiation damage, measured in terms of the thermoluminescence induced by subjecting the sample to a fixed dose of radiation, and

        k = proportionality constant.

Once an object has been heated to a temperature of 400° to 500°C and its electrons have emitted their thermoluminescent light, no further light may be obtained by reheating after a relatively short time. Consequently, recently fired ceramic ware or freshly cooled lava, both of which have all electrons in stable sites, should show no thermoluminescence.

The basic principle is, therefore, straightforward, but there are a number of uncertainties that must be investigated or circumvented before it can be definitely stated that thermoluminescence will provide a means of dating pottery. Some of the major uncertainties are as follows:

1)   Is the radiation damage caused primarily by a bombardment, or is it a combination of a, β, and γ particles?

2)   How many metastable electrons are lost, especially near the surface, during the passage of time?

3)   How, and how much, do the susceptibilities of clay to radiation damage vary?

4)   How do the differing transparencies of clays affect the detection of the photons emitted on heating?

5)   Does the bombardment from radioactivities in soils cause significant radiation damage to potsherds from external sources?

6)   What is the effect of grinding the pieces of pottery, a necessary preliminary to thermoluminescent detection?

Our first concern has been to assemble apparatus sufficiently sensitive and reliable to make a quantity of measurements. Initially, instruments were obtained from the Department of Physics, but they have gradually been replaced with more appropriate components with funds from the National Science Foundation.

Experimental Procedure [6]

Samples of pottery are received usually in the form of fragments, and are cataloged and washed. The grinding of each sample is done in the following fashion: Approximately 10 to 15 grams of clean potsherds are crushed to a size below 30 mesh and are then placed in a small ball mill and ground to less than 200 mesh. Experiments with prebaked samples have demonstrated that the thermoluminescence induced by the grinding is negligible. Also, we have found that exposure to light causes no effect.

A portion of the ground sample is used to measure its relative radio-activity. We have assumed that the major radiation damage is caused by α bombardment or is proportional to it, and have, therefore, constructed special low-background zinc sulphide screens and associated components for this low-level detection of α particles. The α emissions are counted in infinitely thick layers with the result that comparative values only are obtained.

For the detection of the thermoluminescent photons emitted on heating, our preliminary experiments indicated that rapid heating rates of thin layers of powdered potsherds would allow detection of the maximum light output. Since the accumulation of metastable electrons is very small, high sensitivity is required to detect the light output in the visible range.

The apparatus for detection of thermoluminescence is shown below in figure 3.

Samples are mounted on a 3 by 3 inch square of heavy duty aluminum foil by means of the silk screen technique. This is done by mixing a portion of the ground sample with a carrier, silicone oil [7] which is both chemically and thermally stable up to 600°C and which helps to produce a thin uniform layer on the foil. The size of the sample deposited on the foil is ¾ of an inch in diameter. (This size was dictated by the area that can be heated uniformly by our furnace.) The foil on which the powdered pottery is mounted is pressed into the sample holder with the sample facing

[6] Most of this procedure was described by E. K. Ralph and M. C. Han, in *Nature* *210*, 245–247. Since then (16 April 1966) the main improvement has been the installation of the linearly programmed heating control system. The main advantage of precise linear heating is that a given temperature peak of a glow curve will occur always in the same position on the temperature axis of the X–Y recorder, as well as the fact that the reproducibility of replicate runs is improved greatly.

[7] A type of silicone oil which we have found suitable is Duxe Silicone (500 centistokes) made by Duxe Products, Cincinnati, Ohio.

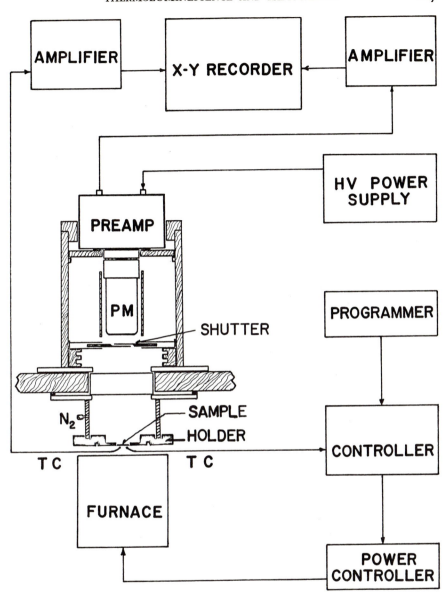

FIG. 3. Block diagram of the glow curve apparatus.

upward, and the back side of the foil is coated with a layer of graphite for maximum heat absorption. The holder is then placed on the furnace and is heated linearly in a nitrogen atmosphere by means of a programmed control system from a temperature of 70° up to 450°C. Two thermocouples are located in direct contact under the back side of the foil, one for the purpose of recording the temperature and the other for the feed-back of the control system. The light emitted during this process is detected by the photomultiplier tube. The signal from the photomultiplier and that from one of the thermocouples are fed into two separate ampli-fiers and are recorded on the X–Y axis recorder. This produces the so-called glow curve, which in this case is the natural thermoluminescence (N-TL) produced by the potsherd. About 20 replicate measurements are made for each given potsherd in order to obtain a more representative result. The standard statistical deviation among these 20 now averages from 5 to 7 percent.

The way to obtain a measure of the susceptibility of a potsherd to radiation damage is by the application of an external dose from a source with much greater intensity than the natural bombardment. If one subjects different potsherds to the same dose of artificial radiation, then the result of their glow curves, or their light intensities yielded upon heating, is an indication of their susceptibility to the radiation.

We have found that even though replicate samples were taken from a single piece of pottery that had been ground and mixed thoroughly, there were variations on the order of from 5 to 7 percent. This indicated that the corrections obtained by artificial bombardment should be applied to the identical samples that were measured for natural thermoluminescence. Fortunately, our mounting technique with silicone oil on aluminum foil allows this to be done easily. Therefore, each labeled sample is heated and measured for natural thermoluminescence and it is then bombarded with X-rays (for 60 seconds at 30 kV and 12.7 m amp). After this the artificial glow curve (A-TL) is obtained by reheating the sample. The peak height of this glow curve is used as a correction factor for each individual measurement. Examples of the natural thermoluminescence and artificial thermoluminescence glow curves are shown in figure 4.

Finally, after the rate of a bombardment, the natural thermolumi-nescence, and the artificial thermoluminescence have been obtained, one may calculate the value of the specific thermoluminescence of the given potsherd as follows:

$$\text{Sp.TL} = \frac{\bar{R}}{a} \tag{Eq. 2},$$

where

Sp.TL = specific thermoluminescence
$\bar{R}$ = the average ratio of (N-TL) to (A-TL).

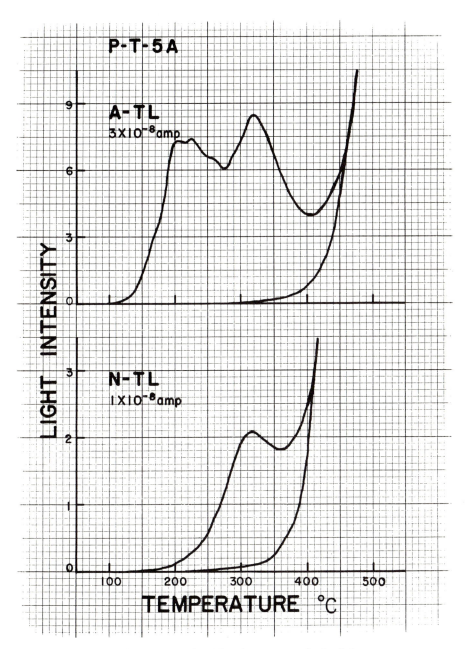

Fig. 4. Examples of the N-TL and A-TL glow curves obtained from measurements of sample P-T-5*A*.

Results and Discussion

The results from X-ray bombardment show that the amount of light intensity emitted is directly proportional to the dose received. Figures 5 and 6 show the results of a pottery sample irradiated with X-rays for different lengths of time.

If one subjects all samples to a fixed dose of X-rays, then one can see that the ratio of natural thermoluminescence to artificial thermoluminescence is an indication of the radiation damage caused by the natural process accumulated through time. Therefore, the specific thermoluminescence of a given sample is directly proportional to its archaeological age, as indicated in equation 1.

For age calibration there are two possible approaches. One is to determine the age directly from the ratio of natural thermoluminescence and natural irradiation multiplied by the inverse ratio of artificial thermoluminescence and irradiation dose as shown below:

$$\text{Age} = \frac{\text{N-TL}}{\text{I}_\text{N}} \times \frac{\text{I}_\text{A}}{\text{A-TL}} \qquad \text{(Eq. 3)},$$

where

I_N and I_A = natural and artificial irradiations, respectively.

This might be considered an absolute calibration, but there is a serious difficulty, namely, that it is not now possible to measure the inherent radioactivity (plus possibly also the contribution from external surroundings) with precision. There is the problem of evaluating the effectiveness of the different types of radiations, α, β, and γ, as well as the actual measurement of these extremely low-level radioactivities.

Fortunately, there is another means of age calibration, namely, using samples of known age. This method may be considered an indirect approach but all factors may be measured with greater precision. The specific thermoluminescence (eq. 2) is determined for each sample of known age, and this value is then plotted versus its known age as shown in figures 7 and 8. The slope of the line drawn through the average values of these determinations then provides the proportionality constant k in equation 1, and the ages of samples of unknown age may then be calculated.

In both figures 7 and 8, the age-calibration line is based upon the samples from A.D. 300 to 800 B.C., that is, those which have been dated firmly by archaeology. The earlier ones are plotted as samples of known age but the ages of these are dependent upon carbon-14 dates of asso-

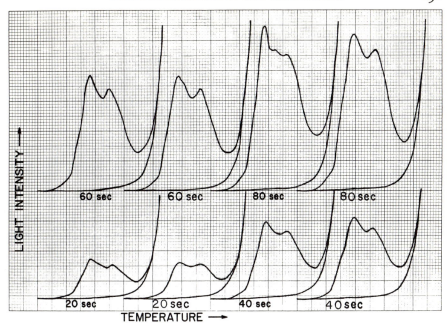

FIG. 5. Artificial glow curves obtained after irradiation with X-rays for different lengths of time.

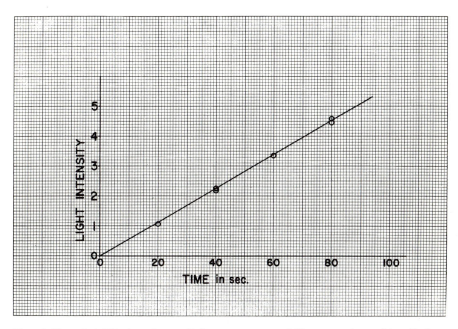

FIG. 6. Plot of A-TL (maximum light output at 320°C) versus time of irradiation.

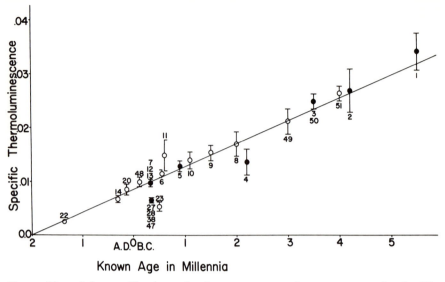

FIG. 7. Plot of the specific thermoluminescence versus known-age samples (1966).

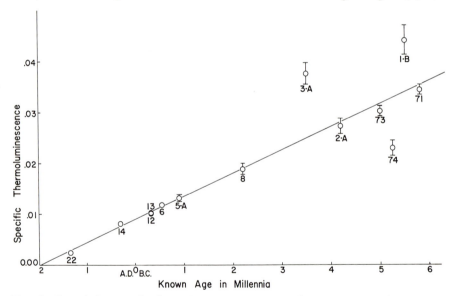

FIG. 8. Plot of the specific thermoluminescence versus known-age samples (1967).

ciated samples. In figure 7 a more complete picture of our measurements of samples of known age is presented than in figure 8. These were made during 1965–66[8] before the installation of our linear programmed heat-

[8] E. K. Ralph and M. C. Han, to be published in the Proceedings of the NATO-USAF Advanced Research Institute on Applications of Thermoluminescence to Geological Problems (1966).

ing system (in March 1967). Even though incomplete, we have shown the data in figure 8 for purposes of comparison. In both figures good agreement is noted between specific thermoluminescence and known ages for samples later than 2500 B.C. For samples earlier than 2500 B.C. there exist the problems of larger uncertainties as well as some scattering of the so-called known-age samples dated by carbon-14 through association only. The scatter appears to be larger in figure 8, but we should like to point out that not all of the sherds for which the average values were plotted in figure 7 have yet been remeasured. (See, for example, numbers 1, 2, and 3.) At this time, the important difference that we note between figures 7 and 8 is the significant improvement in the uncertainty of each measurement as shown by the shorter lengths of the lines representative of the standard statistical deviations. The ages of most samples may now be determined with a precision of ± 200 years.

Although not shown in the figures, pottery made in the past several centuries can be dated with this method, provided that a sufficient amount of natural thermoluminescence can be detected. A few specific examples are as follows:

1) Several supposedly Etruscan statuettes were found to be not earlier than A.D. 1850.[9] These figures emitted natural glow curves but because of their high inherent radioactivity were proved to be of very young age.

2) A tile from Rome,[10] purportedly of classical origin, was dated to be approximately A.D. 1700 and, therefore, probably of the Renaissance period. This tile contained normal radioactivity but, as revealed in its artificial glow curve, was highly susceptible to radiation damage. It therefore was capable of accumulating a sufficient amount of metastable electrons within a relatively short time and could be dated.

These results indicate that there is a good possibility that thermoluminescence will provide a useful dating method for the Renaissance and medieval periods.

[9] Ellen L. Kohler, *Expedition* 9, 2 (1967), 16–21.

[10] The tile sample was submitted by H. B. VanderPoel, and was found in cooperation with Frank E. Brown of Yale University at an excavation within Paul III's cupola in the Church of S. Maria in Aracoeli upon the Capitoline Hill in 1963 at a depth of 4.20 meters.

XIII

TEPHROCHRONOLOGY AND MEDIEVAL ICELAND

S. Thorarinsson

$\mathcal{E}$VERY STUDENT of geology or geomorphology who aims at a quantitative knowledge of geological and geomorphological processes is in need of a time scale, the more exact one the better. The dating methods most successfully applied in postglacial geology, before the carbon-14 method, were G. De Geer's varve chronology, dating back to 1884 and called by him geochronology, a term that should now be used in a collective sense, A. E. Douglass's tree-ring method or dendrochronology, which goes back to 1901, and L. von Post's pollen analysis or palynology, worked out during the second decade of this century. These three methods have in common that they were invented in areas where the possibilities of putting them into practice were very favorable. In central Sweden, where De Geer and von Post worked out their methods, the sections of varve clay suitable for varve measuring are abundant, and this part of Sweden is a border zone between coniferous forests and hardwood forests, so that the climatic changes are clearly reflected by the tree-pollen spectrum in the peat bogs. Douglass's tree-ring method was applied in areas where the climatic conditions determining the growth of trees are rather simple, as the growth in those areas is mainly influenced by a single climatic factor, the precipitation.

But when I as a young and optimistic student of Quaternary geology in 1934 began to put these methods into practice in my homeland, Iceland, two of which I had learned from their Swedish inventors, I found that their application in Iceland presented considerable difficulties. At that time pollen analysis was mainly based on tree pollen. But the only trees in the recent woods of Iceland are birch and some scattered mountain ashes and aspens and it soon turned out that no other species of trees had survived the last glaciation. Further, I found that subglacial and subaerial volcanic activity during the recession of the inland ice cover had disturbed the melting of the ice so as to make the connection of varve diagrams very difficult. But I also found that the volcanism in my country, one of the most volcanically active in the world, offered facilities for establishing a chronology which I have called tephrochronology, a term demanding some explanation. During a volcanic eruption the magma will leave the vent mainly in two ways, either flowing as lava or airborne as pyroclastic ejecta. These ejecta diminish in size with the increasing distance from the volcano. At a great distance from its source a layer of volcanic ejecta will consist of sand or dust, usually called volcanic ash, but near the volcano the same layer will consist mainly of coarse pumice and volcanic bombs. When I wrote my doctoral thesis in 1944 I realized that a collective term for airborne material was needed. It appeared difficult to use "volcanic ejecta" or "pyroclasts" in compound words. Since I did not want to apply the term "volcanic ash" as a collective one, because it is commonly used for a limited grain-size fraction of the volcanic ejecta, the most suitable term appeared to be the Greek word *tephra*. This word means ash, but in one of the oldest existing descriptions of a volcanic eruption, by Aristotle in his *Meteorologica,* giving an account of an eruption on the island Hiera (Vulcano) among the Lipari Islands, he uses the term "tephra" for the volcanic ash that fell on the island and even reached the Italian mainland.[1] This term fits phonetically well with the terms "magma" and "lava," although lava is Sicilian. Tephrochronology is thus a chronology based on the identification and dating of tephra layers.

Every wholly or partly volcanic eruption leaves on the ground a more or less extensive layer of tephra. In extreme cases these layers may spread over enormous areas. Tephra from the eruption of Mount Mazama about 6000 years ago, which gave birth to Crater Lake in Oregon, mantled much of the northwestern United States and adjacent parts of Canada.[2] The tephra layer from the Krakatoa eruption of 1883 covered an area of 827,000 km^2 and the finest dust went all around the earth.[3] Similarly, the tephra from an eruption of Santorini about 1450 B.C. covers about 200,000 km^2.[4] Tephra from the eruption of Quizapú in Chile in 1932 was sampled

[1] Aristotle, Meteorologicorum Liber II. Cap. VIII, *Bibl. Script. Graec. 6,* vol. III (Paris, 1885).

[2] R. E. Wilcox, "Volcanic-ash Chronology," in *The Quaternary of the United States,* H. E. Wright and D. G. Frey, eds. (Princeton, 1965), pp. 807–816.

[3] M. Neumann van Padang, *Catalogue of the Active Volcanoes of the World I,* Indonesia (1951).

[4] D. Ninkovich and B. C. Heezen, "Santorini Tephra," *Colston Papers XVII* (Butterworth's Scientific Publications, London, 1965), pp. 413–453.

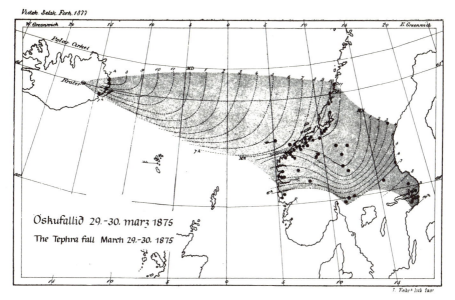

Vidsk. Selsk. Forh. 1877

Oskufallið 29.-30. marz 1875

The Tephra fall March 29.-30. 1875

J. Fehr's lith fast.

FIG. 1. The tephra sector of the Askja eruption 28–29 March 1875. The broken lines are isochrones for the beginning of the tephra fall (from *Mohn*, 1877).

in Rio de Janeiro 3170 km northwest of the volcano.[5] On 30 March 1875, the light of the gas lamps in the streets of Stockholm was obscured by falling dust from the eruption of Askja in Iceland, which erupted on the morning of March 29 (fig. 1). The distance between Askja and Stockholm is about 1900 km. Tephra thrown out from the summit crater of Hekla on the morning of 29 March 1947, was sampled in Finnish Karelia, north of Ladoga, having been transported about 4200 km in the highest strata of the troposphere.[6]

Where the tephra layers have not been stripped off by wind or water, but covered by subsequent soil formation, they appear as more or less distinct horizons in the soil profiles (figs. 6, 17, 21). Owing to their (geologically speaking) instantaneous formation and their frequent very wide dispersal, coupled with usually inconsiderable thickness and characteristic appearance, these layers satisfy every claim as good geological

---

[5] W. Larsson, "Vulkanische Asche vom Ausbruch des Chilenischen Vulkans Quizapú (1932) in Argentina gesammelt," *Bull. Geol. Inst. Uppsala XXVI* (1937), 27–52.

[6] M. Salmi, "The Hekla Ashfalls in Finland A.D. 1947," *C. R. Soc. Geol., Finlande XXI* (1948), 87–96; S. Thorarinsson, "The Tephra-fall from Hekla on March 29th, 1947," *The Eruption of Hekla II, 3* (1954), 1–68. H. Mohn, "Askeregnen den 29de–30te Marts 1875," *Christiania Vidensk. Selsk. Forh., No. 10* (1877), 1–12.

horizons. When exactly dated they are excellent time-stratigraphic markers for archaeology, geology, and geomorphology.

If one uses a widely distributed tephra layer as a chronological key bed, various kinds of human remains such as pottery, tools, farm sites, etc., that are situated just below or above such a layer can be treated as being of approximately the same age even if the artifacts are spaced far apart from one another laterally. The identification of tephra layers in the field is achieved in many ways: by their stratigraphic relation; their color, which in turn is indicative of their chemical composition (fig. 3); and their grain size and thickness, which is up to a certain limit an exponential function of distance from their source. In the laboratory they are identified by determination of their mineralogical, chemical, and physical characteristics such as refractive index of the glass, optical characteristics of phenocrysts, chemical composition, trace elements, etc.[7] The glass shards which are the predominant constituents of most tephra layers, at least at a great distance from their source, have a very characteristic appearance (fig. 2). As for age determinations of tephra layers, those deposited in historical times can often be identified as resulting from eruptions mentioned in written records and can thus be dated more or less accurately according to the accuracy of the records concerned, which in some cases are exact even to the day of the tephra fall.

Eruptions in the Mediterranean dated by written records go back to nearly 700 b.c., but the oldest datings can hardly be regarded as exact.[8] In Japan eruptions mentioned in written records go back about 1300 years and in Iceland to Settlement Time, nearly 1100 years ago. Arab geographers of the Middle Ages mention an eruption in Kaulet Hattab in Yemen which occurred between a.d. 400 and 600.[9] In the Western hemisphere

---

[7] R. E. Wilcox, "Volcanic-ash Chronology," in *The Quaternary of the United States,* H. E. Wright and D. G. Frey, eds. (Princeton, 1965), pp. 807–816; S. Thorarinsson, "Tefrokronologiska studier på Island" (English summary: "Tephrochronological Studies in Iceland"), *Geogr. Ann. Stockh.* (1944), pp. 1–217; S. Thorarinsson, "The Tephra-Fall from Hekla on March 29th 1947," *The Eruption of Hekla 1947–1948 II, 3* (1954), 1–68; R. E. Wilcox and H. A. Powers, "Petrographic Characteristics of Recent Pumice from Volcanoes in the Cascade Range" (Abstr.), *Geol. Soc. Ann. Spec. Pap.* (1964), p. 76; J. Tómasson, "Mineralogical and Petrographical Classification of Icelandic Tephra Layers," *The Eruption of Hekla 1947–1948 I* (1967), 171–183.

[8] G. Imbo, *Catalogue of the Active Volcanoes of the World XVIII* (1965).

[9] M. Neumann van Padang, *Catalogue of the Active Volcanoes of the World XVI, Arabia and the Indian Ocean* (1963).

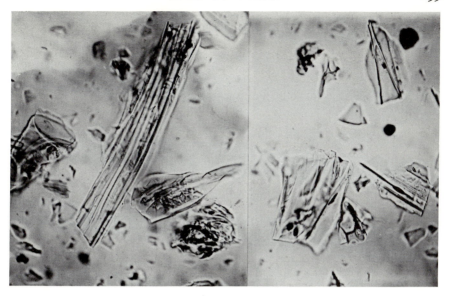

FIG. 2. Tephra (ash) from the Askja eruption 28–29 March 1875, collected in Särna in Dalecarlia, Sweden, 30 March 1875. Magnific. 280✕ (photo: S. Thorarinsson).

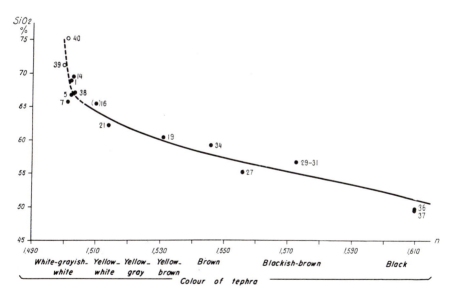

FIG. 3. Relation between SiO_2–content and refractive index of glass and the color of Icelandic tephra.

eruptions dated by written records reach into the fifteenth century (eruption in Atitlan in Guatemala, 1468).[10]

Tephra layers from the oldest eruptions thus recorded in the literature have not yet been identified. In Italy the oldest one recorded and identified is that of the Monte Somma (Vesuvius) eruption of A.D. 79, in Iceland, the Hekla tephra of A.D. 1104. In Japan a layer on the island of Oshima has been identified as tephra from an eruption of A.D. 838 or 886.[11] In other countries the oldest historically recorded and as yet identified tephra layers are much more recent. But the approximate absolute age of a tephra layer can be determined by many other means such as by carbon-14 dating, dendrochronology, pollen analysis, rate of sedimentation, and last but not least with the aid of archaeology.

Tephrochronology in Iceland

In Iceland between 150 and 200 volcanoes have been active during the last 10,000 years, about 30 of which since Nordic settlement began about A.D. 870 (fig. 4). The number of eruptions that have occurred since then is probably about 200. Some of these eruptions have been nearly or wholly effusive or lava producing and have thus formed no tephra layers, but many have been partly or wholly explosive. The most widespread layers are acid (rhyolitic and rhyodacitic) and intermediate (dacitic and andesitic). They are light or brownish in color, and originate from Iceland's few active central volcanoes. Yet some basalt volcanoes, which under normal conditions would mainly produce lava, have yielded large amounts of black basalt tephra as they are covered by glaciers and the contact of the magma with meltwater can cause phreato-magmatic explosions.

The main contributor of tephra layers in Iceland, that have already been dated, is the country's most famous volcano, Hekla, and some words about my tephrochronological study of its eruptions in historical times may exemplify tephrochronological field methods.

Petrogenetically Hekla belongs to central volcanoes with highly differentiated eruption products. Each of its eruptions starts with a violently explosive Plinian phase. Even if the eruption lasts a year or more and

[10] K. von Seebach, "Über die Vulkane Centralamerikas," *Abh. König. Ges. d. Wiss. Göttingen 38* (1892).

[11] K. Nakamura, "Stratigraphic Studies of the Pyroclastics of Oshima Volcano, Izu I. Cyclic Activity of 'Main Craters' and the Absolute Chronology of Pyroclastic Sediments," *Sci. Papers Coll. Gener. Educ. Univ. Tokyo 10, 1,* 125–145.

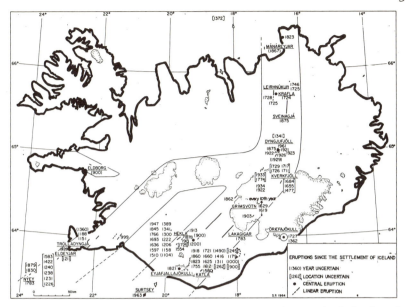

Fig. 4. Map showing the zones of postglacially active volcanoes in Iceland and the volcanoes active since Settlement Time.

produces lava and tephra most of the time, the bulk of the tephra is produced during the first day or even during the first few hours. Thus the main tephra sector of each eruption is rather narrow. By measuring in soil profiles all around the volcano the depth, thickness, and maximum grain size of the tephra layers (fig. 5), and also by noting the color and other characteristics of the layers observable in the field (fig. 6), the individual sectors of Hekla tephra can be discerned. The direction of their axis of maximum thickness is the same as the wind direction above the volcano during the tephra-producing initial phase of the formation. By following the layers where they are found in soil profiles that have been measured all over the country, it has been possible to draw isopach maps showing their extension and thickness, and finally to date them with the help of written records.[12]

In the classical work on Iceland's volcanoes, Th. Thoroddsen's "Die Geschichte der isländischen Vulkane," Hekla's eruptions in historical times number 19, but by combined tephrochronological studies and a

---

[12] S. Thorarinsson, "Tefrokronologiska studier på Island" (Summary in English: "Tephrochronological Studies in Iceland"), *Geogr. Ann. Stockh. XXVI* (1944), 1–215; S. Thorarinsson, "The Öraefajökull Eruption of 1362," *Acta Nat. Isl.,* vol. II, 3 (1958), 1–100; S. Thorarinsson, "The Eruptions of Hekla in Historical Times," *The Eruption of Hekla 1947–1948 I* (1967), 1–170.

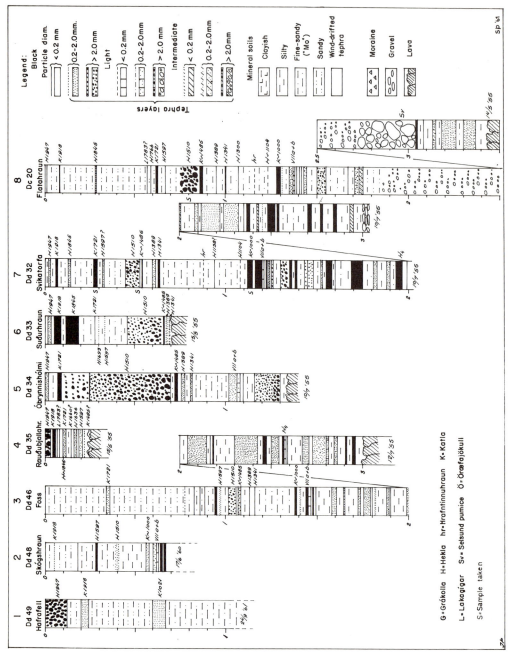

FIG. 5. Soil profiles measured in the Hekla area.

FIG. 6. Section in loessial soil 18 km southwest of Hekla (= profile 8 on fig. 5) (photo: S. Thorarinsson).

critical treatment of written sources this number has now been reduced to 14, and 13 of the tephra layers have been identified in soil profiles. Figure 8 shows in which direction the tephra was spread during the initial phase of each eruption. Figures 9 and 10 are isopach maps of the tephra layer produced by Hekla's first historical eruption. Written records tell us nothing about this eruption except that it occurred in A.D. 1104. (The

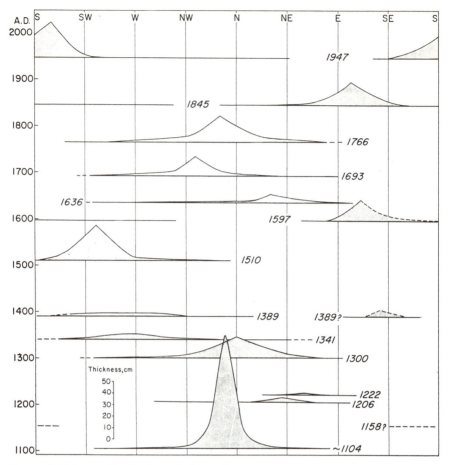

FIG. 7. Thickness distribution of the tephra layers of Hekla's historical eruptions along a circle drawn around the volcano with a radius of 15 km.

dating may possibly have an error of a few years, but is more likely correct.) [13] We know now that the tephra layer, a light rhyodacitic one, such as is produced by Hekla only after a very long period of quiescence, is by far the biggest produced by the volcano in historical times. It covers an area of 55,000 km² on land (within the 0.2 cm isopach) and its volume has been calculated to be about 2.5 km³.

Iceland's largest volcano, the ice-capped Öraefajökull, has erupted twice. The first eruption, in 1362, is by far the biggest explosive eruption in Europe since Vesuvius destroyed Pompeii in A.D. 79. It produced an

[13] S. Thorarinsson, "The Eruptions of Hekla in Historical Times," *The Eruption of Hekla 1947–1948 I* (1967), 1–170.

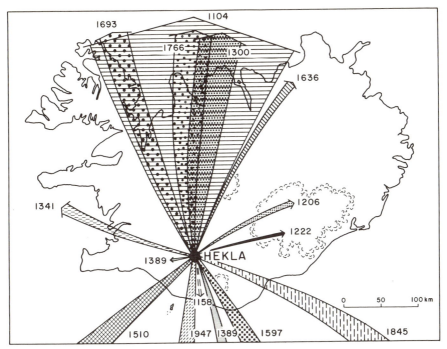

Fig. 8. Map showing in which direction the tephra was spread during the initial phase of each of Hekla's historical eruptions. The width of the arrows is roughly proportional to the volume of the layers.

enormous amount (about 10 km³) of rhyolitic tephra. The extension of the tephra layer on land is shown below.

Hidden beneath the ice cover of Mýrdalsjökull is the volcano Katla, known to have had at least 17 eruptions in historical times. Some of the tephra layers have been identified with certainty, among them two nowhere mentioned in the literature, but it can be calculated from the relation of the tephra layers to other dated ones in soil profiles that one of these eruptions occurred very near the year 1000 and the other about 1485.

An important key horizon in Icelandic soils is a tephra layer found all over middle-south and southwest Iceland (figs. 5, 6, 11, 23). Its source is in the Hrafntinnuhraun area east of Hekla. The layer is easily recognized in the field as its lower part is rhyolitic and nearly white, but its upper part more basic grey. As I did not yet know when writing my doctoral thesis whether it was deposited by one or two eruptions, I designated it as layer VIIa+b. The location of this layer just beneath a layer of charcoal found in the soil around farm sites from Settlement Time shows it to be of approximately the same age as the oldest Nordic settlement in Iceland.

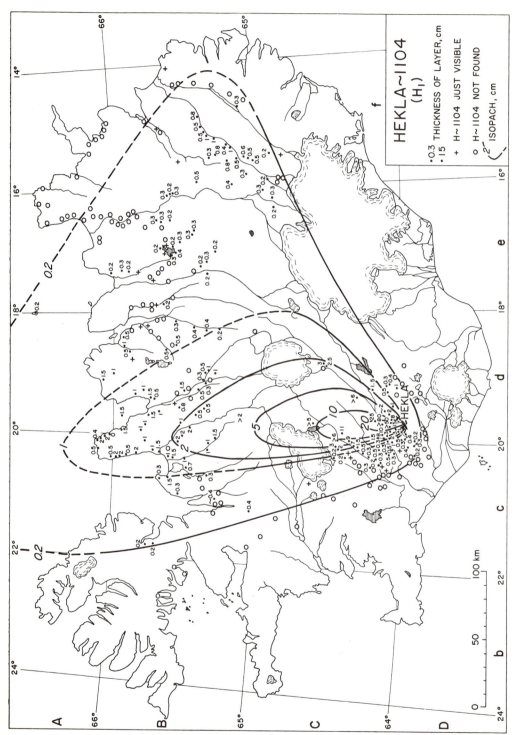

Fig. 9. Isopach map of the Hekla layer H-1104 (= H₁).

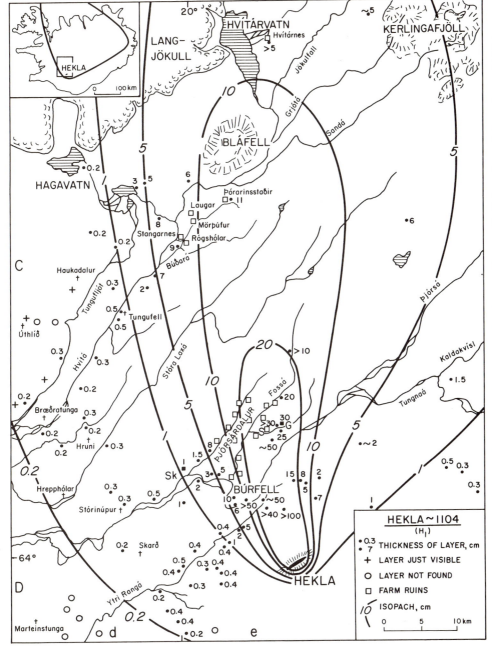

FIG. 10. Isopach map of the tephra layer H-1104, proximal part. Sk. = Skallakot, S = Stöng, G = Gjáskógar.

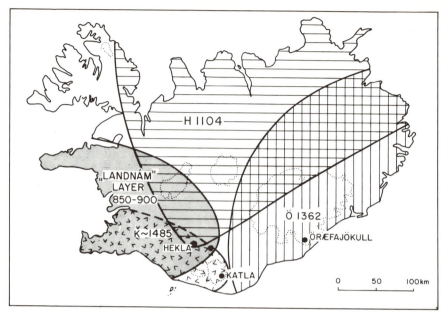

FIG. 11. Four important time-stratigraphic markers in Iceland's medieval soils.

The charcoal itself was formed when the settlers cleared the birch forests around their farmsteads. Pollen analysis supports the conclusion that this layer was deposited between A.D. 850 and 900. It is now often referred to as the "Landnám" layer. Where this widespread and characteristic feature occurs it is easy to tell which part of a soil profile was formed after the beginning of the settlement in Iceland.

The Application of Tephrochronology in Archaeological Research in Iceland

My tephrochronological studies in Iceland began in order to facilitate palynological investigations of the vegetation and climate history of Iceland by establishing a chronology in the peat bogs and a time correlation between them. No doubt the palynological work carried out in Iceland, mainly by Th. Einarsson, has been greatly aided by the dated tephra layers,[14] but for myself tephrochronology soon became an aim in itself.

---

[14] S. Thorarinsson, "Tefrokronologiska studier på Island" (Summary in English: "Tephrochronological Studies in Iceland"), *Geogr. Ann. Stockh. XXVI* (1944), 1–217; Th. Einarsson, "Frjógreining fjörumós í Seltjörn" (English summary: "Pollen Analysis of the Submerged Peat in Seltjörn"), *Náttúrufraedingurinn 26* (1956), 194–198; Th. Einarsson, "Pollenanalytische Untersuchungen zur Spät- und Postglazialen Klimageschichte Islands." Sonderveröff. *Geol. Inst. Univ. Köln 6*

First and foremost, it is a key to the history of Iceland's volcanoes and is intimately connected with the history of the Icelandic nation. In addition it supplies a very useful tool for geomorphological, glaciological, and archaeological research in Iceland.

I will deal here with tephrochronology mainly as an aid in archaeological research in Iceland and include not only excavations but also other research which has increased our knowledge of the conditions of life in medieval Iceland beyond what we can learn from written sources of information. As an introduction a few words outlining the history of the Icelandic nation are in order.

The first known settlers in the country were Irish monks who came as hermits before A.D. 800. Their number was very limited and a real settlement did not begin until about 870 when Nordic farmers and seafarers, mixed with people from the British Isles, began emigration to Iceland in rapidly increasing numbers. The "Landnám" or settlement period lasted until 930. In that year the national chiefs founded a commonwealth by adopting a unified code of law and establishing a parliament. The independent commonwealth of Iceland lasted until 1262 when the Icelanders gave their allegiance to the king of Norway. The Commonwealth Time was on the whole a period of relatively great prosperity. Its intellectual vitality culminated during the thirteenth century when most of the world-famous Icelandic classics were committed to writing.

The period from 1262 to the end of the Middle Ages and onward to 1787 was on the whole a period of decline. Iceland was governed by Norway until 1380 and from then on by Denmark until 1918. From 1602 the Danes had monopolized the trade with calamitous effect. The monopoly was partly abolished in 1787 and wholly in 1854. The total population of Iceland, estimated to have been about 75,000 in 1095, had decreased in number to 50,358 in 1703 when the first exact census was taken (cf. fig. 20).

Tephrochronological Dating of Icelandic Farm Ruins

The most important contribution of tephrochronology to Iceland's archaeology has been its role in the dating of many farm ruins, mainly

---

(1961), 1–52; Th. Einarsson, "Vitnisburdur frjógreiningar um gródur, vedurfar og landnám á íslandi," *Saga* (1962), pp. 442–469; Th. Einarsson, "Pollen-analytical Studies in the Vegetation and Climate History of Iceland in Late and Postglacial Times," *North Atlantic Biota and Their History* (New York: Pergamon Press, 1963), pp. 355–365.

medieval ones, that have been excavated during the last three decades. These excavations have also been of valuable help in the identification of tephra layers. On the whole, tephrochronological research in Iceland has been greatly stimulated by the interest archaeologists have shown.

The collaboration in archaeological and tephrochronological research began in the summer of 1939 when I joined a Nordic archaeological expedition which during that summer excavated a number of farm ruins in the deserted Thjórsárdalur valley in southern Iceland, about 20 km northwest of Hekla (fig. 10). The reports of these excavations were published in the book *Forntida gårdar i Island* (*Ancient Farms in Iceland*) in 1943. The excavation and tephrochronological investigations revealed that the main part of the valley, where about fifteen farm ruins have been found, had been devastated by a great tephra fall from Hekla. Before the excavation the then current opinion was that the devastation in the valley had been caused by an eruption of Hekla in the year 1341. Although I had started tephrochronological work five years earlier, together with H. Bjarnason, I was still rather inexperienced. Identification of the devastating rhyolitic tephra layer in Thjórsárdalur thought to have been produced by the Hekla eruption of 1300 appeared to be wrong. Further tephrochronological studies in the Hekla area after the Second World War proved conclusively, however, that the tephra fall that devastated the valley was Hekla's first historical eruption, in the year 1104. Further, it was recognized that this eruption destroyed not only the valley but also a small settlement on the inland plateau 50 km northwest of Hekla as well as a single farm 20 km still farther inland at Lake Hvítárvatn (fig. 10). The farms buried by the 1104 layer show building customs characteristic of the late eleventh century. Many skeletons excavated in the only churchyard found in the Thjórsárdalur settlement are all from the period 1000 to 1104, Christianity having been adopted in Iceland in A.D. 1000.

Among the farms ravaged in 1104 was that of Stöng (figs. 10, 12). This farm, which was excavated by Aa. Rousell, Copenhagen, is the most outstanding medieval example ever found in Iceland and one of the best preserved, as the rhyolitic pumice had nearly filled the houses so that the walls could not crumble. In this farmhouse, as in nearly all farmhouses built in Iceland until the late nineteenth century, the walls were built of turf and stones which usually were not shaped by man. The Stöng farm and the others that were devastated in Thjórsárdalur in 1104 bear witness to the relative wealth that prevailed in Iceland about the middle of Commonwealth Time.

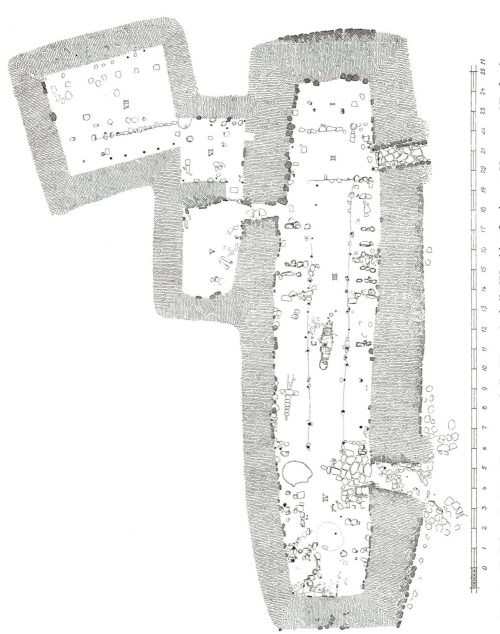

Fig. 12. Skallakot. I, dairy; II, entrance hall; III, main hall; IV, older fire house; V, pantry; VI, fire house; VII, pantry (from *Forntida gårdar*).

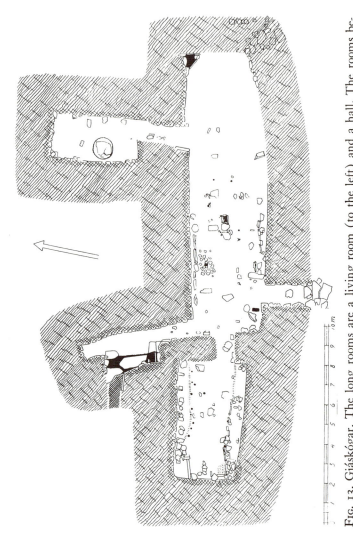

FIG. 13. Gjáskógar. The long rooms are a living room (to the left) and a hall. The rooms behind are a lavatory (to the left) and a dairy.

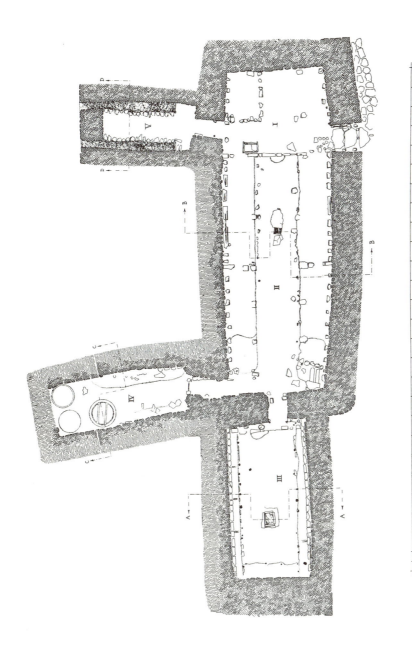

FIG. 14. Stöng. I, entrance hall; II, living room; IV, dairy; V, lavatory (from *Forntida gårdar*).

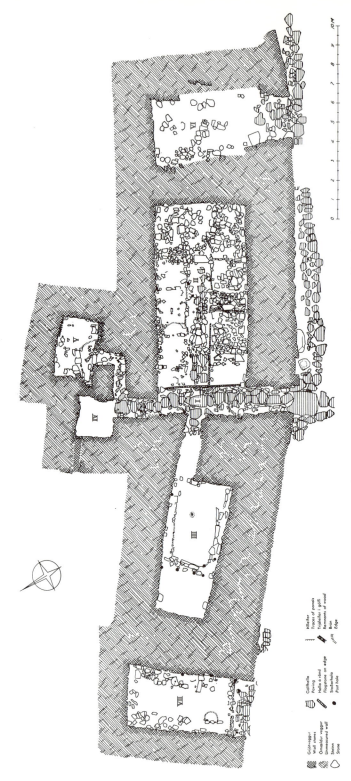

Fig. 15. Gröf. I, passage; II, hall; III, living room; IV, lavatory; V, bathroom; VI, fire house (kitchen); VII, pantry (from *G. Gestsson*, 1959).

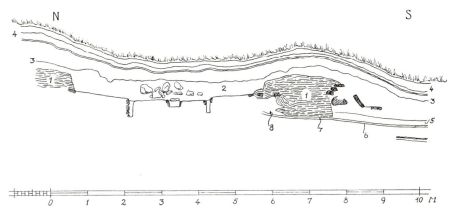

Fig. 16. Section through room III (the main hall) in the Skallakot farm. 1, turf wall with lenses of the "Landnám" layer; 2, loessial soil; 3, Hekla 1104; 4, Hekla 1693, Katla 1721, Hekla 1766.

In the southwesternmost part of the valley, which was not seriously hit by the 1104 eruption, a much more primitive farm ruin was excavated at a location called Skallakot (figs. 10, 12, 16, 17). The relation of this farm ruin to the "Landnám" layer and H 1104 (Hekla eruption of A.D. 1104) shows that it is much older than Stöng and that it was probably built toward the end of Settlement Time.

The present keeper of antiquities in Iceland, K. Eldjárn, who took part in the 1939 excavation in Thjórsárdalur, completed in 1960 the excavation of a farm ruin called Gjáskógar, 2 km northeast of Stöng and 300 m above sea level.[15] Figure 13 is a plan of this farm which was much smaller and somewhat more primitive than Stöng, but not as primitive as the Skallakot farm. Figure 18 is a section through the hall, showing its relation to the tephra layers, from which it can be concluded that this farm, which was the innermost one ever found in this area, was abandoned before Stöng. This point in time can be hardly later than about 1050, as there is a layer of soil between the 1104 layer and the floor, and not earlier than about the year 1000, as otherwise one would find above the floor the tephra layer from the Katla eruption occurring about that time.[16] The farm was not abandoned due to a volcanic eruption, but most likely, as Eldjárn

[15] K. Eldjárn, "Baer í Gjáskógum í Thjórsárdal," Árbók ísl. Fornleifaf. (1961), pp. 7–46; K. Eldjárn, "Two Medieval Farm Sites in Iceland and Some Remarks on Tephrochronology," The Fourth Viking Congress, Aberdeen University Studies 149 (1961), 10–19.
[16] S. Thorarinsson, "The Eruptions of Hekla in Historical Times," The Eruption of Hekla 1947–1948 1 (1967), 1–170.

Fig. 17. The soil cover on the hall floor of Skallakot. I, K 1918; III, H 1766; IV, K 1721; V, H 1693; VI, H 1104 (photo: S. Thorarinsson).

points out, because a farm at this elevation did not prove suitable for agriculture. Thus, to quote Eldjárn: "The habitation in this spot can be interpreted as an unsuccessful attempt at sustaining life by farming beyond the habitable frontier." [17]

During the summers of 1955 to 1957 G. Gestsson, assistant keeper of antiquities, excavated the ruins of a farm named Gröf in the Öraefi district.[18] This ruin was about as beautifully preserved as Stöng, filled as it was by white pumice which I have shown with certainty to have been produced by the great Öraefajökull eruption of 1362. Thus the farm ruin of Gröf shows building customs during the first half of the fourteenth century.

These four farm ruins show a gradual development of the Icelandic turf- and stone-built farms through four centuries, from a settlement type longhouse of simple design via more differentiated longhouses showing a higher building standard to the fourteenth-century farm pointing toward the so-called passage farmhouse. The latter is characteristic of the Iceland

---

[17] K. Eldjárn, "Two Medieval Farm Sites in Iceland and Some Remarks on Tephrochronology," The Fourth Viking Congress, *Aberdeen University Studies 149* (1961), 14.

[18] G. Gestsson, "Gröf í Öraefum," *Árb. Ísl. Fornleifaf* (1959), pp. 5–87.

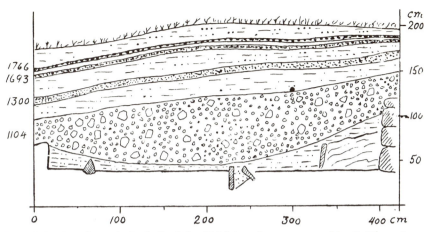

Fig. 18. Section through the hall of the Gjáskógar farm measured by S. Thorarinsson 1949.

of later centuries, consisting of many small houses grouped on both sides of a long passage.

Tephrochronology and Pollen analysis

Pollen analysis combined with tephrochronology has proved an effective method of studying the changes in vegetation caused by the arrival of man in Iceland. Two pollen diagrams of soil profiles near the above-mentioned farm ruins, Skallakot and Stöng, show that the first settlers did grow barley. This we also know from place-names and written records. The occurrence of pollen of oats makes it likely that the settlers also tried to grow this cereal which was important in western Norway at that time. It is possible, however, that oats were not grown intentionally, but only occurred mixed with barley. The pollen diagrams show that the birch woods around the farms were rapidly cleared. The settlers introduced also some plants which no longer grow in Iceland, such as bog myrtle (*Myrica gale*), used for the brewing of ale, and wormwood (*Artemisia*), probably valued for medicinal purposes. Th. Einarsson, who has successfully continued my pollen-analytical studies of the "Landnám" in Iceland, has also found pollen of flax (*Linum usitatissimum*) below the 1104 layer near the episcopal seat of Skálholt in southern Iceland.[19] His dia-

[19] Th. Einarsson, "Vitnisburdur frjógreiningar um gródur, vedurfar og landnám á Islandi," *Saga* (1962), pp. 442–469; Th. Einarsson, "Pollen-analytical Studies in the Vegetation and Climate History of Iceland in Late and Postglacial Times," *North Atlantic Biota and Their History* (New York: Pergamon Press, 1963), pp. 355–365.

grams, like mine, show a sudden increase in weeds with the arrival of man. By more extensive pollen-analytical studies of the soil immediately below and above the "Landnám" layer VIIa+b it ought to be possible to map the vegetational changes caused by the arrival of man and his live-stock in this isolated and virgin country, where no mammal had ever grazed before in Postglacial Times.

Climatic Changes

There are three main indicators of changes in the climate in Iceland in the Middle Ages, namely, the occurrence of arctic drift ice off the coasts of the country, the oscillation of the glaciers, and the history of the grow-ing of cereals. The occurrence of drift ice is reliably and remarkably well recorded in chronicles and other records.[20] More is also known about the oscillation of the glaciers in Iceland during the last 1000 years than in any other country. Tephrochronological datings of terminal moraines have considerably increased that knowledge and tephrochronology has also proved helpful in elucidating the history of cereal growing.[21]

To sum up our knowledge of climate changes in Iceland in the Middle Ages, we find that from about 900 to about 1000 the average temperature was a little higher than in 1900–1930, but hardly higher than in 1931–1960. During the latter half of the twelfth century the climate deteriorated and reached its low between 1250 and 1350. There was probably a slight amelioration in the fourteenth century which lasted at least until 1430. We know very little about the climate during the rest of the fifteenth century, but about the middle of the sixteenth century the drift ice situation is similar to the 1901–1930 period. Finally, the temperature continued to drop and the glaciers to reach their maximal extension of at least 8000 years during the period 1720 to 1890. These temperature changes are schematically shown in figure 19.

[20] S. Thorarinsson, "Klimat. Island och Grönland," *Kulturhistorisk leksikon for nordisk middelalder VIII* (1963), 490; S. Thorarinsson, *The Thousand Years Struggle against Ice and Fire* (Reykjavík: Bókaútgáfa Menningarsjóds, 1956); P. Bergthórsson, *The Drift-ice Thermometer of Iceland* (MS).

[21] S. Thorarinsson, "Tefrokronologiska studier på Island" (Summary in English: "Tephrochronological Studies in Iceland"), *Geogr. Ann. Stockh. XXVI* (1944), 1–217; S. Thorarinsson, "On the Variations of Svínafellsjökull, Skaftafellsjökull and Kviárjökull in Öraefi," *Jökull 6* (1956), 1–15; S. Thorarinsson, "On the Age of the Terminal Moraines of Brúarjökull and Hálsajökull," *Jökull 14* (1964), 67–75; Th. Einarsson, "Vitnisburdur frjógreiningar um gródur, vedurfar og landnám á Islandi," *Saga* (1962), 442–469.

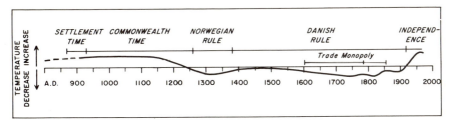

FIG. 19. Temperature changes in Iceland in Historical Times.

Tephrochronology and Settlement Changes

Because of the severity of the climate the inhabitable area of Iceland in Historical Times has never comprised more than about one-fourth of the country. It has been restricted mainly to areas below the 200 m level, to the lowland areas in the south and southwest, to a narrow coastal belt, and to the valleys in the north and east which cut far into the uninhabitable inland plateau (fig. 20). The Icelandic settlement may thus to a large extent be characterized as a pioneer fringe, that is, a border zone to the barren

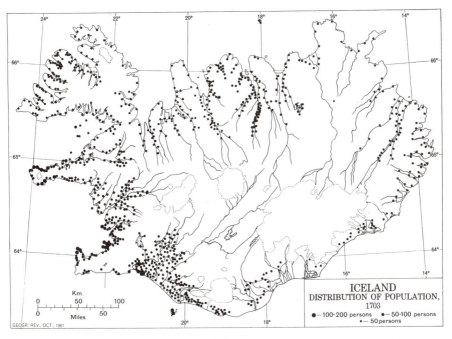

FIG. 20. Distribution of population in Iceland in the year 1703, based on the exact census then taken. A corresponding map toward the end of the Middle Ages would give a similar general picture although showing less concentration on the two southwestern peninsulas and probably a more dense population in the western part of North Iceland.

and deserted inland areas, and as such more susceptible to the influence of man and to climatic changes. Therefore, the frontier between settled areas and the inland *anœcumene* has been unstable, shifting back and forth, but on the whole more retrograde. As a result of these shifts there are many farm ruins found in the frontier areas.[22]

The simplest way to date these changes in those parts of the country where tephra layers are abundant is to apply tephrochronology. Usually it does not take much digging to find whether a farm ruin is older than a certain dated tephra layer or not. It has already been mentioned that the only farms ever to exist on the inland plateau in the south are much older than 1104. It has also been proved by a tephrochronological study that the innermost valley areas inhabited in eastern Iceland were settled long before 1104.

One can now assume as almost certain—and planned additional tephrochronological dates of farm ruins in northern Iceland will show whether this assumption is correct—that already before 1104 and probably even before 1000 the frontier of the Icelandic settlements had reached its most advanced position ever toward the barren interior. Soon thereafter settlements had to be withdrawn somewhat, mainly because these frontier areas proved vulnerable to the destructive influence of man and his livestock.

Soil Erosion in Iceland

In Iceland soil erosion is a more serious problem than in most other countries. Soils are mainly of two types: peat and mineral. The mineral soils are mainly of the loessial type containing a low clay fraction. Consequently, their structure is weak and they are susceptible to erosion by wind and water. Considerable areas of the interior of Iceland have been practically bare of vegetation through the entire Postglacial Time, but the greater part of the land area below the 400 m level had a vegetation cover at Settlement Time, and about 20,000 km² were probably covered with birch forest. Of these birch woods only about 1,000 km² are now left and about half of the area below the 400 m level, or about 20,000 km², is now more or less bare of soil.

Opinions have long differed as to the main cause of the destruction of the forests and the resulting soil erosion. Some students of the problem have put the blame mainly on volcanic activity and deteriorating climate—

[22] S. Thorarinsson, "Population Changes in Iceland," *Geogr. Rev. LI(4)* (1961), 519–533.

Fɪɢ. 21. Soil section near an old farm ruin in Hrafnkelsdalur, East Iceland. A heap of sheep bones rests beneath the undisturbed tephra layers Ö 1362 and H_1 = H 1104 (photo: S. Thorarinsson).

needless to say that the farmers prefer this explanation. Others, among them myself, have maintained that man and his grazing livestock are the main cause. By means of tephrochronology it has now become possible to throw new light on this important problem.[23]

The average rate of accumulation of soil in areas covered by vegetation is an indicator of the soil erosion going on elsewhere as the wind-borne material is partly deposited on the vegetation-covered areas. If one measures the thickness between the depositions of these layers, one can compare the time span with the rate of thickening between other dated layers.

[23] S. Thorarinsson, "L'Erosion Éolienne en Islande à la Lumière des Études Téphrochronologiques," *Rev. Geomorph. Dynamique,* XIII (1962), 107–124.

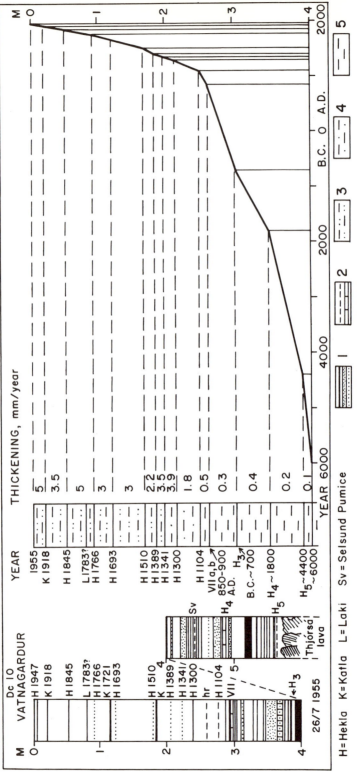

Fig. 22. Soil profile and diagram showing tephra layers, rate of soil thickening and variation in the coarseness of the loessial soil at Vatnagardur, 15 km west of Hekla. The profile to the right is the same as the left one, except that the tephra layers have been excluded. 1, black tephra; 2, light tephra; 3, sandy soil; 4, fine-sandy soil; 5, silty soil.

A typical soil section with many dated layers on the lowland plain west of Hekla is shown in figure 22. Having extracted the thickness of the tephra layers, as they have nothing to do with the accumulation of the soil because of the redeposition of the eroded soil cover, we can construct the diagram to the right which shows the soil thickening versus time. It shows that from the time when soil began to form on the 8000-year-old lava flow Thjórsárhraun, which covers this area, the soil cover increased evenly and on the whole relatively slowly until sometime about or shortly before A.D. 1100, but from then on it accumulated many times more rapidly. Although the Hekla eruption of 1104 may have increased the erosion somewhat in this special area, volcanic activity cannot generally speaking have been the main cause of the increasing rate of soil erosion. We can prove that point by constructing similar diagrams in other parts of the country where the soil erosion began to increase rapidly at this time or even some centuries earlier. This occurs also in areas not at all affected by volcanic activity. On the whole the volcanic activity has not been of a greater magnitude in historical than in prehistoric times.

Figure 23 is a typical profile from a peat bog near Reykjavik. In this profile the tephra layer VII$a+b$ roughly indicates the settlement niveau. A little higher the soil in the bog profile rather abruptly becomes yellowish brown in color. This is due to a highly increased mineral content carried in by wind and water from the loessial soil of the surrounding hills. Thus soil destruction started shortly after the beginning of settlement. The cause can neither be volcanic nor climatic to any decisive degree for climate amelioration began a century later.

The result of the tephrochronological study of the soil erosion is, in short, that during a large part of the Postglacial Warm Period the rate of soil accumulation in Iceland was very even and slow, indicating that soil erosion was then on the whole insignificant. The country was vegetation-covered to a much larger extent than now and there was a fair although unstable equilibrium between the soil-forming and the soil-destructing processes. The climatic deterioration at the beginning of the Nordic Iron Age seems to have accelerated the soil erosion somewhat, but not much compared with the increase that started soon after the beginning of Nordic settlement in the country and which has been continuing on an increasing rate ever since. The main cause of the soil destruction is neither more volcanism nor deteriorating climate; it is in fact man and his grazing animals, especially sheep. But although the rate of soil erosion began to rise shortly after the colonization, it took some centuries before its effects

FIG. 23. Profile in a bog near Reykjavík showing the change in color of the peat soil soon after the deposition of the "Landnám" layer (VII$a+b$) because of increased eolian sedimentation.

began to be seriously felt. As far as soil and vegetation are concerned, Iceland was a better country during the first centuries of settlement than later.

Summing up, as a result of research during the last three decades or so, a much clearer picture exists today concerning conditions in medieval Iceland.

We know better than before how the geographical environment has affected the settlement and vice versa. We know that the country was settled during a period when the climate was about as favorable as it has been during the last few decades and less severe than it became toward the end of Commonwealth Time. We know that at least in some parts of the country the settlements expanded rapidly and reached beyond the frontier that proved habitable and that in the long run they had to be withdrawn. We know that some settlements were destroyed by volcanic activity and we can date their devastation, but we also know that the role of eruptions and other natural catastrophies in the reduction of inhabited areas must not be overestimated and that other processes, working more slowly but continuously, played a greater role. One was a deteriorating climate, but the most important process was probably the destruction of the birch woods and the resulting soil erosion which can be proved to have started shortly after the arrival of man but can hardly have been felt seriously during the first centuries of settlement.

Various paths lead us to the conclusion that the relative opulence prevailing during the first centuries of settlement, which is reflected for instance in the development of the farmhouses, was to a considerable extent due to more favorable conditions than prevailed later. And the subsequent decline is to a considerable degree to be accounted for by deteriorating climate, greater frequency of drift ice, advance of glaciers, increased volcanic activity, and last but not least, increasing soil erosion.

Tephrochronological Teleconnections

At the beginning of this paper I mentioned that tephra from Icelandic eruptions has occasionally been carried to the Scandinavian countries and the British Isles (fig. 1). In fact, it can be identified in the soils of these countries.[24] Although layers are so thin that they can hardly be detected in the field, under the microscope the grains of volcanic ash are easily identified, as they consist of glass of characteristic appearance (fig. 2), especially in countries where practically all rocks are crystalline.

Recently a young Swedish scientist, Christer Persson, has realized my old dream of establishing tephrochronological teleconnection between Iceland and Scandinavia.[25] In Swedish and Norwegian peat bogs he has found horizons containing Icelandic tephra. Measurement of the concentration of tephra grains in the soil (number of grains per the same amount of soil under the microscope), determination of refractive index

[24] S. Thorarinsson, "Tefrokronologiska studier på Island" (Summary in English: "Tephrochronological Studies in Iceland"), *Geogr. Ann. Stockh.*, XXVI (1944), 1–217.

[25] Chr. Persson, "Försök till tefrokronologisk datering av några svenska torvmossar," *Geol. Fören. Stockh. Förh. 88* (1966), 361–395; Chr. Persson, "Undersökning av tre sura asklager på Island," *Geol. Fören. Stockh. Förh. 88* (1967), 500–519; Chr. Persson, "Försök till tefrokronologisk datering i tre norska myrar," *Geol. Fören. Stockh. Förh. 89* (1967), 181–197.

and trace elements, and radiocarbon dating of the organic material associated with the tephra resulted in five acid layers having been identified:
three historical layers—Askja 1875, Öraefajökull 1361, and Hekla 1104—
and two prehistoric ones, H3, 2800 years old, and H4, about 4000 years old.

On the Faroe Islands Danish scientists have started a similar study of
tephra layers, but the results have not yet been published. It is likely that
the tephra from Iceland can also be identified in northern Scotland and
on the Orkney and Shetland Islands.

Combined with pollen analysis these tephrochronological teleconnec-
tions may prove very useful for the correlation of historical events as well
as prehistoric climatic changes, and they may also be expected to facilitate
archaeological research to a greater degree.

Tephrochronology Combined with Other Dating Methods

Since tephrochronology was worked out other dating methods have
been introduced, and especially one of them, radiocarbon dating, is of a
paramount importance. One may therefore ask whether tephrochronology
has not outlived itself. Although the radiocarbon method has to a considerable extent replaced tephrochronological dating, it cannot replace it
entirely. As far back in time as tephra layers are dated exactly by written
records they can be used for more exact dating than is possible by using
the radiocarbon method. And an identifiable tephra layer, whether absolutely dated or not, is an excellent chronological key bed as it is spread
simultaneously over wide areas.

I should also like to underline especially that these two methods com-
plement each other. The approximate age of a tephra layer can often be
determined by radiocarbon dating of organic remains imbedded in the
layer or buried by it. This dating can then be applied to the entire area
where that tephra layer is found, even in places where radiocarbon dating
is not possible, that is, for the dating of artifacts in purely minerogenic
soils. The same holds true for tephrochronology and other isotopic dating
methods.

A combination of tephrochronology and dendrochronology also may
add greatly to the value of these methods for archaeological dating. Trees
are often imbedded in the tephra and dendrochronology is the only
method, except for the use of written records, by which deposits can be
dated exactly to the year. The tephra layer from the Sunset Crater near
Flagstaff, Arizona, has been dated to A.D. 1064. To my knowledge it is the

KRISTIANSUNDSMYREN

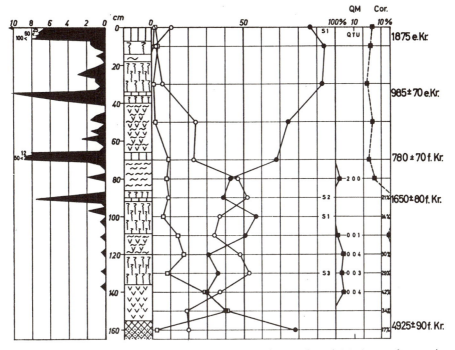

FIG. 24. Ash grain frequency and pollen diagram from a bog (Kristiansundsmyren) in western Norway. The black diagram to the left shows the number of ash grains per half preparation. The uppermost tephra layer is Askja 1875, the three radio-carbon-dated maxima correspond in all probability to three rhyolitic Hekla layers; H 1104 and the prehistoric H3 and H4. In the pollen diagram open squares are *Alnus,* open triangles *Picea,* open rings *Betula,* filled rings *Pinus* and broken line *Corylus* (from *Chr. Persson,* 1967).

oldest tephra layer so far exactly dated in the Western hemisphere.[26] Combined dendro- and tephrochronology has also been applied with success in New Zealand.[27] K/Ar datings may possibly be improved enough to become useful for datings of tephra layers down into the vicinity of 10,000 years.

In Iceland the physicist A. Brynjólfsson (unpublished work) has demonstrated the possibility of combining tephrochronology with dating of recent basalt lava flows by measuring their remanent magnetism. Because of the rather rapid changes in the declination (annual change

[26] T. L. Smiley, "The Geology and Dating of Sunset Crater, Flagstaff, Arizona, New Mex.," *Geol. Soc. Guidebook 9th Field Conf. Black Mesa Basin,* 1958.

[27] A. P. Druce, "Tree-ring Dating of Recent Volcanic Ash and Lapilli, Mt. Egmont, New Zealand," *J. Bot. 4,* 1 (1966), 1–41.

about 6'), a difference of one or two decades in age can be measured. Thus Iceland is on the whole very favored with regard to possibilities of dating. It is really a pity that man arrived so late on this isolated island and that there is no premedieval archaeology.

As to the possibilities of applying tephrochronology in medieval archaeology in other parts of Europe, I have already pointed out that Icelandic tephra layers can be used for this purpose in northwest Europe. Tephrochronology can also be used in parts of Italy and Greece. There is, however, only one eruption in Greece in the Middle Ages that has produced a large amount of tephra, the eruption of Santorini (Thera) in A.D. 726. The tephra produced by the Minoan eruption of Santorini about 1450 B.C. mentioned earlier may have great archaeological significance in its potential effect on eastern Mediterranean history, linked as it is perhaps to the downfall of the Cretan civilization at that time.[28] In early Postglacial Time widespread and thoroughly studied tephra layers are found in the Eifel district in Germany.[29] The youngest of these layers are about 10,000 years old. Similarly, the youngest volcanic activity in the Auvergne is of about the same age.

In Japan tephrochronology has only been applied in prehistoric archaeology, where it has already contributed to some progress.[30] There have also been applications in New Zealand. Tephrochronology combined with radiocarbon dating and tree-ring chronology has considerable unexhausted potential for archaeologists in many Central and South American states as well as in Alaska and parts of the western United States where distinct tephra layers exist.

[28] D. Ninkovich and B. C. Heezen, "Santorini Tephra," *Colston Papers XVII* (Butterworth's Scientific Publications, London, 1965), pp. 413–453.

[29] Hopmann-Frechen-Knetz, *Die Vulkanische Eifel* (Bonn: Wilhelm Stollfuss Verlag, 1962).

[30] S. Kaizuka, Geochronology Based on Volcanic Ejecta and Its Contribution to Archaeology in Japan," *Asian Perspectives V,* 2 (1961), 193–195.

XIV

ARCHAEOMAGNETIC DATING

M. J. Aitken

$\mathcal{T}$HE DIRECTION of the earth's magnetic field is defined by the magnetic declination (the angle between true north and magnetic north) and the angle of dip (the inclination to the horizontal of the magnetic lines of force). The secular variation of these angles over the past few hundred years is known from records of direct observations on suspended magnets, but a fortuitous record is available almost since man discovered fire.[1]

While clay is being baked, the magnetic domains in the ferrimagnetic minerals, magnetite (Fe_3O_4) and haematite (α–Fe_2O_3), are preferentially aligned by the earth's magnetic field, and when the clay cools down this domain alignment remains "frozen," resulting in a weak magnetic moment (specific magnetization in the range 10^{-4} to 10^{-1} e.m.u. per gram) of which the direction is identical with that of the earth's field at the time of cooling. Comprehensive investigation of this phenomenon (thermo- • remanent magnetism) has been made, notably by E. Thellier in Paris from 1933 onward.[2] The magnetization is remarkably stable, certainly remaining constant over archaeological periods, and probably over times on the order of 100 million years. Thermoremanent magnetism is acquired also by rocks on cooling from the molten state; from *paleo*magnetic studies it • has been possible to reconstruct the positions and orientations of the continents during various stages of stabilization of the earth's crust, and also to infer that at some times in the past the earth's field has been in the reverse direction to what it is at present.

---

[1] G. Folgheraiter, "Sur les variations seculaires de l'inclinaison magnetique dans l'antiquité," *Arch. Sci. phys. nat. 8* (1899), 5–16.

[2] E. Thellier and O. Thellier, "Sur l'intensité du champs magnetique terrestre dans le passé historique et geologique," *Ann. Geophys. 15* (1959), 285–286.

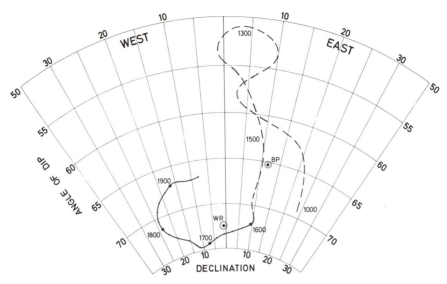

FIG. 1. Secular variation of geomagnetic direction for London from A.D. 1000 onward. Solid curve is data from directly recorded measurements, dashed curve is from archaeomagnetic measurements. (See text for discussion of WR—Wrenthorpe, and BP—Bagot's Park.)

*Archaeo*magnetism refers to measurements made on archaeological material.[3] It should be realized, however, that, except over the past few hundred years, before any dating information can be obtained by this method its time scale must first be calibrated by measurements on archaeological materials of known age and this must be done for each region (of about 500 miles across) in which the method is to be applied. Because the secular variation of the magnetic direction is not a regular, cyclic phenomenon, this calibration process requires at least a half dozen well-dated archaeological structures per century of time scale. Consequently, during the first few years of setting up, the archaeomagnetist has little to offer the archaeologist in return for the sacrifice of his structures except the knowledge that he is providing the geophysicist with data that is otherwise unobtainable.

It is sometimes possible to deduce the ancient magnetic intensity in addition to direction. This is more difficult experimentally and the precision so far obtainable makes it unlikely that intensity measurements will be of any use for dating. The results are of great interest geophysically, however, and show that 2000 years ago the earth's magnetic field

[3] M. J. Aitken, *Physics in Archaeology* (Interscience Publishers, 1961), chap. 7.

intensity was nearly twice the present value; measurements on older samples suggest that this is part of a cyclic variation rather than a monotonic decrease.

Methods

In order for the remanent magnetic direction found in baked clay to be useful in determining the ancient direction, something must be known about its orientation during cooling down. The best material is from structures such as kilns, ovens, and hearths which have remained intact over the centuries of burial. Orientated samples have been extracted from such structures by partially enclosing isolated stumps of baked clay in plaster of paris molds and marking the direction of geographic north on the horizontal surfaces of the molds before the stumps are detached. Each isolated stump is obtained in the first place by cutting with a knife, hacking, or sawing. In this way the ancient declination and the ancient angle of dip can both be determined. In the case of bricks and tiles it is sometimes possible to deduce the ancient angle of dip although the specimens are not found in the position in which they cooled down; this is possible when one face of a rectilinear specimen was on a horizontal floor during baking and there are a dozen or more similar specimens available. Similarly, if a pot was baked standing upright on a horizontal floor, it can be used to find the angle of dip; unfortunately, except for heavily glazed and ornamented Chinese pottery, these circumstances are not common.

Two types of laboratory instrument can be used for measurement of the remanent directions of the samples. In the "spinner" magnetometer the sample is rotated (e.g., at 300 revolutions per minute) inside an electrical coil system and by determining the phase of the minute alternating voltage that is induced by the rotating magnetic movement of the sample, the direction of magnetization can be deduced. In the "astatic" magnetometer the sample is held near to one of a pair of small magnets which are mounted antiparallel at either end of a rigid vertical bar which is suspended on a quartz or phosphor-bronze fiber; because the torques on each magnet due to the earth's field are equal and opposite, the system only deflects if a sample is brought near to one of the magnets, and by measuring the deflection for various orientations of the sample, the direction of magnetization of the sample can be deduced. Both systems are sensitive to external magnetic and vibratory disturbance despite various compensating devices—in general the astatic type is the more delicate of the two. The spinner type also has the advantage that it can be more readily designed for measurements on large samples (up to 20 cm across), but it has the disadvantage that considerable centrifugal force is experienced by the sample during measurement and this raises problems in mounting.

The remanent directions found in a group of samples from the same structure show appreciable dispersion about the mean, the degree of dispersion varying from structure to structure, sometimes being correlated with the type of structure. One cause of this dispersion is the distortion of the earth's field by the magnetism of the structure itself, so that samples of strongly magnetic material often give poor results. Another cause of dispersion is the occurrence, since last cooling, of relative movement of different parts of the structure. In either case it is essential to take at least a dozen well-distributed samples.

Results

Archaeomagnetic projects are currently in operation in various parts of the world—Japan, India, USSR, Czechoslovakia, Poland, France, England,[4] and the southwestern United States. In the United States the structures used have been Indian fire pits and these have been found by R. L. Du Bois (University of Oklahoma) to be good archaeomagnetic material, in general showing less dispersion than the more substantial pottery kilns which have been the main concern of the archaeomagnetic work in England. In what follows discussion is restricted to the post-A.D. 900 part of the investigations in England. A large amount of data is available for the Roman period also but the change of direction during that period was rather too weak for any dating application to be possible.

The secular variation for London as deduced from archaeomagnetic measurements for the period A.D. 1000 to 1600 is shown in figure 1. From 1600 onward the curve represents the directly recorded data collated by Bauer in his paper of 1899. It should be noted that the usually quoted "Bauer curve" differs a little from the curve in figure 1 during the seventeenth century. This is because the Bauer curve is the best fit of two sinusoidal functions to the raw data and during the seventeenth century there was a significant deviation (about one degree in angle of dip) between the best fit and the raw data; it is satisfying to find that the archaeomagnetic results support the latter rather than the former.

[4] M. J. Aitken and H. N. Hawley, "Further Archaeomagnetic Measurements in Britain," *Archaeometry* 9 (1966), 187–192.

Although the change of magnetic direction during the period is strong enough to allow fairly precise dating, straightforward application is prevented over much of the period A.D. 1150 to 1500 by the repetition in time of the same direction. Thus, for example, both in the early thirteenth century and in the late fifteenth century the angle of dip was about 60° and the declination between 5°W and 10°E. Before a magnetic date can be given during the period in which ambiguity occurs, it is necessary for the archaeologist to decide whether the date is before or after A.D. 1300. This repetition of direction is an unfortunate drawback of magnetic dating; in other parts of the world the difficulty may be more or less acute, not necessarily occurring over the same periods.

The archaeomagnetic curve is based on about thirty structures; the reliability and precision of the archaeological dates for these is variable and in most cases the dates are derived from studies of the pottery styles found associated with the structures. To the extent that archaeological ideas about the chronology of pottery styles are revised from time to time, so will be the time scale of the reference curve and any magnetic dates based on it. Consequently, the approach to using archaeomagnetism must be a cautious one in which the remanent magnetic direction found in baked clay of a structure is considered alongside the archaeological evidence as an additional attribute which the excavator must square with his estimate of the date. At worst it is useful as a means of establishing nonsimultaneity of two different pottery types; at best it can approach straightforward dating.

The foregoing limitation does not necessarily apply in general. For instance, the archaeomagnetic time scale in the southwestern United States is based upon dendrochronology, and in England the time scale from A.D. 1600 onward is based upon directly recorded observations. In conclusion two examples are given of the positive way in which archaeomagnetism can give useful chronological information.

The first is a clamp kiln at Potovens, Wrenthorpe, in Yorkshire, excavated by P. Brears and identified from documentary evidence as that used by Robert Glover and his son between 1630 and 1679.[5] Sixteen magnetic samples were extracted from the floor of this kiln and measurement gave the average ancient direction as:

Angle of dip—72.3° ± 0.4, declination—1.0°W ± 0.7 .

[5] P. Brears, "Excavations at Potovens, near Wakefield," *Post-Medieval Archaeology* I (in press).

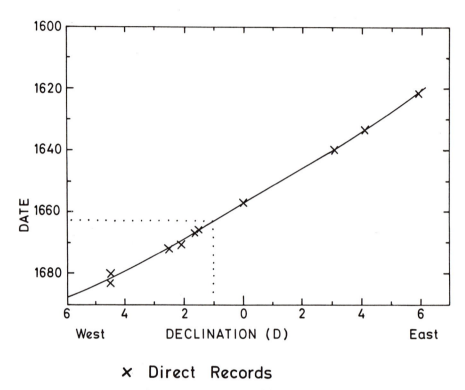

x Direct Records

FIG. 2. Archaeomagnetic dating of kiln at Wrenthorpe.

The limits quoted are at the 68 percent confidence level and represent the standard errors of the means. Reference to figure 1 shows that this average places the last firing of the kiln close to the middle of the sixteenth century. That the observed angle of dip is too shallow to fit the directly observed data by somewhat less than a degree could be due to magnetic refraction effects, but the difference is barely significant (indeed the closeness of agreement can be regarded as a tribute both to the archaeomagnetic method and to the precision of early geomagnetists). The magnetic date is considered in more detail in figure 2 where the archaeomagnetic result is compared with the directly recorded declinations. At the 68 percent level of confidence the magnetic date is A.D. 1663 ± 8.

The second example is a glass furnace excavated by D. Crossley at Bagot's Park, Staffordshire.[6] The most positive documentary evidence

[6] D. W. Crossley, "Glassmaking in Bagot's Park, Staffordshire in the Sixteenth Century," *Post-Medieval Archaeology I* (in press).

was an agreement, dated 1585, to lease four sites to immigrant glass-makers from Lorraine. On the other hand, the type of furnace and the style of the sparse fragments of pottery found suggested a date earlier than the middle of the sixteenth century. The question of whether the furnace was pre- or post-1585 was important in determining the degree of emphasis that should be placed on the native glassmaking tradition. The average remanent magnetic direction found in thirty-three samples extracted from the furnace was:

Angle of dip—65.6° ± 0.2, declination—12.0°E ± 0.6.

By reference to figure 3 it will be seen that this implies a date of last cooling certainly earlier than 1585, and probably around the second quarter of the sixteenth century. Additional documentary evidence has subsequently come to light that a number of glassmaking families were in fact living within a quarter of a mile of the site in the early sixteenth century.

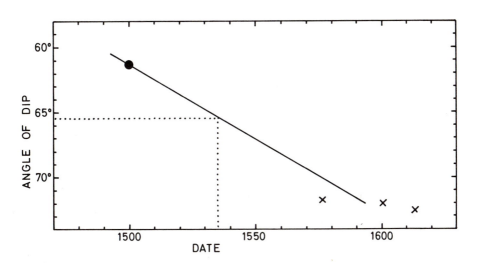

● Cistercian ware kiln at Potterton

✕ Direct records (Norman, Gilbert, Ridley)

Fig. 3. Archaeomagnetic dating of glass furnace at Bagot's Park.

Part Two

Tracing Methods

XV

THE POSSIBILITY OF MEASURING VARIATIONS IN THE INTENSITY OF WORLDWIDE LEAD SMELTING DURING MEDIEVAL AND ANCIENT TIMES USING LEAD AEROSOL DEPOSITS IN POLAR SNOW STRATA

C. C. Patterson, T. J. Chow, and M. Murozumi

*W*HEN LEAD is smelted in blast furnaces, hot gases in the furnaces carry a considerable fraction of the lead up into the atmosphere in the form of fine particles. Although the amount lost is modified by smelting conditions and attempts to recover the fume, an approximate value for the fraction actually lost might be about 1 percent. These particles are mostly removed from the atmosphere by rain or snow. Roughly speaking, meteorological conditions average out over a year, and precipitation mechanisms are highly effective in removing suspended aerosols, so that total concentrations of lead particles in the atmosphere respond within about a year to changes in smelting activities. An average of a year's accumulated precipitation will show little variation from year to year if smelting remains constant, but this accumulation will change from year to year if the intensity of smelting changes. In recent decades, an additional source of lead in the atmosphere has been the burning of leaded gasoline. The fraction of lead produced each year which is burned in automotive and aviation fuels increased from zero in 1923 to 15 percent by 1955. In contrast to the low yield from smelter fumes, about 75 percent of lead in gasolines is converted to long-lived atmospheric aerosols after combustion, so that there has been a recent additional increase in the concentrations of lead in the atmosphere from this new source. As shown in figure 1, a record of the increase in lead content of the atmosphere is preserved as progressively younger and dirtier layers of snow in the polar regions of the earth.

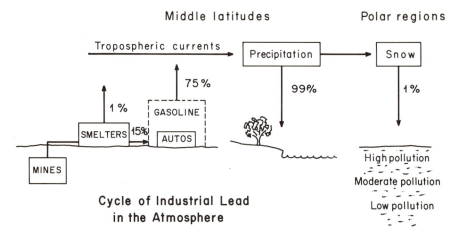

FIG. 1. Industrial lead cycle in the atmosphere. Percentages given are crude estimates.

Recently M. Murozumi, Tsaiwa J. Chow, and I (C. C. Patterson) measured the concentrations of lead in the upper two centuries of snow layers near the north and south poles.[1] We detected a large decrease in lead content going down to the older snows near the north pole, but the lead contents of the snows near the south pole were so small that only a slight decrease was noted. We also showed that there were no similar changes in the amounts of rock dust and sea salts with time, and that the concentrations of these substances were too low to account for the amounts of lead present. We were thus able to detect recent lead pollution of the atmosphere and distinguish between relatively unpolluted southern hemispheric air and strongly polluted northern hemispheric air. The advantages of going to the thick ice shields in polar regions are that the yearly accumulations there are slight enough, so that hundreds of years are accessible and the rate of horizontal flow of compressed snow and ice is insufficient to distort and mix hundreds of yearly layers (the disadvantages are that the pollution effect is greatly diminished, and collection of the snow samples there is difficult and costly). These findings suggest that it may be possible to examine frozen records of ancient atmospheres for changes in the intensity of industrial activity. Lead is particularly suitable for this purpose, because in past millennia one of the fundamental indices of economy, silver, was obtained by smelting it out of lead. For

[1] Discussed at the Sixtieth Annual Meeting of the Air Pollution Control Association, Cleveland, Ohio, 11–16 June 1967: "Changes in Concentrations of Common Lead in North Polar Snows with Time," M. Murozumi, T. J. Chow, and C. C. Patterson.

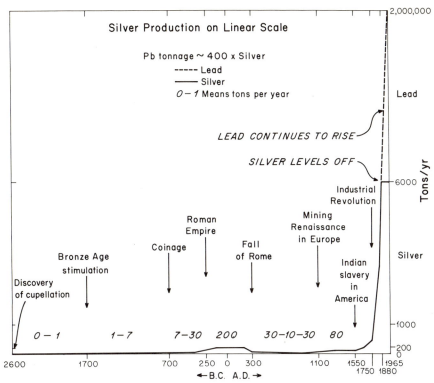

FIG. 2. Total world silver and lead production since the earliest times. Figures are preliminary.

each ton of silver produced, some 400 tons of lead metal, on the average, were first smelted from ores and then cupelled, or oxidized, in a separate operation to yield the eagerly sought after silver which is more difficult to oxidize. In ancient times uses were gradually discovered for the enormous masses of pure lead that were made available by this operation, and thus was born the industrial utilization of lead. Lead metal was easily recovered from the oxide by simply smelting it with charcoal.

The reconstruction of world silver production and, as a corollary, world lead production, in ancient times would be of considerable interest to the economic historians. In a very approximate manner this can be done from evidence based on slag heaps whose sizes and ages have been estimated. The solid curve in figure 2 shows the approximate production of silver in the world since silver was first smelted in northeastern Turkey 4600 years ago.[2] This curve also expresses very well (but in different units) the

---

[2] Preliminary figures. A full discussion and evaluation of these data is being written and will be published.

approximate world production of lead, except for the period after the Industrial Revolution. The 400 to 1 relationship does not hold very well between lead and silver during that last interval, for, in fact, silver production leveled off at about 6000 tons per year after 1880, while lead production continued to climb, as shown by the dotted extension, to some 2,000,000 tons per year at present.

Considering what has been discovered about the variation of lead in polar snow strata, would it be possible to check the magnitude of silver-lead production during the time of the Roman Empire by actual measurement? Also, would it be possible to determine the time of minimum production during the medieval period? It seems feasible, but further development of present techniques would be necessary. The data already collected can be used to show how this could be done.

Figure 3 shows, near the north pole, the seasonal variation of calcium, potassium, and lead concentrations in a single year's accumulation of snow found by Murozumi, Chow, and Patterson. Most of the calcium and potassium came from clay dusts. It can be seen that in the midsummer and fall the concentrations of aerosols were low, while in the winter and early summer they were high. These large variations, which are a function of meteorological conditions, can be smoothed out by mixing

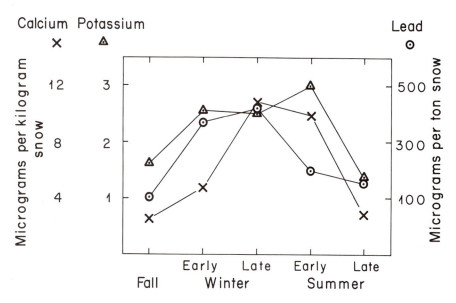

FIG. 3. Seasonal variation in chemical composition of snow at 80 km ESE of Camp Century, North Greenland (76°50′N, 58°30′W).

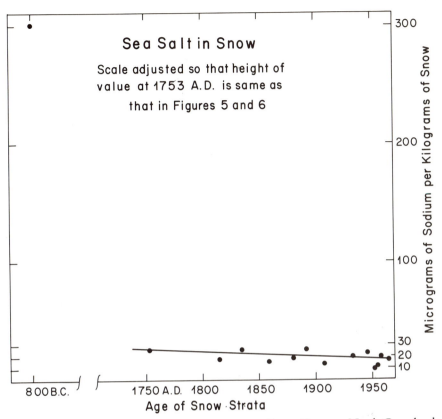

FIG. 4. Year to year variation of sodium in snow at Camp Century, North Greenland (77°10′N, 61°08′W) (A.D. 1753 to 1946), and at 80 km ESE of Camp Century (1952 to 1965). High value is from ancient ice at west edge of shield near Camp Tuto (32 km E of Thule, Greenland). Virtually all of the sodium in all samples is derived from sea salts, not clay dusts.

into a single sample snow accumulated during a period of three or four years. Unfortunately, Murozumi et al. were unaware of this effect and the year-to-year samples which they collected and analyzed each spanned and were a mixture of about one and a half year's accumulation which accentuated, rather than smoothed, this seasonal effect.

Figure 4 shows the concentration of sodium found in the snow as a function of time which at this location is largely derived from sea salts. It can be seen that for a span of 200 years there is no systematic increase of salt. Some of the variation is probably due to the samples at different time levels having different proportions of autumn and winter snows in them because each sample, covering about a year and a half, was taken with a

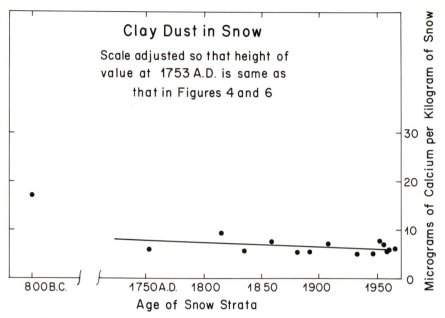

FIG. 5. Year to year variation of calcium in snow at Camp Tuto, Camp Century, and 80 km ESE of Camp Century. Most of the calcium is derived from clay dusts.

stratigraphic uncertainty greater than that interval. It will be noted that the oldest sample, dated at about 800 B.C. by carbon-14,[3] contains very much greater amounts of salt. This is because all the samples except that one were taken from locations in the interior of the Greenland ice sheet, where salt and dust from local seas and shores do not tend to penetrate, but the old sample was taken from a horizontal tunnel drilled into the edge of the ice sheet near the sea and shore, and it came from material highly contaminated with locally derived salts and dusts.

Figure 5 shows that calcium, representing clay dusts, is also affected by the improper sampling. The dust content clearly did not change with time at the interior location, although the old ice sample taken from the shore location was more dusty.

Figure 6 shows that the variation of lead in north polar snows increases dramatically with time. We also note that the salty and dusty millennia-old ice contains the smallest amount of lead. The lead concentration observed in it is within a factor of three of that naturally expected from the

[3] H. Oeschger, B. Alder, H. Loosli, C. Langway, and A. Renaud, "Radiocarbon Dating of Ice," *Earth and Planetary Science Letters,* vol. 1, no. 194 (1966). Our sample is from near "location 1." Considering the much older age of "location 2," our sample may be older, rather than younger, than 800 B.C.

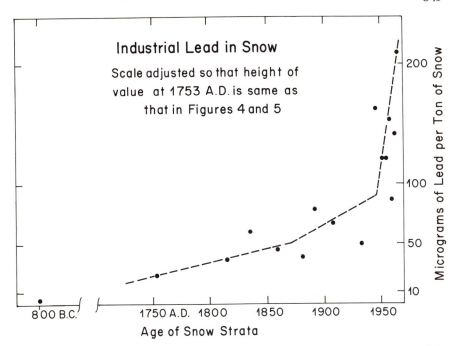

FIG. 6. Year to year variation of lead in snow at Camp Tuto, Camp Century, and 80 km ESE of Camp Century. Lead from natural sources is significant in all of these samples. Most of the lead assigned to the 5000-year-old sample is probably contamination from industrial lead on the walls of drums and bottles, and was never in the snow. Nearly all of the lead assigned to the 1753 sample is industrial smelter lead actually in the snow. Snow from the Antarctic has assigned lead concentrations similar to the low value found for the 5000-year-old Greenland sample.

salts and dusts present (the extra amount probably originates from the plastic drums and bottles). We would therefore expect 800 B.C. snow from the interior to have a lower natural lead content, corresponding to its lower dust content. This would be less than one unit on the scale shown, or less than one part per trillion of snow. The large scatter of the points from a smooth curve does not reflect year-to-year variations. They result from a difference in proportions of autumn and winter layers in the samples which covered somewhat more than a year. For this reason it is not clear whether the observed lead curve faithfully reproduces the world lead production curve. Roughly, lead in north polar snow appears to increase by a factor of about four after 1750 and before 1940. After about 1940, there seems to be a sharp, additional increase by another factor of two or three. This is about what we might expect from the known increase in burning of leaded automotive fuels during recent decades. Certainly, the data could be greatly improved by repeating the experiment using care to mix snow from about three years' accumulation at each dated level.

This information only covers the period since the Industrial Revolution, however. Referring back to figure 2, it can be seen that in approximate terms the level of lead production in Roman times was about equal to the level at the start of the Industrial Revolution boom in 1750 (lead lagged behind silver in 1750, because a lot of silver was then being taken from nonlead ores, so the silver curve in figure 2 lies somewhat above a lead curve for that time). This means that the 1750 lead point in figure 6 should correspond to what could be observed for a Roman lead production peak to appear if it existed. If lead production during medieval times were on an order of magnitude less than production during Roman times, however, it would be difficult to detect a two- or threefold minimum during the medieval period, since it would probably lie close to natural lead concentrations according to present analytical techniques.

An experiment designed to check by actual measurement the silver production or industrial activity in Roman and medieval times would consist of three phases: the development of analytical techniques, the digging of a shaft, and the collection of samples.

At the present time the levels of lead contamination in laboratory analytical procedures are too high, but they can be reduced. The sample size is on the order of 50 liters of water. Four to six samples of this size are needed at each dated level for a proper evaluation of the lead concentration. For Roman times a 50-liter melted snow sample from northern Greenland would contain only 0.6 microgram of lead. Before analysis each sample is melted in a separate 30-gallon plastic drum and shipped from the collection site to the laboratory in a 13-gallon plastic bottle. Although in past experiments these containers were cleaned in vats of nitric acid, rinsed with pure water, filled with pure argon to displace lead-contaminated air, and sealed in plastic bags equipped with breathing filters, they were first shipped from the factory to the laboratory in the midst of auto traffic and were each thereby sprayed, literally, with thousands of micrograms of lead before they were cleaned. Upon evaluating the data it has become apparent that these very large containers, first contaminated and then carefully cleaned, apparently contributed about 0.05 microgram of lead to each sample, which is too much, compared to that in Roman time samples, for accurate measurement. By collecting the plastic containers at the factory as they come off the production line and sealing them in plastic bags for shipment to the laboratory, that source of contamination could be eliminated. At the present time about 0.1 microgram of lead contamination is added to a 50-liter sample during analysis. The various sources and magnitudes of this contamination are now known (mainly reagents) and promising methods for reducing it by a factor of ten have been proposed. Although it has not yet been done, it is reasonable to suppose that techniques could be developed for the collecting, processing, and analysis of 50 liters of ice meltwater with a total contamination of about 0.01 microgram of lead. For medieval times, 50-liter snowmelt samples from the interior of northern Greenland should contain about 0.05 microgram of industrial lead, which means that measurement capability for the lowest-expected concentrations should be above contamination background, providing suitable conditions for reasonably accurate measurements.

The necessarily large size of the samples requires that the ice be mined out in the form of large blocks from a shaft. In the previously sampled arctic location, the inclined shaft was 1000 feet long and 300 feet deep, while it was 300 feet long and 150 feet deep at the antarctic location. The shafts were driven with electric chain saws and electric hoists. Samples were taken from the faces of short, horizontal adits driven into the walls of the shafts. To prevent contamination, the investigators, at the time of collecting the blocks, were encased in plastic suits and gloves and worked with teflon-handled, stainless steel tools that had been cleaned in nitric acid. The freshly removed ice blocks were exposed only a few moments before being sealed in plastic drums. They were melted on electrically heated baths and syphons transferred the water to large bottles. The shafts extended through about 200 annual snow layers. The difference in shaft depths was due to the difference in rates of snow accumulation at the two locations.

A section of more than 2000 annual layers of snow could be sampled by a shaft 1000 feet deep in the northern Greenland ice sheet near the central interior where snow accumulation is minimal. A 6-foot-diameter vertical shaft could be rapidly excavated with a steam drill, which is simply a large heater, or ice melter, fed by steam. Snow shields in polar regions become impermeable a short distance down, and as the ice shaft filled with meltwater it could be pumped out with an electric pump which followed the heater down. The major requirements would include: a headframe with attached pulleys, electric winch, and drums capable of handling a five-ton load for a length of 1500 feet; generators capable of delivering 100 KW with accessory transformers and transmission lines; several large diesel fuel bladders and accessory pumping equipment; a diesel steam generator; a diesel snow melter with auxiliary storage tank and tractor skip loader; several thousand feet of high-pressure, flexible, linked steam hose plus several thousand feet of high-pressure, linked water hose capable of withstanding a pressure of 1000 psi; several thousand feet of low-resistance electric cable; hut enclosure for the headframe assembly, hut enclosure for the generator and snow melter assembly; subsistence and communication units for six working plus four emergency men. After the shaft had been dug, an elevator would be installed on the headframe in place of the steam melter, and the shaft would be wired for power. Short, horizontal adits would be excavated from the walls of the shaft with electric chain saws at appropriate levels. The debris removed by this operation could be dumped into a previously prepared, bell-shaped sump at the bottom of the shaft which had been melted and pumped out when the shaft was dug if it was decided that this would not set up unduly hazardous stresses. If it would be too hazardous, then the debris from the side adits would have to be hoisted out, which would require additional time. In the sample-collecting stage the following year, a laboratory hut would be installed, the ice blocks would be collected, melted, and aliquoted into bottles. It would be difficult to dig the shaft and collect the samples in one season. Even though the work would be within areas unexposed to storms, it might be too exhausting and tedious to be carried out by a wintering-over party. The additional hazards of such an operation might not be balanced by a sufficient diminution of the wall closure hazard. The shafts and adits could be dug in one season and samples from thirty to forty locations could be taken the following summer.

Wall closure above an 800-foot depth might not exceed 20 percent in a year. Below that depth, wall closure could be compensated for by enlarging the shaft diameter below that level initially, anticipating about 50 percent closure within 15 months. For the small, void volumes and rounded cross sections involved, it seems likely that only plastic flow closure without rupture would ensue. Some consideration might be given to the shape of adits that would avoid concentration of stresses and spalling.

The number of required air flights would be small. Operating from Thule, round-trip air time for a ski-equipped C-130 to the shaft site would not exceed four hours, allowing one hour for unloading and pretakeoff runway packing runs. This short weather prediction time should permit an adequate number of supply flights to be tightly bunched early in the season. In the first season the freight flights might consist of four to bring in the huts plus supplies, two for fuel, and two for auxiliary equipment. In the second season the flights might consist of one for subsistence and personnel, two for container delivery, two for water sample pickup, and two for equipment retrieval. Much material would be abandoned. The skip loader might be used to prepare the runway, but it is likely that the expense of jato takeoffs would be required in most instances. The cost of the operation, excluding air transportation and some borrowed major equipment which would include both an electric and a steam generator, winches, huts, subsistence and communication equipment, and vehicles, might come to $200,000 for supplies and salaries for analytical development, collecting, and analysis. The time involved would amount to about two years for development, two years for collecting, and two years for analysis. Time and costs must be provided for in the development of the headframe, steam melter, elevator, water pump linkages, and removable cable shackles for the attachment of water, steam, and electric lines to the hoist cable. Although this appears to be a rather extensive operation for one experiment, it could be coupled with several congruent ones.

There are other substances besides lead which might be used as atmospheric indicators of the intensity of industrial activity in medieval and ancient times. Vanadium is one. Like lead, it is a rare element and does not occur naturally to any great extent in air, but it is concentrated in the ash of coal and other carbonaceous fuels. It is virtually certain that the vanadium content of snows would reflect the increase that has occurred in the rate of coal burning. Elements such as iron would record the increase of iron smelter production, but the natural iron content of the atmosphere is high because it is abundant in clay dusts, and the natural iron background in snow might be too high. On the other hand, copper might be a good possibility. It could be measured by neutron activation. Murozumi et al. used very large volumes of water for their samples, and upon melting their samples in large, separate, very clean, white drums, they observed faint, dark, carbonaceous rings where the water surface had been. The rings' intensity faded out as the ages of the snow layers from which samples were taken increased to three or four decades. It may be that a sensitive chromotographic technique could be developed which would detect an organic atmospheric constituent of burned fossil fuels.

A number of physical property studies of ice under extreme pressures, previously impossible with coring techniques, could be carried out. Wintering-over parties could make use of the surface site for more typical studies.

In any case, it seems perfectly feasible to measure relative changes in silver production and industrial activity at various times several thousand years ago. The lead experiments that have already been carried out and cited above were supported in several seasons at Camp Tuto and Camp Century, Greenland, as part of the operations of the U.S. Army Cold Regions Research and Engineering Laboratory at Hanover, New Hampshire. Laboratory work and supplies were funded by the U.S. Atomic Energy Commission and the U.S. Public Health Service. Lead measurements at Byrd Station in the Antarctic were funded by the Antarctic Research Program of the National Science Foundation and the U.S. Atomic Energy Commission.

XVI

CHEMICAL STUDIES OF ISLAMIC LUSTER GLASS

R. H. Brill

$\mathcal{L}$USTER DECORATIONS are thin metallic films applied to the surfaces of ceramic objects. Since its beginnings, possibly as early as the fourth century A.D., but certainly by the ninth century, the technique of film application has seen frequent use down to the present day. In different times and at different places it has been used to produce a wide variety of colors and appearances, ranging from highly reflecting mirrorlike surfaces to faintly perceptible iridescences. Numerous kinds of colored stains and glazes have often accompanied luster effects and in some cases have so enhanced the ornamentation that these stains and glazes themselves have come to be termed "lusters" even though metallic films may not be present.

Because lusterwares vary so much in style and are broadly distributed geographically—and even more so because of the somewhat complicated technologies involved in making them—there must be many cases where analysis and examination of ancient fragments would be of use to those concerned with medieval studies. The historical spread of the technique has been much discussed by art historians, and both the technology and matters of stylistic identification are usually treated as being well understood. Such may very well be the case. Laboratory studies of sufficiently large numbers of representative wares, however, would undoubtedly prove very worthwhile either for verifying the existing theories or for answering questions about problematical pieces. Analysis of the luster glazes themselves and analysis, X-ray diffraction, and petrographic examination of the fabrics would all probably be helpful.[1]

---

[1] In preparing for this study, a literature search indicated that few, if any, analyses had been made of luster decoration on glass and only a few of pottery of Islamic origin. However, realizing that analyses or studies of this sort might well have been published in places familiar only to Islamic scholars, the accompanying bibliography should not be relied upon as being complete. One analytical study

The scope of the present paper, however, is not intended to be so all-encompassing. The work described here has been confined to one very limited aspect of luster decoration. The main objective has been to see what could be learned about one specific group of luster glass fragments.

There are four significant lines of glass research which converge on the group of fragments studied here. In the first place, the glasses were most likely made in the Islamic glass factories at Fustat, near present-day Cairo. Therefore, the analysis of the glasses themselves should be fitted into the systematic cataloging of compositions of ancient glasses that are being developed.[2] Future analysis of groups of luster glasses (and their glazes) from different parts of the Islamic world might well show compositional differences that could be helpful in characterizing the wares made at different factories.

Even a casual examination of the most common type of luster decoration on Islamic glass, a deep transparent amber stain, suggests that it is a silver stain. Thus Islamic luster glass can be considered to form a historical link connecting the earliest known use of silver and/or gold in ancient glass, for coloring a small group of Late Roman dichroic glasses,[3] with the use of silver for making the yellow-stained glasses of the cathedral windows of Western Europe.

The chemical formulation of the Islamic luster glazes also is of some interest from the viewpoint of the history of chemistry, for there is at least one extant recipe for luster glazes for pottery in the early Persian

---

appears in an appendix to F. Sarre, *Die Ausgrabungen von Samarra, Band II* (Berlin), pp. 95–100. Also a series of early papers were presented by L. Franchet, who concerned himself with the technology of Islamic luster glazes. See, for example, *Comptes Rendus*, vol. 141 (1905), 1020–1022, 1237–1240; *Ann. Chim. Phys.* (8), 9 (1906), 37, 227; *Trans. Brit. Ceramic Soc.*, vol. 7 (1907), 71.

[2] The most noteworthy of these is that being compiled by E. V. Sayre and R. W. Smith. See, for example, E. V. Sayre and R. W. Smith "Compositional Categories of Ancient Glass," *Science*, vol. 133 (9 June 1961), 1824–1826, and "Some Ancient Glass Specimens with Compositions of Particular Archaeological Significance," (BNL-879 T-354) Brookhaven National Laboratories (July 1964). Other large bodies of analytical data are being compiled by M. A. Besborodov in Leningrad and by the author at The Corning Museum of Glass. Analyses up to 1957 have been tabulated and reinterpreted by Earle R. Caley in his *Analyses of Ancient Glasses, 1790–1957* (New York: The Corning Museum of Glass, 1962).

[3] R. H. Brill, "The Chemistry of the Lycurgus Cup," paper no. 223, *Comptes Rendus, II*, VIIth International Congress on Glass, Brussels, 1965, International Commission on Glass.

literature, and others are known from Hispano-Moresque and Italian sources.

The fourth line of research is of a fundamental chemical nature, and deals with the broad question of the nature of the colorants used in ancient red, orange, and yellow opaque glasses. Two of the types of luster studied here are red opaque and yellow opaque stains.

In the sections that follow we shall review the history of luster decoration, describe the samples studied, record the results of several types of experiments, and interpret the experimental results in terms of the lines of research indicated above.

It must be added that these results can only be considered provisional, because experimental work is still in process as this paper is being prepared.

The History of Luster Decoration

Although the topic has been much discussed, leading authorities do not agree upon either the place or date of the origin of luster decoration. Indeed the discussion has at times become so lively that one not well versed in all the arguments hesitates to comment even casually upon the question. The most favored authoritative dates range from the eighth-ninth century back to as early as the fourth-fifth century A.D., and the favored places of origin seem to be Egypt, Persia, and Mesopotamia.[4] Although questions of origin are sometimes finally relegated to unimportance, it does seem that in this case the question could ultimately be of considerable importance in the history of glass—even if not so in ceramics. The question is sharpened by the viewpoint of Lamm that the technique of luster decoration originated with the "glass painters of Egypt." It would be of value to determine the place and date of origin of such a readily recognizable decoration, because this could perhaps be of help in

[4] From the many possible references, we single out here a few containing general discussions of lusterwares. R. Ettinghausen, "An Early Islamic Glass Making Center," *Record of the Museum of Historic Art,* Princeton University, vol. 1 (1942), 4–7; A. W. Frothingham, *Lustreware of Spain,* Hispanic Society of America, New York (1951); C. J. Lamm, *Oriental Glass of Medieval Date Found in Sweden and the Early History of Lustre-Painting* (Stockholm, 1941). See esp. pp. 18–33; A. Lane, *Early Islamic Pottery* (London: Faber and Faber, 1947), pp. 14–20 *passim;* A. V. Pope and P. Ackerman, *A Survey of Persian Art,* vol. II (Oxford University Press, 1939), pp. 1469, 1487–1498, 1545–1558, and esp. 1701–1702; Hans E. Wulff, *The Traditional Arts and Crafts of Persia* (M.I.T. Press, 1966).

telling us to just what extent glass craftsmen did move around in ancient times, and more importantly it might help to clarify our pictures of the ways in which the ancient and indigenous glass industries of the Near East developed into those of the Islamic Period.

We might observe here that the recent discovery at Fustat of the earliest known dated piece of luster glass, a beaker bearing the date of 771–772,[5] lends some support to the view that the technique originated with the glass painters of Egypt.

There were several well-known centers producing luster-decorated pottery, and possibly glass, during the Islamic Period. Some of these were Baghdad and Basra in Iraq, Kashan in Persia, and Fustat in Egypt. The art spread westward via North Africa, and inspired the famous Hispano-Moresque ceramics which reached an artistic peak in the fifteenth century, and to Majorca and Italy where it was incorporated into majolica ware.

Description of Samples

This research was prompted by a group of Islamic luster glass fragments in the collection of The Corning Museum of Glass. Unfortunately, the exact provenience cannot be rigorously proved, but since the fragments were obtained in Cairo, and since they are very similar to types of luster glass excavated at Fustat in great quantities, we believe it is reasonable to assume that they either were made in the factories known to have existed in Fustat, or at least that they came from the extensive rubbish heaps there. Thirty samples were selected for analysis from a group of approximately 700 fragments, and numerous others were examined.

There are three distinct types of glass represented. The first, the most common type of Islamic luster glass, bears a deep amber transparent stain on transparent base glasses which are either very well decolorized, or tinged with the characteristic aqua or pale greenish colors produced by iron (figs. 1, 2).

The second type is a dense yellow-orange opaque stain on either a dark blue transparent base glass or, more rarely, on a greenish glass slightly stronger in color than the aqua mentioned above (fig. 3). It should be noted that this yellow color is definitely due to a stain, that is, the color results from a fine dispersion of colorant particles beneath the surface of

---

[5] George T. Scanlon, "Fustat, 1965," *Newsletter,* no. 54 (June 1965), 3–6, American Research Center in Cairo.

FIG. 1. Fragment of blown-glass vessel, amber stain on pale greenish glass, 10th-11th century, probably made at Fustat. Similar to sample 1014-1020.

FIG. 2. Fragment of blown-glass vessel, amber stain on colorless glass, 10th-11th century, probably made at Fustat. Similar to samples 1010-1013.

the glass.[6] None of the glasses used in this study has the structure of enameled glasses, where a distinct and separate body of decorative material stands raised in relief above the surface of the glass. The third type is a bright red opaque (or translucent) stain on a deep olive-colored transparent base glass (fig. 4).

[6] Stains fitting this description have been termed "fused-in enamels," but this is a very misleading description and is actually inconsistent with the definition of enamels. This becomes apparent, however, only after one is familiar with the chemical nature of the staining process.

FIG. 3. Fragments of blown-glass vessels, yellow opaque stain on dark blue transparent glass, 9th century, probably found at Fustat. Similar to samples 1022-1025.

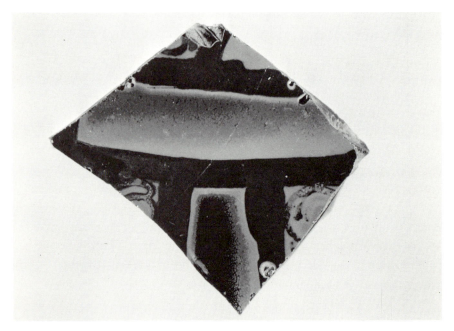

FIG. 4. Fragment of blown glass vessel, bright red opaque stain on transparent olive glass, 9th century, probably found at Fustat. Similar to samples 1027-1029.

Although these descriptions have been stated in terms of pure colors, the yellow and red stains sometimes show a mottled effect containing other colors, as well as superimposed decorations in amber. On the amber-stained fragments milky halations often outline the painted designs. The fragments selected for analysis were examples of the purer, more saturated colors, free of the transient color effects, and showing no macroscopic weathering.

It is notable that only a small proportion of the fragments in the total collection actually show a distinct metallic luster. The color effects by far dominate the luster effects in the decorative motifs. Thus the use of the term "luster" in describing these glasses might be questioned. It is likely, however, that the surface appearances of these glasses could have been much more lustrous or metallic when they were new, because a loss of luster through volatilization could well have occurred over the centuries. Only about 15 percent of the fragments now show a distinct luster, in some cases mirrorlike but in most cases only ephemeral. In view of this, and because of chemical evidence presented in a latter section, we shall refer to the decorations on these glasses as stained regions rather than luster regions, keeping in mind, however, that they are commonly called luster decorations in the archaeological and historical literature.

On the basis of stylistic considerations, Richard Ettinghausen [7] is of the opinion that the amber-stained fragments analyzed here date from the tenth to the eleventh centuries, with the decolorized base glass possibly being somewhat later than the greenish glass. He feels that the yellow- and red-stained fragments, again based on stylistic considerations, are earlier, dating probably from the ninth century or possibly the very early tenth century. Axel von Saldern,[8] who originally cataloged these fragments, shares these views.

The fragments are all of blown vessels, with thicknesses ranging from about 1 mm up to as great as 4 mm. Rims, bases, and wall fragments are all represented. The exact shapes of the vessels have not yet been reconstructed but it is expected that they are the usual cups, beakers, bowls, and small pitchers.

A detailed catalog of the samples studied is appended at the end of this text (appendix 1, p. 375).

As supporting experiments we have also analyzed the luster glazes on four pieces of Hispano-Moresque wares, which were very kindly provided

[7] Professor, Institute of Fine Arts, New York University.
[8] Curator, Kunstmuseum, Düsseldorf, Germany.

by Miss Maria Manuela Soares de Iliveira,[9] and a piece of seventeenth-century stained glass from Nürnberg, supplied by A. G. Frenzel.

Microscopic Examination

Microscopic examinations of many examples from this group of fragments established two important facts. The first is that the colorants within the stained regions lie beneath the surface of the glasses themselves. The colored regions do not in any case protrude or stand in relief above the surface of the base glass, as do enamel decorations. Neither could they be applied to glass which was marvered in. These stains are an entirely different class of decorations than enamels or marvered-in threads. The color of the stained zones seems for the most part not to extend much beyond a depth of 20 microns (0.02 mm) below the surface. In the case of the yellow stain, the color can be seen to be due to a dispersion of fine particles appearing to have a yellow color individually. At the highest magnification available (400×) the shapes of the particles could not be resolved, but they seemed to be approximately regular and of uniform size. The largest measure about 0.3 micron across.

The red stains were found to be due similarly to a fine dispersion of particles, again apparently of regular shapes, with the largest measuring about 0.3 micron across. These grains, however, show distinct metallic reflections. The color-producing particles are usually below a zone of transparent glass which lies just adjacent to the surface of the glass. The occasional small bubbles trapped in the colored zones are spherically shaped. Sometimes they are associated with devitrification crystals, an indication that the glass was reheated after forming, and are surrounded by zones of transparent glass. These transparent zones are undoubtedly localized zones of oxidized glass.

Representative specimens of the red and yellow glasses have been examined by Edward Korda and Raymond Fritz, both of Corning Glass Works, using a scanning electron microscope. These studies have not yet been completed, but we hope to determine more accurately just what are the shapes and dimensions of the colorant particles in each type of glass.

Chemical Analysis

Four types of chemical analysis were carried out on the selected fragments. First, X-ray emission analyses were made of masked-off stained

[9] Curator, Fundação Calouste Gubenkian, Oeiras, Portugal.

regions on the fragments. This technique is well suited for this type of analysis, because the primary exciting X-radiation does not penetrate more than about 50 microns (0.05 mm) beneath the surface of the sample being analyzed. Thus the analysis obtained is essentially that of the stained surface regions rather than of the unaltered base glass below. Two independent sets of analyses were made of these stains. The first was made by Charles A. Jedlicka of Lucius Pitkin Laboratories in New York City, using a Norelco X-ray spectrograph with a tungsten target and LiF crystal. The second was by Donald Stephenson and Mrs. Dorothy Kimble of Corning Glass Works. They used a General Electric X-ray spectrograph, model XRD-6, with a chromium target and LiF and EDDT crystals. The results were only qualitative, because it would be very difficult to express the concentrations in quantitative terms. Actually, since there is obviously a variation in the compositions of the lusters, quantitative results would not be particularly more helpful anyway. A few complete scans have been made, but in most cases only partial scans were made, because we were interested primarily in establishing the presence or absence of specific elements. The effective applicability of X-ray emission analysis under the conditions used was limited to atomic numbers greater than 16, that is, to sulfur and the elements following it in the periodic table.[10]

Before the X-ray emission analyses were carried out, Jedlicka had removed parts of the stained regions and made emission spectrographic analyses of the stains. These samples consisted of mixtures of both stained and some unstained glass, but by comparison with spectrographic analyses of the base glasses beneath the stain it was possible to determine by this independent method the principal constituents of the colorants in the stained regions. These results are summarized, along with those from the X-ray emission analyses, in table 1.

Following the analyses of the stained regions, samples were removed from the unstained regions of the same fragments and semiquantitative spectrographic analyses were made of the base glasses. These samples were analyzed with four reference glasses used routinely in our analyses.[11]

[10] Actually, because of their high concentrations aluminum and silicon could also be seen.

[11] These reference glasses are the same as those being used in an international analytical round robin. They are described in "Interlaboratory Comparison Experiments on the Analysis of Ancient Glass," paper no. 226, *Comptes Rendus, II,* VIIth International Congress on Glass, Brussels (1965), International Commission on Glass.

TABLE I
Analyses of Stains*
Partial Results; X-ray & Spect.

Color	Major	Minor—Trace †
Amber (11)	Cu, Ag	Sn, Pb, As, Bi, Au, Hg (?)
Yellow (6)	Cu, Ag	Sn, Pb, S, Ni
Red (3)	Cu, Ag	Sn, Pb, Au, Bi, Sb (?)

* Elements not present in base glasses.
† Sn in 11 stains, others in 1-5 stains (nf: Zn, Sb).

Samples of the same fragments were then analyzed by flame photometry to obtain quantitative values for Na_2O, K_2O, and CaO and MgO. Combined results of the spectrographic and flame photometric analyses of the base glasses are given in table 2. The samples there are grouped according to the colors of the base glasses and/or the types of their stained decorations.

From the analyses in table 1, it is apparent that the main constituents of all three colors of stain are silver and copper. In the eleven amber stains analyzed, silver and copper were present in about the same concentrations. Among the yellow opaque and red opaque stains there was more copper than silver in some examples, and about the same amount in others. The luster stains on the four pieces of pottery analyzed were very rich in copper but no silver was detected.[12]

The minor and trace components are variable from piece to piece even among samples of the same color type. As a result, we plan more systematic and comprehensive analyses of all of these stains. The most common occurrences are tin and lead. The presence of tin is known to be beneficial for the developing of copper-red stains [13] and it could well have been so in this instance. This cannot be taken as proof, however, that the craftsmen were necessarily aware of the fact that tin has this beneficial effect, because tin would have been introduced accidentally if the original source of copper in their formulations were bronze rather than copper or copper minerals. The copper–tin ratio seems to be consistent with this explanation in the cases where we could estimate it.

[12] The pottery glazes themselves were found to be essentially tin glazes containing also lead, zinc, calcium, potassium, iron, and titanium. Some also showed arsenic and were colored with cobalt.

[13] For an excellent survey of the chemistry of color in glasses, as well as a very comprehensive bibliography on the subject, see W. A. Weyl, *Coloured Glasses,* (London: Dawson's, 1959).

TABLE 2
Analyses of Base Glasses*

	Colorless, amber (4)	Pale green, amber (4)		Aqua, amber (3)	Dark blue, yellow (4)	Olive, red (3)
SiO_2	64	64	58	61	59	55
Na_2O	17–20	17–20		17–20	17–20	17–20
CaO	7.5	7–8	12–15	12–15	9.5	9.0
K_2O	3.8	4		1.2	2	2.5
MgO	2.6	2.5		1.0	5	5
Al_2O_3	1.6	2.2		2.2	3.0	7–9
Fe_2O_3	0.42	0.45		0.75	1.3	1.0
TiO_2	0.07	0.09		0.27	0.25	0.40
CuO	–	–		–	0.1–0.4	–
CoO	–	–		–	0.09	–
PbO	–	–		–	0.01–0.1	0.05
BaO	0.05	0.07		0.04	0.02	0.04
SrO	0.04	0.04		0.02	0.03	0.03
ZrO_2	–	–		0.01	0.03	0.08
MnO	0.9	0.7		0.1–0.4	0.8	0.25

* At the time of publication the results of our quantitative analyses were not yet available. Therefore, the results presented in this table are composite spectrographic and X-ray emission analyses of each type of glass. The samples are described by the colors of the base glasses and stains. Numbers in parentheses are the number of analyses of each type. SiO_2 by difference.

A fuller investigation of the other minor-trace elements, such as gold, mercury, arsenic, and sulfur (seen only in our X-ray emission analyses and not spectrographically), might shed some light on the formulations of the stains. We might anticipate learning whether or not gold played a part in the process, whether realgar and orpiment were used, to what extent sulfur or sulfates were present, and whether the silver was introduced as an amalgam.

From the analyses of the base glasses in table 2, it can be seen that the glasses themselves are of the expected soda-lime-silica type, with the usual impurities such as K_2O, MgO, Al_2O_3, and Fe_2O_3.[14]

[14] For readers unfamiliar with the chemistry of ancient glasses, or with the nature of glass as a material, the two following references might be useful. R. H. Brill, "Ancient Glass," *Sci. Amer.* (Nov. 1963), pp. 120–130, and R. H. Brill, "A Note on the Scientist's Definition of Glass," *J. of Glass Stud.*, vol. IV (1962), 127–138.

There are four noteworthy features. For the most part the K_2O and MgO contents are on the order of 2–4 percent, which places them in the high K_2O–high MgO type of glasses in Sayre's system of classification.[15] This is quite reasonable because of the suggested Fustat provenience. (The low K_2O–low MgO type contains on the order of tenths of 1 percent of each.) These classifications are at present more applicable to earlier glasses, because relatively few examples of glasses of this late date have as yet been analyzed. Sayre has found among some Islamic weights he analyzed (15 samples) and some Islamic luster glasses (6 samples of unspecified dates) that there is about an equal division among high and low K_2O–MgO types.[16] Thus, along with our own results, one might see considerable promise that analysis of the base glasses might some day serve to differentiate between luster glasses from different regions and dates of origin.

A second characteristic is that the glasses have been decolorized with manganese. That manganese has been used is consistent with earlier analyses. The only exceptions are those three fragments that show the strongest greenish color. This provides an excellent example of how efficient ancient glassmakers were in their decolorizing processes. The group of eight glasses cataloged as colorless and very pale green do contain an appreciable amount of iron—about 0.45 percent. Without a decolorizer this much iron would yield a distinct green color.

A third observation is that the blue base glass is colored primarily by cobalt, and although cobalt had already been used by glassmakers for some twenty-three centuries, it usually was accompanied by more copper than is present in these glasses. This clearly indicates that a ready source of cobalt was at hand and that it was freely used, since it did not have to be adulterated with copper. One would have expected it to be adulterated if the blue glass had been made, for example, in Persia, instead of Egypt. Perhaps the most interesting result of these analyses is that the glasses bearing the yellow and red stains appear to have distinctly different base compositions from the "colorless" glasses. In the first place, the MgO values are considerably higher—up to about 5 percent—and the Al_2O_3 in the red glass is very high, being estimated to be 7 and 9 percent. The

---

[15] See n. 2.

[16] E. V. Sayre, "Refinements in Methods of Neutron Activation Analysis of Ancient Glass Objects through the Use of Lithium Drifted Germanium Diode Counters," paper no. 220, *Comptes Rendus, II,* VIIth International Congress on Glass, Brussels (1965), International Commission on Glass.

number of glasses analyzed is small and one cannot therefore be completely certain yet that the results are significant, but the indication is that the red-stained glass, and possibly the yellows, are of different origin than the ordinary amber-stained glasses. We already suspect them of being of earlier date but the alumina-rich composition puts one more in mind of the glasses made in more northerly regions, for example, the region of the Caspian Sea. This provides further encouragement for making a more comprehensive analytical study of luster glasses. There is some reason to believe, too, that the alumina-rich base glass might be more receptive to copper staining.

X-Ray Diffraction

X-Ray diffraction patterns were obtained for samples representing the three basic colors of stains. The determinations, which were made by Hans Holland and John Geiger of Corning Glass Works, are summarized in table 3, and the results are easily understood when compared to the chemical analysis and observed color effects.

The amber stain is caused by colloidal particles of metallic silver. The red stains are due to metallic copper, in one instance covered over with an observable silver stain having a blue turbid color. The yellow-orange stains were found to contain only Cu_2O. As explained below, the association of a yellow color with Cu_2O, instead of its familiar red color, is probably a particle-size effect.

Reheating Experiments

Samples of the three colors of stained glass were reheated under two different conditions. When the base glass is heated in an oxidizing flame just sufficiently to soften and round off the sharp edges, the color of the

TABLE 3
X-ray Diffraction Results

Sample	Color	Phases detected
1018	Amber	AgO
1022	Yellow-orange	Cu_2O (Poss. trace AgO)
1022	Amber over yellow	Cu_2O, AgO
1024	Yellow-orange	Cu_2O, trace CuO
1027	Red	CuO,
1029	Red	CuO, AgO

yellow and red stains disappears as the grains of the colorants go into solution. With reducing conditions the yellow is converted to a red color. Under magnification this red color can be seen to be associated with particles that appear identical to those in the red-stained glasses. In all cases, including the amber transparent stains, a film forms on the surface which shows a metallic luster or multicolored effects that resemble metal-oxide coatings. Upon more prolonged heating (1 hr at 600°C) in a closed container, the amber stain is deepened in its transmitted color, and shows a greenish yellow reflected color, due to light scattering. The yellow opaque stains tend to darken slowly upon longer heating at 600°C, but after 20 hours the yellow color disappears entirely. All the glasses blister somewhat in the stained regions upon reheating, apparently due to the evolution of dissolved gases from the stained zones.

Fluorescence

Under shortwave ultraviolet irradiation (2537Å), approximately two-thirds of the amber-stained glasses show a lemon-yellow fluorescence (fig. 5). In about half of these cases the fluorescence is very strong, in other cases it is only moderate, but still considerably more pronounced than the usual fluorescences of ancient glasses. The fluorescence appears only on the sides of the fragments that have stained decorations, and is much weaker under longwave (3660Å) ultraviolet. The yellow fluores-

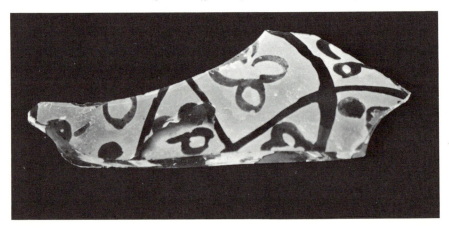

FIG. 5. Fragment of luster glass similar to that in figure 2, but photographed under shortwave ultraviolet irradiation. Bright regions record the lemon-yellow fluorescence from the unstained regions between the stained decorations, which do not themselves fluoresce. Stray visible light and ultraviolet filtered out. (15 min. exp., f/3.5, Plus X film.)

cence is also qualitatively different from the colors usually seen and is certainly due to the presence of colloidal silver. It is very striking, however, that there is no fluorescence in the amber-stained regions themselves, although the milky halation zones outlining the amber regions do fluoresce.

It is a little puzzling why the fluorescence should be so prominent in the unstained regions of the stained surfaces. Apparently, volatilization during the firing process led to the deposition of very finely divided silver in the regions between the painted designs. The bright fluorescence there must be due more to the fine subdivision of the silver rather than to the

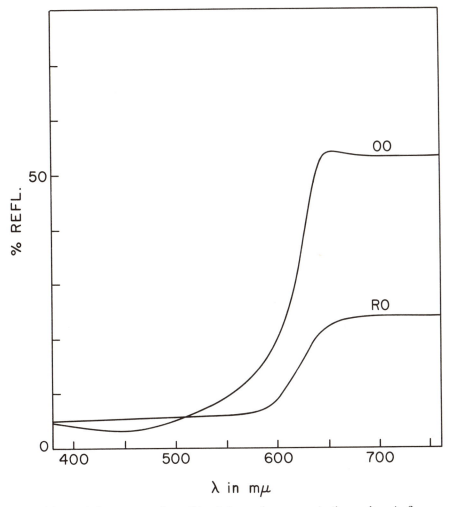

FIG. 6. Transmission spectra of two Islamic luster fragments similar to those in figures 1 and 2, compared to known silver-stained glass.

amount of silver present. There is much more silver present in the painted regions, but the fluorescence efficiency is much diminished because of the larger particle sizes and possibly also because the presence of copper there quenches the fluorescence.

The yellow- and red-stained glasses show no fluorescence.

Transmission and Reflectance Spectra

Transmission and reflectance spectra of the stained regions were obtained by Roland French of Corning Glass Works. These are reproduced in figures 6, 7, and 8, along with curves representative of some glasses from other periods.

In figure 6, curves I_1 and I_2 show the transmission spectra of two amber stains on the Islamic fragments. Both were run against the unstained portion of the same fragments as references, thus compensating for the aqua color of the base glasses themselves. These spectra, therefore, are of only the stain coloration. Curve N_1 is for the bright lemon-yellow–stained portion of the seventeenth-century Nürnberg window which on analysis for silver showed only a trace of copper. Curve N_2 is for an orange-stained region from the same window which contains a considerable amount of copper, as well as silver. Qualitatively, the transmissions of the two Islamic amber stains look more like the orange glass N_2 than the pure silver stain having curve N_1. The two stains must have something in common to give them similar colors and the analysis suggests that it may be the presence of copper.

Figure 7 shows reflectance spectra for one of the Islamic yellow-stained fragments (curve YO), and for one of the Islamic red-stained fragments (curve RO_1). It is believed that the rather sharp cutoff in reflectance at about 600 millimicrons, for the yellow stain, is characteristic of the color of cuprous oxide, the phase known to be present from X-ray diffraction. This is confirmed by the reflectances of two experimental glasses, also known to be colored by Cu_2O, which are shown in figure 8. These are two samples of the same glass given different heat treatments which, in turn, produced different colors. (This is another reason for our belief that the color of Cu_2O-containing glasses is dependent upon the particle sizes.) The same sharp cutoff is found on these curves, as in the yellow-stained Islamic glass.

On the other hand, the reflectance of the red-stained Islamic glass (RO_2 in figure 7) has a qualitatively different shape than the red Cu_2O-containing glass. It is known to be colored by a dispersion of metallic copper crystals, as was shown by X-ray diffraction.

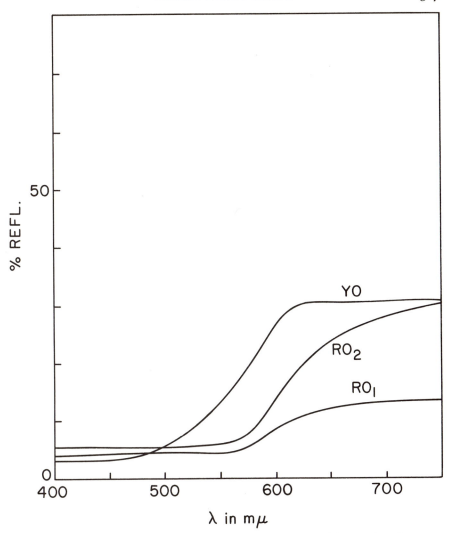

Fig. 7. Reflectance spectra of yellow-opaque stained region of luster glass fragment similar to those in figure 3, and red-stained region of fragment similar to that in Figure 4.

Duplication Experiments

There are at least two, and possibly more, recipes given in the early literature for luster glazes to be applied to pottery.[17] We have selected one as a starting point for some experiments to duplicate the luster effects observed on our Islamic fragments. Of course, there is no reason to believe that the recipe we have selected should necessarily correspond to that used

[17] An Italian recipe by Cipriano Piccolpasso (1524–1579) appears in J. R. Partington, *A History of Chemistry*, vol. 2 (London: Macmillan, 1961), 77–80.

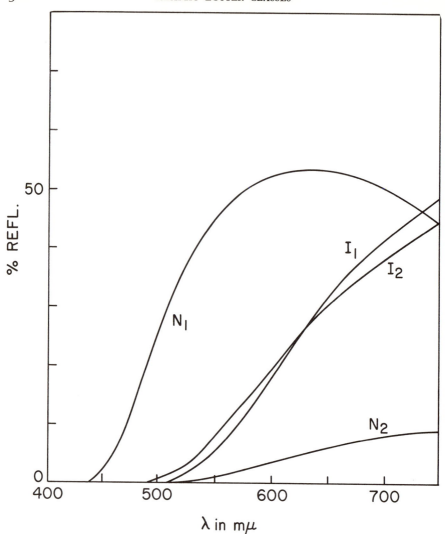

FIG. 8. Reflectance spectra of polished surfaces of two experimental glasses colored by Cu_2O. The upper curve is for a bright orange opaque sample and the lower curve for a bright red opaque sample. Samples differed only in heat treatment following their forming in small crucibles.

by the craftsmen who decorated the pieces we happened to analyze. Nevertheless, one can hardly resist the temptation to guess at the chemicals referred to in the recipe and follow out the directions to see what will happen.[18]

[18] We are probably not the first to have yielded to such a temptation. From the discussions of Franchet, it appears that he made some experiments as did probably the workers mentioned in n. 19.

The recipe to which we refer was recorded by Abdallah Ibn Ali Al-Kashani at Tabriz, in 1300–1301. He was one of a family of famous potters then producing luster pottery in Kashan. The recipes were part of a text translated and interpreted in 1935 by H. Ritter, J. Ruska, F. Sarre, and R. Winderlich.[19] While this recipe was specified for luster decoration of pottery, the text does refer elsewhere to transparent wares.

The author is very much indebted to Martin Levey,[20] a noted historian of chemistry, who retranslated the recipe from the Persian and made valuable suggestions as to the identifications of some of the chemicals involved. In general Levey's translation agreed with that cited above, but he pointed out that the German version is not quite literal and contains some interpretations that are not explicitly stated in the Persian text.

To elaborate on all the reasoning that went into the choice of ingredients used in our experiments would require more space than is warranted here, and so we have simply presented the recipe in English, and along with this is a preparation used in one of our duplication experiments (appendix 2, p. 376).

In the first trials made, the paint was applied to small plates of a commercial soda-lime glass which approximates fairly well the analyzed compositions of the Islamic glasses. One notable difference in composition, which could have an effect on the susceptibility of the glass to taking a stain, is that the trial glasses were much lower in iron than the ancient glasses. Since iron might have been the principal internal reducing agent available to the migrated silver ions (see the chemical mechanism discussed below), the ancient glass might have taken the stain more readily. Our later trials, still under way, are being made on thin rolled sheets of experimental melts[21] which more closely resemble the Islamic glasses, having been patterned after the analyses in table 2.

The sample glass plates, with the applied paints, were wrapped in insulation material and placed in ceramic boxes with small pieces of wood, to maintain a slightly reducing atmosphere. The boxes were placed in a large electric furnace, brought slowly from room temperature to 650°C, and held at that temperature. Draw samples were removed at various

[19] H. Ritter, J. Ruska, F. A. Sarre, and R. Winderlich, "Orientalische Steinbecher und Persische Fayencetechnik," *Istanbuler Mitteilungen, Herausgegeben von der Abteilung Istanbul des Archäologischen Institutes des Deutschen Reiches*, Heft 3, Istanbul (1935).

[20] Dept. of the History of Science, State University of New York at Albany.

[21] These glasses were melted by A. A. Erickson, Manager of Melting Technology, Corning Glass Works, to whom we express our appreciation.

intervals ranging up to 13 hours. A second set of heat treatments was carried out at 600°C with times ranging up to 65 hours.[22]

The sample plates of commercial glass painted with the synthetic ancient preparation, though spotty because of uneven application, developed yellow and amber stains after 15 to 30 minutes at 650°. After more prolonged heating the surfaces tended to take on a yellow-greenish translucency. The appearance, however, was more like that of a surface-devitrified glass than a proper stained surface. In isolated spots ruby-red transparent patches appeared, but neither did they resemble the red-stained regions of the ancient glass, which have a greater opacity. No strongly lustrous metallic films were observed, but faint interference colors were sometimes seen.

The experiments on the synthetic Islamic glass produced amber transparent stains resembling the ancient ones. Occasional traces of a metallic luster showed in small unevenly spaced patches, and a pale greenish yellow opacity developed after longer heating. It did not resemble, however, the best yellow opaque stain seen on the ancient pieces, but was more like the mottled regions of less carefully painted background areas.

It was interesting to see that the ancient formulation did produce an amber stain not unlike that on the Islamic fragments. On the other hand, it must be admitted that it is not a very tricky process and almost any silver salt can be used to make a silver stain of sorts, even if not one suitable for fine decoration.

Interpretation of Results

From all of the foregoing evidence it is clear that the amber transparent decorations are essentially silver stains, and that both the yellow and red are copper stains. Both the chemical nature of these stains and the mechanisms by which they form are quite well understood,[23] but there are some ramifications in the cases of these ancient examples which need to be discussed.

When a silver salt is painted onto the surface of a glass, and then fired, silver ions migrate into the glass by an ion-exchange mechanism, replacing sodium ions which occupy modifying positions in the silicate network of the glass structure. The exchange occurs readily because the silver ion is

[22] The heat treatments were carried out by William Edminster and Fred Krome, both of Corning Glass Works.
[23] W. Weyl, op. cit., passim.

approximately the same size as the sodium ion, and has the same charge. Under even mildly reducing conditions the migrated silver is chemically reduced and precipitates out as a colloidal dispersion of metallic silver. (The presence of ferrous ions or other reducing species appears to help the reduction along.) The glass then takes on a yellow transparent color due to the absorption of blue light by the very small silver particles. As the heat treatment continues, additional particles may form, and the existing particles grow somewhat larger, causing the yellow color to deepen to an amber, which can become strong enough to be called brown. As the particles grow beyond some critical size, the absorptive amber color is augmented by a yellowish green reflective appearance due to light scattered from the colloidal particles. As the particles grow still larger, the scattering becomes more important than the absorption, and a smoky blue-gray turbidity appears. This turbidity can become so dense that the transmission color, a dull red, can be viewed only with very intense illumination.[24]

In the case of copper stains, the colors are somewhat more difficult to produce and the mechanism seems to be less straightforward. Copper has less a tendency to migrate into the glass than does silver. It also appears that when the copper does get into the glass its reduction to metallic copper is more difficult to bring about, and its final state is more sensitive to chemical factors than that of the silver. Nevertheless, when the process does take place and a colloidal dispersion of metallic copper is thrown down, a transparent ruby-red stain results. If the heat treatment is extended, the particles grow to sizes that are large enough to display the color characteristics and reflection of bulk copper. The glasses then take on a livery color and eventually can grow into aventurine glasses, that is, brownish glasses in which flecks of metallic copper can be seen without the aid of any magnification.

Upon refiring under the correct conditions, it is also known that these metals, particularly the copper, can migrate out to the surface again and deposit as a mirrorlike coating of metallic copper.

The descriptions above are sketchy as far as chemical details are concerned and there certainly are questions involved which have not been completely resolved, but in general those are the processes that occurred in the decoration of the ancient amber and red stains we have studied.

The presence, and ultimate fate, of the copper in the ancient silver stain

[24] The color of the Termancia Cup in the collection of the Museo Arqueologico Nacional in Madrid is due to the presence of large particles of silver.

might be explained in several ways. It is possible that the copper was in the formulation for no useful purpose but that it was merely an extraneous constituent included for magical purposes or because the processes simply were not understood. It is much more likely, however, that the copper did perform a specific function, and there are two reasonable ways in which it could have been helpful.

It must first be noted that the observed strong amber is a much more suitable color for the decoration of such vessels than a thin yellow stain which would not stand out as prominently. Therefore, the copper may have contributed to deepening the silver color. The seventeenth-century stained glass window from Nürnberg also analyzed showed a high concentration of copper in the orange-stained portion of the glass, whereas the light yellow regions contained only silver. This is an indication that copper was actually used deliberately to deepen the ordinary yellow color of silver stains at that time. The same means might have been used for the Islamic glasses. (See also the discussion of the transmission spectra.)

The mechanism by which the copper could alter the color of the silver stain might involve a plating out of some copper onto the surface of the colloidal silver crystals or of some solid solution in them. This could alter the optical constants of the silver and cause a change of color. The X-ray diffraction data showed only the presence of metallic silver. The silver lines were broadened, however, due either to their small size or possibly to the presence of copper.

A more logical explanation of the presence of copper is that whereas the silver contributed the color of the stain, the copper was reduced in the smoky atmosphere of the firing and was deposited ultimately on the surface forming the overlying luster part of the decoration.

It is not quite so simple to account for the yellow and red opaque stains, unless one is satisfied simply to dismiss them as being copper stains.

In the case of the reds, the stains are very much like the copper-ruby stains used for making some ruby glasses today, and during the past century. This is confirmed by both the X-ray diffraction data and microscopic examination. It will be recalled that the Islamic red stain has something of an opaque appearance. This is because some particles have grown to rather large sizes. Probably these are accompanied by crystals of colloidal dimensions, too small to be seen under the microscope. In true ruby glasses, which are transparent, only the smaller particles are present.

It is the yellow stains that pose the most interesting chemical problems. Our findings show the color to be due to a dispersion of very fine cuprous oxide crystals. To make this stain was a rather tricky process. It was first necessary to introduce a good deal of copper into the glass by migration from the surface. (Note that the yellow stain sometimes occurs on base glasses that do not contain any copper to begin with.) Then the reduction had to be taken only to an intermediate state of Cu_2O and not taken so far as to produce primarily metallic copper. A third requirement was to arrest the growth of the cuprous oxide grains at a small enough particle size so that they would still show their yellow-orange color and not go over to the familiar bright red color characteristic of cuprous oxide in bulk phase or larger-grained dispersions.

The presence of silver could have been beneficial in creating this yellow-orange form of cuprous oxide, since it may have led to the formation of a large number of crystal nuclei which, if they acted as crystallization nuclei for the cuprous oxide, would have produced a dispersion of many small particles rather than fewer larger ones which would tend to give the red color.

To fit the yellow and red stains into the overall historical picture of yellow and red colorants used in ancient glasses, it should first be pointed out that up until this time red and yellow occurred only in true opaque glasses colored throughout, and not in the form of surface stains. Red opaques were made from the earliest times by precipitating out crystalline dispersions of cuprous oxide, which has a bright red color.[25] X-ray diffraction studies of such red opaques show that they most often contain mainly Cu_2O but sometimes also some CuO. We have also seen a few which contain primarily CuO. Opaque yellow glasses were used in the earliest glass vessels we know, the cored vessels of the Eighteenth Dynasty in Egypt and in their counterparts in Mesopotamia. These glasses were colored by suspensions of yellow pigments,[26] first lead antimonate ($Pb_2Sb_2O_7$) and after the second to fourth centuries A.D. a lead-tin oxide ("$PbSnO_3$").

Interestingly, however, there is a class of ancient orange and yellowish orange glasses that have been shown by X-ray diffraction to contain only

[25] The nature of these red opaques is discussed in a paper dealing with the use of lead in glasses in ancient times. R. H. Brill, "Lead Isotopes in Ancient Glass," presented at the Fourth Congress of Journées Internationales du Verre, Venice (1967). (To be published in the forthcoming proceedings.)

[26] W. E. S. Turner and H. P. Rooksby, "A Study of Opalizing Agents in Ancient Glasses Throughout 3,400 years," *Glastechnische Berichte, 32k,* VIII (1959) 17–28; R. H. Brill and S. Moll, "The Electron Beam Probe Microanalysis of Ancient Glass," *Recent Advances in Conservation* (London: Butterworth's, 1962), pp. 145–151.

cuprous oxide.[27] These invariably consist of very fine-grained crystals measuring not larger than about 0.1–0.3 micron across. We have found such colors in Egyptian, Iranian, Roman, and Byzantine glasses, dating from as early as about 900 B.C. up through Byzantine times. We have also accidentally made several such glasses in attempts to duplicate the ancient red opaque. Although our research on this problem is not yet complete, we are presently of the opinion that this difference of color (yellow instead of red) is a particle-size effect. This opinion is based upon direct experimental observations that fail to show the presence of any crystalline phases other than cuprous oxide in some of these glasses, and also upon theoretical considerations dealing with the color of cuprous oxide and other crystals.[28]

This leads then to the view that the orange opaque glasses of antiquity— and the yellow stain studied on the Islamic fragments—were made by precipitating cuprous oxide and arresting the growth of the crystals at the yellow-orange stage. This does not mean to imply, however, that the glassmakers of early times could necessarily produce this orange color every time they set out to do so, because their control of their processes could not have been so precise. Undoubtedly, however, patient and determined tinkering could have substituted for precise control. The control of the Islamic glass decorators in making the yellow stains must have been much more reliable than that of the earlier makers of the bulk orange glasses. The Islamic glass decorators had to be more successful more of the time because of the economics of their production. The earlier glassmakers could always use their misfired reds and browns anyway, since they were happy to have a full color palette of mosaic tesserae, or could easily remelt their small molded figurines and start all over again. Could the secret of the Islamic glass painters' control have been in their use of silver in the stain?

The principal historical significance of the findings presented here is that this use of silver forms an important link connecting the use of silver and/or gold in coloring a small group of early dichroic glasses,[29] and the much later separate use of silver for making yellow-stained glasses for cathedral windows in Western Europe. Depending upon the dates one accepts for these types of glass, the gap between them ranges anywhere

---

[27] See n. 25. Also additional unpublished results by the author.

[28] There is a series of papers dealing with this subject by S. Nikitine. See, for example, "Experimental Investigations of Exciton Spectra in Ionic Crystals," *Phil. Mag.*, ser. 8, vol. 4 (1958), 1–31.

[29] This group of objects is discussed in detail in the reference in n. 3.

from about five to ten centuries. The dichroic glasses (the Lycurgus Cup, the Termancia Cup, a diatretum fragment, and a fragment from Sardis) all have been dated from the fourth-fifth century up to the seventh-eighth century. An attribution of the invention of silver staining for cathedral windows has been made to Jacob of Ulm (Jacob Griesinger, 1407–1490) in the fifteenth century, but some windows said to be silver-stained are dated at least a century earlier. A dichroic fragment from Behnesa in Egypt[30] is the only silver-containing glass known to this author which bridges this gap. It is dated, though uncertainly, to the ninth-tenth century. It now appears that this glass could be more directly related to the luster glass studied here, than to the other dichroic glasses mentioned above. In fact, occasional fragments of "misfired" luster glasses show a dichroism much like that seen in the Behnesa fragment.

In light of all this the use of silver in the Islamic luster glasses dated from the ninth-eleventh century helps to complete the technological link. This must be one more of the chemical arts preserved from the Greek and Roman world and later passed on to the West by Arabic alchemists and craftsmen. The careful preservation of the techniques and continuing study of the behavior of gold and silver in glasses was assured by the alchemists' preoccupation with those metals.

The red stains are important historically because (along with the yellow) they appear to be the earliest known use of a copper stain on glass. This type of staining may have been an antecedent of the use of copper as the colorant in the ruby-stained glass windows of Western Europe, which were to appear some 250 years later. In searching for other technological connections it could well be that the red stains might not have developed from the ancient Mediterranean world at all but rather from attempts to imitate the red glazed ceramics imported into the Near East from China. Such attempts probably accounted for the early red luster glazes on ceramic wares from Samarra, Mesopotamia.

APPENDIX 1

Catalog of Samples

1010   Rim fragment, *colorless* glass with amber stain. (51.1.145 X)
1011   Rim fragment, *colorless* glass with amber stain. (51.1.145 XI)
1012   Rim fragment, *colorless* glass with amber stain. (51.1.145 XIII)

---

[30] This fragment is also discussed in the reference in n. 3. It is no. 691–1905 in the collection of the Victoria and Albert Museum.

1013   Body fragment, *colorless* glass with amber stain. (51.1.146 XII)

1014   Rim fragment, very pale greenish glass with amber stain. (51.1.145 XIV)

1015   Rim fragment, very pale greenish glass with amber stain. (51.1.145 IX)

1016   Body fragment, very pale greenish glass with amber stain. (51.1.145 XII)

1017   Body fragment, very pale greenish glass with amber and pink (metallic) stains on both sides. (51.1.161 I)

1018   Base and pontil fragment, aqua glass with amber stain. (51.1.145 XIX)

1019   Body fragment, aqua glass with amber stain. (51.1.145 VI)

1020   Body fragment, aqua glass with amber stain on both sides. (51.1.150 II)

1021   Base fragment, pale blue glass with amber stain on both sides. Shows halo effect. (51.1.173)

1022   Base and pontil fragment, deep blue glass, with amber stain and yellow opaque stain. (51.1.159)

1023   Wall fragment, deep blue glass, with yellow opaque stain and red stain. (51.1.155)

1024   Wall fragment, deep blue glass, with dense yellow-orange opaque stain, and yellow-green streaked appearance on reverse. (51.1.152 II)

1025   Wall fragment, green glass, with dense yellow-orange opaque stained bands. (51.1.149 VI)

1026   Rim fragment, pale green glass with yellowish-brown (and red-streaked) opaque stain on both sides. (51.1.149 III)

1027   Rim fragment, olive glass with red opaque stain and red-stained bands. (51.1.162 IX)

1028   Rim fragment, olive glass with red opaque stained characters on concave surface and greenish-yellowish-red mottled convex surface. (51.1.162 XIV)

1029   Rim fragment, olive glass with red opaque stained exterior and red-stained interior. (51.1.162 X)

APPENDIX 2

Early Persian Recipe

The recipe given below was recorded by Abdallah Ibn Ali Al-Kashani at Tabriz in 1300–1301. This English translation is from the German version published in 1935 by Ritter, Ruska, Sarre, and Winderlich (see footnote no. 19).

The preparation process for the glaze is as follows: One takes 1½ parts yellow and red arsenic, 1 part silver or gold marcasite, ½ part yellow vitriol from Tabas, and ¼ part burnt copper, which are pulverized and made into a paste. ¼ of this is ground together with six dirham of pure burnt and pulverized silver, and pulverized 48 hours until the powder is extremely fine. This is then dissolved in grape juice or vinegar and painted on the vessels as you wish and is put again into a second oven made especially for this purpose, and then fired there for three days with little smoke so that they take on "the color of two fires." And when they are cooled one takes them out and rubs them with wet earth, so that the gold color becomes apparent. Other people add to the glaze certain things like red lead and verdigris, but instead of this, simple bloodstone with burnt silver does the same thing. The parts of this that are exposed to a constant fire will glow like red gold and shine like the sun.

From certain assumed identifications of the ingredients mentioned in the above text we prepared the mixture shown below. The materials were weighed, mixed, and ground thoroughly in a mortar and pestle with a small amount of 1:1 vinegar and grape juice. Additional vinegar-grape juice mixture, thickened with a small amount of gum arabic, was added until a paint of usable consistency was obtained.

Mixture Prepared to Duplicate Early Persian Recipe:

3.0 silver carbonate
2.5 silver chloride
2.5 silver sulfate
2.0 silver sulfide

40.0 cupric sulfate
3.0 cupric sulfide
10.0 cuprous chloride

5.0 ferric sulfate

2.5 zinc chloride
0.5 zinc sulfide

0.5 sulfur

15.0 yellow ochre

5.0 arsenic disulfide

Cu/Ag ratio approx. 2.7
Cu/Zn ratio approx. 16.

XVII

PHYSICAL AND CHEMICAL PROPERTIES OF SOME MEDIEVAL NEAR EASTERN GLAZED CERAMICS

J. D. Frierman

T HE HISTORY of Near Eastern ceramics is intimately linked with the social history of the region. At the time of the Islamic conquests of the seventh and eighth centuries the prevalent ceramic tradition was one in which relief-decorated, unglazed slipwares predominated. A small amount of lead-glaze ceramics was made in Egypt and elsewhere in the Near East—Georgia in Transcaucasia, for instance, and Byzantium. All of these continued the traditions of later antiquity. In the East, the Sassanian tradition of blue or turquoise alkali silicate glazes also continued a tradition, one that began in the third millennium B.C. These traditions did not long survive except in the most remote areas. From the beginning of the ninth century A.D. Chinese ceramics made their appearance in the Near East and remained the dominant influence in ceramic style for the following millennium. The rise of the Abbasids was reflected in the brilliant development of ceramic art and technology that is so evident in the excavations of their single occupancy capital, Samarra, near Baghdad (836–883). Here we find side by side a vast experimental repertory of glaze formulations—lead glazes of several varieties, alkali silicate glazes, a wide variety of lusterwares and other overpainting techniques, and the use of tin as an opacifier. All of this existed in order to produce local imitations of the T'ang ceramics, which were ably done, and also to give vent to the same kind of imagination and invention that appears in the contemporary *Thousand and One Nights*.

In the eleventh century the Seljug Turks invaded the region, and in their wake came a new school that produced what may be the most colorful and beautiful ceramics made outside of the Far East. Luster was raised to a high art in Iran, especially in Kushan. The old T'ang three-color wares were reinterpreted, faience reappeared in new forms and

379

colors that rivaled the Sung porcelains they imitated; but this dramatic flowering was to be short-lived, for during the first half of the thirteenth century the Mongols swept in from Central Asia and this was reflected in the discontinuation of the most sophisticated types and techniques.

The late thirteenth and the fourteenth centuries witnessed a slow artistic recovery; the most symptomatic ware was the blue- or black-painted wares which were covered with a transparent glaze that ran the colors a little and had a crackle, once again echoing the work of Chinese potters. Although luster and other overglaze ceramics were made again, and both the pots and techniques became widely diffused, the dominant trend in the Near East was to remain the blue-and-white of the Ming, so much admired and collected by the Ottomans. This taste was still dominant in the ninteenth century. Even in the briefest discussion it is clear that each major historical event was mirrored in new or transformed styles. It appears that not only were there iconographic and stylistic changes, but that these changes were paralleled by technological changes which ought to be demonstrable by objective physical and chemical observations.

Since these studies are based almost entirely on small shards, where normal art historical methods become tenuous, an analogous method is very welcome. The use of shard studies is essential in the western United States because of a total lack of large, representative medieval Near Eastern study collections and the absence of scientifically excavated materials. Generous colleagues, however, are always willing to supply us with collections of shards even if they may be small and not characteristic. Is, then, the ubiquitous bluish green shard with the slightly deteriorated surface second-century Parthian or fifth-century Byzantine or eleventh-century Transcaucasian or thirteenth-century Crusader or Rhenish or fourteenth-century Mamluk? Since they look very much alike, how can we determine their provenience and how they were made?

An interest in physical and chemical properties of Near Eastern glazed ceramics is not new. In 1914 Sarre had a fine representative series of shards from his great excavation at Samarra analyzed at the Technische Hochschule, Berlin, and another group was examined by Hans Arnold.[1] Wet chemistry was used and the analysis was for silicic acid, clay, TiO_2, Fe_2O_3, CaO, MgO, alkali as K_2O, and weight loss on heating to 100°C. The firing temperature was estimated by heating the shards and visually

---

[1] F. Sarre, *Die Ausgrabungen von Samarra II (Die Keramik von Samarra)* (Berlin, 1925), pp. 95–100.

noting when the glazes became fluid. Although these analyses were quite rudimentary, they are still one of the largest published groups. In the ensuing years a few more analyses appeared: three Parthian samples from Dura, two Egyptian glazes, one lead, and one an alkali silicate on faience. But with this meager activity little more is known of these materials than was known in 1941 when Florence E. Day and Frederick R. Matson complained about the lack of accuracy in describing and reporting on Islamic glazes and ceramics.[2]

Discussed below are those methods which are more or less generally available at scientific institutions and with which a good measure of success was achieved. Ideally, inexpensive, nondestructive, rapid, and reasonably accurate analytical techniques offer the greatest promise in elucidating the provenience of large numbers of samples as they exist to-day in the world's collections.

Analytical Methods

Visual examination. While the specimen is under the binocular microscope it should be examined for transparency (on sandblasted or weathered glazes the surface appears to be opaque when it is actually transparent), interesting mineral or other inclusions, and for the technique of decoration. It is well to note that even the most completely deteriorated glaze, if carefully scraped away, will reveal areas of the original glaze. Careful examination will generally reveal whether a slip has been applied under the glaze.

Firing atmosphere. The firing atmosphere is extremely important in plain wares, but since all our wares were fired in an oxidizing atmosphere with the exception of the final low-temperature firing of luster, it is less important here. These wares were generally evenly and thoroughly fired in an updraft beehive kiln. The final firing was generally between 1000° and 1200° C. Many of the vessels, possibly the majority, were fired twice.[3] The first time they were fired with the slip and the underpainting, then they were glazed with a colorless glaze and refired, the color being derived from the underlying colorant.

The color of the clay body depends on the degree of oxidation or

[2] F. E. Day, in *Ars Islamica VIII* (1941), 17–18; F. R. Matson, in ibid., pp. 61–62.

[3] V. V. Dzhaparidze, *Keramiķuli c'armoeba XI–XIII ss. Sak'art'veloshi* (ark'eologiuri masalebis mikhedvit) (T'bilisi, 1956).

reduction during the firing. Perlman and Asaro have shown that the amount of iron oxide is secondary. In their brilliant analysis of material from Tepe Sialk III, IV, V (Necropolis A), and VI (Necropolis B) it was demonstrated that a reducing atmosphere produces a very light buff, almost white with a slight greenish tone; that a smoky reducing atmosphere produces a dark gray or black surface; and that an oxidizing atmosphere produces various shades of pink, pink-buff, or red-brown although the amount of iron oxide remains the same.

It is possible that some of the very white faience bodies might benefit from a slight reduction at the end of the firing. This will become apparent when additional analyses of faience bodies have been carried out giving the amount of Fe_2O_3 in the bodies, or by reduction firing of some high iron specimens.

Hardness. One of the easiest tests is the determination of hardness on Moh's scale. This is the well-known method used in geology, which employs a set of rock samples of known hardness graduated from 1 (talc) to 10 (diamond).[4] This fine technique fulfills many criteria of desirability as it is inexpensive, almost nondestructive, rapid, and reasonably accurate. The hardness of most medieval Near Eastern glazes being between 4 and 5.5, the clay of the bodies, depending on whether the test is taken on a weathered or fresh surface, is between 2.5 and 3.5. Any wares with a body hardness of 6 or more can be safely assumed to be Chinese imports. On occasion, however, one finds exceptions such as the Palestine Crusader wares in which some of the clay bodies are as hard as or harder than their glazes.[5] This we believe is an important and unique trait introduced from Western Europe where stone wares were being developed. Greater accuracy and less destruction result if this determination is carried out under a binocular microscope.

Mineralogy. Generally, mineralogical examinations are more useful for the clay body than for glazes, but in glazes that are fired at about 1200°C inclusions of undigested material are visible and a great help in determining how the glaze was actually made. Palestine Crusader glazes are filled with clearly visible fragments of quartz and plagioclase feldspar which are also abundantly represented in the clay body. On the basis of coarse quartz and feldspar, we can make a reasonable reconstruction of the Crusader glazes which are remarkably uniform.

[4] F. A. Wade and R. B. Mattox, *Elements of Crystallography and Mineralogy* (New York, 1960), pp. 140–142.

[5] J. D. Frierman, in *Israel Exploration J. 17* (1967).

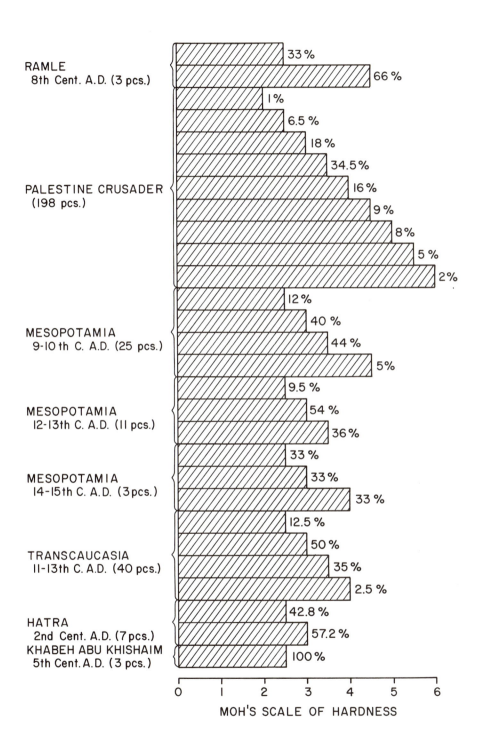

RAMLE
8th Cent. A.D. (3 pcs.)

33%
66%

PALESTINE CRUSADER
(198 pcs.)

1%
6.5%
18%
34.5%
16%
9%
8%
5%
2%

MESOPOTAMIA
9-10th C. A.D. (25 pcs.)

12%
40%
44%
5%

MESOPOTAMIA
12-13th C. A.D. (11 pcs.)

9.5%
54%
36%

MESOPOTAMIA
14-15th C. A.D. (3 pcs.)

33%
33%
33%

TRANSCAUCASIA
11-13th C. A.D. (40 pcs.)

12.5%
50%
35%
2.5%

HATRA
2nd Cent. A.D. (7 pcs.)

42.8%
57.2%

KHABEH ABU KHISHAIM
5th Cent. A.D. (3 pcs.)

100%

0 1 2 3 4 5 6

MOH'S SCALE OF HARDNESS

Empirical Formula

PbO	60.
SiO$_2$	28.
MgO	.25
Fe$_2$O$_3$	1.
Al$_2$O$_3$	4.
Na$_2$O	1.50
K$_2$O	.75
CaO	1.50

97.00 plus either additional
Fe$_2$O$_3$ or CuO as colorant.

This suggests that it was made out of a certain naturally occurring igneous PbO, very rich in quartz and containing a little plagioclase feldspar and the colorant. The uniformity is the result of this simplicity.

Index of refraction. These glazes are rarely homogeneous enough to give good results. One can separate lead from alkali silicate glazes, but it is difficult to accurately determine the lead content of the glaze.[6]

		Index of refraction ($=$ 1.59)		PbO (%)	PbO (%)*	D*
Caesarea	D1	1.625	Green	59.0	43.8	1.6157
	D2	1.625	Yellow	61.0	43.8	1.6157
	C4	1.64	Green	62.0	49.3	1.6450
	D2	1.69	Green	61.0	58.1	1.6836
Athlit	B2	1.758	Light brown	58.7	63.8	1.7278
	A2	1.796	Dark brown	58.5	68.9	1.7800

* G. W. Morey, *The Properties of Glass,* ACS Monograph series, no. 77 (New York, 1938), p. 374, table XVI, 7 (Optical Properties and Densities of Glasses in the System PbO-SiO$_2$).

Chemical analysis. Microanalytic techniques using small quantities of glaze have been consistently used by us in determining the lead content by the lead iodate method.[7] This is necessary for Pb concentrations over 35

[6] Our samples (below) show an inverse relationship between PbO and index of refraction when compared to standards. The refraction index was determined by David L. Weide, Curator, Geology Museum, UCLA. The PbO was obtained by X-ray fluorescence spectrometry.

[7] A. I. Vogel, *A Textbook of Inorganic Quantitive Analysis* (New York, 1961), p. 592.

percent when optical emission spectrography becomes inaccurate. Similarly, "wet" analysis is also recommended for manganese and cobalt.[8]

The low-energy X-ray fluorescence spectrography recently developed at the Lawrence Radiation Laboratory, University of California, Berkeley, seems to be an important improvement for all elementary determinations, especially in glazes (see below).

Optical emission spectrography. This is the most commonly available and gives the broadest coverage of elements. Its disadvantages are that it is destructive, although it uses small amounts, that it does not give good results on either lead or silicon, and that it involves a good deal of art. In cases where good standards exist and a skillful technician is in charge, excellent results can be obtained. This technique is highly recommended for the light elements up to atomic number 20 (calcium). With uniformly accepted standards for this class of materials, our results would be much improved. It seems unlikely though that the development of such standards can be justified in the light of recent revolutionary developments in analytic techniques, that is, in low-energy X-ray fluorescence spectrography and neutron activation analysis.

X-ray emission spectrography. This can be used as a nondestructive method of great importance, in that the object is in no way marred. Most of these devices require, however, some type of specimen preparation such as grinding and embedding a small sample or, in other cases in which this is unnecessary, where the geometry of the equipment will allow objects of only quite limited size to be introduced. The advantage of these machines is that they are often connected to computers that give a readout of the elements in percent or parts per million. These machines can usually scan the spectrum from calcium or titanium.

X-ray fluorescence spectrography. This remarkable development is by far the simplest and most rapid of all spectrometers. The device is nondestructive and, since it can be adapted to several orientations, it can be used on objects of any size or shape. The 0.6 keV high resolution detector is said to make analysis of chlorine and argon possible, and all higher elements can be measured. Excellent results on all glaze samples examined were obtained but they were inconclusive with respect to the clay bodies. I will refer the reader to Bowman's detailed exposition later in this volume.

[8] Ibid., pp. 566, 604.

Neutron activation analysis. This process requires about 100 mg of powdered clay. For the thirty-three elements that it scans, the accuracy is dramatic; and the results that have been forthcoming from clay body samples will revolutionize the objective determination of provenience in the near future. It has not been used on glazed materials as yet, but there can be no doubt that it will be a major tool in solving the vexatious problems of provenience. Again, I defer to Perlman and Asaro's work, in which they discuss their remarkable development in the following paper.

Applications

These methods have permitted us to analyze 40 samples by a combination of optical emission and wet chemistry for lead. They formed the control group for over a hundred X-ray fluorescence studies. We were able to enhance the original work (wet chemistry) by adding a number of undetected elements, especially strontium, zirconium, and barium through X-ray fluorescence spectrometry. Best results would be forthcoming from a procedure that included optical emission spectrography up to calcium; X-ray fluorescence thereafter; and, if provenience is an issue, neutron activation analysis. Of course, hardness testing and a careful examination under a binocular microscope must precede all other activities.

As a result of these studies, we can now visually separate lead from alkali silicate glazes.[9] This is based on the difference in color that a colorant has in a glaze that contains predominantly basic oxides (PbO, Na_2O, K_2O, CaO, MgO) and the same colorant in a glaze that is predominantly an acidic oxide (SiO_2). Thus manganese oxide in an acidic, alkali silicate glaze is a rich purple; in a basic, high-lead glaze, it is light brown in low concentrations and black-brown in high concentrations. The green glazes all contain a high percentage of lead oxide (50–60%). The same amount of copper oxide (2–5%) that produces the greens in lead glazes produces the lovely and characteristic sky-blue azure in an alkali silicate glaze. Iron oxides are generally used in lead glazes. They produce various browns, blacks, yellows, and occasionally orange. It is well to note that one must be careful to test browns and blacks to determine whether they are actually manganese or iron as they can be deceptive. Manganese is common in the glazes of Transcaucasia and Iran, but has not been detected on contemporary Crusader wares in Palestine.

[9] J. D. Frierman, in *Bedi Kartlisa XXIII–XXIV* (1967), 175.

The polychrome glazes are of the same two types, and composition of the glaze determines the potter's palette. The lead glaze, which tends to be yellowish, can be ornamented in green, brown, yellow, orange, and cobalt royal blue. The alkali silicate glazes, which are clear, have pink and purple, turquoise and azure blue, and a darker blue (cobalt). For the rare intermediate type glazes which contain 15–20 percent PbO, it is necessary to check the spectrograph, for they are blue-green intermediate between the azure and the green. All the glazes when on clay bodies have the same superficial appearance and properties; only their color gives an indication of their composition.

A high silver content (AgO 0.1–1%) occurs in those areas where de-silvering lead was not consistently practiced. We have found two such areas, the Lake Sevan region of Armenia at the end of the twelfth and the beginning of the thirteenth century and Crusader Palestine.[10] Brill had noted this in lead glasses as an inconsistent occurrence, but it apparently can also be a cultural trait.[11]

The problem of the alkali silicate glazes and faience (which is an alkali silicate glaze on a synthetic body made of a fritted, finely ground quartz and a little very plastic clay to make it workable) is an interesting one. These are among the earliest glazed wares made dating from the third millennium B.C. They were consistently produced until the ninth century A.D. when both glaze and body disappear. They are said to return in the eleventh and twelfth centuries. It is difficult to believe that techniques in use for three millennia can disappear for 150 years and then reappear in their original form. If indeed it can be shown that lead-glazed earthen-ware entirely displaces alkali silicate glazes as well as faience during this period, it is still possible that they survive as beads and enamels, which was the original use of these materials. Further excavations and wide-scale analysis will have to answer this question.

The nature of faience is that the body and the glaze have almost identical constituents. In the case of the body, plastic clay is added; in the glaze, a colorant. A rapid test of this is to hold an X-ray spectrograph of the body and glaze together and see that only the colorant differs. We have found about 6 percent lead in a sample from Lake Sevan. It was too small to separate the glaze from the body, but it would be very interesting to know whether the lead was in the frit or not.

[10] J. D. Frierman, in *Israel Exploration J. 17.*
[11] R. H. Brill and J. M. Wampler, in *Amer. J. Archaeol. 71* (1967), 73, n. 22.

Apparently the Crusaders made neither faience nor alkali silicate glazes; however, their conquerors, the Mamluks of Egypt, did. The Crusaders fired high; the Mamluks did not. The Crusaders did not desilver lead, and their wares are notable for the quantities of coarse quartz in body and glaze. At present this coarseness seems unique in the Near East.

The late L. A. Mayer, Islamic archaeologist of Hebrew University, Jerusalem, claimed that it was impossible to differentiate the Crusader wares from the subsequent Mamluk products, except where there are obvious iconographic indications such as crosses or inscriptions.[12] Today it seems possible that with more modern analytical techniques they might be separated.

[12] J. Praver, Hebrew University, Jerusalem, 1967. Personal communication.

XVIII

DEDUCTION OF PROVENIENCE OF POTTERY FROM

TRACE ELEMENT ANALYSIS

I. Perlman and F. Asaro

*T*HE WORK REPORTED here was undertaken on the premise that pottery clay from each area has a distinctive chemical composition. If this is so, the ubiquitous ceramics of archaeology can be assigned places of origin independently of other characteristics such as style.

Others have had this thought; in particular, the elaborate study of Mycenaean and Minoan pottery by Catling, Richards, and Blin-Stoyle[1] should be mentioned. These workers employed spectrographic analysis and concentrated on nine elements which include some of the minor constituents as well as such major elements as aluminum, calcium, magnesium, and iron.

In the study to be reported here, we have used neutron activation analysis and have measured some thirty elements, but the approach is conceptually similar. In both studies pottery itself was analyzed with the objective of deriving internal correlations. This may be thought of as a classical archaeological approach which depends upon some distinctive uniformity within an area applying both to the geochemical history of the clay beds and to the treatment of raw materials by the potters. In a parallel but separate study which we have started, we are attempting to obtain information of another kind which should help in the interpretation of the first study. The questions we hope to answer include (1) how uniform in composition is raw clay within a discrete clay bed and within an area of supposed geochemical uniformity, (2) what happens to the composition in preparing it for making pottery, and (3) what happens during firing. This second approach is, in a sense, more fundamental but

[1] H. W. Catling, E. E. Richards, and A. E. Blin-Stoyle, in *Annual of the British School of Archaeology at Athens 58* (1963), 94–115.

it is beset by a serious difficulty of a practical nature. There is a wealth of potsherds of known archaeological context, but it is almost impossible to locate with certainty the clays from which they were made. The study can still be made using modern materials and from the results one can get some guidance in the interpretation of the ancient pottery. These problems in the diagnostic use of chemical makeup have been discussed by Shepard [2] in her critical review of the Catling, Richards, and Blin-Stoyle paper.

It was mentioned that we used neutron activation analysis and obtained data on more than thirty elements. Attempts have been made in the past to use this technique on pottery [3] but the results seemed to be of limited value. The difference lies in the recent development of equipment for measuring gamma-ray spectra which is far superior to the best available at the time of the earlier studies. This dramatic change will be more fully described further on.

The basic constituents of pottery clays are hydrated aluminum silicates metamorphized in the weathering of certain igneous rocks. Within the basic aluminum silicate structure are found some minor constituents present to the order of a fraction of 1 percent to several percent. The raw clay used for pottery contains, in addition to the clay minerals, residual components of the original rock and other materials that are picked up during the transport of the clay by surface water. Conversely, secondary clay beds may be deficient in some of the components of the primary rocks because of settling during transport of the fine clay particles. Finally, tempering materials of one kind or another are deliberately added to the clay in order to obtain workable plasticity and to provide porosity and diminish shrinkage during firing.

Although the major constituents of pottery clay may well provide clues as to origin, results obtained through the years do not appear very encouraging. Attention was therefore addressed to the many trace elements which undoubtedly appear in any geochemical substance, clay included. The technique, in principle capable of satisfying this objective, is neutron activation analysis. Any element subjected to neutron irradiation has a finite (and fixed) probability of reacting with neutrons, and at least one of the isotopes will be partially converted to a radioactive form. In principle, each radioactive species is distinct from all others, and the

[2] Anna O. Shepard, foreword to fifth printing of *Ceramics for the Archaeologist,* pub. 609, Carnegie Institution of Washington (1965).

[3] E. V. Sayre, A. Murrenhoff, and C. F. Weick, Brookhaven National Laboratory, Report no. BNL–508 (1958); V. M. Emeleus, in *Archaeometry 3* (1960), 16.

measurement of the distinctive radioactivity can be related quantitatively to the abundance of the element in the specimen. As is true for any other scheme of analysis, neutron activation analysis does not measure all elements with equal sensitivity, and as a practical matter there are a sizable number for which the method is not suitable. Nevertheless, where it can be applied it is capable of yielding considerable accuracy and, most importantly, a considerable number of elements can now be determined simultaneously. Before turning to how this is done on pottery, it is worth pointing out why neutron activation analysis is unique in its sensitivity to what we term "trace elements." Speaking in general terms, the composition of rocks mirrors the composition of the earth's crust, and elements that are rare in nature will be the trace elements of rocks. It is just these elements which react most readily with neutrons and hence are most sensitively detected. This fact has been used to account for the cosmic abundances of elements. At some stage in the genesis of elements they were subjected to huge numbers of neutrons; those which react readily were largely burned out converting to those which react slightly. For the purposes of our analysis of pottery, this is most fortunate, because the radioactivity from the handful of major constituents will not completely mask the radioactivity from the many trace elements. It will be seen that even with this fortuitous regulatory system the problems are severe enough.

The study reported here was conducted with archaeological materials, but the methodology rather than the possible archaeological significance will be stressed. A somewhat similar analysis has been made by Gordon et al.[4] on rock samples. From the start, we have received valuable guidance and encouragement from archaeologists Jay D. Frierman of UCLA and Robert Rodden of Berkeley. These colleagues also selected the shards with careful attention to their archaeological context. They will, of course, play dominant roles in the analysis of the information in terms of its archaeological significance. Hopefully such papers will be ready for publication in the not distant future.

Neutron Activation and Gamma-Ray Spectroscopy

The measurements of the radiations from neutron-activated species can be explained most simply by an example, and the element iron has been

[4] G. E. Gordon, K. Randle, G. G. Goles, S. B. Corliss, M. H. Beeson, and S. S. Oxley, in *Geochim. et Cosmochim. Acta* (to be published).

selected. Iron as found in nature is made up of four stable isotopes. Only one of these, Fe^{58}, reacts with neutrons to give a radioactive isotope suitable for measurement. It turns out that Fe^{58} comprises only 0.31 percent of iron, and its probability for reacting with neutrons is not very high. The result is that iron is not detected with great sensitivity. This is a fortunate circumstance, because pottery contains about 4 percent iron, and if it were strongly activated, it might mask a number of the other elements. The product of neutron reaction is Fe^{59} which decays with a 45.6-day half-life and has a distinctive "spectrum."

Figure 1 shows a decay scheme for Fe^{59}. The diagram indicates that Fe^{59} decays to Co^{59} by β emission and that only a very small percentage (0.3%) of the decay events goes directly to the ground state of Co^{59}. Most of the decay events lead to several distinct excited states. The energies (in million electron volts) at which these lie above the ground state are indicated. Excited states such as these very quickly lose their energies by the emission of monoenergetic gamma rays. These are shown schematically by the vertical arrows. The energies are discrete as are the relative amounts to be observed, and these constitute the gamma spectrum for Fe^{59}.

The process and equipment for measuring the gamma-ray spectrum might be described as follows:

(1) Gamma rays impinge upon a "detector" which absorbs some of the photons converting the energy of each into an electrical pulse proportional to the photon energy.

(2) The electrical pulses are sorted electronically according to size and accumulated in a memory circuit.

(3) When a large number of events have accumulated the stored information can be read out.

Although not every photon enters the detector and not each one entering gives up its full energy, the system can be calibrated with standard radioactive sources so that the data may be interpreted directly in absolute numbers of Fe^{59} atoms. A straightforward but tedious calculation tells one how much iron was in the specimen irradiated with neutrons.

Nothing has yet been said about how faithfully the detector responds to gamma-ray energy. Up to the present day almost all results reported on neutron activation analysis were based on measurements with the *sodium iodide scintillation counter* as the detector. Figure 2 displays the spectrum so obtained for Fe^{59}, and we see the five peaks corresponding to the five gamma rays. The parts of the curve lying below the peaks are of consider-

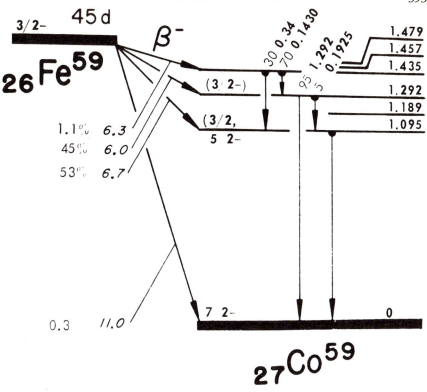

XBL 6711-6077

FIG. 1. Decay Scheme of Fe^{59}

able importance in gamma-ray spectrometry but will not be discussed here. If we focus attention on only the two prominent peaks at 1.095 and 1.292 MeV, we see that they are quite well resolved, but the instrument gives a spread of energies for each rather than a monoenergetic spike. This is a limitation of the detector and is given quantitative expression by designating the width of the peak at the position of half of its maximum. In this case the peak widths are about 75 keV and the separation between the peaks is close to 200. Suppose now that we were not dealing with pure Fe^{59} but that the spectrum contained many other gamma rays. We could only determine these accurately if each were separated by several peak widths from any other. Without further elaboration of this point, one can say categorically that the sodium iodide detector is unsuitable for the analysis of a complex mixture of elements such as that in pottery.

Starting a very few years ago, the semiconductor materials silicon and germanium have been developed as gamma-ray counters of superior

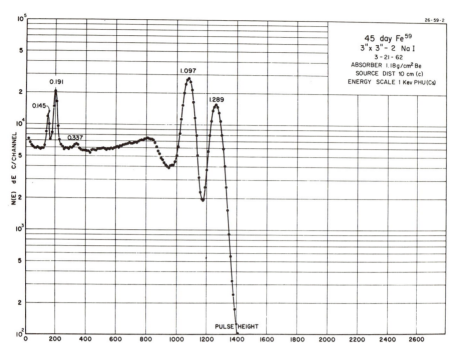

Fig. 2. Gamma-ray spectrum of Fe^{59} taken with a sodium iodide counter, R. L. Heath, "IDO-16880-2 AEC Research and Development Report," *Physics,* TID 4500, 31st ed., August 1964.

resolution. Instead of a peak width of 75 keV, a good germanium counter can give 2 keV. The description of such counters and the attendant sophisticated electronics would take us rather far afield from our present purposes and will be omitted.[5] It may, however, be instructive to show a part of the gamma-ray spectrum of irradiated pottery taken with each system. The section of the spectrum in figure 3 includes the two prominent gamma rays of Fe^{59} already discussed.

The lower scan of figure 3 was taken with our germanium system and covers about 20 percent of the energy range encompassed in a single measurement. The two peaks of Fe^{59} are, of course, still separated by 200 keV, but this separation is now about eighty times the peak width. It is seen that pottery also shows a number of other peaks some of which have been labeled and others unlabeled. The upper scan represents the identical measurement with a good sodium iodide system. For a mixture

---

[5] For a popular account of semiconductor counters and their applications, see J. M. Hollander and I. Perlman, in *Science 154* (1966), 3745.

as complex as this, such spectra are quite unusable because of the relatively poor resolution. The undulations observed are the envelopes over the most prominent gamma rays. It may be mentioned in passing that the parts of the spectrum not shown here are much more congested with gamma-ray peaks.

Analysis of Pottery

Neutron activation analysis may be applied to virtually any kind of material, but the optimum conditions are set on the basis of the radioactivities produced. The following prescription for analyzing pottery was arrived at by considering, in addion to the nature of activated pottery, the equipment at our disposal and, above all, by the requirement of automation to cope with the large number of analyses envisioned. In setting down this prescription it is hoped that the general outlines will be intelligible to those who have never handled a problem such as this, but interspersed will be a number of vital details which will only be understood by those already familiar with equipment and concepts relevant to gamma-ray spectra.

Sample preparation. The surface of the shard was cleaned over an area of 1 cm² using a sapphire scraper, and the remainder was masked with tape to avoid contamination from dust. A drill was fashioned from a rod of synthetic sapphire whose base could be placed in the chuck of an ordinary electric hand drill. The first portion of the powder drilled was discarded and then a sufficient quantity of more powder removed to provide a sample of 100 mg. After showing on several specimens that no weight loss resulted from oven drying, this step was eliminated.

Approximately 100 mg of powder was weighed, mixed with 50 mg of cellulose, and compacted into a pill using a hand-operated hydraulic press with stainless steel dies. The pills (1 cm $\times$ 1.5 mm) were wrapped in aluminum foil and packaged in an aluminum capsule for irradiation. Each batch contained in addition two pottery pills to which a measured amount of gold chloride had been added during the mixing stage to serve as the neutron flux monitor. The material was dried before pellets were pressed.

Irradiation and measurement schedule. Irradiations were carried out in the Triga Reactor in the University of California Department of Nuclear Engineering at a flux of approximately 8×10^{13} neutrons/cm²-sec. The initial irradiation of each batch was carried out for 1 min in a plastic capsule, and gamma-ray analysis was started about 75 min thereafter. Each pill was measured for 30 min except for those containing gold monitors

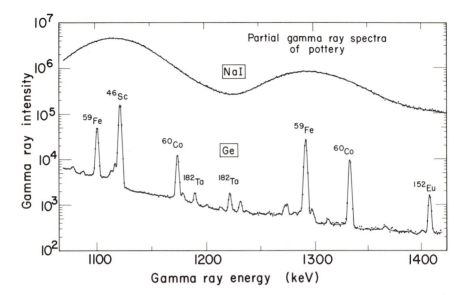

FIG. 3. Partial gamma-ray spectra of pottery. Top curve spectrum taken with good NaI detector, lower curve spectrum taken with good Ge detector.

for which 5-min counting was sufficient. This irradiation and measurement regime accentuated certain radioactivities with half-lives in the range of one to several hours and permitted the decay of those in the range of a few minutes. This choice eliminated the possibility of analyzing for aluminum and of obtaining (at best inaccurate) values for magnesium and vanadium.

The elemental analyses which were obtained in this campaign were dysprosium, manganese, sodium, and potassium. Samarium, strontium, and barium were also obtained, but better analyses for these elements resulted from the next stages.

The pills from the 1-min irradiation were repackaged and on a later day reirradiated for a period of 4 hours or, more recently, 8 hours. Because of the greatly extended irradiation time new monitors with considerably lower amounts of gold were used. These samples were analyzed for 50 min each after a cooling time of either 7 or 8 days. The principal reason for waiting one week was to permit the decay of the sodium radioactivity, which is quite intense and diminishes the accuracy with which lesser components can be determined. This period of waiting, rather than a larger one, accentuates radioactivities with half-lives on the order of a few days. The elements obtained here were samarium, ytterbium, titanium, uranium, lanthanum, bromine, arsenic, calcium, and gold.

Rather good numbers were also obtained for iron and scandium and less accurate numbers for cesium, antimony, and europium. All of these latter elements, however, were better determined in the final stage.

The long-lived radioactivities were best determined by waiting until those mentioned above had diminished by decay. Consequently, after a further delay of at least two weeks the same pills were again analyzed with a running time of about 6 hours for each. These measurements yielded results for antimony, europium, iron, scandium, zinc, tantalum, cesium, nickel, zirconium, strontium, barium, hafnium, chromium, thorium, terbium, iridium, and cerium. In all, thirty-three elements were determined covering most of the periodic system and including almost all distinctive chemical types.

In separate iradiations, known quantities of all the above elements were irradiated and measured under identical conditions. This standard procedure for activation analysis obviates the necessity for specifying neutron cross sections which may vary from reactor to reactor, and also removes the necessity for knowing gamma-ray abundances and counterefficiencies. The use of standard-size samples eliminates uncertainties in the solid angle subtended by the detector. Finally, it is not necessary to know the neutron flux in the reactor, as the gold monitors serve to normalize the different exposures. These will be mentioned further when the accuracies of the measurements are discussed.

Table 1 summarizes what has been said about the elements detected and gives further information useful to someone who wishes to do similar measurements. Also given is a set of results from a single piece of pottery to indicate typical abundance values. *We must stress* that an error as listed is not the true error but simply that part which comes from the statistics of radioactive counting. Those who are used to making such measurements will see reflected in these numbers the intensities of the photoelectron peaks measured and the relation of these intensities to the backgrounds under the peaks. In some cases, the indicated errors shown are a fraction of 1 percent. On the basis of independent measurements from duplicate samples and from the agreement of gold monitors, we feel that it would be prudent to say that none of the abundances shown should be considered more accurate than 5 percent.[6] At the expense of

[6] Evidence has accumulated over the course of this project which casts doubt on the comparability of "absolute" abundances obtained over a period of time within the errors mentioned here. Although the origin of this drift is not definitely understood, we have enough built-in cross-checks to permit corrections to be made. The

considerable labor, errors should be reducible nearly to that of the statistical errors shown, but it is our judgment that this is not worthwhile. Although not proved, it is quite likely two pots which we would classify as identical because they were made at the same time from the same clay bed would vary in composition by several percent.

The validity of errors shown for those elements which have larger uncertainties are also in question but for other reasons. A large statistical error implies in most cases that the peak height is small compared with the background. Suppose that the peak intensity is 1000 counts above a background of 20,000 counts. This measurement has a statistical error of $\pm$ 20 percent. The background is the envelope of Compton distributions of all gamma rays and can change slightly in height and shape, depending upon variations of the constituents. If at the place we choose for background subtraction there has been a shift of only 1 percent, this would introduce an additional 20 percent error in our analysis. As experience is gained it will be possible to learn how to handle the background problems more judiciously, and such refinements would indeed be worth the effort because the work need be done only once for all measurements.

Data accumulation and processing. Gamma-ray spectra are taken by recording the number of pulses corresponding to a certain small-energy interval in a storage unit called a channel. The instrument used for the present study contained 1600 channels. The lower limit of pulse heights accepted and the pulse amplification can be fixed; in this case the lowest energy accepted was 50 keV and the upper limit 1700 keV. Accordingly, the energy interval per channel was slightly greater than one kilovolt. The detector employed was a germanium counter of approximately 5-cm^3 volume. The detector with its attendant electronics produced gamma-ray peak widths of about 2.5 keV for the higher-energy gamma rays.

In measurements such as these there will be low-intensity peaks of value as well as strong peaks; so in order to accumulate statistically valid numbers of counts, it is desirable to count samples that are highly radioactive. The stronger a sample is the more "coincidences" occur, a term

---

nature of the problem is such that, whatever the cause, it can be eliminated by changing our method for monitoring the neutron flux. We propose to make up a "synthetic pottery" of known composition and to use samples of this for monitors in each irradiation in place of the gold pills. Each gamma-ray peak can then be compared with the corresponding peak in the specimens being analyzed. This system will involve minor changes in data processing but will eliminate errors introduced by shifts in neutron energy distributions and shifts in behavior of the analyzing equipment.

TABLE I

Neutron Activation Information for a Typical Pottery Specimen

Element	Isotope examined	Half-life	γ-ray chosen (keV)	Abundance of element in pottery	Statistical error
Dy	^{165}Dy	2.3h	95	1.94×10^{-6}	0.05×10^{-6}
Mn	^{65}Mn	2.6h	847	4.84×10^{-4}	0.16×10^{-4}
Na	^{24}Na	15.0h	1369	1.020×10^{-2}	0.005×10^{-2}
K	^{42}K	12.4h	1524	2.0×10^{-2}	0.18×10^{-2}
Sr	^{87m}Sr	2.8h	389	3.1×10^{-4}	0.4×10^{-4}
Sm	^{153}Sm	1.9d	103	4.92×10^{-6}	0.01×10^{-6}
Ti	^{47}Sc	3.4d	159	3.06×10^{-3}	0.09×10^{-3}
Lu	^{177}Lu	6.7d	208	7.4×10^{-7}	0.1×10^{-7}
Yb	^{175}Yb	4.2d	397	2.88×10^{-7}	0.08×10^{-7}
U	^{239}Np	2.3d	278	1.12×10^{-5}	0.03×10^{-5}
La	^{140}La	1.7d	1596	1.56×10^{-5}	0.01×10^{-5}
Br	^{82}Br	1.5d	554	3.4×10^{-6}	0.3×10^{-6}
As	^{76}As	1.1d	559	8.7×10^{-6}	0.4×10^{-6}
Ca	^{47}Ca	4.5d	1298	1.31×10^{-1}	0.06×10^{-1}
Au	^{198}Au	2.7d	412	1.9×10^{-8}	0.15×10^{-8}
Sb	^{124}Sb	60d	1692	2.1×10^{-6}	0.1×10^{-6}
Eu	^{152}Eu	12.7y	1408	5.1×10^{-7}	0.1×10^{-7}
Co	^{60}Co	5.3y	1332	1.25×10^{-5}	0.01×10^{-5}
Fe	^{59}Fe	46d	1292	3.35×10^{-2}	0.01×10^{-2}
Sc	^{46}Sc	84d	1120	1.210×10^{-5}	0.002×10^{-5}
Rb	^{86}Rb	19d	1077	6.4×10^{-5}	0.2×10^{-5}
Ta	^{182}Ta	115d	1222	1.25×10^{-6}	0.05×10^{-6}
Cs	^{134}Cs	2.0y	796	7.4×10^{-6}	0.1×10^{-6}
Ni	^{58}Co	71d	810	9.4×10^{-5}	1.1×10^{-5}
Zr	^{95}Zr	66d	756&723	1.5×10^{-4}	0.2×10^{-4}
Ba	^{131}Ba	12.0d	496	4.1×10^{-4}	0.2×10^{-4}
Hf	^{181}Hf	42d	482	2.96×10^{-6}	0.05×10^{-6}
Cr	^{51}Cr	28d	320	1.38×10^{-4}	0.01×10^{-6}
Th	^{233}Pa	27d	312	8.45×10^{-6}	0.04×10^{-6}
Tb	^{160}Tb	72d	298	2.9×10^{-7}	0.1×10^{-7}
Ce	^{141}Ce	32d	145	1.90×10^{-5}	0.01×10^{-5}
Ir	^{192}Ir	74d	316	$<5 \times 10^{-10}$	

relating to a pulse starting through amplifier and analyzer before recovery from the previous pulse. Such pile-up pulses must be rejected as much as possible, because they broaden peak widths and diminish the accuracy of the measurements. Technical points concerning this matter are the following. The irradiation schedule outlined above was geared to produce sample strengths of less than 7000 counts per second. In general, the corresponding "dead time" of the instrument was 25 percent or less. The dead time and the count rate were recorded for each measurement, and a small correction factor (determined empirically) was applied to the peak intensities. The separate application of this correction is a necessity of the manner in which the data are processed.

The processing of the data started with the emptying of the data storage unit onto magnetic tape. This reproduced all the information stored in the 1600 channels in form suitable for computer analysis. The analyzer was stabilized automatically by a digital threshold stabilizer which effectively held a preselected peak dead-center on a particular pair of channels. This stabilization meant that from measurement to measurement the positions of the various peaks would not drift significantly, and the computer might be instructed to add specific channel data to obtain the peak intensities. Instructions were also given as to which channels were to be used for subtraction of the background for each peak. Different ways of handling the background subtraction arose from the detailed shape of the curve in the vicinity of a peak and the presence or absence of other peaks nearby. A number of background "options" evolved and the use of these became a part of the computer program and instructions. The dead-time correction mentioned above arose in part from the fact that at large dead times the peaks were broadened somewhat and some of the stored counts appeared in channels outside of those which the computer was instructed to add. For a few elements, the best peak for analysis contained some counts from the tail of nearby peaks. The amount of this tailing depended upon the amount of the element producing the interfering peak. The computer program also included the calculation of how much was to be subtracted from the final abundance of the element in terms of the abundance of the interfering element.

In addition to the determination of the numbers counts (peak intensities) for each of the peaks analyzed, the computer program included the calculations all the way to the final printout of the abundance of each element in the pottery. Those familiar with these simple but tedious computations will recognize the involvement of the following factors: integrated neutron flux, abundance and cross section of the stable isotope which becomes transmuted, abundance of the specific gamma ray from each radioactive isotope, gometry factor and counting efficiency for the detector, and decay correction for the activated species. Although all these factors are implicit in any determination, some are handled indirectly by use of standards consisting of known amounts of the elements. For example, there is within the calculation a product of the neutron cross section, gamma-ray abundance, and counting efficiency of the gamma ray—all constants for a particular gamma ray and analyzer assembly. In comparison with a standard, any two of these may be fixed arbitrarily and the "errors" so incurred absorbed in the third factor. Since other workers would follow similar procedures, the ultimate analytical results should be strictly comparable even though (for example) the cross sections employed are different.

Although we have analyzed over 250 shards at the present writing, the standardization process was deferred and is not yet in final form. The examples of analyses to be given are therefore unfortunately not absolute values. Some of the constants which we shall determine by means of the standards were taken from the literature, and these can be at variance from what we shall determine. For illustration, the values given for the element lanthanum will not change relative to one another, but the absolute values will have to be revised. By the same token, inferences on the relative amounts of *different* elements will have to be deferred. Only when meaningful absolute values can be put down will it be possible to compare our analyses with those done in other laboratories.

Statement of the Archaeological Problem

Before looking at some actual analyses, it may be well to set down the presently conceived limitations on what the analyses could possibly show. First, a few words should be said about the geochemical basis for judging provenience of pottery. Considering the complexity of the parent rocks and the sensitive fractionation possible in the formation of clay beds, it is possible that no two sources of pottery clay will prove to be the same if a large number of elements are compared. If so, then even a single source of pottery clay may prove to be inhomogeneous. We can only conjecture about this point at present, because nothing has yet been done to explore such variations. The reasons for temporarily ignoring this problem are very much the same as those stated by Catling, Richards, and Blin-Stoyle.[7] They, as we, confine their attention to the finished pottery, because it may be no simple matter to relate pottery directly to clay beds. In most instances it might be quite difficult to satisfy oneself that one is actually sampling the sources from which the ancient potters drew their materials. Further, one cannot be sure how they processed the raw clay, removing

[7] H. W. Catling, E. C. Richards, and A. E. Blin-Stoyle, in *Annual of the British School of Archaeology at Athens 58* (1963), 94–115.

some materials and adding others. There need be less uncertainty concerning the problem of what happens to the composition during the process of firing, because this matter could be explored by experiment. Despite the complexities envisioned, the prospects of getting meaningful information are by no means hopeless. As an example, some conclusions may be drawn on uniformity to be expected within a clay bed by simply sampling and ignoring pottery association.

For the time being, we are therefore relying upon the traditional approach in archaeology, that is, the development of internal correlations to establish the norm for uniformity. Superimposed upon this is the desirability of any external cross-checks which can be elicited. All in all, this calls for a rather lengthy development in which the boundaries of reliability are set by an accumulative process rather than a definitive settlement at one time.

One other point should be mentioned which is perhaps unique to the type of analysis under discussion. Much of the information obtained concerns trace elements present in the parts-per-million range. The inadvertent contamination of our specimens is a real problem and must be guarded against. For example, antimony found to the extent of 1 ppm corresponds to an amount of only 0.1 microgram in a 100-mg sample. If we employ normal diligence, abnormal values do not occur very often, as experience has shown, but they do occur. Where such cases occur, an independent sample should be run. A more difficult problem, and a more interesting one, is the possibility of contamination at the source. There is abundant evidence that ancient peoples used a variety of substances in concentrated state: ores for metallurgy, pigments for decorating, cosmetics, materials for glass—to name a few. It is quite conceivable that pottery would be contaminated significantly, particularly when a rich source of an element corresponded with a trace element in the pottery clay. Evidence for this type of contamination may be difficult to single out unless incidents are repetitive, but where it is obtained one has information of archaeological value.

Results

Some representative analytical results are presented in histogram form in figures 4–8 below. It should be borne in mind in viewing these that the variations in content for a particular element from a particular site cannot be attributed to lack of precision in measurement. Some of the factors that could cause such variations in pottery composition have already been

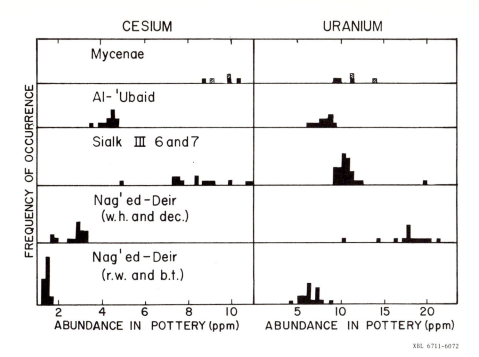

XBL 6711-6072

Fɪɢ. 4. Cesium and uranium composition of pottery excavated from various sites. Crosshatched data represents pottery excavated at Kea.

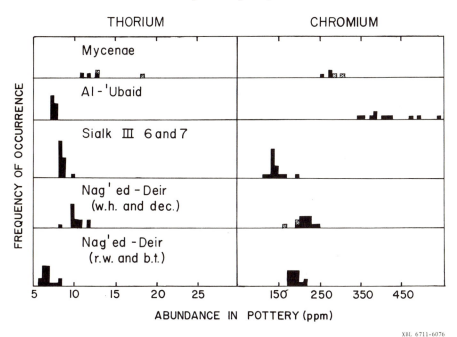

XBL 6711-6076

Fɪɢ. 5. Thorium and chromium composition of pottery excavated from various sites. Crosshatched data represents pottery excavated at Kea.

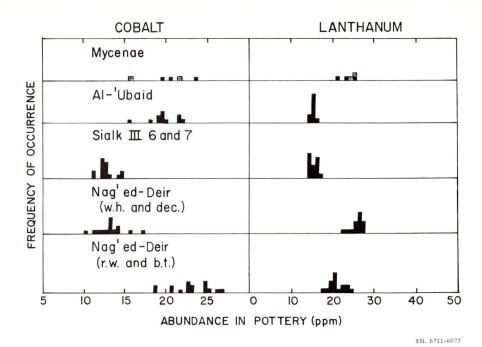

COBALT LANTHANUM

FREQUENCY OF OCCURRENCE

Mycenae

Al-'Ubaid

Sialk III 6 and 7

Nag' ed-Deir
(w.h. and dec.)

Nag' ed-Deir
(r.w. and b.t.)

ABUNDANCE IN POTTERY (ppm)

Fɪɢ. 6. Cobalt and lanthanum composition of pottery excavated from various sites. Crosshatched data represents pottery excavated at Kea.

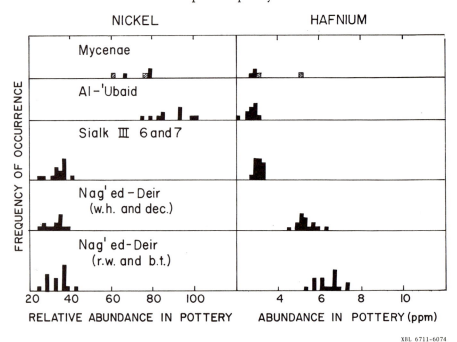

NICKEL HAFNIUM

FREQUENCY OF OCCURRENCE

Mycenae

Al-'Ubaid

Sialk III 6 and 7

Nag' ed-Deir
(w.h. and dec.)

Nag' ed-Deir
(r.w. and b.t.)

RELATIVE ABUNDANCE IN POTTERY ABUNDANCE IN POTTERY (ppm)

Fɪɢ. 7. Nickel and hafnium composition of pottery excavated from various sites. Crosshatched data represents pottery excavated at Kea.

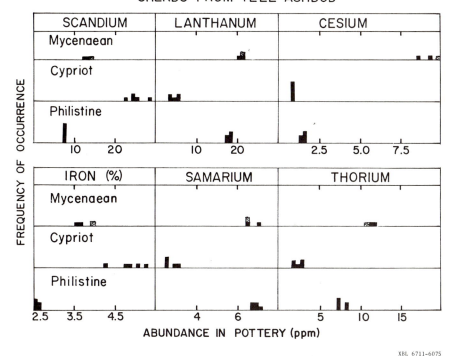

FIG. 8. Partial composition of pottery excavated at Tell Ashdod. Crosshatched data represents sherds excavated at Mycenae.

mentioned. In selecting data for these figures, some have been included specifically to illustrate these points. Each set shown, however, is complete in the sense that no pieces of the type selected have been left out. For example, all of our measurements of the red ware and black-topped ware from Nag' ed-Deir have been included.

The particular elements chosen for illustration represent only about one-fourth of those for which we have data. Among those omitted are some such as arsenic, which seem to be rather chaotic, and others which represent some of the more prominent constituents of clay. Some fifteen elements not shown, however, are probably as useful diagnostically as the eight that appear.

A brief description of the material examined follows:

(1) "Nag' ed-Deir" refers to a predynastic cemetery in Upper Egypt, and materials are from the large Reisner Collection in Berkeley. The selection of representative shards was made by Robert Rodden. Typologically the shards fell into several groups.

(*a*) "Red ware" (r.w.) or "plum ware" is characterized by a fairly coarse texture and a heavily burnished slip of high iron content.

(*b*) "Black-topped ware" (b.t.) is similar in composition to the red ware, and the data for these types have been combined.

(*c*) Decorated ware (dec.) refers to contemporaneous pottery with a hard pink body decorated with red pigment.

(*d*) "Wavy-handled ware" (w.h.) is of the early type in which the handles are pronounced. In later evolutionary states this handle degenerated into a decorative motif. In large part the compositions of these specimens were the same as for the decorated ware and were so combined.

(2) "Sialk" refers to the site in northern Iran which had a long occupation period stretching from 6000 B.C. to A.D. 1000. Materials representative of most of the strata were selected by Jay Frierman, and in due course all the analytical results will be presented along with the inferences of archaeological value. For the present purposes, we are showing only combined pieces from levels III 6 and III 7 which are often typologically indistinguishable.

(3) "Al 'Ubaid" is a site in southern Bablyonia slightly inland from the Euphrates river, and our shards date approximately from 4000 B.C. These materials came from the collection of the Museum and Laboratories of Ethnic Arts and Technology at UCLA and were obtained by J. D. Frierman.

(4) "Mycenae" is too well known to require description. The few pieces so far analyzed were obtained for us by J. D. Frierman, and not all are of known provenience.

(5) In figure 8 are presented some data taken from shards excavated by Dothan at "Tell Ashdod" in the southern coastal region of Israel. These also were obtained by Frierman. Ashdod was a Philistine city of about 1400 B.C., and the few shards analyzed fell distinctively into three typological groups: (*a*) Philistine local, (*b*) Cypriot imports, and (*c*) Mycenaean imports.

In examining the data of figures 4–7 it should be borne in mind that the present stage of this study is not aimed at settling any archaeological problem. Materials were selected whose origins were surmised to be correct and which were typologically distinctive. Whether or not some of the spread in values will ultimately prove to be an unplanned-for excursion into archaeology we do not know.

First, a mere glance at the Nag' ed-Deir material shows that the two categories which can be easily distinguished by visual examination are also quite different in composition. We wish to point out, however, that we already have abundant evidence that such clear correlations are not universal. From sites neighboring on Nag' ed-Deir in Upper Egypt we have typologically similar specimens that are significantly different in composition, and we have found the (inadvertent) intrusion of a shard in the Sialk collection which has not been previously described but which definitely "belongs" to Sialk in its chemical makeup. Reiterating, it is not our purpose here to pursue such leads of archaeological interest. Only one further point will be mentioned and this relates to the few shards designated "Mycenaean." Of these, three were excavated at Mycenae and two (crosshatched in the figures) were found on Kea.

Returning to the data, it is seen that Nag' ed-Deir red ware is the lowest of all in cesium and quite low in thorium. On the other hand, this particular pottery is the highest of all in some other elements not shown here. Sialk and Ubaid overlap in hafnium and lanthanum, are somewhat different in uranium and thorium, and are distinctly different in nickel, chromium, and cesium. Mycenae and Sialk are both high in cesium but are distinctly different in nickel and chromium. Gross comparisons of this nature can be continued by the reader and, as already mentioned, could be done with many other elements not shown here. The objective, however, is to pursue this matter in much greater detail by applying it to materials which are typologically indistinguishable or which have not been "typed" with certainty at all.

In figure 8 we have analytical results on six elements for three types of shards found at Tell Ashdod. This is a rather remarkable set in that there is virtually no overlap between any of the three types for any of the elements. There were only two shards of Mycenaean type. The third, presented as a crosshatched marker, was selected arbitrarily from a small group excavated at Mycenae. Examination of the other data (not shown here) produced fifteen other elements which had similar differences, not including elements which generally vary coherently with those selected. For example, these fifteen elements did not include any rare earth elements, because this type is already represented by lanthanum.

We wish to thank again R. Rodden and J. D. Frierman for their invaluable participation in this study and for the use here of some of the results before the more complete exposition in archaeological context. We are also indebted to our assistants Mrs. Helen V. Michel and Miss Susanne Halvorsen for their skilled and painstaking efforts in almost all phases of this work. This study would not have been possible without the contribution of Duane Mosier in setting up the electronic pulse-height analyzer and the interface equipment which permitted computer processing of the data. We are also indebted to Lawrence Ruby and Leonel Stollar of the University of California Department of Nuclear Engineering for the many carefully controlled irradiations in the Berkeley Research Reactor.[8]

[8] This work was performed under the auspices of the U.S. Atomic Energy Commission.

XIX

RAPID X-RAY FLUORESCENCE ANALYSIS OF ARCHAEOLOGICAL MATERIALS

H. R. Bowman, R. D. Giauque, and I. Perlman

*T*HE GREAT improvement recently in solid-state photon detectors and associated electronics has led to the development of a rather new type of X-ray fluorescence spectrometer. The instrument appears to be particularly suited to the rapid nondestructive analysis of a large number of articles and artifacts. The system takes advantage of the very high resolving power of these semiconductor detectors which makes it possible to measure and distinguish the individual characteristic X-rays of various chemical elements excited in a specimen by a primary source of gamma radiation. The main features of this instrument which may appeal to the archaeological investigator are as follows:

(1) It is relatively easy to use and operate. Many objects can simply be held in front of the detector housing for the analysis. The data resulting from these analyses are presented in a form that is relatively easy to interpret.

(2) It provides a rapid means of nondestructive qualitative and semi-quantitative analysis of the chemical materials in a large number of artifacts. Many times only one or two minutes are needed for each analysis.

(3) The instrument is portable. It could be taken into a museum and set up in a few minutes. It can even be taken into the field for an on-the-spot analysis of artifacts. If an object cannot be moved, then the unit can be brought up to the object to be tested.

(4) Preliminary results indicate that the instrument can be used for quantitative analysis.

A detailed description of the equipment has been given in *Science*[1]

[1] Harry R. Bowman, Earl K. Hyde, Stanley G. Thompson, and Richard C. Jared, in *Science 151* (1966), 562.

where it is compared with the more conventional X-ray fluorescence analysis equipment, and only a brief description of the general principles involved will be given here. Figure 1 shows the arrangement of the apparatus schematically. The source of gamma radiation at the lower left is usually either I^{125} or Am^{241}. Gamma rays from the source impinge on the sample to be tested while the detector is shielded by lead from the direct rays. The characteristic K X-rays and L X-rays that are excited in the sample are then detected by the X-ray detector and give rise to electrical impulses proportional to the X-ray energies. The electrical pulses are amplified and then stored in a multichannel analyzer. The stored information can be printed or plotted out at the end of the run giving a permanent record of the X-ray energy spectrum.

The X-ray detectors and the first transistor (F.E.T.) of the preamp (fig. 1) are kept at liquid nitrogen temperature which reduces the electronic noise and results in the very high X-ray energy resolution. The lower X-ray energy cutoff of the instrument is determined by this electronic noise as well as by the window on the detector housing and the air between the window and the sample. At present the latter two causes prevent us from detecting X-rays with energies lower than those of calcium.

In the analyses presented here we used both the lithium-drifted silicon and germanium-type solid-state detectors, although either type could have been used for all the measurements. The X-ray detectors were originally developed for nuclear spectroscopy where the products of nuclear reactions are analyzed in terms of atomic number through their self-induced X-ray energies. The X-ray fluorescence spectrometer as an analytical tool is a fortuitous product of this nuclear work.

The fact that the instrument might be of use to analyze archaeological artifacts was suggested first by Jay Frierman from UCLA, who sent a large number of articles to use in an evaluation program. With the help of Robert Rodden from the University of California we were able to obtain a number of early Egyptian artifacts to further this evaluation. More than one hundred items were analyzed, and a few of the results will be shown to illustrate the technique.

In figure 2 we show a photograph of the equipment along with a predynastic Egyptian spear which is being analyzed. The accumulation of data can be seen on the oscilloscope screen even while the measurement is in progress. A plot of the results from a two-minute analysis of this spear is shown in figure 3. We are able to identify copper, arsenic, and

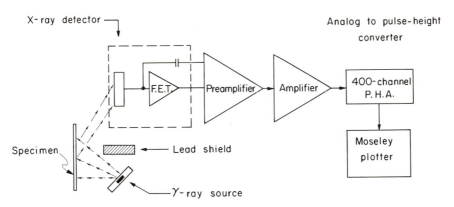

FIG. 1. Schematic arrangement of the apparatus for exciting and measuring the characteristic X radiation of archaeological samples.

silver in the spearhead. The arsenic and silver intensities are very low compared to that of copper and represent only about 1 percent arsenic and and 0.1 percent silver when these results are compared to results obtained from the analysis of standard alloys. The standard alloys were usually made by melting and mixing pure metals in a ceramic crucible. Arsenic in a range of around 1 percent was found in a number of the dynastic and predynastic copper artifacts.

The artifacts from this collection all came from burials and along with them were found many ore specimens including those of copper. Over 100 bits of copper ore were examined and none contained arsenic in detectable amounts. One can say for sure that arsenic in the copper objects was not accidentally introduced through copper ores of the types found and, by inference, that it was added deliberately.

X-ray fluorescence analysis is particularly sensitive to surface conditions and the surface materials. This is illustrated in figure 4 where the two sides of an early dynastic bronze mirror were analyzed. Side "A" indicates about a 12 percent tin-bronze content while side "B" indicates about 4 percent tin-bronze content. At first it was thought that this variation was the result of selective corrosion of side "A" shown in the photograph in figure 4. Further analysis using the "source target assembly" (to be described later) seems to indicate that there is a thin layer of tin on side "A." This assembly allows one to vary the energy and hence the depth of penetration of the exciter radiation. Additional useful information could be obtained by a more detailed analysis of the surface layer and of

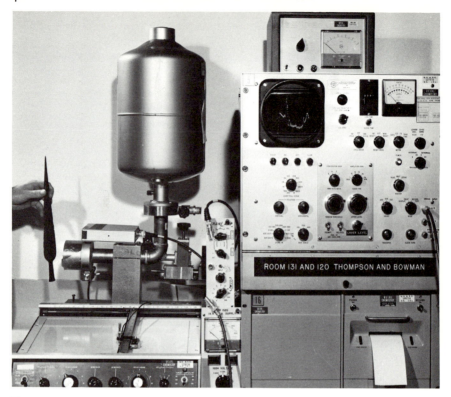

FIG. 2. A predynastic Egyptian spearhead being analyzed with the X-ray fluorescence spectrometer.

material bored from the body of the mirror. The point to be made is not that this problem has been resolved but that a very rapid scan of the X-rays did turn up a problem of potential archaeological interest.

In many cases the gamma radiation can be concentrated or focused onto a particular part of an object to test for local nonuniformities. The article in figure 5 labeled "late dynastic bronze clamp" was used to demonstrate this effect. When the gamma rays were focused onto the labeled location, exceptionally intense iron X-rays were observed. The arrows pointing to the iron on the left side may indicate the use of an iron hinge pin and the other two locations imply the use of iron rivets or brads to fasten the hinge to a second material. The clamp or hinge is only about 2 inches long. This technique could probably be developed so that a small beam of γ-rays ($\sim$1 mm dia) could be used to scan an object and produce an X-ray contour plot of the different elements in or on the surface of the articles. The appearance of iron on this particular object sheds considerable doubt as to whether it belongs in such an early context.

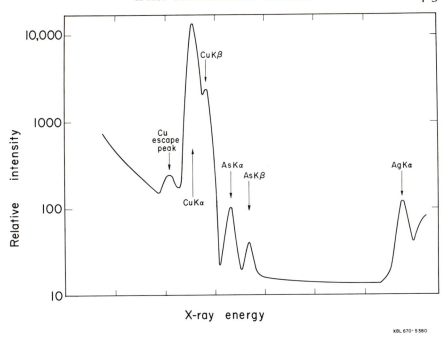

Fig. 3. The X-ray energy spectrum obtained from a two-minute analysis of the spearhead shown in figure 2.

The article shown in figure 6 was labeled "late dynastic metal tube." The X-ray analysis on the right indicates that both the walls and the bottom of the tube were made of the same materials, namely, a tin bronze with a small amount of lead that may be on the surface of the tube. The X-ray shadowgraph (in the center) suggests that the walls and the bottom were cast as one piece and also shows three separate zones of materials within the tube. These materials have the appearance of metal slags. The top zone is rich in lead, the second zone is a tin-lead composition, and the bottom zone is a tin-copper mixture. One is tempted to suggest that this metal tube was used to reduce small amounts of tin or lead ores. The lower wall has either been melted or corroded away, probably melted.

Preliminary measurements indicate that the X-ray fluorescence technique can be used for more quantitative results if one is willing to sacrifice a small amount of the materials to be tested. About 100 mg of the material can be ground into a powder, incorporated into a cellulose matrix, and pressed into a wafer. The wafer is then placed in a standard sample holder and attached to what is called a source-target assembly. This assembly is shown in figure 7. The gamma-ray source which is not critical in this method is encapsulated in a thin aluminum annular ring about 1 inch in

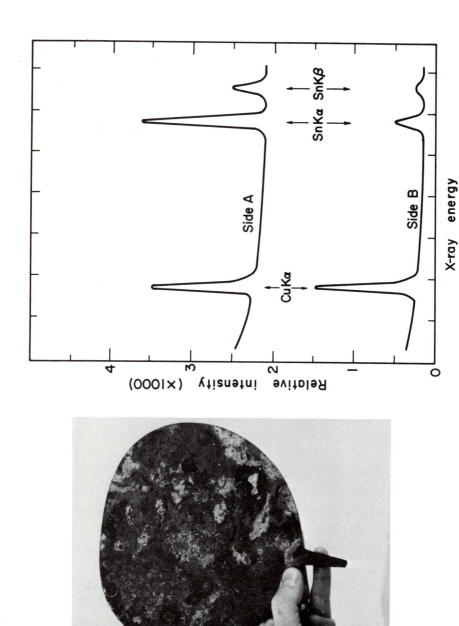

Fig. 4. The X-ray energy spectra obtained from the two sides of an early dynastic Egyptian bronze mirror. Side "A" is shown in the photograph.

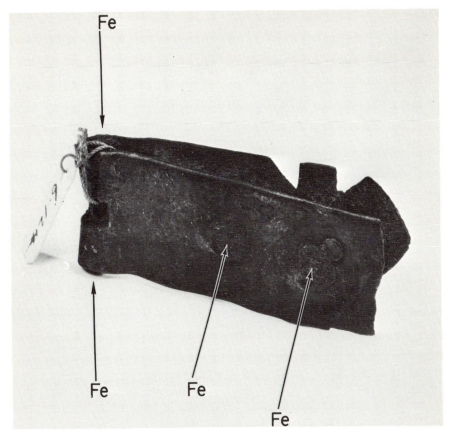

Fig. 5. A late dynastic Egyptian bronze clamp. Iron was detected at the labeled locations.

diameter. The isotope Am^{241} was chosen in this case because of its long half-life. The gamma rays and neptunium L X-rays from this source impinge upon a secondary target material which can be made of any element and excites the characteristic X-rays of that element. The targets are made from metal powders, oxides, or other suitable compounds of the elements mixed with a minimum of epoxy resin. The target X-rays, which are nearly monochromatic, impinge on the wafer and in turn excite X-rays of their constituents. The target materials can be chosen to have their characteristic energy just above that of the absorption edge of the element to be determined in the wafer, thus ensuring high analytical sensitivity. This general approach was originally developed by Rhodes and is described in more detail in his "Review of Radioisotopes in X-rays Spectrom-

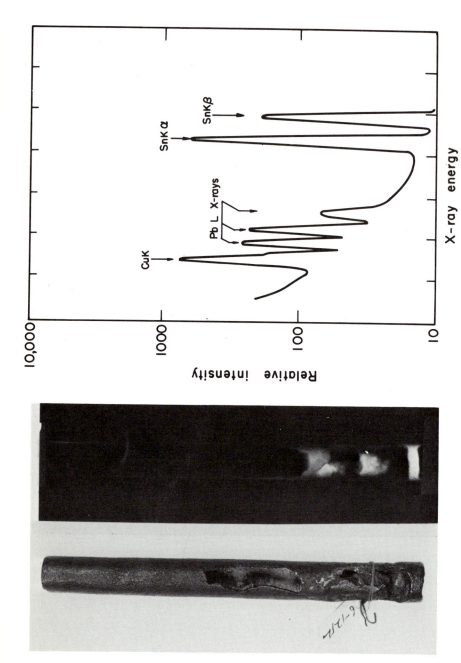

FIG. 6. A late dynastic Egyptian metal tube. The X-ray shadowgraph, in the center, shows the outlines of the tube walls and bottom along with three zones of material within the tube. The X-ray spectra of the outer wall of the tube shown on the right are similar to the spectra obtained from the bottom of the tube.

Source-Target Assembly

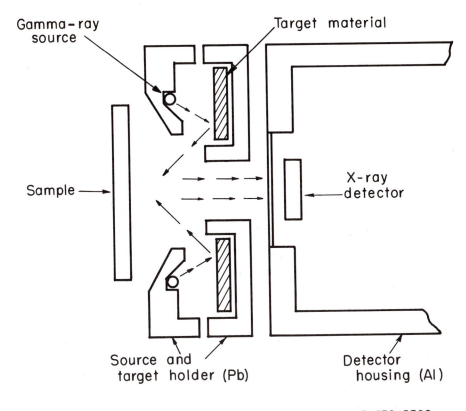

Gamma-ray source

Target material

Sample

X-ray detector

Source and target holder (Pb)

Detector housing (Al)

XBL670-5398

FIG. 7. Schematic arrangement of the source-target assembly.

etry"[2] which appears in *The Analyst*. The article also reviews the many difficulties encountered in X-ray fluorescence analysis. The three main sources of difficulties are due to effects usually called "matrix absorption, matrix enhancement, and particle size." These are well-known effects in conventional X-ray analysis, and the approach to their elimination is similar in both the conventional and present techniques, because the effects occur in the sample.

A number of early sub-Saharan African glass beads (from Mapumgu-bwe) were used to evaluate this method.[3] These analyses hopefully will

[2] J. R. Rhodes, in *The Analyst 91* (1966), 683.
[3] We are indebted to J. Desmond Clark for placing these beads at our disposal and informing us of their significance.

TABLE I

Comparison of Glass Beads Analyzed by X-Ray Fluorescence

Sample no.	Sample	Sample origin	Fe	Cu	Zn	As	Sn	Sb	Pb
A–1	Brownish red beads	Mapumgubwe; S. Limpopo, Rockshelter	1.3%	1.7%					4.3%
A–2	Pink beads	Mapumgubwe; S. Limpopo, Rockshelter						.5%	25.5%
A–3	Light blue beads	Mapumgubwe; S. Limpopo, Rockshelter				1.6%		.5%	21.9%
A–5	Blue beads	Mapumgubwe; S. Limpopo, Rockshelter				3.7%		.1%	27.4%
A–6	Long light green beads	Mapumgubwe; S. Limpopo, Rockshelter		1.1%		2.1%		<.05%	32.5%
A–7	Dark blue beads	Mapumgubwe; S. Limpopo, Rockshelter		2.2%				1.2%	9.8%
A–8	Long dark blue beads	Mapumgubwe; S. Limpopo, Rockshelter		2.8%				1.8%	10.8%
A–10	Bluish green beads	Mapumgubwe; S. Limpopo, Rockshelter		1.2%				.5%	12.7%
A–12	White beads	Mapumgubwe; S. Limpopo, Rockshelter						2.1%	13.6%
C–1	Black beads	Mapumgubwe; Skeleton 23	.9%			4.2%		.1%	.1%
C–2	Light blue beads	Mapumgubwe; Skeleton 23	1.5%						<.1%
D–1	Yellow beads	Mapumgubwe, Eastern area; Ex. 7, no. 1, Skeleton 14	1.0%				1.0%		
D–2	Amber beads	Mapumgubwe, Eastern area							5.9%

No.	Description	Locality						
D-3	Turquoise beads	Ex. 7, no. 1, Skeleton 14	.7%		.4%	1.5%		9.5%
		Mapumgubwe, Eastern area	1.1%	1.5%		1.4%		.3%
D-4	Apple green beads	Ex. 7, no. 1, Skeleton 14	.8%	1.5%		1.2%		6.9%
		Mapumgubwe, Eastern area						
D-5	Blue beads	Ex. 7, no. 1, Skeleton 14	1.5%					<.1%
		Mapumgubwe, Eastern area						
D-6	Black beads	Ex. 7, no. 1, Skeleton 14	1.0%					<.1%
	Maximum metal content if none reported		<.2%	<.2%	<.1%	<.1%*	<.1%	<.1%

* <.3% if more than 5% Pb is present.

give results on some of the constituents of glass which will be of some diagnostic value. The time required for the analysis of each of these specimens typically was 10 to 30 minutes, and improvements are quite possible
by using stronger sources and X-ray detectors of higher-energy resolution
than the system thus far employed. The initial results are presented in
table 1 and show quite clearly that, aside from the coloring matter, a
number of different types of glasses appear. The A series all contain lead,
and in all except one case antimony was present, presumably added for
opacity. Four of the nine specimens contain substantial amounts of
arsenic.

Four of the D series contain substantial amounts of lead; the others
contain smaller or undetectable quantities. All but two of the D series
contain tin, but none antimony. Two of the D series (D5 and D6) contain
neither lead nor tin and are very similar to the C series. The turquoise
beads (D3) were visibly inhomogeneous, and further effort at segregation
was attempted under magnification. The segregated beads were significantly different in copper content but otherwise seemed to be of the same
type of glass. The ember beads were the only ones showing some zinc.
Of special significance for archaeologists is the fact Skeleton 14 from
Mapumgubwe has beads of two quite different compositions, namely,
those of D1-4 and D5-6. The latter shows similar composition to the beads
with Skeleton 23. This suggests that the beads traded up the Limpopo
River to Mapumgubwe came from at least two different sites.

Returning to the A series, it will be noted that the substances responsi-
ble for the colors in A-2, A-3, and A-5 were not detected by this technique.
Also A-1 was significantly lower in lead than other members of the series.
These beads were the only ones which were laminated, consisting of
Indian red material over a colorless core. It may well be that one of the
layers contains little or no lead.

In conclusion we would like to emphasize that the instrument and the
techniques have only recently been developed and will no doubt be improved with further application. We believe it has a potential use in the
field of archaeology, although it is still not clear which problems are most
suited to it. We feel that the archaeologist himself will be able to use the
instrument in the laboratory, the museum, or the field, and that perhaps
he will be the one to determine the manner in which this instrument can
be best applied to his problems. With this in mind we would like to
restate the main features that may appeal to the archaeologist:

(1) The equipment is relatively easy to operate.
(2) It provides a rapid nondestructive means of identifying the elemental materials in a large number of articles.
(3) It is portable and can be taken into museums and even into the field.
(4) It can be used for more quantitative results when more time and care are involved in sample preparations.[4]

[4] This work was done under the auspices of the U.S. Atomic Energy Commission.

XX

MAGNETIC PROSPECTING

M. J. Aitken

$\mathcal{M}$AGNETIC PROSPECTION has been used for the location of iron-ore deposits since the end of the last century, and subsequently, with the development of very sensitive measuring techniques, other aspects of geological structure have been mapped out in this way. One major advance in technique was the development, by Packard and Varian (1954), of the proton free-precession magnetometer, which provided a rapid and accurate means of mapping magnetic anomalies and which, after transistorization, was easily carried by one man. The idea of using it on a smaller scale for the location of buried archaeological remains was put forward in 1956 by J. C. Belshé, who suggested in particular that this would be a good way of finding ancient pottery kilns. The first archaeological trial was made by the Oxford Archaeological Research Laboratory in March 1958, with the object of locating any pottery kilns that lay in the route of a new trunk road, where a two-mile-long stretch bordered the Roman town and camp of Durobrivae. Kilns producing "color coated" ware had been found previously in the region, and it was a matter of considerable concern to Romano-British archaeologists that any more that lay in the route of the road should be located before they were lost forever.

Thus the first trial was also an application of critical importance and the success of it stimulated great interest in the technique. In the next four years alone some fifty sites in Britain were surveyed with the proton magnetometer,[1] and elsewhere the technique has been widely used too— by R. Linington for the Lerici Foundation in Italy and other countries, by

---

[1] M. J. Aitken, *Physics and Archaeology* (London: Interscience, 1961), chap. 2; M. J. Aitken and M. S. Tite, "Proton Magnetometer Surveying on Some British Hill-forts," *Archaeometry* 5 (1962), 126; M. J. Aitken, "Magnetic Location," sect. 53, in *Science in Archaeology*, Brothwell and E. Higgs, eds. (London: Thames and Hudson; New York: Basic Books, 1963), p. 555.

Elizabeth Ralph for the University Museum, Philadelphia, notably in looking for the lost Greek colony of Sybaris in southern Italy, by I. Scollar for the Landesmuseum, Bonn, by A. Hesse for the French C.R.N.S. in Nubia, by M. Tite [2] for the Oxford Research Laboratory in Nigeria, and by Glenn Black and R. Johnston for the Ohio Archaeological Society at Angel Rock, as well as by a number of other institutions and individuals. In the last year or two, its use has been extended to underwater archaeology.[3]

The features detectable by magnetic prospection fall into four main categories:

(1) Pits and ditches;

(2) walls and tombs;

(3) kilns, furnaces, ovens, and hearths;

(4) iron objects.

The reasons why these features produce magnetic anomalies will now be outlined.

Magnetic Anomalies

Archaeological features are detectable by magnetic prospection when they produce a significant disturbance, or anomaly, in the normal value of the earth's magnetic-field strength. A feature produces such an anomaly when its magnetic properties differ from those of the adjacent strata: such a difference may arise because of a different percentage of iron oxide, or because of changes in the *condition* of the iron oxide (the average amount of iron oxide in the earth's crust is 6.8%). Whereas *haematite* (α Fe_2O_3) is only very weakly ferrimagnetic, *magnetite* (Fe_3O_4) and *maghemite* (γ Fe_2O_3) are appreciably so. The magnetic susceptibilities of the two latter are many times greater than those of the former, so that if the iron oxide in the soil filling of a pit, or ditch, is in the form of maghemite, whereas the iron oxide in the adjacent natural is in the form of haematite, the induced magnetization of the feature is higher than that of its surroundings. This produces an increase in the magnetic-field strength above ground level. Haematite can be converted to maghemite by successive reduction and oxidation.

[2] M. S. Tite, "Magnetic Prospecting near to the Geomagnetic Equator," *Archaeometry* 9 (1966), 24–31.

[3] E. T. Hall, "The Use of the Proton Magnetometer in Underwater Archaeology," *Archaeometry* 9 (1966), 32–44.

Two mechanisms by which this happens in natural topsoil have been suggested by E. Le Borgne [4]—first, alternating periods of wetness and dryness, and second, the cumulative effect, over centuries, of ground clearance by burning. Both mechanisms are favored by a high humus content in the soil.

PITS AND DITCHES

As a result of these mechanisms on sedimentary geological formations, the topsoil is appreciably more magnetic than the substrata. Thus if a pit, or ditch, is dug into limestone, clay, chalk, gravel, etc., and allowed to silt up, a magnetic anomaly is created. Alternatively, if a pit has been used for food storage, or as a repository for domestic rubbish or human excreta, it is likely that its humus content will be higher than the topsoil, and so the magnetic anomaly correspondingly enhanced. It seems that the blackness and dirtiness of the soil filling of a feature is a good guide to the strength of an anomaly. The size and burial depth of the feature is important also; in typical conditions, it is not possible to detect a pit smaller than a meter across and a meter deep when it is buried beneath a meter of overburden. If the overburden is less, then the minimum detectable size is less also. Of course, if a pit, or ditch, has been refilled with the sterile material which was excavated from it before any silting has occurred, then no anomaly is produced and the feature is not detectable.

WALLS, FOUNDATIONS, AND TOMBS

The anomaly from a pit, or ditch, is produced because the archaeological feature is more magnetic than the adjacent natural. This is described as a "normal" anomaly, and corresponds to an increase in the magnetic-field strength. When a substantial limestone wall is buried in soil that is appreciably magnetic, then the feature constitutes a region of reduced magnetization, and a "reverse" anomaly is produced, corresponding to a decrease in field strength. For such an anomaly to be detectable the magnetic susceptibility of the natural soil must be appreciable (say, 10^{-3} emu per gram); this is the exception rather than the rule in Britain, but often the case in countries bordering the Mediterranean at any rate. If the wall is built of brick or basaltic rock, then it may be detectable on account of its own "thermoremanent magnetism."

[4] E. Le Borgne, "Les proprietés magnetiques du sol, Application a la prospection des sites archaeologiques," *Archaeo-Physika* (Bonner Jahrbuch 15), 1.

Empty tombs, like walls, produce a reverse anomaly. This is because air has replaced the natural soil. On the other hand, a tomb filled with humus-rich soil would be expected to produce a normal anomaly. Obviously, for a partially filled tomb there is a degree of filling for which the two effects cancel out, and the anomaly is zero. In such cases, however, it is still possible that the associated stonework, etc., will produce an anomaly close by. The detection of Etruscan tombs has been extensively studied by Linington[5] in Italy.

KILNS, FURNACES, OVENS, AND HEARTHS

The anomalies due to these features arise because of the phenomenon called *thermoremanent magnetism*. This occurs in material, particularly clay, when it cools down from being heated to a temperature of several hundred degrees Celsius. It again concerns the few percent of iron oxide naturally present, and rather than constituting a chemical change in condition, it is a physical one. Before heating, the magnetic domains of the iron oxide are randomly orientated, whereas, as the temperature rises, more and more of them are able to align along the direction of the lines of force of the earth's magnetic field. On cooling, the magnetic domains remain "frozen" in this lined-up situation, thereby producing a weak permanent magnetism. As explained in an accompanying paper, thermoremanent magnetism is the basis of "magnetic dating" in which the changing direction of magnetic north is used to determine the age of pottery kilns, etc.

The anomaly due to the thermoremanent magnetism of a kiln or furnace is usually stronger than that due to a pit, whereas that due to a hearth is usually smaller on account of the smaller bulk of material present.

IRON OBJECTS

Iron in metallic form produces a very strong magnetic disturbance. In some circumstances it is possible to detect ten kilograms of iron at a depth of five meters. This high sensitivity to iron is usually inconvenient, because near to any present-day habitation there is often a litter of horseshoes, nails, wire fencing, and the like, which may obscure the weaker archaeological anomalies.

[5] R. E. Linington, "The Use of Simplified Anomalies in Magnetic Surveying," *Archaeometry* 7 (1964), 3–13; R. E. Linington, "An Extension to the Use of Simplified Anomalies in Magnetic Surveying," *Archaeometry* 9 (1966), 51–60.

It should be emphasized that the magnetometer is not sensitive to any metal other than iron, steel, cobalt, and nickel. Thus treasure hunters after gold and silver must use an electromagnetic method (see below).

VOLCANIC GEOLOGY

Igneous rocks possess thermoremanent magnetism, acquired as they cooled from the molten state. For recent basalts this is liable to be strong and the disturbances from the rocks themselves may mask the archaeological anomalies. On the other hand, granite is very much weaker magnetically, and this is likely to be the case, too, with other plutonic rocks.

THE DIURNAL VARIATION

A complication of magnetic surveying is that due to ionization currents in the upper atmosphere small erratic changes in the magnetic-field strength occur from time to time, at any one location. During a "magnetically disturbed day" these temporal changes may be comparable with the spatial changes due to archaeological anomalies. In these circumstances, it is necessary to use a second detector kept in a fixed position in order to monitor the changes due to this "diurnal variation" (the changes are the same over a wide region), or to use a gradiometer type of instrument. On ordinary days, however, and with archaeological anomalies of average strength, this procedure is not necessary, although it does facilitate interpretation.

Suitable Instruments

The proton magnetometer.[6] The detecting element for this instrument is a bottle of water (or some other hydrogen-rich liquid such as methyl alchol) around which is wound an electrical coil. The coil and bottle are encapsulated and mounted on a short staff.[7] The coil is connected to the transistorized electronics by a long cable. In order to measure the magnetic-field strength, the protons (the nuclei of hydrogen atoms) are first polarized by a current of about one ampere through the coil and then allowed to exhibit free precession. The frequency of this free precession is exactly proportional to the magnetic-field strength. The precessing protons

---

[6] M. J. Aitken, *Physics and Archaeology* (London: Interscience, 1961), chap. 2.
[7] E. T. Hall, "Some Notes on the Design and Manufacture of Detector Heads for Proton Magnetometers," *Archaeometry* 5 (1962), 139–145.

induce a minute alternating voltage in the coil and this is fed to the electronics for amplification and measurement. In most instruments the sequence of polarization and measurement is programmed automatically to repeat itself every two or three seconds. The reading is presented in digital form as a five-figure number of which one unit is usually made equal to one *gamma* (100,000 gamma = 1 oersted).

Two operators are needed, one to move the detector bottle from point to point over the area being surveyed, the other to record the readings. With practice about 600 readings can be taken in an hour; of course, it is not necessary to record all five figures of the reading; at most only the hundreds, tens, and units are needed. The spacing at which readings are taken depends on the size of the features expected; typically the spacing is between two and five feet.

To interpret the readings, it is necessary to decide on a rough average reading and look for deviations from this average. The level of deviation that is significant varies from site to site, because there is a random fluctuation (often described as "soil noise") due to irregularities of the topsoil. In figure 2, which shows the deviations from the average over an area containing a pottery kiln and a ditch, the "soil noise" is seen to be about $\pm 5\gamma$. The level of the soil noise is roughly proportional to the magnetic susceptibility of the soil; consequently, on sites of strong soil noise the anomaly due to an actual feature is strong also.

The differential proton magnetometer. Difficulties arising during days on which the "diurnal variation" is strong have been mentioned earlier. Similar interference can arise from electric trains and trams run from DC supplies. One method of avoiding this sort of trouble is to use two detector bottles (one fixed, the other to be moved over the area) and design the electronics to calculate the difference in reading between the two. Such instruments have been developed by I. Scollar [8] at Bonn and by J. Mudie [9] at Cambridge. Scollar's instrument also has facilities for direct punch-tape output so that the readings can be fed to a computer for analysis and interpretation. This highly sophisticated approach is very advantageous when large areas are to be surveyed, but for small areas of limited accessibility the bulkiness of the equipment may outweigh the advantages.

[8] I. Scollar and Krückeberg, "Computer Treatment of Magnetic Measurements from Archaeological Sites," *Archaeometry* 9 (1966), 61–71; I. Scollar, "A Contribution to Magnetic Prospecting in Archaeology," *Archaeo-Physika* (Bonner Jahrbuch 15), 21.

[9] J. D. Mudie, "A Digital Differential Proton Magnetometer," *Archaeometry* 5 (1962), 135–138.

FIG. 1. The proton magnetometer in operation. One operator moves the detector bottle from point to point on the large-scale string mesh that is laid over the area being surveyed while the other operator records the reading indicated for each point.

The proton gradiometer. This instrument[10] is also a form of differential magnetometer but the two detector bottles are fixed at either end of a staff (between 4 and 10 feet long) which is usually held vertically. The upper detector bottle, being remote from any buried features, can be regarded as a reference and the instrument indicates when the magnetic-field strength at the lower bottle deviates from this reference.

In the *"Max Bleep"* and the *"Wreckfinder"* the electronics have been reduced to a minimum. This reduces the cost of the instrument to a fraction of that for the standard proton magnetometer, but on the other hand, the indication is a little more difficult to interpret, being semiquantitative.

The caesium gradiometer.[11] This utilizes the magnetic properties of atomic caesium. It is considerably more complex than the proton magnetometer but it is more sensitive (easily detecting changes of 0.1 gamma) and gives a continuous reading of the field strength.

[10] M. S. Tite and M. J. Aitken, "A Gradient Magnetometer, Using Proton Free-Precession," *J. Sci. Instruments 39* (Dec. 1962), 625–629.

[11] E. K. Ralph, "Comparison of a Proton and a Rubidium Magnetometer for Archaeological Prospecting," *Archaeometry 7* (1964), 20–27.

PROTON MAGNETOMETER READINGS AROUND POT KILN.

Anomalies in 1 gamma units

DITCH

N

|————— 50 feet —————|

1	-2	3	10	4	-3	6	2	6	5	8	4	-1	-2	-8	-6	-7
1	-2	2	9	3	1	7	11	19	18	17	7	2	3	-5	-4	-4
2	0	7	7	2	8	16	24	35	45	34	15	1	-4	-4	-8	-5
2	3	11	4	6	16	32	50	74	91	69	20	-2	-4	-6	-10	-7
4	6	12	4	10	21	33	47	74	95	67	22	-2	-5	-5	-5	-5
2	7	7	7	13	23	28	36	45	36	15	-3	-5	-6	-6	-5	-4
2	13	4	6	10	19	18	21	2	-9	-15	-8	-9	-3	-3	-5	-5
6	10	2	1	4	4	3	-8	-18	-21	-16	-12	-9	-3	-4	-4	-3
7	6	0	-2	-5	-6	-11	-16	-18	-15	-14	-11	-4	-1	0	-2	-2
11	2	1	0	-1	-4	-7	-9	-7	-7	-4	-2	1	1	2	-2	0
5	-1	1	2	0	-3	-6	-6	-6	-5	-4	-1	-1	1	2	-1	1
2	3	2	1	0	-1	-5	-7	-8	-7	-6	10	-32	15	0	1	1

IRON

FIG. 2. Sample results from a proton magnetometer survey over an area that contains a pottery kiln, a ditch, and a piece of surface iron. The figures shown (units in one gamma) indicate the deviation of each reading from the reading to be expected over undisturbed ground. The appreciable "reverse" anomaly lying to the north of the circular "normal" anomaly is characteristic of the magnetic disturbance from a pottery kiln. The actual kiln lies roughly midway between the two.

The convenience of the caesium gradiometer is a strong advantage over the proton magnetometer, but except on sites where the soil noise is abnormally low there is not much advantage in the high sensitivity. The instrument can be used in the gradiometer configuration, as a differential device, or with a single detector.

The fluxgage gradiometer.[12] The detecting elements are thin strips of high permeability mu-metal. These measure the component of the magnetic-field strength parallel to their length, and consequently a single

---

[12] J. C. Alldred, "A Fluxgage Gradiometer for Archaeological Surveying," *Archaeometry* 7 (1964), 14–19; M. J. Aitken and J. C. Alldred, "A Simulator-Trainer for Magnetic Prospection," *Archaeometry* 7 (1964), 28–35.

detector would be extremely directionally sensitive. However, by fixing a detector at either end of a rigid rod in the gradiometer configuration this difficulty can be overcome—though in order to make the rod sufficiently rigid it needs to be of complex design requiring competent mechanical facilities for its construction. The instrument has the advantages of continuous indication and insensitivity to power-line interference; the detecting staff, however, is heavier to carry than for the other instruments mentioned, and the sensitivity so far obtained with this type is barely three gamma. In searching for kilns this is no disadvantage but for weaker features it would be.

The pulsed magnetic induction technique ("DECCO").[13] All the preceding instruments are "passive" in the sense that they detect the local field arising from the magnetization of the feature by the earth's field. In "DECCO" repeated pulses of magnetic field are transmitted into the ground and immediately following each pulse a receiver coil is switched on. Any decaying magnetic fields that are present after the switchoff of the transmitter pulse induce a voltage in the receiver coil. Such fields can be produced by decaying eddy currents in metal objects and also by a subtle short-term remanent magnetization (the so-called magnetic viscosity) in soil. Thus the instrument, although designed as a metal detector (hence the name—*Decay of Eddy Currents in Conducting Objects*), can in fact locate the same types of soil feature as a magnetometer. As a metal detector it is somewhat more sensitive than conventional types and has particular advantages for underwater archaeology.

The soil conductivity meter ("The Banjo").[14] This is an electromagnetic instrument consisting of a transmitter coil and a receiver coil rigidly fixed at either end of a rigid staff (about 3 feet long) which is held horizontally. The planes of the two coils are perpendicular so as to minimize direct reception. The transmitter coil is powered at about 4 Kc/s and the receiver is tuned to the same frequency. Soil features are detected by a change in the strength of the receiver signal; the name of the instrument implies that this variation is due to enhanced electrical conductivity but it is probable that the magnetic properties of the soil also

[13] C. Colani and M. J. Aitken, "Utilization of Magnetic Viscosity Effects in Soils for Archaeological Prospection," *Nature 212* (1966), 1446; C. Colani, "A New Type of Locating Device, I—The Instrument," *Archaeometry 9* (1966), 3–8; C. Colani and M. J. Aitken, "A New Type of Locating Device, II—Field Trials," *Archaeometry 9* (1966), 9–19.

[14] M. Howell, "A Soil Conductivity Meter," *Archaeometry 9* (1966), 20–23.

play a part. The electronics involved in this instrument, being in the continuous-wave, audiofrequency category, are much simpler than in the preceding instruments. The soil conductivity meter (SCM) holds high promise for widespread use in archaeological prospecting as long as the features sought are fairly near the surface.

Site Application [15]

The degree of usefulness of magnetic prospecting on any given site is difficult to predict without actual trial on that site, but there are some general practical, geological, and archaeological considerations that are worth noting.

Practical. The difficulty of surveying near to any forms of present-day habitation has already been mentioned. This arises because of the strong magnetic effects from accompanying iron litter that mask the weaker anomalies due to soil features. Iron litter can also be a hazard in remote localities; for example, iron wire associated with vine growing may linger long after the plants themselves have been removed. Power lines, railways, radio transmitters, and iron fences are some other hazards to be looked for.

Even when the surface is free from iron, weeds, undergrowth, bushes, or rocks may make it impracticable to carry out a survey because of the difficulty of moving the connecting cable of the instrument. There is also the need to have some form of marking out of the surveyed area—either tape measures or a mesh of strings stretched for example between pegs on a 50-foot grid system. Obviously the latter system—which allows maximum speed of coverage—is only feasible on large, clear areas. It should be emphasized, however, that it is only in such circumstances that reliable predictions can be made: a few spot measurements here and there on a site are usually misleading.

Archaeological. The technique is one for locating the presence of some abnormality in the ground rather than for determining its nature. It can delimit the extent of the abnormality, but to find out what it really is almost always requires excavation. Thus on a complex site that has been occupied intensively the technique is not likely to be of value: there will be abnormalities everywhere. Its real value is in finding a few isolated features on a site that is mostly blank—for example, occupation remains

[15] M. J. Aitken and M. S. Tite, "Proton Magnetometer Surveying on Some British Hill-forts," *Archaeometry* 5 (1962), 126; M. J. Aitken, "Magnetic Location," sect. 53, in *Science in Archaeology*, Brothwell and Higgs, eds. (London: Thames and Hudson; New York: Basic Books, 1963), p. 555.

within the ramparts of a large hillfort; or in finding distinctive features among a background of minor ones—for example, strongly magnetic pottery kilns, or features recognizable by their geometry such as long walls and ditches. Finally, it is a technique for site *exploration* rather than site *discovery;* the latter remains the province of aerial photography. Although the speed of ground coverage is very rapid compared to coverage by trial trenching and can approach one or two acres per day, there are some 600 acres in every square mile!

Geological. The geology of a site is important from two points of view. First, it partially determines the strength of an anomaly from a given size and shape of feature. Second, some types of substrata give rise to "geological" anomalies.

The anomaly strength is affected also by the humus content and amount of burning in the topsoil—that is, the intensiveness and duration of occupation—but it is usual to find that sites on limestone are "strong" sites, whereas those on clay, chalk, and gravel tend to be weaker.

The occurrence of geological anomalies is frequent on basalt (because of its thermoremanent magnetism) and where the geology is highly disturbed. Sites on limestone are good as long as the surface of the rock is regular. In hot climates the rapidity of degradation may be such as to give the surface a pitlike nature and the resultant anomalies are indistinguishable from a high concentration of man-made pits.

APPENDIX

Some Commercial Suppliers of Prospecting Equipment

Askania	Conti Elektro Askania-Werke Berlin-Mariendorf Germany	(Proton magnetometer)
Barringer Research, Ltd.	304 Carlingview Drive Rexdale Ontario Canada	(Proton magnetometer)
Compagnie des Compteurs	12 place des Etats-Unis Montrouge Seine Boite Postale 56 France	(Proton magnetometer)

Littlemore Scientific Engineering Company	Railway Lane Littlemore Oxford	(Proton magnetometer) (Pulsed magnetic induction technique)
Forster	Institut Dr. Forster 741 Reutlingen Grathwohlstrasse 4 Western Germany	(Fluxgage gradiometer)
Nonesuch Expeditions Ltd.	100 Park Street London, W. 1	(Soil conductivity meter)
Varian	Quantum Electronics Division 611 Hansen Way Palo Alto, California U.S.A.	(Proton magnetometer) (Caesium gradiometer)
Wardle & Davenport, Ltd.	Leek Staffordshire	(Proton gradiometer— "Wreckfinder")

U.S. Agents: M. & E. Marine Supply
                    Co.
               P. O. Box 601
               Camden, N.J.

Addendum

ADDENDUM

CORROSION IN ARCHAEOLOGY

I. Cornet

Corrosion Fundamentals

THE ARCHAEOLOGIST in the field and the curator in the museum are often faced with corrosion problems involving metal artifacts. Simply stated, corrosion is the deterioration or destruction of a metal due to chemical or electrochemical reaction with the environment. The mechanism of corrosion is the same as that found in an ordinary electric dry cell, such as a flashlight battery. Such an electrochemical cell consists of two electrodes, connected by a conductor of electricity, and in contact with an electrolyte. The electrode where corrosion occurs is called the anode; in the case of the flashlight battery this is commonly zinc. The electrode which does not corrode is called a cathode; in the flashlight battery it is normally a carbon rod. An electrolyte is a solution that contains ions; in the flashlight battery there is an ammonium chloride solution absorbed in sawdust or clay. When a metallic conductor connects the anode and the cathode the circuit is complete. The electrochemical cell may consist of two different kinds of metal, or they may be different areas on the same piece of metal. There are differences of electrical potential between the two electrodes in an electrolyte, which arise from the nature of the electrodes. For example, there is a difference in reactivity of iron relative to copper; or there may be differences in reactivity in a piece of bronze due to cold work in a deep-drawn or hammered part relative to an adjacent undeformed area. Any such differences give rise to differences in potential when an electrolyte is present.

Metals such as iron and steel, or pewter or brass, tend to react and corrode. Philosophically, one may say they tend to revert to compounds, such as the ores from which they were originally obtained. This tendency to react is determined by the nature of the metal as well as by the conditions and nature of the environment—that is, temperature, concentration of salts, and the like.

When corrosion occurs metal at the anode is converted to metal ions. Under certain conditions, for example, for steel in a waterlogged saline marsh, the metal ions may actually dissolve and travel some distance from the metal from which they came. In the case of the same metal in an aerated soil, the ferrous ions which form will be converted to iron oxides on the metal surface and remain as a scale on the metal.

For an electrochemical cell to function, all its elements—the anode, the cathode, the electrolyte, and the electrically conducting circuit—must be present. If there is no electrolyte, for example, there is no corrosion—as can be the case with a piece of steel in dry desert air: it can remain shiny and uncorroded for a long time. The rate of corrosion and its extent may also be determined by barriers, such as films or patina which form on copper alloys; or by other resistance factors such as are provided by a lacquer or enamel coating. While there are some well-understood quantitative relationships concerning corrosion factors, the archaeologist will often find corrosion is an art as well as a science!

Summarizing, an electrochemical cell consists of two electrodes, one or more ion-conducting electrolytes, and an electron-conducting path between the electrodes (fig. 1). If there is asymmetry of electrodes, of electrolytes, or of both, a difference of potential will exist, current will flow through the circuit, oxidation (corrosion) will occur at one electrode (called the anode), and reduction will occur at the other electrode (called the cathode). Thus, if iron and copper are the electrodes placed in saltwater, iron becomes the anode and corrodes if there is an electrical connection between the two metals. The electrodes may be of the same metal; if there is a difference in temperature between the electrodes, or if there is a difference in stress between the electrodes, a difference in potential will be present which can cause corrosion.

If the electrodes are of the same metal, and the temperature and other physical factors are the same, there may still be a difference in potential due to asymmetry of electrolytes. For example, if one copper electrode is placed in a concentrated copper sulphate solution and another copper electrode is placed in a dilute copper sulphate solution, with ionic and

[1] W. M. Latimer and J. H. Hildebrand, *Reference Book of Inorganic Chemistry* (3d ed.; New York: Macmillan, 1951); G. N. Lewis and M. Randall, *Thermodynamics* (2d ed., rev. by K. S. Pitzer and L. Brewer; New York: McGraw-Hill, 1961); Herbert H. Uhlig, *Corrosion and Corrosion Control* (New York: John Wiley, 1963).

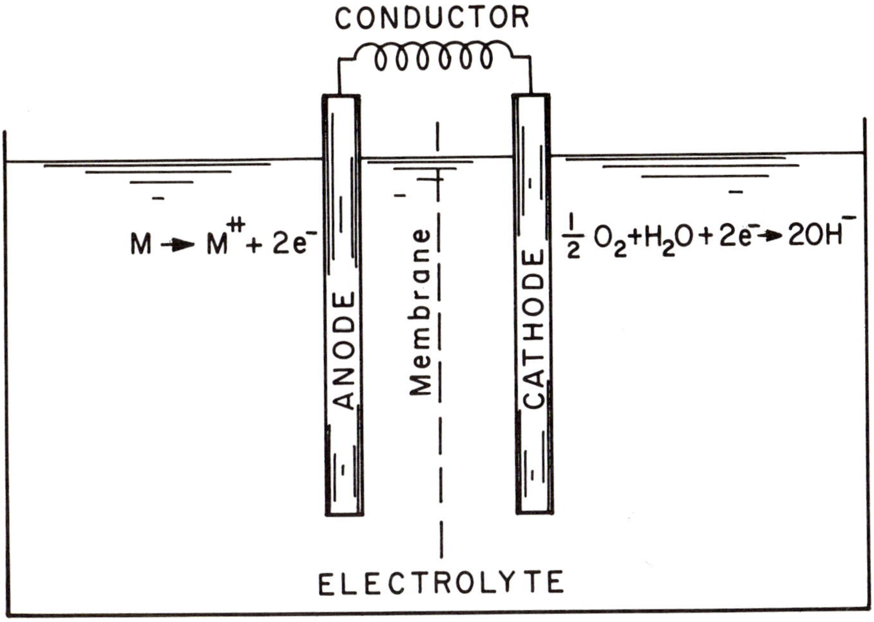

CONDUCTOR

$$M \rightarrow M^{++} + 2e^-$$ — ANODE — Membrane — CATHODE — $$\frac{1}{2}O_2 + H_2O + 2e^- \rightarrow 2OH^-$$

ELECTROLYTE

FIG. 1. An electrochemical cell. The reaction shown at the cathode, where oxygen is being reduced, is for illustrative purposes.

electronic conductors present, current will flow. This would be called a copper-ion concentration cell. Two steel electrodes will have a difference of potential of about ½ volt if one electrode is in an aerated saltwater and the other is in deaerated saltwater.[2] This is called an oxygen concentration cell. The steel in the deaerated solution will be anodic and corrode. The semipermeable membrane between the electrolytes surrounding the cathode and anode may be a piece of filter paper, a pile of sand, or any barrier to ready circulation of solution.

Corrosion Rates

Representative corrosion rates in various environments are shown in table 1.[3] Different metals respond differently. Steel corrodes five times more rapidly in seawater than in soil, and ten times more rapidly in seawater than in air. Such average corrosion rates refer principally to a wasting away of metal. Steel exposed in soil may pit at much more rapid rates than table 1 indicates. If steel is in contact with copper, in seawater, for

[2] E. Schaschl and G. A. Marsh, "Concentration Cells and Aqueous Corrosion," *Corrosion,* vol. 16, no. 9 (Sept. 1960), 461–467T.

[3] Herbert H. Uhlig, *Corrosion and Corrosion Control* (New York: John Wiley, 1963).

TABLE I

Representative Corrosion Rates in Air, in Seawater, and in Soil

Environment	Corrosion rate					
	Steel		Zinc		Copper	
	mdd *	mpy †	mdd	mpy	mdd	mpy
Rural atmosphere	—	—	0.17	.034	0.14	.023
Marine atmosphere	2.9	.532	0.31	.063	0.32	.052
Industrial atmosphere	1.5	.274	1.0	0.202	0.29	.047
Seawater	25	4.56	10	2.02	8	1.29
Soil	5	.915	3	0.606	0.7	.113

* mdd = milligrams per square decimeter per day.
† mpy = mils per year (1 mil = 0.001 inch).

Atmospheric tests on 0.3% Cu steel, 7½-year exposure, from C. Larrabee, *Corrosion 9*, (1953), 259. Atmospheric rates for Zn and Cu, 10-year exposure, from Symposium on Atmospheric Exposure Tests on Non-Ferrous Metals, A.S.T.M., 1946. Seawater data from *Corrosion Handbook*. Soil data for steel are averaged for 44 soils, 12-year exposure, for Zn, 12 soils, 11-year exposure; for Cu, 29 soils, 8-year exposure—from *Underground Corrosion*, M. Romanoff, circ. 579, Bureau of Standards, 1957. (Based on H. H. Uhlig, *Corrosion and Corrosion Control*.)

example, the corrosion rate of the steel will be greatly increased and the corrosion rate of the copper greatly decreased, due to galvanic effects.

Table 1 and similar data must be used with caution. The corrosivity of atmospheres may vary fiftyfold for steel exposed in Khartoum, Egypt, compared to Congella, South Africa, as shown in table 2.[4] Soils may vary widely in corrosivity.

The metals of major concern here are gold, silver, copper, lead, tin, iron, and zinc.[5] Generally, these metals occur as alloys[6] although it is

[4] C. P. Larrabee, "Corrosion of Steels in Marine Atmospheres and in Sea Water," *Trans. Electrochem. Soc. 87* (1945). Based on field tests of the Iron and Steel Institute Corrosion Committee reported by J. C. Hudson in *J. Iron Steel Inst. 11* (1943), 209, with additional data; U.S. Corps of Engineers, "Corrosion Control," EM 1110–1–184, 1 August 1962.

[5] H. J. Plenderleith, *The Conservation of Antiquities and Works of Art* (London: Oxford University Press, 1956).

[6] Hanna Jedrzejewska, "Sampling Precautions in the Analysis of Metallic Antiquities," *Studies in Conservation*, vol. 7, no. 1 (Feb. 1962), 27–31; R. M. Organ, "Are Analyses of Uncorroded Ancient Alloys Representative?" *Studies in Conservation*, vol. 7, no. 2 (May 1962), 48–54.

TABLE 2

Relative Corrosivity of Atmospheres
Twenty Locations Throughout the World*

Location	Type of atmosphere	Losses of weight † in grams			Relative corrodibility ‡
		Max.	Min.	Mean	
Khartoum, Egypt	Dry inland	0.28	0.05	0.16	1
Abisco, North Sweden	Unpolluted	0.72	0.34	0.46	3
Aro, Nigeria	Tropical inland	1.53	0.74	1.19	8
Singapore, Malaya	Tropical marine	1.74	1.05	1.36	9
Basrah, Iran	Dry inland	2.17	0.68	1.39	9
Apapa, Nigeria	Tropical marine	2.94	1.47	2.29	15
State College, Pa.	Rural			3.75	25
South Bend, Pa.	Semirural			4.27	29
Berlin, Germany	Semi-industrial	4.83	4.55	4.71	32
Llanwrtyd Wells, B.I.	Semimarine	6.22	3.40	5.23	35
Kure Beach, N.C.	Marine			5.78	38
Calshot, B.I.	Marine	7.19	4.22	6.10	41
Sandy Hook, N.J.	Marine, semi-industrial			7.34	50
Congella, S. Africa	Marine	11.13	5.61	7.34	50
Kearny, N.J.	Industrial marine			7.75	52
Motherwell, B.I.	Industrial	9.39	6.57	8.17	55
Vandergrift, Pa.	Industrial			8.34	56
Pittsburgh, Pa.	Industrial			9.65	65
Sheffield, B.I.	Industrial	13.40	8.74	11.53	78
Frodingham, B.I.	Industrial	23.40	10.37	14.81	100

SOURCE: U.S. Corps of Engineers, "Corrosion Control"
EM 1110-1-184
1 August 1962

* C. P. Larrabee, "Corrosion of Steels in Marine Atmospheres and in Sea Water," *Trans. Electrochem. Soc. 87*, 1945. Based on field tests of the Iron and Steel Institute Corrosion Committee reported by J. C. Hudson, in *J. Iron Steel Inst. 11* (1943), 209 with additional data.

† Losses of weight sustained by 5.1 × 10.2 cm (2 × 4 in.) specimens made of open-hearth iron (0.007% copper) are used as a criterion (1.03 dm² of surface).

‡ Frodingham, British Island = 100.

not clear from the composition whether the alloys were intentional or fortuitious. Except for pure gold, all these metals and their alloys are subject to corrosion in the environments to which most archaeological specimens are exposed.

Factors Influencing Corrosivity of the Atmosphere

The metals and alloys of interest here are quite resistant to corrosion in clean dry air. Freshly bared metal surface is immediately covered by a layer of sorbed gas; oxygen molecules on the active metal surface form oxygen ions, and the metal is soon protected by an oxide film. The oxide film thickness increases with time according to logarithmic, cubic, or parabolic rate laws at ambient temperatures.[7] The film formed is highly protective.

Why then are some atmospheres so much more corrosive than others? Temperature and relative humidity are obvious factors. Generally, the most striking differences in the corrosiveness, however, are the result of pollution in the atmosphere: sulfur dioxide, sodium chloride, hydrogen sulfide, and particulate pollution.[8] The objects that museums now treasure have generally been exposed to dust, smoke, sea spray, or sulfurous gases. Volcanoes, forest fires, breaking seas, and salt fogs are natural sources of air pollution.[9] Combustion processes provide the major source of sulfur dioxide in metropolitan areas. Hydrogen sulfide generally originates in industrial processes.

Particulate pollution includes dust from various sources. Dust from windstorms, if it is not saline, is less corrosive than dust from some smelting process. Soot is especially corrosive, because it is highly surface-active and often at the time of formation has absorbed sulfur dioxide, sulfur trioxide, or inorganic acids. Such particulate pollution can promote rapid corrosion even inside a building.[10]

[7] Herbert H. Uhlig, *Corrosion and Corrosion Control* (New York: John Wiley, 1963); Ulick R. Evans, *The Corrosion and Oxidation of Metals: Scientific Principles and Practical Applications* (London: Edward Arnold, 1960), pp. 492–494.

[8] Ulick R. Evans, *The Corrosion and Oxidation of Metals;* pp. 492–494; Israel Cornet, "Material Damage," sect. 15, *Combustion-Generated Air Pollution,* ed. E. S. Starkman, 21–30 June 1967, University of California, Berkeley.

[9] Gordon Nonhebel, "Characteristics of Solid and Gaseous Pollutants," *Air Pollution.* Based on papers given at a conference held at the University of Sheffield, September 1956, *Butterworth's Scientific Publications* (1957), ed. M. W. Thring.

[10] Ulick R. Evans, *The Corrosion and Oxidation of Metals: Scientific Principles and Practical Applications* (London: Edward Arnold, 1960), pp. 492–494.

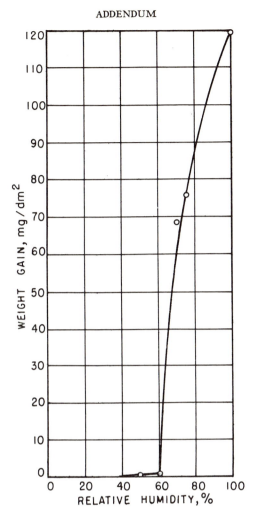

FIG. 2. The effect of critical humidity. Corrosion of iron in air containing 0.01 percent SO_2, after fifty-five days' exposure. There is a great increase in corrosion rate when the relative humidity exceeds what is termed a critical humidity.

Critical Humidity

It has already been noted that the metals of interest to us do not corrode in clean dry air. Experiments show that when an atmosphere becomes sufficiently humid corrosion rates increase greatly, as shown in figure 2. The relative humidity at which this increase in corrosion rate occurs is called the critical humidity. The critical humidity for iron and steel is normally considered to be 60 percent.[11] For chloride-contaminated copper

[11] Herbert H. Uhlig, *Corrosion and Corrosion Control* (New York: John Wiley, 1963); Ulick R. Evans, *The Corrosion and Oxidation of Metals,* pp. 492–494.

or bronze objects the critical humidity may be below 50 percent RH[12] (relative humidity).

Theoretically metal specimens will be stable if maintained in environments at less than the critical humidity. In June 1967 I noted that various rooms in the Louvre were maintained at 43 to 55 percent RH; this was more for paintings such as the Mona Lisa rather than for the metal specimens. A word of caution is in order. The critical humidities cited have been obtained generally by tests with simplified systems, such as steel exposed in air plus water vapor plus sulfur dioxide. Specimens may have picked up complex contaminants from prior exposure to soil or to human handling. Such specimens may have been stable in a Spanish castle or in a Turkish mosque, but they may start to corrode when exposed to what is normally regarded as a satisfactory museum atmosphere. Soot and soluble metal chlorides would be among the contaminants which should be removed from a specimen surface to assure stability.

Further Comments on Atmospheric Corrosion

It often turns out that metal exposed under partial shelter corrodes more rapidly than when exposed in the open. This is particularly true in marine coastal environments. The partially sheltered specimen cannot be washed by rain but can be covered by windblown sand, dust, and spray, and can absorb moisture from salt-laden fogs and highly humid air.[13]

Mechanisms

What mechanisms account for the corrosion phenomena observed? One approach is to consider the contaminants as catalysts in corrosion reactions.

Thus sulfur dioxide is readily oxidized by oxygen of the air to form trioxide which absorbs water vapor to form sulfuric acid on an iron or other metal surface. The sulfuric acid then catalyzes oxidation of the metal in the following manner:[14]

$$Fe + H_2SO_4 + 1/2\ O_2 \longrightarrow Fe\ SO_4 + H_2O \tag{1}$$

$$Fe\ SO_4 + H_2O + 1/4\ O_2 \longrightarrow 1/2\ Fe_2O_3 + H_2SO_4. \tag{2}$$

[12] R. M. Organ, "Aspects of Bronze Patina and Its Treatment," *Studies in Conservation,* vol. 8, no. 1 (Feb. 1963), 1–9.

[13] F. L. LaQue, "Corrosion Testing," Twenty-fifth Edgar Marburg Lecture, presented on 29 June 1951, before the 54th Annual Meeting of the ASTM. Reprinted from *Proc. ASTM,* vol. 51 (1951), 495–582.

[14] Herbert H. Uhlig, *Corrosion and Corrosion Control* (New York: John Wiley, 1963).

The second reaction has regenerated sulfuric acid which is then available to attack more metal.

Copper withstands exposure to water containing carbon dioxide, sodium bicarbonate, and oxygen. However, adding as little as 10 ppm (parts per million) of sodium chloride or 40 ppm sodium sulfate promotes pitting and increases the corrosion rate.[15] One may postulate reactions such as the following:

$$2\ Cu + 1/2\ O_2 + 2HCl \longrightarrow 2\ Cu\ Cl + H_2O \qquad (1)$$

$$2\ Cu\ Cl + 1/2\ O_2 + H_2O \longrightarrow 2\ CuO + 2\ HCl. \qquad (2)$$

The basic carbonate of copper $CuCO_3 \cdot Cu\ (OH)_2$ (malachite) is less soluble and more stable than CuO (cupric oxide) in water of pH lower than 8.6. The malachite film is fairly protective, but local concentration cells may be set up due to differences in oxygen and chloride concentration, and active pitting can occur in which the pits actually have pockets of acid.[16] A copper or bronze specimen exposed to a humid atmosphere may corrode in much the same manner as in water, since some contaminating salts such as certain chlorides are hygroscopic and will absorb enough moisture to give active corrosion sites.

There is another approach to mechanisms which stems from advances in our knowledge of the solid state.

Oxidation of Metals

When metals such as iron or copper oxidize, they are covered by an oxide film composed of oxygen and metal ions in an orderly array, called a lattice.[17] Simple experiments show that metal ions diffuse preferentially from the metal-oxide interface through the lattice to the oxide-air interface, but that oxygen ions do not readily move from the air interface to the metal interface. When an iron surface is painted with chromic oxide (Cr_2O_3) slurry and then oxidized in a furnace, the green-colored chromic oxide layer is found to be buried under iron oxide. Iron atoms have migrated around or through the green chromic oxide, reacted with oxygen at the air-oxide interface, and buried the green marker layer.[18]

[15] Malvern F. Obrecht and Marcel Pourbaix, "Corrosion of Metals in Potable Water Systems," *J. Amer. Water Works Assoc.* (Aug. 1967), pp. 977–992.

[16] Idem.

[17] Herbert H. Uhlig, *Corrosion and Corrosion Control;* Ulick R. Evans, *The Corrosion and Oxidation of Metals,* pp. 492–494; O. Kubaschewski and B. E. Hopkins, *Oxidation of Metals and Alloys* (New York: Academic Press, 1962).

[18] L. B. Pfeil, "The Oxidation of Iron and Steel at High Temperatures," *J. Iron and Steel Inst.,* vol. 119 (1929), 501.

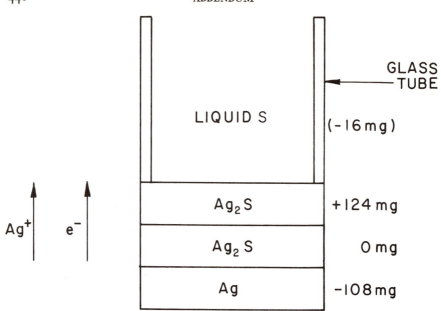

Fɪɢ. 3. Formation of silver sulfide from silver and liquid sulfur, 1 hr., 220°C (after Wagner). This experiment shows that Ag+ rather than S−− ions migrate through the Ag₂S. Note that the semiconductor Ag₂S conducts both Ag+ and e−.

The oxidation of silver by sulfur gives a similar picture. Wagner [19] exposed two weighed wafers of silver sulfide (Ag₂S) over silver metal, with molten sulfur above the top wafer, in a furnace at 220°C. After one hour of exposure he found that the silver metal had lost weight, the silver sulfide wafer in contact with the silver had not changed in weight, but the silver sulfide wafer in contact with the sulfur had gained weight equal to the loss of silver from the metal plus the loss of sulfur from the molten sulfur. Silver ions and electrons had migrated through the semi-conductor silver sulfide layers to react at the sulfide-sulfur interface. This experiment is shown in figure 3.

Figure 4 shows oxide lattices with some defects. If the bottom of the cuprous oxide (Cu₂O) lattice lies on a copper metal surface, a copper ion can hop into the little open square, called a cation vacancy. There is no occupant present in this lattice position, and a positively charged copper ion will be happy to find a vacant lattice site near some highly attractive negatively charged oxygen ions. This game of musical chairs results in the cation vacancy migrating into the copper metal. The coalescence of

---

[19] C. Wagner, in Z. Physik, Chem. B21 (1933), 25.

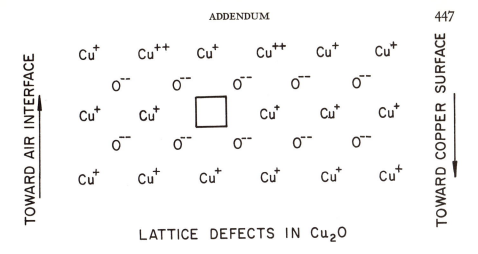

LATTICE DEFECTS IN Cu_2O

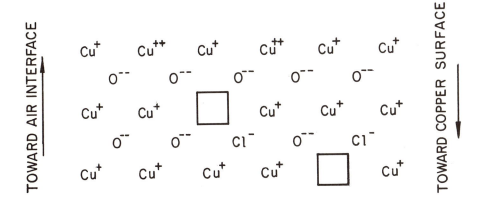

LATTICE DEFECTS IN Cu_2O, Cl^- PRESENT

FIG. 4. Lattice defects in cuprous oxide. The presence of cation vacancies facilitates the movement of cuprous ions, Cu^+, from the copper surface to the air interface.

numerous such vacancies forms voids or cavities in positions formerly filled by metal atoms.

It is easy to see how chloride ions will affect a lattice such as that of cuprous oxide. Two singly charged chloride ions will displace one doubly charged oxygen ion, but the chloride ions will occupy the sites formerly filled by two oxygen ions. To maintain electrical neutrality two cuprous-ion (Cu $^+$) lattice sites must be left vacant. The presence of additional cation vacancies makes it easier for copper ions to diffuse through the oxide lattice and thus renders the oxide film less protective.

Experiments have shown that when copper or zinc or iron are exposed first to an atmosphere containing sulfur dioxide or chloride ion they will corrode at a more rapid rate than if the initial exposure is in an atmosphere free of these contaminants. The difference in corrosion rate will be marked even after long periods of exposure.[20]

When thick scales form on metals such as iron or copper there is a tendency for layers of the scale to crack or spall off from time to time.[21] This is partly due to the fact that the outside layers of scale are at a higher state of oxidation, forming ferric oxide compared to ferrous oxide, or cupric oxide compared to cuprous oxide. Differences in the coefficients of thermal expansion and in other physical properties accompany these differences in chemical composition. Mechanical or thermal cycling thus tends to crack or spall off outer layers of thick scale. Once the scale is cracked or spalled off, however, the lattice defects of the underlying oxide film again strongly influence the rate of corrosion.

Let us examine scale formation on iron at high temperatures. Figure 5 shows oxide scale formed on iron wire after 14 hours at 1500°F (805°C) in pure oxygen.[22] Figure 6 shows schematically steps in the oxidation of a small iron wire.[23] First the oxide scale grows freely to some critical thickness, vacancies diffusing into the metal. At the critical thickness excess vacancies in the metal require a sump; this is provided in the second step by separation of a portion of the oxide on one side. With a small wire the oxide can adhere on the side opposite the separation. Step 3 shows another oxide film forming, and step 4 shows another separation. Iron keeps diffusing through the adherent oxide film, to oxidize on the outside of the film,

[20] W. H. J. Vernon, in *Trans. Faraday Soc., 19* (1924), 886; *23* (1927), 159; *31* (1935), 1678; in *Trans. Inst. Chem. Eng., 17* (1939), 171; in *Korr. Met., 14* (1938), 213; in *Chem. Ind.* (1943), p. 314; F. L. LaQue, "Corrosion Testing," Twenty-fifth Edgar Marburg Lecture, presented on 29 June 1951, before the 54th Annual Meeting of the ASTM. Reprinted from *Proc. ASTM,* vol. 51 (1951), 495–582.

[21] Herbert H. Uhlig, *Corrosion and Corrosion Control* (New York: John Wiley, 1963); Ulick R. Evans, *The Corrosion and Oxidation of Metals: Scientific Principles and Practical Applications* (London: Edward Arnold, 1960), pp. 492–494; B. F. Dunnington, F. H. Beck, and M. G. Fontana, "The Mechanism of Scale Formation on Iron at High Temperature," *Corrosion,* vol. 8 (Jan. 1952), 2–13.

[22] B. W. Dunnington, F. H. Beck, and M. G. Fontana, "The Mechanism of Scale Formation on Iron at High Temperature," *Corrosion,* vol. 8 (Jan. 1952), 2–13.

[23] Idem.

as shown in step 5, and finally all of the iron is gone, as shown in step 6. If the piece of metal is thick, internal laminae or cavities may act as vacancy sumps, or the metal surface may retreat partly, leaving a loose iron oxide between its original and final positions.

Reactions at ambient temperatures progress much more slowly than in a furnace, but the mechanism may be similar. Thus there are reports of archaeological specimens found covered with quantities of corrosion products which when cleaned carefully reveal in places what appear to be original surfaces still showing tool marks.[24]

Corrosion of Metals in Water

Natural waters contain dissolved salts, such as sodium chloride, and dissolved gases, such as oxygen. Normally water becomes more corrosive as the salt content increases.

Seawater is of major interest to us. Many archaeological sites are near the sea, and specimens have been and are still being found in abundance in sunken ships and sunken sea coasts. Unfortunately, the ordinary data of the corrosion engineer may not be too applicable to archaeological structures. Engineering data are obtained for panels held in various zones: totally submerged, tidal zone, splash and spray area, mud zone, coastal atmosphere. Also data are available for structures such as piling which extend through many zones. Engineering data are usually obtained for carbon steels, cupronickel, monel, and similar alloys, selected primarily for service in ship hulls, propellers, pump impellers, or for structures such as piling or offshore drilling platforms.[25]

Archaeological specimens tend to be metals or alloys of chemical composition which may or may not correspond to the composition of engineering alloys. However, the exposure tends to be rather special. Archaeological specimens often come from the holds of ships which sank with coins and treasures in leather and wooden chests, with swords in leather scabbards, with assorted human accompaniments.[26] Decay of organic material buried under shallow mud or sand cover is anaerobic, with a plentiful supply of hydrogen sulfide and other sulfides present. Silver corrodes to form silver sulfide under these conditions.

[24] R. M. Organ, "Aspects of Bronze Patina and Its Treatment," *Studies on Conservation,* vol. 8, no. 1 (Feb. 1963), 1–9.

[25] Herbert H. Uhlig, *Corrosion Handbook* (New York: John Wiley, 1948).

[26] Kip Wagner, "Drowned Galleons Yield Spanish Gold," *National Geographic,* vol. 127, no. 1 (Jan. 1965), 1–37.

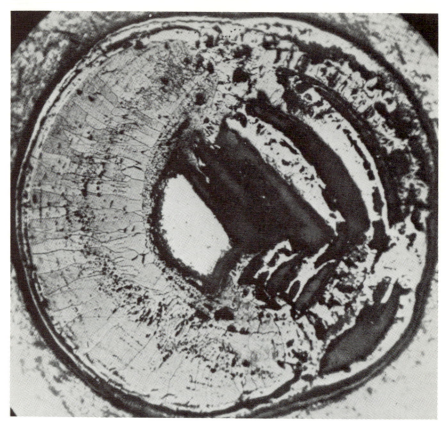

Fɪɢ. 5. Oxide scale on iron wire after fourteen hours at 805°C in pure oxygen. 100×. Etchant 20 percent HCl. Cf. ref. 20.

Massive objects like cannonballs or cannon will persist. When these are brought up from the sea and cleaned of overlying material, the surfaces are still covered with a chloride-containing rust. Such surfaces may be observed to weep on humid days, the soluble chlorides absorbing enough moisture to deliquesce and form beads of liquid on the surface.

Galvanic effects become particularly important in a high conductivity electrolyte like seawater. A piece of iron in contact with copper or bronze will furnish cathodic protection in seawater, so the copper or bronze will be well preserved while the iron is consumed. (Cathodic protection is the reduction or prevention of corrosion of a metal surface by making it cathodic, for example, by contact with a less noble metal which acts as a sacrificial anode.) An alloy of silver and copper will have the copper selectively corroded, leaving a surface enriched in the more noble silver. Any of the metals such as iron, copper, or silver in contact with gold will

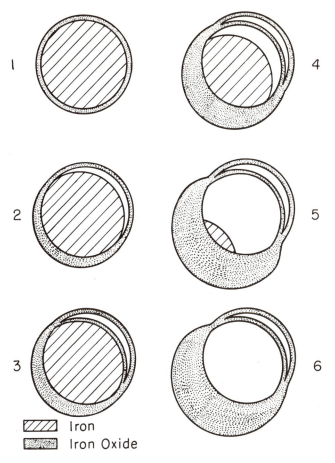

Oxidation of a Small Iron Wire

Fɪɢ. 6. Schematic diagram showing steps in oxidation of a
small iron wire. Cf. ref. 20.

be accelerated in corrosion, and sometimes the gold ornamentation of, for example, a sword hilt will be found buried under layers of corrosion products and accretions.

Corrosion in Soils

Soils are perhaps the most heterogeneous of environments to be considered. Dry sandy soils can be quite protective to metal objects. On the other hand, when the U.S. Army had some surplus defective shells to dispose of and these were unsafe to process, the shells were gently laid in a New England cranberry bog where the acid soil could perforate the brass shell casings in less than five years and ultimately consume the metal. Half-inch thick steel pipe has perforated in thirteen years, despite a ¾-inch thick cement mortar coating, in saline soil in the San Francisco Bay Area, but this rate of corrosion was probably due to long-line electric current flow.

Pitting is generally a prominent feature of corrosion in soils.[27] Since the environment tends to be chemically reducing, iron forms soluble ferrous ions which diffuse away from the iron surface. Figure 7 shows some pipe as removed from a soil exposure site, before and after cleaning.[28] Copper, silver, and lead may be expected to behave differently, in that the corrosion products may remain on the surface of the objects and respond to electrochemical reduction treatment.

Some Special Problems

The question is occasionally asked whether one can use corrosion to date specimens. The previous discussion has already indicated that a vase exposed in an Egyptian tomb shows less corrosion in a thousand years than a vase exposed twenty years in the isles of Greece. There will be subtle differences in the composition and microscopic structure of films formed on the two vases, but as far as loss of metal is concerned a 50 to 1 difference in corrosion rates could be observed.

There will be special cases, however, where corrosion may be quantitatively useful. An isolated silver coin partly corroded to silver sulfide in the sea under shallow cover may be such a case. Knowing the temperature and assuming it to be uniform for centuries, one may estimate a corrosion rate, assuming diffusion control. Since one can check the date of many coins, and use carbon dating and other techniques on surrounding remains, the applicability of corrosion dating can be tested and verified. It would be particularly interesting to find a metal object with internal voids or cavities produced by diffusion of vacancies, rather than by cores in casting, to check whether corrosion rates obtained at high temperatures can be extrapolated to ambient temperatures with confidence. It should be remembered that when an object corrodes in the sea encrustation of marine organisms and precipitates of various kinds make the system far different from what one encounters in a laboratory test.

Another group of problems encountered deals with preservation of

[27] Melvin Romanoff, *Underground Corrosion*, National Bureau of Standards Circular 579 (issued April 1957).

[28] Irving A. Denison and Melvin Romanoff, "Corrosion of Nickel Cast Irons in Soils," *J. Res. of National Bureau of Standards*, vol. 51, no. 6 (Dec. 1953).

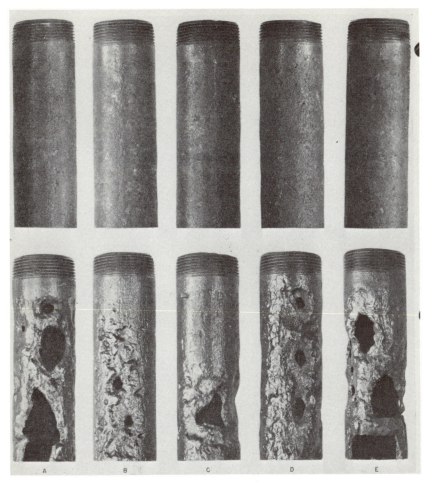

Fig. 7. Condition of cast iron exposed to highly corrosive soils before (top row) and after (bottom row) removal of the corrosion products. Exposure was for eleven years, approximately. A. Lake Charles clay at El Vista, Tex.; B. Muck at New Orleans, La.; C. Tidal marsh at Charleston, S.C.; D. Docas clay at Cholame, Calif.; E. Merced silt loam at Buttonwillow, Calif.

archaeological specimens indoors. Silver and copper specimens are tarnished by atmospheres containing as little as 2 ppm (parts per million) hydrogen sulfide. If the specimens are delicate and precious, it is not desirable to keep cleaning and polishing them. Under such circumstances cloth, paper, and even paint in display cases should be selected with caution to avoid sulfide-containing material. Sulfide-absorbing or anti-tarnish chemicals should be used to condition the environment if air pollution is a problem.

Sometimes organic acids liberated from wood in cabinet work constitute a problem. Acetic and other organic acids may come from oakwood, for example, and such acids catalyze the conversion of lead to sugar of lead in the presence of water vapor and carbon dioxide of the atmosphere. Lead and pewter objects deteriorate rapidly where acetic acid contaminants are present.[29]

Another problem the corrosion expert hears of deals with bronze disease. Ulick Evans[30] has described the outbreak of this problem at the Fitzwilliam Museum shortly after World War II. He attributed this outbreak to acetic acid absorbed from wood shavings in which the bronzes had been packed. The acetic acid penetrated through cracks in the patina, which was mainly basic copper chloride, attacking the copper to give soluble copper acetate. The copper acetate was then converted into basic carbonate or basic sulphate by acid constituents of the atmosphere, regenerating acetic acid to produce further attack on the bronze. To remedy the situation a local electrochemical cell was set up, applied to every corrosion site in turn, in which the bronze was made the cathode relative to a zinc anode, and the negatively charged ion was coaxed to come out of the corrosion pit toward the positively charged zinc ions being formed. This type of electrochemical coaxing is often helpful, because the trouble-causing negatively charged ions such as chloride or acetate ion concentrate deep inside the pits where positively charged cuprous ion is being formed. Chloride ion is normally the problem.[31] Washing with distilled water or even with sodium bicarbonate solution is a slow process, and may take months or even years to leach out the troublesome contaminants.

[29] Ulick R. Evans, *The Corrosion and Oxidation of Metals* (London: Edward Arnold, 1960), pp. 492–494.

[30] Idem.

[31] R. M. Organ, "Aspects of Bronze Patina and Its Treatment," *Studies in Conservation,* vol. 8, no. 1 (Feb. 1963), 1–9.

Index

Page numbers in italics refer to illustrations

457